At Pyramid Lake

BERNARD MERGEN

UNIVERSITY OF NEVADA PRESS

RENO & LAS VEGAS

University of Nevada Press, Reno, Nevada 89557 USA
Copyright © 2014 by University of Nevada Press
All rights reserved
Manufactured in the United States of America
Design by Kathleen Szawiola

Library of Congress Cataloging-in-Publication Data
Mergen, Bernard.
At Pyramid Lake / Bernard Mergen.
pages   cm
Includes bibliographical references and index.
ISBN 978-0-87417-939-2 (pbk.) — ISBN 978-0-87417-940-8 (e-book)
1. Pyramid Lake (Nev.)—History. 2. Pyramid Lake Region
(Nev.)—History. 3. Pyramid Lake Region (Nev.)—Social life and
customs. 4. Pyramid Lake (Nev.)—Environmental conditions.
5. Pyramid Lake Region (Nev.)—Environmental conditions.
I. Title.
F847.W3M47 2014
979.4'93—dc23   2013043941

The paper used in this book meets the requirements of
American National Standard for Information Sciences—
Permanence of Paper for Printed Library Materials,
ANSI/NISO Z39.48-1992 (R2002).
Binding materials were selected for strength and durability.

This book has been reproduced as a digital reprint.

To the memory of Katharine Norrid Mergen
(1910–97)

MAP

This book is a history of an extraordinary place, Pyramid Lake, Nevada. The lake's beauty and abundant resources have for centuries attracted Indians, white ranchers, farmers, fishermen, agents of government bureaus and private businesses, and tourists of all types. Their connections to the lake and to each other provide the stories I tell in the following chapters.

The stories are fascinating and important in two ways. First, they are little-known episodes of western American history. There is only one other book about the lake in print, *As Long as the River Shall Run: An Ethnohistory of Pyramid Lake Indian Reservation,* by Martha C. Knack and Omer C. Stewart, a history of the Pyramid Lake Paiutes and their struggle to preserve the lake's water. My book builds on that history, adding the histories of white squatters, scientists, artists, and tourists. Second, the stories are a microcosm of political and cultural forces such as the dispossession of the Indians, racism, the expansion of irrigation agriculture, urbanization, tourism, the shift from conservation to environmentalism, and the extension of civil rights that have shaped America in the past 150 years. My focus in *At Pyramid Lake* is on the ways the lake has been and continues to be perceived, depicted, and managed in the context of these forces. The central question to be answered is how a place often described as mysterious, primitive, and unique became part of vast systems of water and wildlife management, experiments in social planning, economic development, and environmental protection. Some answers are found in the profiles of the many colorful characters associated with the lake. The stories of Pyramid Lake are full of wonder and paradoxes, conflict and reconciliation, spiritual quest and struggle for survival.

The title *At Pyramid Lake* was suggested by my poet daughter, Alexa, during a walk in the Yolo Bypass Wildlife Area. The simple two-letter preposition solved my search for a title that would convey the subject of the book clearly, but complicate it sufficiently to alert the reader to the paradoxes in my stories about the lake and its people. "Primarily, *at* expresses the relation of *presence or contact in space and time,* or of *direction toward,*" write the editors of the indispensable *Webster's New International Dictionary of the English Language* (2nd ed., 1934).

Presence *and* contact in space and time with Pyramid Lake and surroundings is the subject I explore through brief histories of the people at the lake: the Kuyuidokado, white squatters and their political allies, dude ranchers, fishermen, missionaries, scientists, poets, artists, and tourists. My sources are published accounts, manuscripts, conversations, and personal memories. I have tried to keep myself in the background, but I am part of the lake's history and I use the personal pronoun when necessary. This book is a history of and a tribute to the lake I know. A full history of the Pyramid Lake Paiutes, the Kuyuidokado, remains to be written.

I was fortunate to have lived at Pyramid Lake for a brief period of my childhood in the late 1930s and early 1940s and near the lake, in Reno, for another fifteen years, through the 1950s. My strong emotional attachment to the lake is also a legacy from my mother, Katharine Norrid Mergen, and the stories in this book are infused with her presence.

Fifty-five years ago I took a Greyhound bus from Reno to Berkeley for a meeting with a committee interviewing applicants for Woodrow Wilson Fellowships. The committee was composed of University of California professors who were bemused by my request to pursue graduate work in something called American studies, and they appeared baffled by my explanation that such an academic field would allow me to combine the study of anthropology, history, and literature. "Why would you want to do that?" one august committee member asked. "Well," I replied, "I would like to place American Indians in the context of American history." There was a collective gasp, and my interlocutor sternly replied, "That's not possible." There were murmurs of assent.

Despite this inauspicious exchange, I received the fellowship and began my meandering path through American labor history, the material culture of play and recreation, and environmental history. The trail has led back to my impulsive response to an unanticipated question. This book is partially an attempt to show the interview committee they were ill-informed and to thank them for planting an idea that kept driving me to prove them wrong.

In a book dependent on primary sources, print and manuscript, some readers may question the absence of footnotes. I wrote *At Pyramid Lake* for both scholars and the literate public. Having written several books in which footnotes attach themselves to almost every sentence like ticks in a dog's ear, I wanted to give the reader unencumbered pages. I have tried in every instance of quoted or paraphrased material to indicate the source in the text. Readers should easily be able to find the original source by consulting the references. If not, e-mail me: mergen@gwu.edu.

My deepest thanks goes to the Pyramid Lake Paiute Tribe, three of whose members contributed to this book in vital ways: Ben Aleck, collections manager, Pyramid Lake Paiute Tribe Museum and Visitor Center; Ralph Burns, storyteller, Pyramid Lake Paiute Tribe Museum and Visitor Center; and Michelle McCauley, who has been active in promoting Paiute culture and language, especially among young people.

Second only to the oral knowledge preserved by tribal members are the written records concerning Pyramid Lake cataloged and maintained by the staff of the Special Collections of the University of Nevada, Reno, Library. Two archivists who helped me immeasurably over several summers of research are Donnelyn Curtis, head of Special Collections, and Jacquelyn Sundstrand, Manuscripts and Archives librarian. Without the interest and encouragement of Donnie and Jacque, this book would not have been possible.

Three other manuscript and archival collections were indispensable, and I thank the archivists and staff of the Nevada State Historical Society and the Harry Ransom Center, University of Texas at Austin, for their assistance. The third repository of essential records turned out to be a closet in the offices of the Environment and Natural Resources Division of the US Department of Justice in Sacramento, California, where Stephen Macfarlane, senior trial attorney, invited me to examine them. These documents were copies of federal records compiled in the 1970s in an unsuccessful effort to reopen the Orr Ditch Decree to secure a federal reserved water right for Pyramid Lake. I believe these were some of the materials used by Martha C. Knack and Omer C. Stewart in writing *As Long as the River Shall Run*. Steve's good memory and interest in my project saved me a long search for the originals of these records in federal archives across the country.

My alma mater, the University of Nevada, Reno, remains a collegial and welcoming place. Elizabeth Raymond and Bill Rowley have contributed to this book in many ways, some of which are made clear in the text. Peter Kopp took time from graduate studies to organize a panel at the Western History Association annual meeting in 2010, allowing me to present some of the ideas developed in this book. Professor Eugene Moehring, University of Nevada, Las Vegas, made comments on my paper that greatly improved this book.

While thanking colleagues at the university, I want to express my gratitude to Matt Becker, senior acquisitions editor, University of Nevada Press, for his careful attention to this book. Annette Wenda's careful copyediting is greatly appreciated. I also thank two anonymous readers for the University of Nevada Press for their constructive criticism of an early draft of my manuscript.

Other Nevadans provided friendship, wisdom, and insights into the history of Pyramid Lake. Dee and Fred Kille, Nevada historians, made my research trips even more enjoyable than they already were. Hal Klieforth, meteorologist emeritus of the Desert Research Institute, collector of Nevada's past, has been an adviser for three of my books. Tom Strekal's insights as a fisheries biologist for two government agencies were invaluable.

Internationally, Raili Põldsaar and Krista Vogelberg, the organizers of the Fifth International Tartu Conference on North-American Studies, May 7–9, 2001, deserve my thanks. I am also grateful to the American Studies Association of Turkey and especially to Ann Weldon, public affairs officer, US Embassy, Ankara, who made it possible for me to present my thoughts on *The Misfits* to a knowledgeable audience at the annual conference of the ASAT in Izmir, Turkey, in 2002.

Finally, my closest advisers: Claudia, my wife and editor; Alexa, my daughter and second pair of eyes and ears throughout the research and writing of this book; and Andrew, my son and provider of insights into legal and environmental history.

My profound gratitude to you all.

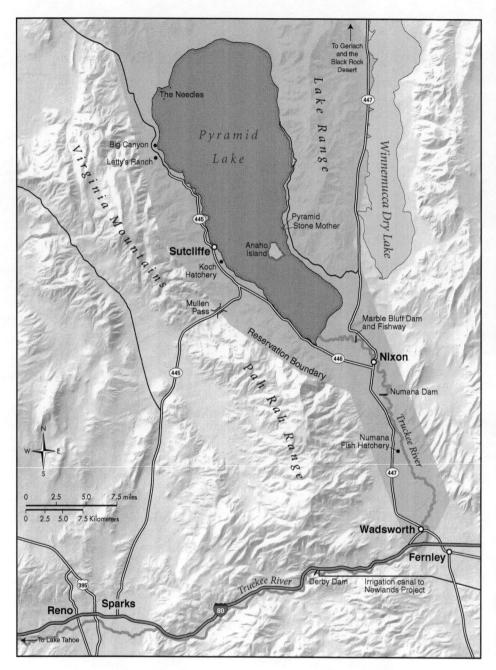

Map of Pyramid Lake, the reservation, and the lower Truckee River.

Introduction

Located in the sagebrush desert 35 miles north of Reno, Pyramid Lake is an unexpected expanse of water 30 miles long and roughly 4 to 11 miles wide. By scientific measurement its deepest point is 335 feet. In the imaginations of the lake's many admirers, it is bottomless. Its color changes across the full visual spectrum of blue from violet to green. The principal source of Pyramid Lake's water is the Truckee River, which flows 100 miles from Lake Tahoe in the Sierra Nevada. Pyramid Lake has no outlet, and in many years more water evaporates than enters the lake; consequently, its water is slightly saline. Pyramid Lake is a remnant of Lake Lahontan, an inland sea that filled a large part of the Great Basin during the Pleistocene geologic era, 2.5 million to 12,000 years ago. The lake is home to two noteworthy fish, a bottom-feeding sucker known as cui-ui and Lahontan cutthroat trout (LCT), a species of lake salmon. The cui-ui, sacred to the Numa (Paiute), is an ancient fish found only in Pyramid Lake. Lahontan cutthroat trout, sought by sportfishermen, grow to more than four feet and can weigh up to forty pounds.

Pyramid Lake is also remarkable for the many large tufa deposits that border the lake. Tufa is a rock that forms when springs beneath the lake surface discharge calcium that mixes with carbonate dissolved in the lake's water. The calcium carbonate creates a reef-like formation. Since the rocks cannot grow above the level of the lake, geologists use them to measure the depth of the lake in the past. The immense tufa pyramid that gives the lake its English name and a smaller monolith that has broken into pieces resembling a seated woman covered by a shawl, with a round open container beside her, known as Stone Mother and Basket, are the most memorable works of nature at the lake.

I HAVE ALWAYS THOUGHT that there should be a clock for Pyramid Lake, a clock similar to the one on the cover of the *Bulletin of the Atomic Scientists* indicating how close we are to the midnight (high noon?) of nuclear annihilation. The Pyramid Lake clock would be set at 11:45 in 1844, tick to 11:50 in 1905, tock

1

Pyramid Lake's Pyramid Is Larger By Far Than Most People Believe

THE HOTEL MAPES Nevada's tallest building, would look like this if it stood beside Pyramid's famous pyramid. The picture below shows the two in exact scale. The pyramid is more than 400 feet in height, and the hotel is 126 feet high. Harry Drackert has a similar picture at his Pyramid Lake store, which compares the big rock with the Hotel Riverside. It was after seeing his picture that the Journal got the idea for this one. (Journal photos)

Photomontage of John C. Frémont's pyramid and the Mapes Hotel in Reno. The photo's caption read in part: "Pyramid Lake's Pyramid Is Larger by Far than Most People Believe." *Nevada State Journal*, April 3, 1955, 26. Courtesy Nevada State Historical Society.

to 11:55 in 1967, surge to 11:59 in 1985, and fall back to 11:45 in 2013. Some old threats are still around, new ones continue to emerge, but some safeguards are in place.

The lake provides its own chronology of decline in the bands of older dark and more recent white rock exposed as the water level drops. Photographs of the lake's shore, and prominent features such as the pyramid, clearly reveal the nearly 100-foot lowering of the lake in the past century. The roughly 30-foot rise in the lake since the mid-1980s is harder to chart visually, except, perhaps, in the submerged picnic tables at Warrior Point.

The pyramid has inspired other measurements. A photomontage appearing in the *Nevada State Journal* on April 3, 1955, placed the Mapes Hotel, at 12 stories then the tallest building in Nevada, against the 360-foot pyramid to provide a sense of scale. The original caption with the photo indicates that the reader may not realize how large the pyramid is. This, in turn, implies that many Nevadans and tourists knew the hotel better than they knew the lake and its pyramid. The photo promotes tourism to both the lake and Reno. But this seemingly simple pictograph may send other messages to receptive viewers. When I showed it to students in Professor William Rowley's Native American history class at the University of Nevada, Reno, in April 2011, they perceived a "grandeur of nature over puny works of man" theme. Others noted that both the pyramid and the hotel lacked contexts. Absent from both newspaper and classroom discussion was the Paiute perspective. The Indians call the rock "wono," a large overturned basket. In some legends the basket conceals a mermaid whose breath appears as steam from the rock's hot springs. Conversely, the Mapes occasionally revealed the stripper Lili St. Cyr, veiled in steam from her onstage bath. Two cultures, two revealing legends.

The *Journal*'s photo is one more variant of historian Leo Marx's idea of "the machine in the garden," where human technology reshapes nature's landscape. Explorer John C. Frémont had claimed that the lake's pyramid was older and larger than Egypt's Cheops, the Great Pyramid of Giza. While the pyramids were both more than four thousand years old, Cheops (480 feet) was higher. Reno's own pharaoh, Charles Mapes, and his Sky Room–topped temple were dwarfed by both pyramids.

The Mapes Hotel was demolished in January 2000, despite protests by preservationists. The 30-story pyramid-shaped Luxor Hotel and casino was built in Las Vegas in 1993. At 365 feet it matches the lake's pyramid, but the hotel's twin ziggurat towers and 110-foot sphinx bid to eclipse Frémont's dreams of empire. The lake's pyramid endures, while the lake itself and the river that feeds it have become part of a vast technology of dams, reservoirs, sewage treatment plants, water and fish management regimes, and electronic monitoring—an "organic machine," to borrow historian Richard White's astute description of the Columbia River.

Pyramids, their mysteries and imagined powers, have inspired pseudoscientific theories for centuries. Some of this nonsense has appeared at the lake from time to time and is related to dreams of utopia. The unlikely juxtaposition of lake and desert, commented on by almost every visitor, has always made Pyramid Lake a place for dreaming of a better future. From Numa origin stories to the recurrent proposals for resort developments, the history of the lake has been tinged with visions of an ideal community—peaceful, prosperous, and in harmony with nature. The Edenic, utopian, lake appears in one form or another in each of my chapters.

CHAPTER 1, "Survival of the Numa and Pyramid Lake," looks at the lake and its people from the moment of white contact to the present, focusing on the threats to their survival and the response of the Kuyuidokado. Following current usage, I use Numa (also spelled Numu) as a synonym for Paiute, recognizing that Numa means "the People" in Numic languages and that Paiute is a name imposed by whites. I use Paiute because it is more commonly used in the historical records and will be understood without any negative connotations by most readers. Kuyuidokado is used when referring specifically to the Pyramid Lake Numa/Paiutes.

The voices of the oppressed are seldom heard, while those of Indian agents, journalists, politicians, and anthropologists fill thousands of pages. I have tried to infer what life on the reservation was like from the sources at hand, but this part of the story needs a Numic speaker. I reflect on the meanings of the legend and tufa formation Stone Mother and on Indian dances performed for the public at powwows.

Chapter 2, "The Fate of the Lake," looks in more detail at the post–World War II era, the National Congress of American Indians, the Bureau of Indian Affairs' (BIA) renewed attempt to terminate the reservations, the Indian Claims Commission (ICC), the role of anthropologists in defining Indian identity, and the first attempts by the Paiutes to bring private development to the lake.

Chapter 3, "The Lake and Its Totem," examines the "Pyramid Lake Task Force" of 1969–71, the Senate hearings in the 1980s, and the "water wars." The tales that make up my story of the lake are both extraordinary, as when its very existence is at stake, and mundane, when it is just a fish story. But what a fish story! The listing of the cui-ui as endangered on the 1967 endangered species list gave the Pyramid Lake Paiute Tribe one of its most powerful legal tools to provide more water for the lake and prevent its further decline.

Chapter 4, "Railroads, Ranches, and Dudes," is about some of the interlopers who have made the lake and its resources their own despite the efforts of the Kuyuidokado to remove or control them. Some of them trespassed within a year or two of the creation of the reservation in 1859. Later the squatters claimed they did not know the land had been removed from homesteading. Most did not care, acting on the oldest of principles, that possession is nine-tenths of the law.

The railroads were not bad neighbors, but they also took without asking. They took Congress's land grants and assumed they were valid everywhere they wanted to lay track. Twice, in 1868 and again in 1912, they sliced off acres of the reservation for routes east and west, north and south. The railroad was a squatter on wheels. Where farmers and ranchers attempted to create a pastoral landscape and conformed to the cycles of time set by crop and cattle, the railroad introduced the Kuyuidokado to steam power, rapid transportation, and time measured by watches. Indians who chose to live in the settlement that became Nixon lived for almost fifty years in relative silence, while those who settled in Wadsworth grew accustomed to the bells and whistles of passing locomotives. When the railroads declined, they took away more than rails and buildings; they removed the future of a way of life they had introduced.

This chapter includes personal reflections based on my family's connection with the Southern Pacific Railroad and my mother's friendships with some of the white squatters on the west side of the lake. There are stories within stories about the Kitselmans, about Harry Drackert, and about the guest ranches.

Chapter 5, "Squatters and Sportsmen," inquires into the conflicts between the Pyramid Lake Paiutes and the white ranchers and farmers on reservation land along the Truckee River from Wadsworth to Nixon. Some were real farmers who worked the land; others were absentee speculators who found land seekers willing to buy without asking for legal proof of ownership. I use the Senate hearings of 1937, in which Senator Pat McCarran made his first of several attempts to strip the Paiutes of their lands along the Truckee River north of Wadsworth, as a way into the politics of the Indian Reorganization Act (IRA), the Bureau of Indian Affairs, and their impacts on the Pyramid Lake Tribe.

Land trespass, as Martha Knack and Omer Stewart explain in *As Long as the River Shall Run: An Ethnohistory of Pyramid Lake Indian Reservation* (1984, updated 1999), their exemplary account of the Kuyuidokado's struggles to preserve the lake and their way of life, was just one of many transgressions. Fish trespass was equally devastating to the Natives' scarce resources. Non-Indian commercial fishermen took thousands of tons of Lahontan cutthroat trout from the lake between 1869 and 1929. Impoverished, the Indians also fished commercially, hastening the extinction of the native trout, forcing them to depend on state and federal hatcheries to restock the lake with sometimes incompatible species. Paradoxically, the end of commercial fishing opened opportunities for sportfishing. Sportsmen are the flip side of the squatter coin. They stay at the lake a few days to a few weeks a year. They are willing to pay for licenses, gear, supplies, and boat rentals, but they expect the lake to be managed for their pleasure and it is. Part of the sportsmen's identity is rooted in their consumption of the lake's resources for leisure. Recreation is a business that now brings northern Nevada more revenue than agriculture ever provided.

Readers will notice a shift from the historical narrative in the first five chapters to a more topical arrangement in chapters 6–10. My intent in these chapters is to present descriptions of the lake by journalists, artists, scientists, and others that expand on the stories chronicled earlier. They may in a sense be digressions, but my central point is that the lake's historical sources are fragmentary and personal, more about place than about time as in conventional history.

Chapter 6, "Pyramid Lake Observed," is about sojourners, writers, and artists at the lake, including photographer Timothy O'Sullivan, humorist Dan De Quille, geologist Israel C. Russell, geographer Harold W. Fairbanks, painter Gilbert Natches, novelist Walter Van Tilburg Clark, and three local poets. Their observations cover a century of the lake's history, providing a sense of permanence and change.

Chapter 7, "Pyramid Lake, Mustangers, and *The Misfits*," uses the essays of reporter A. J. Liebling and the short stories, novel, and film script of playwright Arthur Miller to discuss some of the meanings of frontier, cowboys, and love. The story of the movie has never been placed in the larger context of Liebling's *New Yorker* articles "The Mustang Buzzers" or the history of the feral horses as symbol and pest. The two writers raise a number of issues about myths of both the Old and the New West that are relevant to the lake as fable—the timeless lake, the unpredictable lake, the healing lake, the lake indifferent to human fate.

Chapter 8, "Pyramid Lake Proclaimed," picks up the thread of chapter 6, extending it to the present. The focus of the writers and artists considered here is on making the lake known to the public. Some of the paintings and photographs of the lake by Hildegard Herz, Robert Caples, Fletcher Martin, Gus

Bundy, Jonas Dovydenas, and Richard Misrach have become iconic. *Nevada Highways* magazine was an important medium for both visual and prose images of the lake. Journalist Basil Woon wrote sympathetic sketches of the lake and its residents whom he saw as doomed. Biologist Sessions Wheeler and ethnographer Margaret Wheat were the first to write popular books about the lake. Their legacy endures. Last in this chapter I consider some maps of the lake and the information they add to our understanding of place and time.

Chapter 9, "Seekers in the Desert," is about the spiritual attraction of deserts as a place of escape and renewal and the ways in which Pyramid Lake fits into Old World systems of belief. Nevada writer Idah Meacham Strobridge wrote about deserts east of Pyramid Lake, providing some understanding of the area's appeal. The boundaries between the latter-day desert fathers and Paiute shaman are as porous as the reservation's borders were in the 1860s. Although the Paiute religious leader Wovoka and journalist Dan De Quille were products of very different cultures, they both created elaborate fables of desert life that share a sense of wonder about nature.

Chapter 10, "Pyramid Lake as Theater," continues the theme of the desert as spiritual place by examining the life of the actor-turned-missionary Brother David and the motion picture directors—Henry King, Robert Wise, and George Stephens—who saw in the lake and its surrounding deserts the Salton Sea, the Gobi, and the Sea of Galilee. I conclude with a look at the absurd and humorous side of life at the lake, the seekers of Pyramid Power and other paranormal phenomena. Religion, ritual, performance, entertainment, play—their defining circles overlap like a Venn diagram.

This is the chapter where I come closest to the work of Professor Richard V. Francaviglia, whose books on Great Basin cartography, spiritual geography, and orientalist symbolism have fascinated me. He enjoys looking through one end of the telescope and seeing the whole Great Basin and millennia of religious traditions. I look through the other end and see one small lake and a little more than a century. He seems most comfortable in the eastern basin, I in the western. We agree that landscapes contain multiple stories and that belief in a place requires believing the stories about it, but he and I part company on specifics, such as his assertion that Stone Mother's tale is about loss. I believe the legend and the stone formation are also about power. Stone Mother may have wept for her banished children, but her tears created a lake that gives her other descendants a bountiful home, while her tufa monument provides a compelling symbol of Kuyuidokado identity and survival.

* * *

At Pyramid Lake asks the reader to join the author in remembering the lake as she or he knows it, from personal experience, reading, or rumor. If I have learned anything in fifty years as a professional historian, it is that there is no final draft of history. To borrow an old Soviet joke that historian Larry Levine revived, "The future is certain, it is only the past that is unpredictable." Pyramid Lake's past is unpredictable because there is so much we do not know about its history, nor do we always agree on the meanings of the evidence we have.

Seek with me some understanding of Pyramid Lake. Sojourn there with this book in mind and let the sky and water transform what needs transforming. Celebrate the survival of the lake and its people. And don't forget to pay the tribe for your permit.

ONE

Survival of the Numa
and Pyramid Lake

The people and the fish are inextricable. The archaeological evidence of human habitation along the shores of what is now Pyramid Lake dates back at least ten thousand years. Whether these early lake dwellers were the direct ancestors of the people who call themselves Numa (People), and who are called Northern Paiute in the anthropological argot of Euro-Americans, or whether they were one of the many peoples who lived and vanished in the sands of the Great Basin before a band of Numa named the tasty black lake suckers kuyui and themselves Kuyuidokado—kuyui eaters—will probably never be known.

What we do know is that the hundred or so Numa families who lived more or less permanently at Kuyui Pah (Pyramid Lake) when the exploring party of Captain John Charles Frémont arrived in January 1844 not only took the name of their favorite fish, but organized their lives around the kuyui's annual spring spawning runs up the Truckee River. The Kuyuidokado fished with spears, nets, and weirs; children, men, and women participated in the catching, cleaning, preservation, and eating of the fish. Prayers were offered and answered, tired fishermen relaxed in sweat lodges, dancers celebrated the cycles of life of fish and humans. The Kuyuidokado managed the lake like a well-tended garden, carefully observing the habits of fish and water fowl, cultivating patches of tules and cattails for building material and snacks, traveling in the autumn to nearby mountains to hunt rabbits and deer and gather pine nuts.

In January the kuyui were dormant in the mud of the lake bottom, so the Indians offered the weary explorers their less favored fish, a kind of "salmon-trout" whose flavor Frémont found "superior, in fact, to that of any fish I have ever known." Despite his appreciation of the free meals, the newly promoted captain had bigger fish to fry. Favoring history over ecology, or even gastronomy, the "Pathfinder" named the lake for a three-hundred-foot rock formation that reminded him of the Great Pyramid of Cheops and, he hoped, reminded readers of his journal of his Napoleon-like conquest of the West. The Numa, blissfully unaware of pyramids of any kind, called the rock "wono," an overturned

conical basket. This rock formation and many others are known geologically as
tufa deposits. These deposits are formed of calcium carbonate ($CaCO_3$) emitted
by springs at the bottom of the lake. Since the tufas cannot grow above the level
of the lake, they provide a record of the depth of prehistoric Lake Lahontan of
which Pyramid Lake is a remnant. Before they hardened, the mineral deposits
branched and formed nodules, crystals, tubes, and similar shapes, creating reef-
like structures. The tufas of Pyramid Lake were, writes geologist Larry Benson,
formed between twenty-six and thirteen thousand years ago and are unique in
terms of their size and beauty. As they have broken apart over time, they have
assumed shapes that stimulate human viewers to see figures and faces, pyramids
and baskets.

In 1844 the Kuyuidokado's lake was slightly larger than it is today, perhaps
40 miles long and 10 to 20 miles wide. (Even today you could drop the island of
Manhattan—13 miles long and 2.3 miles wide—into Pyramid Lake, and all but
the tallest buildings would be covered.) The level of the lake plunged more than
90 feet in the last century, but regained around 30 feet beginning in the 1980s,
thanks to several wet years and improved water management on the Truckee
River. Lacking an outlet and subject to constant evaporation, the lake's water
is saline, but only about 17 percent as salty as the ocean. The lake's shores are
mostly treeless, the nearby mountains gray-green with shadscale, rabbitbrush,
and sagebrush. In spring the hills brighten with yellow blossoms. Vegetation,
including willows and cottonwoods, is thicker in the delta at the south end of
the lake where the Truckee River enters. Today, invasive plant species such as
tamarisk (planted by the US Navy in the 1940s as camouflage for ordinance) dot
the lake's western shore, and alfalfa and its associated weeds—Russian knap-
weed and yellow starthistle—grow in plots near the river. Puncture vine (*Tribu-
lus terrestris*) is found along the old Southern Pacific Railroad right-of-way (railroads are always a path for invasion) on the west side of the lake.

The Natives of Pyramid Lake were hospitable to Frémont's party, and there
is no indication in his journals that they were surprised to see pale strangers
or horses. Linguistically related Indians to the north, south, and east had been
encountering trappers and traders for a half century. Thomas Layton's pioneering article on horse use in the northern Great Basin gathers evidence that Indians along the Lassen Trail stole immigrants' horses for food, while tribes along
the Humboldt River were riding by the 1820s. Exactly when the Kuyuidokado
got horses is unknown, but they were mounted by 1860. The Paiute word for
horse was *Ti'-hig*, according to explorer John Wesley Powell, but the term for a
rich man was *I-wau'-hig Kai-yus* (Many horses have) and *Kai'-hig Kai-yus* (No

horses have) for a poor man. *Cayuse* (English spelling) is a common noun for "horse" in western America and also denotes an Indian tribe in Oregon, indicating that both the word and the animal were borrowed from there. Trading and theft were reliable ways of acquiring horses.

A tantalizing item in the May 6, 1857, *San Francisco Daily Evening Bulletin* refers to a "Dutchman" who was considered a "white chief" by the Pyramid Lake Paiutes. The story notes that he was branded and run out of town for horse stealing. A white man who stole horses might be a valuable ally. Could this be the "German," Snyder (named by the press the "white Winnemucca"), who accompanied Sarah Winnemucca, Captain Truckee's granddaughter and "Chief" Winnemucca's daughter, to boarding school in San Jose in 1860? Names and identities were fluid on the frontier as the conquest began, with English names replacing Paiute. Thocmetony became Sarah Winnemucca, her grandfather became Captain Truckee, and Wovoka, a Paiute spiritual leader, was also known as Jack Wilson.

There is no doubt from the account by Sarah Winnemucca that Captain Truckee, who joined Frémont in California during the brief war with Mexico, was a realist who knew that resistance to white encroachments would be futile. His granddaughter, who became an important advocate for Numa rights, but had almost nothing to say about Pyramid Lake, claimed that her grandfather's name meant "all right" in Numic. He eagerly offered his services as a guide to immigrants as well as to Frémont, learned their language, and ordered his grandchildren to attend school and learn the immigrants' customs. In the first decades of contact, when the numbers of invaders were few, Captain Truckee's strategy of keeping the strangers moving on to California worked satisfactorily, but by 1860 Winnemucca and Numaga, the Kuyuidokado war chief, had an impossible task. Gold- and silver-mining prospectors and would-be ranchers began flooding into Paiute lands. As historian Ferol Egan recounts in *Sand in the Whirlwind: The Paiute Indian War of 1860*, a series of transgressions by whites against the Indians, including rape and murder, led the Paiutes to retaliate. Whites then mounted a force of 750 vigilantes. On May 12, 1860, the Paiutes ambushed 105 of the ersatz army, killing between 50 and 76 men, including their titular leader, Major William Ormsby, erstwhile friend of Captain Truckee.

Less than a month later, more than 500 volunteers under "Colonel" Jack Hays and more than 200 regular army troops from California under Captain Joseph Stewart attacked a force of perhaps as many as 600 Paiutes and allies, killing 4, according to their leader, Numaga, before the Indians disappeared into the rugged terrain east and north of the lake. Other claims put Indian losses at 160, with white fatalities at 3 or 4. Violence continued for five years, culminating in the massacre, by troops under the command of Captain Almond B. Wells, of at least 32 Paiute women and children, including one of Sarah's brothers, at Mud Lake on March 14, 1865.

Myron Angel, an early Nevada historian, estimated that between 1860 and 1870, 30 whites and 287 Indians were murdered in interracial conflicts. The prolific Virginia City diarist Alfred Doten estimated the total Paiute population at 2,000 at the time of the "War," but never mentions the battle again, indicating how insignificant it was for the conquerors. Thanks to the research of Nevada archaeologist Donald R. Tuohy, we have a good idea of Kuyuidokado demographics. Whatever the consequences of the battles, the population of Pyramid Lake Paiutes was decimated in the years between 1860, when Indian agent Major Frederick Dodge estimated their numbers at 1,550, and 1866, when agent H. G. Parker put the population at 700. Starvation, disease, and flight to more remote areas surely account for some of the loss. Moreover, the decline continued. The census of 1880 counted only 396 Kuyuidokado. A century later the resident population was only a little higher. A 2010 census finds 1,330 enrolled members of the Pyramid Lake Paiutes.

The Pyramid Lake Reservation was created in November 1859, when the commissioner of Indian affairs and the commissioner of the General Land Office accepted the recommendation of Major Dodge to provide a home for some 600 Indians. (The figure here may mean adult Indians, or Dodge was fiddling with the numbers to assure Bureau of Indian Affairs officials in Washington that this was a minor request.) "These are isolated spots," Dodge wrote, "embracing large fisheries, surrounded by Mountains and Deserts, and will have the advantage of being their home from choice."

Despite Dodge's good intentions, the relatively small parcel of land (originally twenty-five to fifty-three miles wide, now an irregular rectangle about fifty-five miles north to south and five to twenty miles east to west) surrounding the lake and about fifteen miles of the Truckee River was a Procrustean bed into which the Paiutes were expected to fit regardless of their size. The following 150 years is a record of daily struggles by the tribe to preserve this fragile spot.

In August 1860, after the hostilities, Colonel Frederick Lander, chief engineer for the Federal Wagon Road and special Indian agent, met with Numaga and arranged a truce. No peace treaty was ever signed, but the legal status of the reservation was confirmed March 23, 1874, by executive order of President U. S. Grant. With the legal status of the reservation unclear from 1859 to 1874 (in the minds of land-hungry whites), and with little enforcement of Indian claims by the Bureau of Indian Affairs, white squatters began to move in by 1861. Murder of Indian farmers to acquire land on the reservation went unpunished. The reservation was surveyed in 1865, but no map was published by the government until 1868. Tribal members survived by selling fish to restaurants in Reno and Virginia City, making attempts at farming, and hiring themselves out to local ranchers.

In 1868 the Central Pacific Railroad, following the valley of the Truckee River eastward, reached the reservation and laid out the town of Wadsworth, naming it in honor of a fallen Union army officer and further erasing Indian claims to the place. In an uncharacteristic gesture of goodwill toward the Paiutes, from whom they had taken several hundred acres of reservation land, the directors of the railroad allowed Indians to ride on the roofs of freight cars for free. Although this benefit lasted only about twenty years, it gave enterprising Paiutes a way to visit relatives, enlarge their hunting and gathering grounds, and market their fish. Free passes for "Bucks" and "Squaws" were offered by other railroads, when approved by Indian agents. "Because of the railroads," writes anthropologist Alex Ruuska, who studied the spread of the Ghost Dance by rail,

Pyramid Lake Paiutes with members of the Fortieth Parallel Survey, summer 1867. Photograph by Timothy O'Sullivan. Courtesy of George Eastman House, International Museum of Photography and Film.

"native peoples could temporarily remove themselves from unwanted surveil-lance, traverse greater distances, increase their work opportunities, and expand their social, political, and ritualistic connections."

RESERVATION LIVES

By 1872 the Pyramid Lake Paiutes were shipping an estimated forty to one hundred tons of fish annually to markets as far away as San Francisco. Most of the catch was the "salmon-trout," now identified as the Lahontan cutthroat trout (*Oncorhynchus clarki henshawi*). In an effort to prevent the Indians from profiting from their industry, the Nevada Territorial Legislature had, in 1861, defined trout as a sport fish, legally catchable by hook and line only, prohibit-ing the Indians' traditional use of weirs, spears, and nets. With numbers of Lahontan cutthroat trout declining, the California Fish Commission began stocking brook trout and whitefish in the Truckee in 1875 and the Nevada Fish Commission began planting Sacramento perch in the lake in 1877, without con-sulting the tribe. White commercial fishermen, encouraged by these and other actions, greedily descended on the lake. The Indians and some of the BIA agents responded as best they could. On December 21, 1877, a US marshal and deputies exchanged gunfire with poachers. Two years later twenty-five members of the US Cavalry evicted some white fishermen, and troops were back in 1884 in a futile effort to prevent trespass on the reservation.

Thanks to the prodigious research of John M. Townley, we know how rapidly a fleet of fishing and pleasure boats on Pyramid Lake expanded in the 1870s. The *Nevada State Journal* and the *Reno Evening Gazette* kept their readers up-to-date on nautical affairs, although some of their claims are suspect. In 1876, for example, it was asserted that a thirty-eight-foot steamer capable of running up the Truckee to Wadsworth was under construction. In the following year it was reported that a twenty-four-foot steamer yacht with a four-horsepower engine was coming from Buffalo, New York. By 1879 forty-five boats were said to com-pose the lake's fishing fleet.

On March 11, 1880, the *Nevada State Journal* reported on the opening of the Griswold Trout Cannery, a white-owned fish-processing facility in Wadsworth. An article in the *Reno Evening Gazette* on June 24 of the same year described various methods of fishing, and the reporter claimed that he caught eighteen trout, with a combined weight of fifty pounds, in two hours of trolling. Tons of fish continued to be shipped annually, but the noticeable decline in stocks brought the attention of state authorities. Even the lowly kuyui was noticed, and renamed. The *Gazette* reported on March 3, 1881, that a California Fish

Commission ichthyologist had, in 1869, identified the Pyramid Lake "Cooy-ouie" as *Catos tomus* (reclassified in 1883 as *Chasmistes cujus*). Twelve days later in an article titled "A Fish with Hooked Bones," the paper quoted Washoe and Paiute Indians on the meaning of "cooyouie" and corrected its transcription to "gooyoue." Although whites did not like the taste of what they came to call cui-ui, they soon claimed bragging rights to the fish found only in their state and shortened the Paiute pronunciation, "cooey-ooey," to "kwee-wee."

In another effort to prevent Indians from competing with white fishermen, the Nevada Legislature passed a law in 1891 forbidding Indians to ship fish to market. Ever resourceful, the Kuyuidokado used their own wagons, but reservation income fell by two-thirds. The legislature passed other restrictions, including prohibiting sales of fish throughout most of the year. Demonstrating how well they had adapted to capitalism, the Paiutes made "gifts" of their fish to chefs in Reno, accepting payment only in the legal season. The struggle for control of fishing on the reservation continued well into the 1930s when the Lahontan cut-throat trout became extinct. Frustrated by the Pyramid Lake Tribe's opposition to the gathering of trout spawn for artificial propagation, the state asked the US Bureau of Fisheries to take over in 1930, but opposition continued because the real issue was not the trout, but water for the lake, which had been drastically reduced since 1905 when the Bureau of Reclamation completed Derby Dam and began diverting most of the Truckee's waters to farmers in the Newlands Reclamation Project. Much of the irrigation water is used to grow alfalfa for cattle feed. The question remains, how do we measure the benefit of subsidized cow chow, or alfalfa sprout salads for humans, against the cost to the beauty and cultural value of the lake?

GLIMPSES OF RESERVATION LIFE at the end of the nineteenth century and beginning of the twentieth can be found in newspaper accounts of visits by whites on holidays and the reports by Indian agent Lorenzo Creel, whose papers are preserved in the Special Collections of the University of Nevada Library. In these records Creel is sympathetic to the Indians, but his comments also reveal unconscious racism and obscure the psychological and cultural devastation taking place as the river and the lake were exploited.

On March 9, 1899, the *Reno Weekly Gazette and Stockman* published a lengthy report on the Pyramid Lake Reservation by Jeannett Miller. Framed by reports on blizzards in the East and US military skirmishes in the Philippines, Miller's article paints a rosy picture of "Uncle Sam's" efforts "to lift the poor Indian from his savagery." As John Toby, a tribal policeman, brings her down the Truckee from Wadsworth to the unnamed village that would become Nixon in 1912, she learns the names of the Paiute "owners of 'farms' along the river"—Andy Jackson, Whisky Ben, Black Frank, Old Dick, Bronco Jim, Rawhide Henry, Pussy Abigins, Honest Jim, Spanish Joe, Captain Dave, and Winnemucca Natches—heads of families who were born just before or just after the creation of the reservation forty years earlier. Their names are wrenched from those we find in the "Stick Census" of 1880, cataloged by Tuohy. In that enumeration, each head of a household was given some peeled sticks of coyote willow (*Salix exiqua*) stained with red ochre to represent each member of his or her family: Whe-á da (Old Hickory/Andy Jackson?), To zouac (Whiskey Ben), Koo-zoue-doüb (Pussiaba Jim or James).

Miller writes that she was met by the Indian agent, Major Spriggs, who introduced his staff—a clerk, a physician, a general mechanic, the school principal and three teachers, a seamstress, a matron and her assistant, a cook, and a post trader. Thirteen government employees and contractors supervised "a little less than six hundred Piutes," only 475 of whom resided at the lake. The clerk, physician, principal, mechanic, industrial teacher, and post trader were men, the rest of the staff women, presumably unmarried.

"The story of Hiawatha was being used as the basis of a reading lesson in the primary grade and seemed very appropriate," Miller writes, "but the dull grind of grammar and geography as ordinarily taught must have little meaning to these children of the brush, and can hardly be as beneficial as lessons in carpentering, blacksmithing, and farming." She attended a session of the "Indian Court," where Dave Gibson (Mahwee), Lee Winnemucca, and Billy Frazer were trying a man for stealing another man's wife. The judges, Miller notes, were appointed by the agent and their decisions subject to his approval. The government provided wagons and farm implements and employed about 40 men to construct an irrigation ditch and improve the fishway between the lake and the river. Miller concludes: "The Piutes are a happy-go-lucky class, and the cares of life seem to trouble them but little. It is no wonder that they take no thought for the morrow, since Uncle Sam looks out for their aged and sick, gives them farms to live upon and Pyramid Lake for a fish pond, and in short, fondles each young Piute in the lap of luxury."

The patronizing tone of this article is echoed in an editorial-page notice in the *Reno Evening Gazette*, October 26, 1916, under the headline "A Neglected Attraction." "For the last five years at Nixon, the postoffice of the Pyramid Lake Reservation, 'baby shows' and child welfare exhibitions have been given every year under the direction of the superintendent, J. D. Oliver, along with all the other incidentals of an animal fair—live stock, farm, domestic art and science. Appropriate prizes have been given to the aborigines and are thought much of." In the spirit of Wilsonian-era Progressivism and Nevada boosterism, the writer continues: "The truth is Reno does not appreciate the proximity of the Pyramid Lake Reservation as it should. It would be a great drawing card if properly advertised and would attract tourists from all parts of the country."

Papooses, ponies, and poults must have given the judges, reporters, and tourists much amusement. Baby shows for the white middle class were nothing new, of course—P. T. Barnum had staged them at his museum in New York City beginning in 1855—but they were criticized as being degrading to women, despite their popularity. Dark-skinned families had been put on display at the world's fairs of 1876, 1893, and 1904, as evidence of American benevolence, masking the nation's imperial ambitions. Baby shows continue to be part of county fairs around the country, and Paiute mothers may have been complicit with agent Oliver. They were proud of their babies, and prize money came in handy.

By 1922 the Progressive movement in the state had instituted a home-demonstration program that presented a "Ranchers and Homesteaders Institute" at Nixon. The program began at 1:00 P.M. with an invocation by deaconess Lucy N. Carter of the Episcopal Indian Mission, followed by the singing of "America" by the Indian Glee Club. Dr. M. M. Carmichael, school physician, lectured on "trachoma among Indians and its treatment" and on flies as disease carriers, followed by a workshop on making fly traps. Tribal member Harry Mitchell performed a clarinet solo, and Indian children sang songs, followed by a talk titled "How I Teach Little Indians to Help Around the House," by Mrs. J. W. Jackson, housekeeper of the day school. In the evening Miss Mary E. Stilwell, the state home-demonstration leader, gave a presentation of social games.

Another view of reservation life at the beginning of the twentieth century comes from the memoir of Janette Woodruff, who spent almost thirty years in the service of the BIA. *Indian Oasis* is her account of teaching and nursing on the Crow (Apsáalooke), Pyramid Lake, and Papago (Tohono O'odham) Reservations. She arrived in Wadsworth in July 1908 when Lorenzo Creel was still the agent and left for Arizona in December 1915 when J. D. Oliver was agent. Creel's instructions to her were vague and impossibly ambitious—"Live right here among them to show them how to do better." Since the departure of the Southern Pacific Railroad shops in 1904, Wadsworth had fallen into economic decline and its population diminished, but Indians "still went gathering gold in the debris and tangled weeds that marked the once-flourishing Chinatown, or stealthily crept to the garbage piles behind lonely Chen's

Paiute woman with baby in a cradle board. She is displaying other examples of her craftsmanship, including a beaded belt. Photograph by E. H. Linton, 1907. Courtesy Nevada Historical Society, ETH 752.

restaurant to forage for a meal." Chen and his compatriots were most likely workers laid off after the completion of the Central Pacific Railroad, which had recruited them in the 1860s. Woodruff describes an Indian community plagued by poverty and disease. Funerals, usually for children, take place every few pages of her book.

When Woodruff stepped off the train, Wadsworth was a charred remnant of an arson that destroyed more than half of the town's business section. As reported by the *Reno Evening Gazette,* July 22, 1907, a "fire-fiend," with a grudge against Constable Milo Crosby for shooting his friend for resisting arrest, ignited a blaze that destroyed Jim Crosby's saloon, another saloon, E. W. Griswold's home and warehouse, the post office, a Chinese bakery and restaurant, Crosby's blacksmith shop, and several other residences and businesses. The "fiend" was arrested after he "proceeded to fill up on whisky at an Italian saloon just across the street from the building he had fired." This story is fascinating for what it reveals about the reservation's largest town—so many Crosbys, so many saloons (segregated by ethnicity), but apparently no Indians— and how the reporter ties the incident to an expected visit by Secretary of the

Interior James R. Garfield, son of the assassinated president. Quoting H. W. Esden, owner of the Wadsworth Power, Light & Water Company, the story concludes: "We intend to entertain Secretary Garfield despite our loss and to have him do something for the town in regard to the opening of the Pyramid Lake Indian Reservation and also in regard to the irrigation scheme in this state." Schemers trying to wrest land from the Pyramid Lake Paiutes needed little prompting.

Woodruff quickly established her school, provided breakfasts for the students, and organized a sewing circle for a group of young women. These "Madonnas of the Wigwam," as she calls them, became her guides to Paiute life. She learned a little about the importance of the "Que-wees," pine nuts, mud hens, and rabbits in their diet. She was bemused by Bull Tom, an older man who collected cast-off clothing from whites in Wadsworth to make costumes for the dances he performed at the Fourth of July celebrations at Nixon. "With baubles, fringe, lace, a confusion of colors, and a pair of steer horns cocked on his forehead, he could at least attract attention. Some few admired him; some laughed at the comical figure he cut, and followed him because of the irresistible attraction of his outlandish garb." She also notes that the young men of the tribe were especially disdainful of Bull Tom for being old-fashioned. This seems a classic case of multiple cultural misunderstandings. Woodruff had no knowledge of Paiute customs; her eight years with the Crow provided her only frame of reference. The young men may have seemed embarrassed by Bull Tom, but they may have been objecting less to his traditionalism than to his performing as an "Indian" for whites. "Modern" Paiutes may wear Levi's and denim shirts, but the costume conceals a variety of attitudes.

By her first Christmas, Woodruff seems to have learned to appreciate Paiute behavior and humor. She had persuaded a young man to play Santa Claus and dressed him in a costume trimmed with cotton. As he was handing out presents, his coat caught fire. Woodruff, Creel, and another employee quickly snatched off his jacket and cap and extinguished the flames. "That was one time," Woodruff writes, "I fervently thanked Providence for an Indian audience."

No one shouted "Fire!" or even made the slightest commotion. As a striking contrast, the few whites who were sitting beyond the open door in my apartment, bolted pell-mell the minute they saw the flames, and did not return till the danger was well over. As for the Indians, they all sat as still as statues, fascinated by the spectacle, apparently regarding it as just another number on the program. . . . In this incident there was a comic element for the Indians as well. They joked, too, but after their own fashion. One young fellow voiced the sentiment of others when he expressed his reactions to the fire scene. "Gosh!" he drawled, "Santa might help himself little bit. Didn't even know enough to take off false face."

Jokes often contain layered meanings. Woodruff and the young Paiute may have chuckled for different reasons. The conclusion of Woodruff's recollections of life at Wadsworth concerns the ways in which white and Indian medicine and religion were merged in the daily lives of the Natives. She is critical of the arrogance of a woman doctor who tried, unsuccessfully, to bully the Indians into submitting to smallpox vaccinations. Woodruff finds much to admire in the Paiutes' ability to live in two worlds. As her reference to "Providence" rather than "God" in the Christmas fire episode suggests, she was more of a freethinker than a conventional Christian. No missionaries are mentioned in her memoir, though Episcopalians had been active since the 1890s, maintaining churches in Wadsworth and Nixon. What the Paiutes made of doctrinal disputes among white people is difficult to determine, but Woodruff's faith was clearly that of the Social Gospel, and her legacy was a foundation for John Collier, Alida Bowler, and the Indian Reorganization Act.

A fascinating glimpse of Indian-Anglo relations at this time is provided by a visitor to the reservation who took part in an early-autumn mud hen (American coot or *Fulica americana*) drive. Written by E. F. Creel, certainly a relative of superintendent Lorenzo D. Creel, the four-page typed account is rich with detail on the methods of the hunt and the festive atmosphere created by both whites and Indians. The hunt took place at what the diarist calls Carmelita Lake. The lake is described as being at the south end of Pyramid Lake, a pond about a mile long and a half mile wide. It appears on the 1864 map by Eugene Monroe; on later maps it is labeled Duck Lake. The mud hens, ducks, killdeer, and other wetland fowl fed on Indian rice grass and other marsh plants in the river delta. Soon the birds became too fat to fly. "At one end of Carmelita Lake," E. F. Creel writes, "the rowboats were manned by the younger, stronger and best shots of the Tribe."

> These boats formed a fleet as it were and all started at once so as to sweep the lake. Some of the boats falling behind formed a second row, to close in the rear, one man rowing and another shooting from each boat. The surface of this lake was fairly covered with Mud Hens and looking up and down the course there was presented to the eye one dark colored mass of the fowls. One could hardly see the waters but the boats ploughed through and the firing was almost constant, and

the hens fell thick and fast when trying to fly away which some of them did; many Hens floated in toward the shore, some dead and others only injured.

Creel describes how men, women, and children dispatched the wounded birds with sticks. "Many of the Hens swam to the shore and attempted to fly to the other lake but owing to their being so fat they could fly only a short distance and most of them dropped exhausted in the sand and sage brush from whence they were quickly gathered in by the Indians, so that while the shooting was being carried out on the lake, the Mud Hens were being slaughtered in number by the Indians on the banks of the lake and out in the sage brush."

At the conclusion of the hunt, the birds were taken to camps, where the women skinned and dressed them for cooking or dried them for consumption later in the year. Except for the use of guns, the hunt was similar to those described by Margaret Wheat in *Survival Arts of the Primitive Paiutes,* her lovely homage to life in the Great Basin before the arrival of whites. Traditionally, men would catch ducks and other waterfowl with nets, or use their tule rafts to drive the birds from the lake to the shore, where they were killed by young men with something like a hockey stick. E. F. Creel assures us that the hunt did not seem to diminish the number of mud hens on the lake and that the Indians usually had three or four of these drives during October and November. They were occasions for gossiping, storytelling, and "fun and merry-making generally," especially for children, who were given time off from school to be "Indians in the old time way."

Creel's vignette is significant in a number of ways. The writer avoids the sentimentalism often found in writing by "friends of the Indian" in this period. The slaughter of the mud hens is accepted as part of the cycle of life. Whether the "ecological Indian" is myth or historical fact is an important question still being debated. What the account of the mud-hen drive reveals is that technology matters: people with guns can kill more birds than people with sticks. Presumably, little was wasted in either the pre- or the postfirearms period. Meat not consumed at the festival was smoked for future dining. The mud-hen drive was part of the endless cycle of hunting and gathering and required an understanding of the ecology of the place—when to expect the migratory birds, when the pine nuts would ripen, when the cold weather would drive game down from the mountains, and, above all, when the fish would spawn. Food came to the Paiutes, or at least met them halfway. Despite what Senator Pat McCarran would later assert, the Kuyuidokado were not nomadic in the usual sense of this term, which is used to describe people with no fixed abode. Although they traveled to hunt and to gather pine nuts, Pyramid Lake was home to the cui-ui eaters.

* * *

AMID THESE GOOD TIMES, however, some conflict occurred. In the *Reno Evening Gazette,* June 14, 1915, a banner headline announced: PYRAMID LAKE INDIANS BELLIGERENT; THREATEN TO BURN WHITES' BOATS. The lede continued the alarm: "Unrest among the Pyramid Reservation Indians, which caused them to display an inclination and desire to destroy property belonging to white persons on the Reservation and lake, manifested itself yesterday when 30 bucks appeared at The Willows, threatened to tear down the fences around the James Sutcliffe ranch and removed from the lake two boats belonging to white persons, threatening to burn them if they were placed on the lake again." The leader of the protest, George Green, told Sutcliffe that whites had no right to fish in Pyramid Lake and no right to place boats on the lake. Sutcliffe's reply was to go to Indian agent J. D. Oliver, who signed an order declaring the protesters "off the reservation" and directing them to return to Nixon. The final paragraph of the story suggests that the Indians were also protesting the arrest of their licensed trader, C. S. Crosby, for testing what they considered an unfair state law that placed all the fish in the lake except the cui-ui under state control and made it illegal for the Indians to sell any fish. An adjacent story, illustrated with a photograph of a young woman carrying the Stars and Stripes, invited Nevadans to observe Flag Day. For the Kuyuidokado, as one of their leaders would later observe, the cui-ui is the flag.

The *Gazette's* alarmist tone in its account of the confrontation between Indians and trespassing fishermen may be explained by memories of the deadly 1911 skirmish with "Shoshone Mike" in northern Washoe County and by news from southeastern Utah where, in early 1915, a conflict between cattlemen, Mormon settlers, and dispossessed Paiutes culminated in several deaths. Armed encounters and killings between whites and Indians in San Juan County, Utah, did not end until 1923, according to Steve Lacy's *Posey: The Last Indian War.* Better leadership on the Pyramid Lake Reservation and a less bellicose white citizenry spared northern Nevada from having the dubious distinction of providing the setting for "the last Indian war."

H. W. Philipson, a farmer hired by the BIA to help Paiutes at Pyramid Lake improve and enlarge their farms, filed a report on June 26, 1922, describing the condition of fifty-four families who were trying to make a living off their land. This document, also from the Creel papers in Special Collections, is rich in information on daily life on the reservation at this time. Each of the families is identified by the name of the head of household. Other family members are enumerated; a few are named. One family was headed by a widow. If there were children in school, Philipson mentions whether they were in the day school at Nixon or boarding at the Stewart Indian School in Carson City. He was, of course, primarily interested in the kinds of crops and acreage and the number, kind, and condition of livestock. The figures are impressive. There was a total of at least 325 acres of alfalfa. Almost every family had a garden. More than 100 horses and 160 cattle were counted. Most families had only 2 or 3 horses and cows, but Willie Oday had a herd of 49 beeves. Sam Kay and John Wright had followed the agent's advice and gotten into the poultry business. Kay had 60 turkeys, Wright 150.

Philipson makes some intriguing observations about a man he calls W. M. Roberts. "He has a frame house and his family consists of a wife and no children in accordance with the example of some of the best white people," the BIA farmer notes. Was Philipson alluding to the founding of the Birth Control League (later Planned Parenthood) by Margaret Sanger the year before his report? Immediately after his remark on family planning, Philipson adds that Roberts "also owns a touring car with yellow wheels and a black body." Philipson's inclusion of this detail suggests that car ownership by Kuyuidokado in 1922 may have been a novelty. Clearly, Philipson singles out this detail as both an anomaly and a sign of assimilation, illustrating what historian Philip Deloria calls "Indians in unexpected places." Third, the BIA farmer notes that Roberts, "a model rancher . . . had hardly finished planting his spring crop when more urgent work in the way of being a dancer in an exhibition in Sacramento called him to that place. His fame in this line proved so great that his aid was solicited in presenting some acts for a moving picture firm. This however he declined feeling that his example as a farmer here was of far greater value to his people."

Federal Indian policy equated good Indians with farming, bad Indians with fishing. The blatant disregard for the fishing rights of the Paiutes by agent J. D. Oliver was typical. In 1925 his predecessor, Lorenzo D. Creel, complained about Oliver to California congressman John E. Raker, who was working on legislation to improve water use on the Truckee. Ironically, this was the same Congressman Raker who wrote the act that dammed the Hetch Hetchy Valley to provide water for San Francisco. The fight to preserve Hetch Hetchy as a companion to Yosemite was led by John Muir, but other conservationists, even some in the Sierra Club, defended the creation of an artificial lake because it would provide recreational boating and fishing.

Similar arguments were used over the years to support the diversion of Truckee and Carson River water into the Lahontan Reservoir that provided water for irrigating the farms of the Newlands Reclamation Project, the first of many irrigation projects in western states funded by the Reclamation Act of 1902 that created the US Reclamation Service. From 1905, when Derby Dam was completed on the Truckee, to the 1990s, when efforts were made to save Pyramid Lake by limiting flows into Lahontan and the Stillwater marshes, proponents of the Newlands Reclamation Project claimed the boating, fishing, and duck hunting in the artificial lake was actually superior to recreation at Pyramid Lake. Creel explained to Raker how the irrigation project had interrupted the spawning of the trout and the "Quiwui" and accused Oliver of profiting from the slaughter of the fish as they floundered at the worthless fish ladders on the small earth dams on the reservation and at Derby Dam.

There is no evidence of a reply from Raker, whose ideas on river management probably did not include challenging the Reclamation Service (renamed the Bureau of Reclamation in 1923) or the Bureau of Indian Affairs for the benefit of a few Indians. The year following Creel's appeal, the Bureau of Reclamation turned over the management of the Newlands irrigation project to a local body, the Truckee-Carson Irrigation District (TCID), whose antipathy toward the Pyramid Lake Paiutes and intransigence in making any improvements in fish or water conservation will be discussed in the following chapters. The draining of a beautiful, bountiful natural lake to create a shallow, more polluted, artificial one is just one of the many ironies that pile up like dead fish.

Throughout their history, the Kuyuidokado were willing to sacrifice the trout for the larger goal of preserving the lake's water level and, for them, the lake's important treasure, the cui-ui. Water was vital to the preservation of the lake, its cui-ui, and Paiute identity, an identity that clashed with western politicians' dreams of turning the desert into a garden through irrigation. The Nevada Fish and Game Commission had begun a program of artificial propagation of trout in 1914, but the Indians forced its cessation in 1923 because they correctly saw that stocking the lake was a way of avoiding the need for greater flows through the river and the restoration of natural spawning upriver. The turmoil created by the conflicting goals of the Indians and the Nevada Fish and Game managers was compounded by the lack of scientific studies of the ecosystem of the lake and its fish and fowl.

A depressing illustration of the problem appeared in the *Reno Evening Gazette*, March 21, 1923, under the headline "Trout Running Up Truckee; Start Yesterday." The story begins with a statement by James H. Vogt, superintendent of the state fish hatchery at Verdi, that 250,000 eggs had been "stripped" from LCT captured while attempting to ascend the river at Derby Dam. Stripping was halted, however, when "forty Piute bucks came down on the war path and objected." Vogt claimed he did not understand the Indians' objections, but pronounced that the new fish ladder "is an ideal one," despite the fact that the *Gazette*'s reporter, aided by Indian agent Lorenzo Creel and a party of observers, found that fewer than half of the spawning fish cleared the dam. Even less fortunate were the pelicans and magpies, "which were numerous a few years ago, Mr. Creel informing the party that the poisoning campaign [I have been unable to discover what the "poisoning campaign" involved or who was responsible] had all but exterminated them." The trout were extinct in Pyramid Lake within two decades.

The passage, June 18, 1934, of the Indian Reorganization Act (Wheeler-Howard Act) that encouraged the creation of tribal councils with the power to negotiate directly with federal, state, and local governments began the long process of breaking the deadlock. The Pyramid Lake Paiutes had been taking steps toward an elected council since 1930 and had elected a twelve-member group and a chair by February 1934. One of the council's first acts was to initiate tribal fishing licenses, appoint wardens, and assert control over the lake's resources. Agreements were reached with the state, and the collection of LCT spawn resumed. By 1948 the Nevada Department of Fish and Game reached an agreement with the tribe to resume stocking the lake experimentally with various nonnative fish, and, by 1960, it was planting "cutbows," a hybrid of rainbow trout and the Walker River strain of Lahontan cutthroat trout. In 1975, after the state turned over the stocking of the lake to the tribe, a strain close to the original Lahontan cutthroat trout had been found and was being released from a hatchery managed on the reservation by the tribe.

Important as it was for revenue, the struggle to control game fishing was a sideshow. The fate of the tribe, the cui-ui, and the lake was in the hands of federal judges in faraway courts. Recognizing that the Newlands irrigation project was causing disputes among water users along the Truckee, the US Reclamation Service initiated, in 1913, a "friendly" suit against the Orr Ditch Water Company, one of the many small businesses furnishing water to farmers in the Truckee Meadows, near Reno. These ditch companies sold stock and charged farmers a fee. The Reclamation Service hoped a "friendly" judge could sort out the conflicting water claims of home owners at Lake Tahoe (source of the water), power companies, city businesses and residents, and farmers and their ever-thirsty crops. Pyramid Lake and the Indians who lived there were an afterthought.

Lakefront property owners at Tahoe insisted their lake level remain stable. Several hydroelectric companies depended on storage in reservoirs for consistent flow through their canals. Because of a severe drought in 1912, members of these two interest groups almost came to blows at the Truckee's outlet in Tahoe City. An early fruit of *U.S. v. Orr Ditch Water Co., et al.* was the decision in 1919, by a US District Court judge in Nevada, to appoint a "special (water) master" to resolve future disputes. Sensing trouble, the big landowners organized the Truckee Meadows Water Users Association to protect their interests, which it apparently did quite well. When the special master issued a proposed decree in 1924, he allowed the Pyramid Lake Reservation 58.7 cfs (cubic feet per second) of water annually for irrigating 3,130 acres, while awarding the Newlands Project 1,500 cfs for 232,800 acres. Two years later the "master" failed to allocate any water to Pyramid Lake. Some water was legally restored to the lake in 1944 when a decree was finally issued in the "friendly" suit, but the court's "Orr Ditch Decree" still failed to provide sufficient water for the preservation of the lake and its fish.

Overfishing by both Indians and whites, dams and irrigation, pollution from timber mills—all these contributed to the decline of Pyramid Lake and its natural resources in the first century after Frémont's arrival. Nevertheless, the Kuyuidokado remained resilient. They costumed themselves in white people's clothes, built houses from whatever lumber they could buy with profits from fishing, and sorrowfully watched their children shipped off to BIA boarding school, even after building their own elementary school in 1878. Parents and children learned English, the men became horse and cattle wranglers, and the women cleaned and did laundry for nearby farms and ranches. They survived, as Margaret Wheat's *Survival Arts of the Primitive Paiutes* subtly reveals, because they were not so "primitive" that they lacked "survival arts." They knew from the moment of contact the limits of their autonomy and remained independent within those limits. Some traditional arts—hunting, fishing, basketry, beadwork on buckskin moccasins and clothing, gathering edible and medicinal plants— remained useful. For their survival course at Stead Air Force Base in the 1950s, the US Air Force employed Paiutes to teach pilots how to find water, identify edible plants, and snare game in a desert environment. The first century was hard, and the second century continued the challenges that Captain Truckee, Chief Winnemucca, and Numaga would have understood. Survival meant keeping your eye on the lake.

STONE MOTHER

And the lake will provide. The lake furnished additional spiritual strength with the appearance—near the pyramid—of a heretofore unseen tufa formation that resembled a hooded figure seated with an open basket. The rocks were dubbed "the Squaw Woman and Her Basket" in the September–October 1938 issue of *Nevada Highways and Parks*. The accompanying photograph, the earliest I have found, mislocated the formation, placing it at the northern end of the lake, suggesting that the editors had not yet visited the site and that it was not well known to local whites. The use of the insulting word *squaw* indicates additional, if widespread, ignorance. The label "Squaw and Basket" persisted in state government publications for thirty years. The Pyramid Lake Tribe quickly asserted its claim to the monument by calling it "the Stone Mother" and working it into their existing origin myth.

The earliest version of the origin story of the Numa in English that I have seen is the one collected by John Wesley Powell in 1873:

> Pi-aish [wolf's brother] said "let's make people" and went down to the shore of the lake. Looking out on the waters which were troubled by the winds he saw a Pa-ha (mermaid or long haired woman) on the water. He beckoned her to come ashore and took her to his own home as his wife. They had three children, two boys and a girl, and the boys even when very young were quarrelsome, and would bite and pinch, and scratch each other. As they grew older they fought with arrows, and were always fighting until they grew to be men.
>
> This made the father, mother, and sister very sorrowful. . . . Then Pi-aish turned to the young men and said "Go away from my sight!" And the next day

Stone Mother and Basket at Pyramid Lake. Photograph by the author, 1998.

he caused a great fog to settle over the land, and when the boys were out on the plain, as was their wont, each tried to find the other that they might renew their quarrels but they wandered in the fog and were lost; and were never seen again.

Then Pi-aish said, "We will raise better people," so he sent Pa-ha back to the lake and married his daughter. They had two boys and two girls and when these were grown the brothers married their sisters, and each pair raised two other pairs, and these again two other pairs until there were a great many people in the country and Pi-aish said "There are too many people living in the valley." And he caused another great fog to settle over all the land and the people went out and were lost and wandered off into distant countries and so all the world was settled.

Allowing for possible distortions of the story by both narrator and translator, some elements of this creation story are revealing. The Numa recognize their kinship with the nonhuman world. When the Numa arrived in the Great Basin, wolves and coyotes were the smartest creatures to greet them. Why not take wolf as an ancestor? Any explanation of creation must also account for differences among people. Additionally, the story acknowledges that conflict and violence are present in life, beginning with siblings. While the Christian account of expulsion from Eden posits fratricide as a consequence of disobedience of the Creator's law, the Paiutes see it as a cause of human diasporas. Commandments are often broken; exile is a way to restore order. Paiutes are pragmatists in the deepest sense, rooting their knowledge in lived experience, recognizing that knowledge is not the same as wisdom.

In their explanation of the origin of human conflict, separating quarrelsome people is the simplest solution, since overpopulation relative to the natural resources needed for survival is a cause of conflict. The fog in which they wander and get lost may be metaphorical, representing all the challenges that individuals face as they learn to survive in an environment indifferent to their fate, but the winter "pogonip," a Paiute word for a mist of ice crystals or frozen fog, is common enough is northern Nevada. *The Annual Report of the Nevada State Weather Service* in 1892 describes the phenomenon in the hills near Virginia City.

It came suddenly; appeared in its greatest beauty on the morning of January 22; filled up the valleys and rolled up the mountain sides, leaving the tops of the largest hills like islands and rocky headlands; its waves tumbled over its shores; late in the afternoon its surface was much agitated by some unknown impulse causing its great waves to roll to the westward; the sky took on a yellow hue, where they tumbled over the eastern mountain rim of the city; Sugar Loaf Mountain became a cone-shaped island, with falls on each side of it. The canyons were slowly filled and the vapor surged up the sides of Mount Davidson, partly covering the city, and causing intense cold where there had been sunshine and warmth before.

Similar scenes must have inspired Numa storytellers for centuries.

THE ELEMENTS in Powell's informant's story—disobedience to parents, family conflict, banishment—can be found in the origin tales told by members of related Numa bands. The Cattail-eaters, whose territory is southeast of Pyramid Lake, located their fractious first family on a peak in the Stillwater Range. The Cattail-eaters' story includes two rock formations as representations of their first parents. This may be a precedent for including Stone Mother in the current Kuyuidokado version of the myth. The wanton destruction of the Cattail-eaters' stone figures, by navy pilots who used them for target practice during World War II, is a bitter reminder of the costs of conquest.

That the twenty-five-foot-tall Stone Mother tufa formation was under at least fifty feet of water until the shrinking lake exposed it in the 1930s accounts for her late appearance in the tribe's origin story, but her fortuitous emergence provided strong visual evidence of their claims to the lake. Coming as it did in a national period of Indian reorganization and cultural renewal, Stone Mother was quickly incorporated into public displays of identity. A brief story on page 3 of the June 28, 1939, *Reno Evening Gazette* illuminates the process:

> The legend of Pyramid Lake will be unfolded here Saturday night as Indians from Pyramid Lake Reservation stage their Reno rodeo pageant at the civic auditorium. The show, "Our Stone Mother," will start at eight o'clock with thirty Paiute Indians taking part.
>
> The story was written in 1937 by Frank Hudson, teacher at the Reservation school, and is taken, he said, from an old folk tale showing how the Paiute forefathers lived before the coming of the white man. The title "Stone Mother" was suggested by a stone formation near the large pyramid, said to resemble a woman with a basket on her back. The Indians, says the legend, called the rock their stone mother.
>
> The legend will be carried out in pantomime and will be followed by the various tribal dances, with a commentator explaining the significance of each. The dances will include the bear, owl, sun, antelope, eagle, circle, flower, wedding or feather, rabbit and war dances. The tribal wedding ceremony will also be depicted and the various tribal songs will be sung.

The performance was apparently successful, as it was repeated in 1940 and 1941 and many times after World War II. I have been unable to discover anything about Frank Hudson, the teacher mentioned in the *Gazette* article, but Kuyuido-kado with whom I have spoken remember him as a white man.

By 1974, when Nellie Shaw Harner, a teacher and native of the Pyramid Lake Reservation, published her history, *Indians of Coo-yu-ee Pah*, Stone Mother was central to the history of the people of Pyramid Lake. In her version the exiled children became the Pit River Indians in Northern California, the Bannocks in Idaho, and the Southern Paiutes of Owens Valley. In her rendering the father dies. The grieving mother wanders off with her basket on her back, sits down, and begins to cry. Her tears form Pyramid Lake. "The area around the Stone Mother," Harner concludes, "is a sacred place to the Neh-muh (Numa) for their meditation and prayer."

The burden the grieving mother had been carrying for centuries could now be put down. The Kuyuidokado had survived, and significant signs indicated that they were going to be stronger than ever. By revising their origin story to include the tufa formation, the Paiutes of the 1930s were simply continuing the tradition of locating their history in the landscape. Stone Mother was a chapter in that history, evidence that even the dimmest white person could see. Photos of Stone Mother appear regularly in brochures, magazines, and websites promoting Nevada tourism and its exotic, mysterious, haunted landscape. Misconceptions continued for some time, however. A writer for *Nature Magazine* in 1942, Marie Lomas, explained that "the Squaw with a Basket . . . was doomed to sit thus for some offense against the gods."

A better, somewhat quirky, interpretation of the Stone Mother appeared in the May 6, 1941, "Reno Revue" column by Gladys Rowley of the *Nevada State Journal*. Rowley begins her piece with an encomium to Pyramid Lake as a place of tranquillity and rest. She mentions the climate, how, protected by mountains on either side, spring comes earlier than in Reno. The tone shifts abruptly when Rowley writes about Stone Mother:

> The Stone Mother of Pyramid be [sic] likened to a vastly larger mass of stone— the Sphinx of another desert of pyramids. In each are the secrets of centuries. Only where the one is nature's work, the other is the work of man—chiseled from solid rock, to perpetuate the features of an Egyptian king who caused it to be built to guard him in death. Where the Indians saw, in one, a sorrowful mother, the Arabs have called the other "The Father of Terrors." . . . Where the one rises from the cool clear waters of a peaceful lake region, where an inescapable serenity is in the very atmosphere—the others form an ancient backdrop to a modern stage setting—for a raging war.

Rowley's apprehensions concerning World War II were well founded. Her older son, a paratrooper, was killed during the invasion of Holland. The popularity of her daily, then weekly, column was based on her ability to link everyday life in Reno with the wider world. In this column she tries to escape her fears, but they follow her to the lake, and in the article she briefly summarizes the legend of the Stone Mother's tears only to conclude that "her placid features tell another story too—of the futility of tears and care." Lounging on the lawn at the Pyramid Lake Guest Ranch and gazing across the lake, Rowley could not escape thinking of recent headlines about the German invasion of Athens and the Anglo-Iraq war. Her May Day sojourn was one of the last anyone would take at the lake for four years.

STONE MOTHER reminds me of "Grief," the name bestowed by tourists on the bronze figure created by the American sculptor Augustus St. Gaudens to commemorate Marian Hooper Adams. Commissioned by her husband, historian Henry Adams, the memorial is located in Rock Creek Cemetery in Washington, DC. St. Gaudens called his figure *The Mystery of the Hereafter.* The statue is a seated, barefoot figure, presumed to be a woman, whose face is obscured by a cloak, the folds of which envelop it like waves or a cloud. In his philosophical autobiography, *The Education of Henry Adams,* Adams archly commented on the memorial:

> He supposed its meaning to be the one commonplace about it—the oldest idea known to human thought. He knew that if he asked an Asiatic its meaning, not a man, woman, or child from Cairo to Kamchatka would have needed more than a glance to reply. From the Egyptian Sphinx to the Kamakura Daibuts [Buddha]; from Prometheus to Christ; from Michael Angelo to Shelley; art had wrought on this eternal figure as though it had nothing else to say. The interest of the figure was not in its meaning, but in the response of the observer.

For Adams, the lesson of the statue was simple—wisdom and peace are achieved through suffering and experience, a lesson the Pyramid Lake pragmatists understood all too well. On a more monumental scale, Stone Mother is the Kuyuidokado's Lincoln Memorial, a shrine to hope and progress born of violence and sorrow. Unlike the larger American society that has turned the public park in front of the Lincoln Memorial into a ceremonial space for protests both serious and ludicrous, the Paiutes have kept Stone Mother, and Frémont's pyramid, relatively inaccessible, controlling the site by means of a washboard dirt road, choosing to perform Stone Mother's story and theirs away from the reservation, or bringing a replica of her to Reno as part of a Fourth of July parade.

Another creative manipulation of the saga of Stone Mother occurred in the testimony of Pyramid Lake Paiute Tribal Council chairman Joe Ely in the Senate Committee hearings February 6, 1990, on the Truckee-Carson–Pyramid Lake Water Settlement Act. "To understand the significance of water to our people," Ely began, "specifically the importance of the Truckee River water, you have to go back to our origins."

> The legend of the Stone Mother tells of the origins of our people. It tells of the settlement of the Tribe, cui-ui tuccatta (cui-ui eaters); it tells of the Lake's origin, cui-ui pah (cui-ui lake); and the origin of its fish, the cui-ui. It tells us that all this creation was simultaneous, that the son of the Stone Mother became our ancestor, that the tears of the Stone Mother became our Lake, that the Lake's shore became our home and its depths the home of our fish, the cui-ui. This legend sets our identity and forever fixes the components that make up our way of life.

Having set up the historical claim to the lake's water, Ely elaborated on the moral and ethical foundations to the tribe's current search for justice.

> When we talk of the water it must be understood that it is a major component of our identity and way of life. These components are the people—cui-ui tuccatta, the Lake—cui-ui pah, and the fish—cui-ui. These are inseparable components and one does not exist without the other. I know one might make light of this significance or write it off as romance, but to us it is everything. As we watched the celebration of the Statute [sic] of Liberty and the controversy surrounding the desecration of the flag, we know that your culture also holds important its own symbols, identities and rituals.

This is just the beginning of an astute, detailed analysis of S. 1554, in which Ely made it very clear that the ultimate goal of the tribe was the reduction in size, if not the complete elimination, of the Newlands irrigation project. They would share the Truckee's water with cities and industry or with farms, but not with both, Ely asserted. Water for Reno, the power company, and wetlands for migratory waterfowl must come from the reclamation project, not the tribe's share of the river. Moreover, Ely insisted, the federal government should admit that its agencies—the BIA, Corps of Engineers, and Bureau of Reclamation—had contributed to the destruction of the lake. This was a bold and skillful performance. Ely was counting on the fact that many of the senators or their staff members were familiar with the legend of the Stone Mother from the national press or from the earlier work of the tribe's public relations firm during the hearings held

Parade float with dancers for Stone Mother and Basket pageant, July 4, 1960. Courtesy Nevada Historical Society, ETH 881.

in 1986 by Senator Paul Laxalt. Ely had used the cui-ui as tribal-flag analogy in an interview with a *Sports Illustrated* writer in 1989. His use of language in telling the significance of the legend of Stone Mother was incantatory, the repetitions of Numic words almost a chant. His analogies between Stone Mother and the Statue of Liberty and the cui-ui and the American flag were striking. His admission that it might all be "romance" eliminated the possibility that it was. He took a sophisticated audience into his confidence, played to their guilt and their tendencies to exoticize Indians, and made them see that oppressor and oppressed had analogous symbols of their identity and equal love of their homeland.

If, by some miracle of climate change and population decline in the Truckee River basin, more water were to pour into the lake, raising its level another thirty feet, would the tribe pay to have Stone Mother moved to higher ground? Possibly. The desecration of the Stone Mother by vandals spraying graffiti led the tribe to close the area to visitors in the spring of 2011. Ben Aleck, a curator at the Pyramid Lake Museum and Visitor Center, pointed out to a reporter from the *Reno Gazette-Journal,* " 'The thing about sacred sites or places, the way most

Indian people believe, is it's all around us. Everything is sacred. This mother earth of ours is sacred.' And whether they're American Indians or not, the Pyramid Rock area is a serene and quiet place that 'should be respected and where people can find solitude.'" Solitude versus the estimated 150,000 visitors annually, this is the conundrum.

DANCES AND POWWOWS

To conclude my brief survey of Kuyuidokado survival, I want to focus on the role of dance and powwows. Flexible and practical more than rigid and sentimental, Paiutes, like many tourists to Reno and Las Vegas, prefer to be *in* a good show, participating more than bystanding—an example of what historian Jacqueline Fear-Segal aptly calls "cultural survival as performance." Pyramid Lake families have been taking part in traditional dance programs at powwows and pageants throughout Nevada and adjoining states since at least the 1920s, although Ralph Burns of the Pyramid Lake Tribe Museum suggested to me that the Indian CCC (Civilian Conservation Corps) brought new dances to Nixon in the 1930s, noting that some ceremonial dress was inspired by Indians of the Great Plains.

On September 5, 1942, the *Gazette* reported on a war-relief rodeo to be held in Reno: "Indians from Pyramid lake [*sic*], dressed in full Indian costume, are scheduled to appear at the rodeo both tomorrow and Labor Day and will also appear at the War Relief rodeo dance at the El Patio ballroom tonight. Also planned is a powwow at Wingfield park tomorrow afternoon following the completion of the first day's events. The committee in charge of the rodeo has estimated that approximately 45 Indians will lead the grand entry at the grounds tomorrow afternoon."

Whether the committee recognized that the Pyramid Lake Tribe was already sending almost all of its young men into military service remains unknown, but a turnout of forty-five performers from a community of about five hundred demonstrates a major effort to engage with the larger society. The Sampson, Frazier, and Winnemucca families were prominent in preserving and creating the Kuyuidokado cultural revival and helped to establish a Paiute presence in the state's tourism promotions. The dance performances by the Pyramid Lake Tribe described below illustrate the importance of dances and powwows in the preservation of Paiute identity.

Tourism became an important source of Nevada's revenue after the war, and state officials were happy to include local Indians in their promotional programs. Ironically, this recognition of the value of the Indians occurred just as

Senator McCarran was pursuing his seventeen-year campaign to give the best agricultural land on the Pyramid Lake Reservation to white farmers. Journalist A. J. Liebling, in his 1954 *New Yorker* magazine series on the tribe's struggle to remove the squatters from the reservation, digresses briefly to describe a dance rehearsal at Nixon that shows that the Paiutes kept their sense of humor in this dismal decade. The Pyramid Lake dancers were preparing for the pageant to be held at the Nevada Admission Day celebration in Carson City, October 31, 1953.

In Liebling's account, Harry Drackert, manager of the Pyramid Lake Guest Ranch, mentions, "The Admission Day committee hired a fellow from Hollywood to write a pageant, and there is a Hungarian girl from there comes up to teach the Indians dances. . . . All Indians in the parade in costume will get fifteen dollars, with five dollars extra for a papoose and the same if mounted on a horse." Liebling accompanied Harry to a rehearsal in the gym at Nixon where he met the Hungarian choreographer, who whispered ecstatically, "They are such preemie-teeves! Real peasants!" As she tried to lead the women in a mock Native dance, her efforts were greeted with giggles and whistles from the high school boys in the bleachers. "Nothing amuses a Paiute more," Liebling observes, "than the sight of another Paiute dressed as an Indian." "When it was the men's turn to do the war dance," he continues, "they hollered and shuffled, yelled like the wild Indians they had seen in the movies, shadowboxed, and did calisthenics, but the Hollywood girl was not satisfied. The only one who pleased her was a fellow who had been in the Seabees in the South Pacific, where he had picked up a couple of Papuan steps."

Liebling teased the frustrated woman by telling her that the Paiutes had not had to do a war dance since 1860, to which she replied, "Ah, zat explains it. Zay have forgotten." Liebling poked fun at the absurd imposition of Hollywood onto the cui-ui eaters, calling the whole affair "some sort of traditional Mary Wigman harvest dance." Wigman was a German choreographer known for appropriating non-Western motifs and employing masks in her performances. Adding insult and injury, the Nevada Admissions Day Committee "cut the Indian-parade rates to five dollars with no bonuses for horses or papooses."

Drackert's "fellow from Hollywood" hired to write a pageant was Basil Woon, and the "Hungarian girl" was Veronica Pataky, a dancer and bit player in Hollywood, best known for a part in the Frank Sinatra–Fred MacMurray 1948 tearjerker *The Miracle of the Bells.* Woon, to whom I will return in chapter 8, was a British-born writer who promoted tourism to Reno and Pyramid Lake in the 1950s. He must have been known to Liebling, and the latter's failure to name him was probably a deliberate slight.

On September 20, 1953, Woon introduced Pataky, "one of the four most beautiful women in Hollywood," to readers of the *Nevada State Journal*. Calling her a television star "better known in the theatrical world as a stager of giant spectacles," Woon quotes her without Liebling's snide reproduction of her middle European accent. "I hope no Indian dancer will think I intend to tell him how to dance!" Pataky avers. "Such dancing has its ritual, its traditions; it is based on factors no one but Indians themselves know." To confirm that Pataky can relate to the beat of tom-toms, Woon adds: "I recall that one of Miss Pataky's own dances—she was considered the top interpretive dancer in Europe not many years ago—was called 'Der Krieg'—'War.'" Woon continues, "In it she danced, or rather walked, around in a circle to the sole music of drums. The dance took seven minutes. In the beginning she was a young recruit, ardent in patriotic fervor, flowers in his bayonet, throwing kisses to his girls as he marched away to war. At the end she was an old broken dying disillusioned veteran, lousy, muddy, bitter, hungry, wanting only death so that he could rest. A Vienna paper the next day said that 'Pataky has danced a better sermon against war than anything ever written in a book.'"

A two-column photograph of Veronica Pataky accompanied the article, and it is easy to see why the sixty-year-old Woon was smitten. He had persuaded the thirty-five-year-old actress, most recently seen in the television series *Ramar of the Jungle,* starring Jon Hall, to lend some glamour to his Nevada Day Indian pageant. On October 30, 1953, an ad appeared in the *Journal* for "Dot-So-La-Lee: An Indian Legend, Cast of More than 200 Indians, written by Basil Woon, Directed by Veronika [sic] Pataky, Produced by the Nevada Day Committee, Spectacular Dances Including the Mysterious & Beautiful Puberty Dance Never Before on Any Stage and the Gigantic Battle of the River of the Washoe-Paiute War, also The Famous Laguna Dancers in the program of Navajo Dances as performed at the Eisenhower Inauguration." Flanked by ads for *Mighty Joe Young* and *Isle of the Dead* playing at the Tower Theater and *Blowing Wild* with Gary Cooper at the Majestic, Woon's fantasy was not out of place by the entertainment standards of the time.

Unknown to either Woon or Liebling, Nevada Indian superintendent Alida Bowler had already introduced professional music and dance instruction to students at the Stewart School in 1935, when, according to John Troutman's excellent history, *Indian Blues: American Indians and the Politics of Music, 1879–1934,* she hired George LeMere, a Ho-Chunk (Winnebago) trained in voice and cello at the Haskell Institute and the University of Miami, to teach there. The history of the Stewart Indian School, established by the State of Nevada and the BIA on 240 acres of land three miles south of Carson City in 1890, is an important part of the Kuyuidokado story, but too lengthy to undertake here. Suffice to say that most of the first Washoe, Paiute, and Shoshone children brought to the boarding school came under protest. An elementary day school was opened in Nixon in 1878, but there was no high school until the spring of 1979. Intermittently, there was a school in Wadsworth, but many students from the Pyramid Lake Reservation went to junior and senior high school in Fernley. Stewart grew rapidly in the 1920s and '30s, boarding hundreds of Navaho, Apache, and Pueblo students, as well as Nevada Indians. Stewart School was closed in 1980, due to budget cuts and the opening of day schools on the reservations. Native attitudes toward Stewart changed from fear and suspicion to pride, as the school came to be admired for its vocational programs, high academic standards, competitive athletic teams, and marching band and arts programs.

Another post–World War II dance pageant of note was announced by an August 18, 1955, headline in the *Nevada State Journal:* "1,000 Persons Expected to Attend Paiute Dance." The Paiute Pageant scheduled for August 28 at a site opposite Drackert's Pyramid Lake Ranch was intended to raise money to build a permanent building at Sutcliffe for future Indian fairs and rodeos. More than thirty-five Indians were expected to participate. "There will be," the story continued, "11 group dances and eight solos by expert dancers of the Tribe, including Chief Thunder-Face, chairman of the Paiute Council and an aging man of fine mien who speaks no English. Those who have seen Gordon Fraser before will be glad to know he will again give his rendition of the Eagle Dance, which is locally celebrated."

Avery Winnemucca was council chairman at this time, fifty-three years old and articulate in English as well as Paiute. The hokum of "Thunder-Face," the last of the monolinguals, sounds suspiciously like the work of the director of the pageant, Nick Jackson, amateur archaeologist, Indian trader, and muralist, who will appear in the next chapter as a commentator on Indian history for a hydroplane race program. A year later, in an article on Nixon in the *Journal,* Woon identified Chief Thunder-Face as Mark Jones, an eighty-four-year-old "patriarch of the tribe." Jones could have created his "Thunder-Face" persona as a joke, or in collaboration with Jackson and Woon. White expectations and Indian humor danced circles around each other.

As dance historians Charlotte Heth and Jacqueline Shea Murphy have clearly shown, dance has played a major role in defining Indian identities. The preservation of preconquest dances helped to maintain religious beliefs. The performance of traditional dances for Wild West shows and tourists was a way for

Kuyuidokado in dance regalia at the Pyramid Lake Guest Ranch, ca. 1955. *Left to right, back row:* Levi Frazier, Paul Wright, Harrison Frazier, Mark Jones, Gordon Frazier, Harry Winnemucca, Roland John, and Harry Drackert. *Front row:* Nina Winnemucca, Lena Wright, Rosabelle Tobey, Grace Frazier and son Douglas, Flora Greene, and Herma Winnemucca. Courtesy Special Collections, University of Nevada, Reno, Libraries.

tribes to come to terms with European culture and commercialism. Despite the BIA's efforts to prohibit Indian dances in the 1890s and again in the 1920s, "the people have never stopped dancing," to borrow Murphy's felicitous phrase. The most important aspect of dance in modern Indian American life is not that it presents some timeless element of Native cultures, but that it allows for innovation, change, and renewal. Indian boarding schools, missionaries, and BIA agents did their collective best to extinguish what they considered primitive and time-wasting activities. Genocide reduced the number of tribal elders who could teach young Indians the chants and steps of the dances.

I use *genocide* in this book in the sense employed by historian Patrick Wolfe in his studies of settler colonialism in Australia, the Middle East, and the Americas. Wolfe sees the elimination of the native by settlement as distinct from military imperial conquest. This was clearly true in the case of the Paiutes, who were dispossessed of their land at Pyramid Lake and throughout western Nevada by squatters who assumed that Indians lacked ownership rights. What the Paiutes lost along with their land was a culture closely linked to place. The genocide was both mortal, when they died of disease or gunshots, and psychological, when they were denied access to their lands, rivers, and lakes. Continuity of life through dances and songs rooted in topography was extensively disrupted by settlement. Yet some of that knowledge was preserved and shared by the survivors. Reduced in numbers and forced to cooperate, widely divergent tribes created a pan-Indian culture in which tribes borrowed dances and musical instruments from each other. What was once a strictly communal activity became public and offered a way for tribes to build on their heritage and exploit white stereotypes.

Murphy tells the fascinating story of white dancer-choreographers Ted Shawn and José Limón appropriating the Hopi Eagle Dance, while Leah Dilworth and Tisa Wenger analyze the spectacle of the Hopi Snake Dance in the contexts of Indian land claims and the aesthetics of modernism. An Eagle Dance is found in many Indian tribes, and Shawn reinterpreted the dance as a masculine version of Anna Pavlova's dying swan. The Snake Dance, on the other hand, has often been dismissed as bizarre even by other Indians. In the late summer of 1960 I was part of a US Forest Service crew fighting the Dog Valley fire. As the fire spread and threatened power and telephone lines northwest of Reno, Indian firefighting crews were brought in from Montana and New Mexico. On a break I talked with the Crow camp man for the team of Crow firefighters. He was quick to dismiss the firefighting skills of the Hopi, "those little guys from the desert." "What do they know about trees?" he scoffed. "I hear they like to dance with snakes." His scorn was accompanied by facial expressions. "When I go to a dance, I want to dance with a woman."

This little moment of Indian humor—how much will the white guy believe?—makes several points relevant to understanding the history of public dance performances by the Kuyuidokado. First, as Heth argues, dance is ubiquitous, found in "every venue, from the most traditional and private places to those most public and accessible." Although it can be commercialized, raising money to build a stadium or simply to supplement personal income, dancing is primarily for reasons—pleasure, healing, bringing rain—that transcend everyday life. Most important, tribal dances tell stories; they are kinetic footnotes to history as preserved in oral tradition and local ecological knowledge.

Look back at the list of dances performed in Reno in 1939—"bear, owl, sun, antelope, eagle, circle, flower, wedding or feather, rabbit, and war dances." What a range of social and environmental factors were assembled. Such dances were originally performed over days of celebration, participation organized by kinship, age, and sex. The public dances were abbreviated, open to young and old, with fancy attire and feather decorations that may or may not have been familiar to their ancestors, but were expected by the white audiences.

The Kuyuidokado danced to save themselves and the lake and inspired a response from socially conscious dancers from a different tradition. In 1975, in the midst of the water wars between the tribe and the irrigation project farmers, an organization called Young Audiences contacted Professor Elmer Rusco of the Political Science Department of the University of Nevada, Reno, about joining with them to apply for a grant from the Nevada Humanities Committee to sponsor a Bicentennial-related dance and discussion program entitled *Who Owns the Water?* The mission of Young Audiences was to bring high-quality music and dance to Nevada high school students. At the time Rusco was involved in monitoring developments in the California-Nevada water compact and other federal and state efforts to end the water wars. The dance program was to be provided by Burch Mann's American Dance Theater of Sherman Oaks, California. As materials in the Pyramid Lake Water Papers in Special Collections reveal, Rusco was skeptical but agreed to help, and the effort paid off.

Mann was the daughter of a Texas oilman who moved to Tulsa, Oklahoma, in 1920 when she was twelve years old. Mann studied dance in Tulsa until she graduated from high school, whereupon she went to New York City and studied under Mikhail Mordkin, a Bolshoi-trained dancer who had been with the Ballets Russes. In New York he organized a company that was a forerunner of the American Ballet Theater. Burch Mann returned to Tulsa in 1930 and married a banker, Joy Holtzman. She taught ballet in Tulsa before rejoining Mordkin in his new company. By the 1950s Mann had retired from the company, and she and her husband moved to Southern California, where she opened her own studio and devoted herself to creating "folk ballets" that would appeal to Americans who laughed at "men in tights." Her career received a boost when she was hired by the producers of the Mickey Mouse Club to choreograph a Mouseketeer production number.

Burch Mann's American Dance Theater, later the American Folk Ballet, began touring professionally in 1965. In 1971 she relocated the company to Cedar Creek, Utah, where it is based at Southern Utah University. She continued teaching into her eighties and died in 1990. *Who Owns the Water?* had four live performances, one in Carson City, January 9, 1976; one in Fallon three days later; and two in Reno, on January 13 and 14. KOLO-TV broadcast a performance on January 11. The program for these performances suggests that it was an ambitious collaboration.

After an introduction by a "humanities consultant" from the Nevada

Department of Education, the American Folk Ballet dancers performed, accompanied by a "poetic narration" by Burch Mann. This was followed by two short lectures, one by Margaret Wheat on the geography of the Truckee and Carson Rivers and the impact of water diversions on fish and wildlife, the other by Robert Hunter, "Washo Indian and Superintendent Nevada Indian Agency, Stewart," on Indian tribes and ownership of the water. The dancers took the stage for a second act, followed by talks by attorneys Leslie Gray and Frankie Sue Del Pappa on urban water needs and Fallon rancher and Nevada assemblyman Virgil Getto, who spoke on agricultural water rights. The troupe did a third dance, and the final speeches were given by Rusco and Richard Sill, who addressed cooperative water management and population growth. There was a "Dance Summary," after which the audience asked questions and voiced their opinions, which were, alas, unrecorded.

The event was well covered by Reno's newspapers. On January 2 the *Reno Evening Gazette* announced that Burch Mann's American Folk Ballet would stage two productions, *Who Owns the Water?* and *Untamed Land,* with a special appearance by singer Jimmie Rodgers (the pop singer, not the "father of country music"). *Untamed Land* was performed in Elko, Winnemucca, Carson City, Yerington, and Reno. On January 7 the *Gazette* reviewed *Untamed Land,* comparing it to the MGM musical *Seven Brides for Seven Brothers,* apparently the reviewer's point of reference for folk ballet. One of the pieces in the ballet was "The Mood of Falling Leaves," which was intended to express the philosophy of the Sioux. The reviewer was impressed, declaring that "the choreographer does with dance what Ravel did with 'Bolero.' She builds from the quiet and soft, delicately and logically to the strong and the powerful. Her work is exciting to watch."

A different reporter covered *Who Owns the Water?* In the January 10 *Gazette,* his odd review begins, "There wasn't, as half expected, a blackface rendition of 'Truckee, How I Love You,' or a snappy buck and wing version of 'How Dry I Am.'" This lede may convey something of local disgust with the long-running political wrangling over water rights and the impending ecological disaster. The reporter recovers his senses to praise the performance and the presentations of the speakers that "seemed to blend into a generalized call for harmony, cooperation, and the realization of the finite nature of our resources." It is doubtful that this kind of well-meaning attempt to blend the arts and public policy achieved very much, but it was part of the effort in the 1970s to right past wrongs.

SACRED VISIONS POWWOW, 2012

On July 20, 21, and 22, 2012, I attended the Fourth Annual Sacred Visions Pow-wow in Wadsworth. The festival's purpose, "Te Nanumu Magodyuku," translated as "Bringing the People Home," was achieved by three days of drumming, singing, dancing, and reuniting with friends and relatives, some of whom had come from as far away as New Mexico and Canada. I estimate that there were at least four hundred spectators during the dances that were performed by more than a hundred men, women, and children dressed in handmade powwow regalia. Many of the attendees camped out near the dance arena, a circular area about one hundred feet in diameter surrounded by a series of lean-tos, joined to form a continuous roof around the dance ground.

I had not been to a powwow since childhood and was struck immediately by the changes over sixty years. The clothing was more colorful and elaborate. The program was more organized. Sacred Visions was a study in paradoxes. On display were tradition and change, family and state, ordinariness and spectacle, informality and organization, heritage and history. The forty-page program amplifies these dichotomies. The mission statement reads: "It is our mission of the Pyramid Lake Sacred Visions Pow-wow Committee to bring all the children of our 'Stone Mother' back home. From the very young to our Elders, families of the North, South, East, and West. For all to forever gather in a good way without pain and suffering, to enjoy and share each other's company through the spirit of our Traditions."

Later in the program there is a page of maxims that constitute a kind of pow-wow creed. A few examples: "Receive and *honor* strangers & outsiders with a good heart, treating your guests with consideration. To serve others, to be of some use to family, community, nation, and the world is one of the main purposes for which human beings have been created. True happiness comes only to those who dedicate their lives to the service of others. Respect yourself and the home you live in (your body). Keep it in good repair, it's the only one you get and as Star Trek Spock says, 'Live Long and Prosper!'" Paiutes easily adopt non-Indian values that do not conflict with their own, they share references from popular culture, but they know that some beliefs such as respect for elders and the natural world need to be reinforced before they are lost in the dizzying pace of technological and economic change.

Fourteen pages of the program are devoted to pictures of and statements by the outgoing Junior Miss and Lil' Miss Sacred Visions, the Tiny Tot Princess and the Lil' Brave, and this year's contestants. The emphasis in these statements is on family genealogy, gratitude for family and community support, and plans for the future. A number of potential conflicts are addressed, if not fully resolved. Competition for first place is balanced by community service. Economic inequality that allows some children to meet the expenses of regalia and travel to powwows is mitigated by the expectation that winners will share their prizes and serve their communities. I could see how much more elaborate powwow dress had become since the 1950s, especially in men's dances such as the Eagle Dance and in boys' and girls' fancy and jingle dances. These garments represent considerable investment in time and money. Like Civil War reenactors, powwow dancers allow those in the audience who lack the time, money, or inclination to be participants, to witness a heritage they claim. Unlike most folklife festivals, pioneer days, square dances, and similar celebrations that seek a momentary revival of the past, Sacred Visions is future oriented. Drum groups compose new songs. Powwow clothing and music are evolving. Respect for traditions is demanded, but tolerance for new behaviors is encouraged. Out of the arena participants and spectators texted messages and shared video games. At one point in the Friday-evening ceremony, prizes were scattered around the arena, and small children were invited to play a game of Red Light Green Light while they gathered rewards. Rows of vendors' tents flanked the ceremonial ground, offering Indian fry bread, cold nonalcoholic drinks, and crafts. Commercial visions coexist with sacred.

Each day's festival began with a grand entry led by a color guard of veterans, mostly from the Vietnam War. American flags, one with the portrait of an Indian superimposed on the stripes, waved in the winds above the announcer's stand. The entrance was through an opening facing east, and the parade, like the dances, moved clockwise around the arena. The order of events was by age, with children under five years of age performing first, followed by girls and boys ages six to twelve, teenagers, golden age (sixty and older), adult men and women (nineteen to thirty-nine), and concluding with senior adult men and women (forty to fifty-nine). These age categories may reflect health problems in Indian communities. The heat and warm clothing clearly took a toll on some contestants. Volunteers were giving away fans in the shape of a bird's tail feathers inscribed "Pyramid Lake Sacred Visions Diabetes Program."

Within this general structure were specialty dances—Rabbit Dance, Cowboy/Cowgirl Dance, and Men's Switch Dance—and a women's Paiute dress competition in which each participant sang two songs in Numic. Grass dances, in which the flowing movement of the fringe on garments is emphasized; fancy

Paiute dancers, Sacred Visions Powwow, July 21, 2012. Photograph by the author.

dancing, which requires elaborate headdresses, multicolored ribbons, and feathered bustles; and jingle dancing, with bells attached to the dancer's clothing were part of the performances of all age groups. Note that there was no war dance, no wedding dance, no dance associated with shamans. Although there were few non-Indians present, some rituals were either too private or otherwise inappropriate for this powwow.

The ritual/show/family reunion was almost seamless; a new dance was announced as another ended. Several drum groups—Bearshield, Echo Sky, Young Chief, and Red Hot Warriors among them—spelled each other, and the music, which has a steady hard beat with complex variations in rhythm as the songs and dances move from beginning to end, was seldom interrupted. An exception occurred on Sunday afternoon when the temperature rose above ninety degrees and dust began to obscure the feet of the dancers. A reservation sprinkler truck drove into the arena and dampened the ground while children ran behind it, cooling themselves in the spray. The dancing resumed with a fancy dance followed by a grass dance and finally a switch dance, in which a male dancer wears female regalia and imitates women's dance steps and bodily motions in a gentle parody. The sole performer in this dance received enthusiastic applause from the crowd and a substantial prize. As the ceremony was coming to a close, the skies darkened and the wind gusted. Someone must have summoned the spirit of Wovoka. There was dust in a whirlwind. A spate of rain soaked the crowd. Perhaps the raindrops were Stone Mother's tears, not in sorrow, but in joy.

The cloudburst ended. The celebrants returned and resumed dancing. Prizes were awarded. "Sa' nu u punedwa,'" as the program advised, not "goodbye," but "see you later." The good humor of the now soggy dancers mirrored that of the powwow organizers who averred in the program: "The Sacred Visions Powwow Committee is NOT responsible for short funded travelers, divorces, accidents or personal liabilities." In next year's program they could very well mention weather as one of the calamities for which they are not liable

The Fate of the Lake

The year 1944, the uncommemorated centennial of Frémont's arrival, coincided with three notable events in the history of Pyramid Lake. The first was the publication of a proposed policy for postwar development of Pyramid Lake and other Nevada reservations. Second was the issuing of a "final" judgment in the thirty-one-year-old suit known as *U.S. v. Orr Ditch Water Company, et al.* The third was the founding of the National Congress of American Indians (NCAI).

On March 31 Ralph M. Gelvin, of the Carson Indian Agency, submitted a 250-page report, *Post War Planning Program for the Carson Jurisdiction,* to Indian commissioner John Collier. The Carson Agency's jurisdiction covered three-fourths of the state of Nevada, a small area of Oregon, and three counties in California—eleven reservations and eight "colonies." In his letter of transmittal to Collier, Gelvin, who had been with the BIA for a decade after studying at Colorado Agricultural College (now Colorado State University) and working in the dairy division of the state's Extension Service, recommended a number of projects for improving farming, ranching, education, and health on the reservations, but cautioned: "The following program does not attempt to plan a utopia of the future but if followed, will undoubtedly increase the economic stability and independence of the Indian people of this jurisdiction. It should permit an increase of Indian participation and responsibility towards the administration of their affairs and a decrease of Indian Service responsibility."

This may not have been what Collier wanted to hear, as his own plans for Indian cultural revival were utopian. In his *Indians of the Americas,* Collier devotes a chapter to Bartolomé de las Casas and attempts to establish Indian utopias in Paraguay and Venezuela in the sixteenth century. Collier may have seen himself as more realistic than Las Casas, but he took the Dominican priest, known as "Protector of the Indians," as an inspiration for his own ambitious programs. Their shared dream of protecting Indians from destructive foreign influences creates a link between Pyramid Lake and the whole history of the conquest of the New World. Gelvin, on the other hand, was no softhearted liberal. To him, the Paiutes, and many Nevadans, were so many dairy cows in need of herding.

"The Indians of this jurisdiction," Gelvin declared, "do not have the traditions and religious customs that are so evident on many other reservations. The early missionary influence is not particularly noticeable. The traditional Indian dances and Indian costumes are conspicuously absent. . . . Nearly every reservation has an annual festival which takes the form of a rodeo. Gambling is common and participated in by both men and women. The State of Nevada is notorious for its gambling and it is therefore not surprising that gambling is so prevalent among the Indians." Only somebody who had not read the newspapers could write that about the importance of dances and fandangos to the Numa. Gelvin shows a good understanding of the problems at Pyramid Lake—erosion along the river, the need to recover land from squatters, proper management of rangeland, and the need to provide each ranching Paiute with at least 60 acres of land—but dismisses fishing and tourism as sources of future income. Gelvin's recommendations seem to have been ignored. Collier left the BIA a year later to be replaced by Dillon Myer, whom Gelvin had to defend before a congressional committee that implausibly suspected Myer of being a communist. Paiute GIs must have wondered about the political world to which they were returning.

The second commemorative moment came September 8, when, after thirty-one years in litigation, the *Orr Ditch* suit was settled in the US District Court in Reno. Judge Frank H. Norcross recognized the Pyramid Lake Tribe's priority rights to water based on the Interior Department's 1859 recommendation of the creation of the reservation, but he set the tribe's total diversion at 30,000 acre-feet of water per year for irrigation, with none for the lake's restoration or preservation. The Sierra Pacific Power Company was allotted almost as much water for municipal, industrial, and domestic purposes for the Reno-Sparks metropolitan area. The Newlands Reclamation Project received water rights to about 300,000 acre-feet to irrigate 74,500 acres. The Orr Ditch Decree invoked the quaint phrase "Duty of Water," a legal term meaning the volume of water required to grow a particular crop in a type of soil. The Bureau of Reclamation identified two types of land on the reservation: bench and bottom. Bottomlands are "those lands with a five-foot soil profile having a holding capacity equal to or exceeding 8 inches and/or a water table within six feet of the surface for a period equal to or exceeding 150 days. If neither of these factors applies, the land is designated as *Bench Land*." Bottomlands were eligible for a maximum of 3.5

acre-feet of water per acre per year, benchlands 4.5. Even if every drop of water did its duty, Pyramid Lake was doomed.

According to Gary Horton's invaluable *Truckee River Chronology*, the annual average flow of the Truckee below Derby Dam is 362,420 acre-feet, just enough to meet the Orr Ditch allocations and far less than Pyramid Lake needs to prevent continuing decline. In dry years between 1973 and 1994, the annual flow was only 4,460 acre-feet. While the irrigators received additional water from upstream reservoirs, virtually nothing went to the lake. Thus, *Orr Ditch* was a temporary setback for the Paiutes and ultimately a disappointment for the Bureau of Reclamation because Judge Norcross had left the door open to future suits by the various parties.

The importance of World War II for the Kuyuidokado and all American Indians cannot be overestimated. The war brought to the forefront three long-simmering issues: citizenship, the legacy of imperialism, and Indian identity. Treated in the nineteenth century as citizens of their own nations, Indians could not vote in most of the states in which their reservations were located or in cities where they lived. Some Indians became citizens by serving in the military or giving up tribal affiliation, but the majority were not granted US citizenship until 1924 when Congress passed the Indian Citizenship Act. Some states refused to allow Indians to vote until 1948. The act did not require relinquishing tribal citizenship, but some Indians were suspicious that the law was just another tactic in the push for assimilation and termination of Indian lands.

Patriotism was a concept broad enough to include most Americans. Many Indians saw three benefits to military service. First, it provided young men and women with badly needed employment. Second, it proved to their sometimes hostile white neighbors that they shared the ideals of peace and freedom for which the government said the war was being fought, that they believed in the "American way of life." Third, military service reinforced the warrior ethos found in most Indian tribes. Young men and women could uphold the tradition of fighting to maintain a way of life for their families and to accrue individual honor. By all accounts American Indians entered the armed services in higher numbers in proportion to their total population than non-Indians. This was certainly true of the Kuyuidokado, who sent more than forty young men to war from a reservation population of fewer than one hundred men between the ages of eighteen and forty. When they returned to a dying lake, a BIA determined to terminate reservations, and a racist senator, some of the Kuyuidokado veterans questioned their place in American imperial history.

The questioning began, as Paul Rosier documents in *Serving Their Country: American Indian Politics and Patriotism in the Twentieth Century,* almost immediately after the war, when Indian men and women realized that the promises of equality and justice were not forthcoming. The founding of the National Congress of American Indians in 1944 was the product of the war's impact on Native society and the third important event of that year for the Pyramid Lake Paiute Tribe. The NCAI opposed the growing support within the US Congress and the BIA for termination of reservations and assimilation of the tribes. The idealism of the Collier administration of the BIA, which also favored assimilation but at a pace set by Indians themselves, was fading. The NCAI organizers believed that the time had come for Indians to set aside their many differences and organize politically as one people. They wanted the federal courts to protect the civil liberties of American Indians and the federal government to address problems of education, health, and unemployment among Indians.

The Pyramid Lake Paiute Tribe joined the NCAI in 1947 at the urging of Dewey Sampson, the first Paiute elected to the Nevada Legislature. He had attended the second meeting of the organization. Membership brought the Kuyuidokado in contact with James E. Curry, an idealistic and ambitious lawyer who had worked for the BIA and other government agencies before becoming an attorney for the NCAI in 1946. The NCAI was still in the early stages of organization when the US Congress, after several years of discussion, created the Indian Claims Commission (ICC) in an attempt to settle the growing number of claims being made by dozens of tribes seeking to reclaim lands lost when treaties were broken. The existing Court of Claims was being overwhelmed. With a new advocacy group eager to make its reputation and a new federal agency hoping to settle all the long-standing disputes and do justice to the Indians, the time was ripe for change.

The background and significance of the ICC are succinctly explained by Harvey Rosenthal in his essay "Indian Claims and American Conscience." Although the US government frequently resorted to military force to remove Indians from their homes and land, national policy was based on "legally" acquiring occupied land by treaty (up to 1871), or by legislation, which sometimes involved negotiations. Reservations were created to confine conquered Natives apart from rapacious settlers. Rosenthal estimates that by 1868, 370 treaties left Native Americans with 140 million acres of the more than 2 billion they had occupied. The General Allotment Act of 1887 helped take away another 90 million acres by the time it was repealed in 1933. Little wonder that President Harry Truman, when

signing the act creating the ICC, referred to the theft of Indian lands as "the largest real estate transaction in history," adding, "We stand ready to correct any
mistakes we have made."

If Truman, who was no friend of Indian self-determination, and members of
Congress who wrote the bill thought a claims commission could settle all the
grievances that Indians had against the federal government for lost land, they
were poorly informed. Created to last just ten years, the ICC had to be renewed
five times before its final sunset in 1978, thirty-two years after its creation. It settled hundreds of claims, but turned many back to the Court of Claims, and left
a legacy of hard feelings that continues to this day. The major problem by all
accounts was that, although it was created as a commission to investigate land
claims and establish facts for negotiated settlements, it quickly evolved into a
court in which Indians and their lawyers could confront government lawyers
over such issues as establishing the "definable territory the Indians occupied
exclusively" and the value of that territory if it was recognized. The process
consumed years for each case and created a new role, and wealth, for academic
anthropologists who had studied various tribes. "Expert" testimony created the
illusion that these ethnographers, archaeologists, and folklorists were bringing
science into the courtroom and that Indians surely would agree with what they
said. The Pyramid Lake Paiutes and their kinsmen throughout northern Nevada
knew differently.

The tribe had already learned how difficult it was to get its own lawyers. In
1938 it attempted to hire H. R. Cooke, a disaffected former associate of Senator Patrick McCarran, to represent them in the senator's 1938 attempt to legal-
ize the squatters' claims. John Collier, probably acting on an old BIA tradition
of "protecting" their wards from unscrupulous lawyers, refused to allow this,
and the tribal council went without an attorney until 1947, when it attempted
to hire James Curry. Again there was opposition within the BIA, but the superintendent of the Carson Agency, E. Reeseman Fryer, supported the tribe, and
he and Curry became burs under McCarran's saddle. The fight that ensued over
the next six years raised the Pyramid Lake situation to prominence but eventually eclipsed it, as it became a brawl between McCarran and Curry, with Dillon
Myer, Fryer, and the National Congress of American Indians left holding their
coats.

The Curry-McCarran brouhaha began in early 1949, when Curry, acting as
the Pyramid Lake Tribal Council's attorney, and Fryer urged the tribe to take
back the land claimed by the squatters along the Truckee by fencing them out.
The white farmers, acting on McCarran's advice, shut off the irrigation water,

which they controlled off the reservation. Curry wanted to go further and told the Indians to take over the ditches, but Fryer, who had a better understanding of the complexities of water law, advised against it. The gathering intensity of the political storm can be glimpsed in an exchange between Pete Petersen, an aide to the senator, and McCarran in September 1949 as quoted by Faun Mortara Dixon in her dissertation, "Native American Property Rights." Petersen sent the senator the names of individuals who were "stirring up animosity against you insofar as your Indian land and displaced persons bill are concerned. They are fomenting trouble with both the Indians and apparently the Jews. My information concerning Indian affairs is that the Indians are primarily being led by Mr. Frier [*sic*], the Superintendent of Indian Affairs and E. P. Carville [a Nevada attorney working with Curry]. I don't know if it would be advisable to have Mr. Frier transferred, but I know he is creating a lot of disturbance among the Indians."

McCarran retaliated, and in October Myer removed Fryer from the Carson Agency. Curry began using his political contacts to intercede, and the transfer was overruled by Truman. McCarran countered by appointing Fryer head of the Division of Health, Education, and Manpower in the State Department's Point Four Program (Technical Cooperation Administration), a position with global responsibilities. "Up and out," this strategy is called. The senator had used this tactic successfully in 1939, when Alida Bowler was promoted to an agency position in Los Angeles, but in that case, according to Stanley Underdal's dissertation, "On the Road to Termination: The Pyramid Lake Paiutes and the Indian Attorney Controversy of the 1950s," her transfer was supported by Dewey Samson, who resented all BIA supervision. Fryer refused the promotion, but resigned from the Carson Agency because, as a professional civil servant, he felt he could not do his job without the support of his immediate supervisor.

Now, McCarran and his allies, including Governor Ernest Gruening of Alaska, whom Curry had opposed when the governor tried to use Native lands for year-round logging, could turn their full wrath on Curry. In late October Dillon Myer canceled Curry's contract with the Pyramid Lake Tribal Council and announced new rules for hiring lawyers for Indian tribes. On October 25, 1950, the *Reno Evening Gazette* reported Curry's countercharge that Myer wanted only yes men as Indian attorneys. In November Curry got the tribe to give him another contract, for a ten-year period. Normally, the BIA limited contracts to two years. Myer asked Curry to accept a compromise—a two-year contract, subject to cancellation on sixty days' notice by the tribe with the commissioner's approval, the hiring of local counsel to work with Curry, and the filing of frequent reports on services rendered. Curry, overestimating his support, refused the offer.

As Thomas Cowger documents in *The National Congress of American Indians: The Founding Years,* Curry took his case to the public by enlisting two old McCarran and Myer haters, former secretary of the interior Harold Ickes and John Collier. Ickes wrote a regular column for the *New Republic,* where he often called Myer and McCarran fascists and denounced Myer as "Hitler and Mussolini rolled into one." Secretary of the Interior Oscar Chapman canceled Curry's contract, despite an appeal from Avery Winnemucca, Warren Toby, and Albert Aleck, who traveled to Washington to meet with the secretary and to ask Senator Clinton Anderson (D-NM) to hold hearings on Indian lawyers. The hearings began in January and ended in September 1952, with the charge that Curry and other lawyers had used their position with the NCAI to solicit lucrative contracts for themselves. During the hearings Ickes died, and Curry's other allies deserted him. The NCAI agreed to keep him on their legal staff until the hearings ended. By early 1953 his career as an Indian lawyer was over, although the Pyramid Lake Paiutes tried to retain him as late as July 20, 1955. Curry politely declined, citing illness, but perhaps taking some pleasure in the recent resignation of Dillon Myer and the end of the strongest wave of termination efforts.

LAWYERS AND ANTHROPOLOGISTS — STUCK IN THE SAND

Return now to those thrilling days of yesteryear (the 1950s) for the final assaults on the Northern Paiute by the Indian Claims Commission and the Lone Ranger of Great Basin anthropology, Julian Steward. The ICC procedure involved three steps: establishing a claimant's title to a parcel of land, establishing its value, and establishing offsets, that is, any previous payments on earlier claims. By far the most difficult and time-consuming was the first, which required establishing the "definable territory the Indians occupied exclusively." If other Indians occupied the same territory, the claim was denied. Moreover, as Rosenthal explains, "Each stage required two interlocutory judgments and a final judgment by the commission, and almost always received motions for rehearing (and appeal after 1961). The final judgment was appealable to the Court of Claims and to the Supreme Court through a writ of certiorari" (this means an order by a higher court directing a lower court to send a record of a case).

Both sides were allowed to call on anthropologists to help establish where Native Americans had been located at the moment of white settlement. Aware that Steward had developed a theory that placed the Great Basin Natives on the lowest level of social development, without organization beyond the family unit, the Justice Department, representing the BIA, contacted him in early 1949 to prepare evidence that would convince the commission to deny their claims. The Northern Paiutes, claiming all of northern Nevada and parts of Idaho, Oregon, and California, were represented by I. S. "Lefty" Weissbrodt, who had worked with Curry on some Alaskan claims and whose brother was the flamboyant Abe Weissbrodt, a prosecutor at the Nuremberg war-crimes trials. Their chief expert witness was the less famous anthropologist Omer C. Stewart.

In retrospect, the epic battle of the academics may seem a little daffy, but cultural anthropology had emerged from World War II with panache, having provided the military with profiles of both enemies and allies, predicting how they would behave in certain situations. Needless to say, anthropologists wanted to prove that they were real scientists. Unfortunately, as anthropologist Marc Pinkoski reveals in a provocative paper, "Julian Steward, American Anthropology, and Colonialism," they were consciously or unconsciously part of the political system of the United States, including its imperial and colonial ambitions.

Steward (1902–72) fled Washington, DC, as a teenager and finished high school at Deep Springs Preparatory School (now College) near Owens Valley, California. He studied at Cornell and the University of California, Berkeley, where he worked with one of the founding fathers of American anthropology, A. L. Kroeber. Steward received his PhD in 1929, with a dissertation titled "The Ceremonial Buffoon of the American Indian, a Study of Ritualized Clowning and Role Reversal." His rival in Great Basin studies, Omer Stewart (1908–91), also studied with Kroeber, focusing on Paiute religion, completing his dissertation in 1939. When the Northern Paiute hearings before the ICC began in early 1951, Steward and Stewart were eager to go a few rounds in a public arena. Pinkoski cites correspondence between Steward and a Justice Department anthropologist that gives an idea of the intensity of feeling:

> Julian,
> We think Omer is going to be the opposing witness. If you could sit in as you did in the Paiute cases it might show him up. Let me know.
> —[Signed] Ralph [Beals]

> Dear Ralph,
> Your scheduled Shoshone hearings for August 26th come just when I shall be leaving the country in connection with my Ford project. While it might give me a certain pleasure to try to embarrass Omer I doubt whether I could bear to sit through another of his performances. I am sure Bob Murphy [one of Steward's graduate students at Columbia University] can do a good job for you.

How Stewart felt about Steward is unrecorded as far as I know, but Stewart seems to have been a nicer man. Where Steward described the Shoshone and Paiutes, whom he found indistinguishable, as representing the lowest level of social organization, without tribal identity, merely "gastric" family groups motivated solely by their need for food, Stewart argued that the Northern Paiute bands occupied a single physiographic province, spoke similar dialects of one linguistic family, possessed cultures and traditions in common, and "without doubt" formed one tribe. "The unity was tenuous," Stewart acknowledged, "but no indications of internal strife were discovered; on the contrary, hunting grounds were shared, and Old Winnemucca, in the early days of white contact, nearly united the bands under one political leadership."

Accepting Stewart's evidence over Steward's, the Indian Claims Commission found for the Northern Paiutes and, on July 3, 1961, awarded them $3,650,000. A second award of $935,000 was given to the Owens Valley Paiutes, and a third, $15,790,000, was awarded the Western Paiutes, including the Kuyuidokado. On April 17, 1980, after years of planning, the BIA finally distributed $45,782,773.24 (the sum originally appropriated plus interest, less attorney fees and litigation expenses) to 9,062 descendants of the Paiutes who lost land in the 1860s and '70s. Individuals received $5,162.52 each, less than a third of the median annual household income of that year.

As Pinkoski points out, the ICC rejected Steward's testimony in every case in which he was an expert witness. Unaccountably, Steward's views of the Native people of the Great Basin remain largely unchallenged in academic anthropology. In fairness to Steward, *The Northern Paiute Indians,* a survey that he and one of his students, Ermine W. Voegelin, prepared in 1956–57 for the government's case, offers a detailed refutation of Stewart's conclusions, based in part on an analysis of the testimony of the Indian witnesses before the commission. Though not always convincing, it reveals that the disagreement between Steward and Stewart on the degree of political organization among the Numa was based on differences of evidence.

Steward's emphasis on the physical environment, what became known as "cultural ecology," led him to miss the enormous changes that took place in the ecology of the Great Basin with the arrival of white settlers. His eye was fixed on precontact times, but most of his evidence was historical. He read back into antiquity a way of life that had been forced onto the Indians of the Great Basin by the immigrants who brought new diseases to both humans and wildlife. Miners and railroad workers destroyed habitats, especially by cutting vast swaths of timber. Ranchers took land and water, and their cattle drove native game from the range. The homeless, starving, begging Indians so despised by Steward were a recent creation. Although he grudgingly acknowledged that cui-ui were important culturally as well as nutritionally, he refused to grant the Paiutes their own cultural identity. "The only ceremony of significance was the 'kuyui-no 'qa', or kuyui fish festival, held by the Paiute at Pyramid Lake at the beginning of the spring run. Lowie [Robert H. Lowie, a University of California anthropologist] says that this dance continued for five nights and was presided over by a special master of ceremonies."

Stewart, whose fieldwork was with Paiutes who slipped easily among the roles of peyote church member, converted Christian, and shaman, better understood that culture is dynamic, not static. Perhaps today, when we understand that natural environments are also in constant change, Steward might revise some of his theories.

Julian Steward's ethnocentrism and personal limitations as an ethnologist are discussed in Richard Clemmer's anthology *Julian Steward and the Great Basin: The Making of an Anthropologist*. Elmer Rusco reviews Steward's 1936 report to John Collier and the BIA on the Western Shoshone, whom Steward disliked almost as much as he disliked John Collier and Omer Stewart. His report, which recommended helping the Indians assimilate as quickly as possible, was suppressed by the BIA, lest his harsh remarks upset negotiations with the Shoshone. Steward's contempt for all the Natives of the Great Basin alarmed Alida Bowler, who knew from experience with the Pyramid Lake Paiutes that Steward had little understanding of the current state of Native culture. Rusco, who was familiar with the role of social scientists in public policy, concludes that Steward violated professional ethics. If he opposed the policy of the agency he was hired to advise, he should have resigned and made his criticisms from outside. Alice B. Kehoe, an anthropologist who studied the Ghost Dance and other Native religious movements, puts her criticism of Steward's negative assessments of the Natives of the Great Basin quite simply by asking, "Where were Wovoka and Wuzzie George?" Her point is that Steward seldom considered human beings in his studies, focusing instead on the physical environment and skimpy archaeological evidence.

I WANT TO MAKE ANOTHER OBSERVATION on Julian Steward that will explain him without absolving him and also offer some understanding of Paiute life in the late nineteenth century. My insight comes from his publication *Two*

Paiute Autobiographies, one of his few attempts to understand living Indians. In 1927–28 he collected life histories from two men he thought were close to a hundred years old, Jack Stewart (Hoavadunuki) of Big Pine and Sam Newland of Bishop, California. Each document is a little less than five thousand words long. Both men begin their autobiographies with memories of learning to hunt. Stewart was taught by his father, but he soon came to think his father was often wrong and he used his own judgment. Newland's father died when he was still a boy, and he claims he never learned to hunt, yet he recalls the dances associated with nut gathering and rabbit hunting and took part in both the dances and the hunts with his brothers-in-law. Stewart is boastful, Newland self-effacing.

Stewart describes many of his dreams in detail in order to explain his special hunting and gambling powers. He says he was twice called to be a doctor (shaman), but refused because he felt the power would shorten his life. He was not reckless in battle, staying at the end of the line so he could escape. He was, nevertheless, adventurous, traveling to the San Francisco Bay Area with white friends and hunting throughout the Sierra Nevada. Newland confined his travels to the mountains around Bishop, gathering food. He fished using the roots of slim Solomon (*Smilacina sessilifolia*) to make a substance that, put in a pool, stupefied the fish, making it easy to catch them by hand. He and his friends stole horses from whites and in a skirmish with US troops he claims he killed an officer. Later he attended a Fourth of July celebration at an army fort. Subsequently, he escaped from four white men who were hunting Indians. He describes himself as a good runner. He concludes his story with a description of salt trading.

Although Stewart's life history is certainly entertaining, I find Newland's much richer in ethnographic detail. Stewart's dreams are interesting, but they seem material for psychoanalysis, not Paiute history. Professor Steward felt differently. He was scornful of Newland. "Sam Newland, a simple prosaic fellow, was less than mediocre in such pursuits as bring social recognition to a Paiute—hunting and gambling. If he possessed any outstanding ability, it was fleetness of foot to get himself away from trouble with which he could not cope. His autobiography is therefore a rehearsal of events familiar to any Paiute Indian and is of value in depicting the culture in actual operation." The famous ethnographer completely missed Newland's modesty, a central feature of Paiute culture.

On the other hand, he was enthusiastic about Jack Stewart. "Stewart represents himself as a remarkably virile and distinguished man who has achieved those values upon which a Paiute Indian places importance. His success results from tremendous physical vigor, manifest even in his old age, much sheer luck, and a vast amount of self-confidence born of innumerable visions. . . . Unlike Sam, he is evidently of a mind predisposed to hallucinations, interpreted as supernatural communications."

The question is why Julian Steward, a high priest among the tribe of anthropologists, seemed to prefer the man who attributed his successes to supernatural powers to the "prosaic fellow" who, when the chips were down, actually killed a white soldier. My answer is that Julian Steward's intellectual kinship with Jack is the similarity between their abstractions. Jack's dreams often served as partial previews of future events, paradigms for his actions. Julian's theories of cultural evolution were meant to be models to explain the advance of one group of humans over another, a paradigm to justify US colonialism. Moreover, Jack was least like a Paiute in his individualism, preferring his dreams to social occasions such as harvest dances. Sam may have lacked Jack's flash, but Sam Newland seems a more reliable informant of Paiute experience during the early contact period, including their fear of white aggression.

THE DECADE OF THE 1950s was a period of transition and hard times for the Kuyuidokado. As a high school student, I barely noticed their plight. As a college student, I became aware of the poverty at Nixon and the decline of the lake, but ardently believed that conditions had to improve. After all, Dillon Myer's reign of terror at the BIA had ended in 1953, and Senator McCarran died in 1954. Besides, I spent most of my childhood and youth on the western side, where my mother took me to Crosby's for a coke, to the guest ranch, and, usually, on to Letty's ranch near the Southern Pacific section foreman's house at Big Canyon, where I once lived with my grandparents Andy and Eunice Norrid, people and places I will revisit in the next chapter.

When I got my driver's license and bought a used Jeep, my lakeside horizons expanded. I must have made my first visits to the pyramid and Stone Mother in the summer of 1953. It was on one of those trips that I briefly metamorphosed from geek to cool by rescuing a popular classmate from Reno High, let's call him "Ace," who had gotten his brand-new Ford Crestline stuck in the sand. He was, needless to say, extremely proud of his ride, which had a customized Continental tire mount instead of a regular trunk. My war-surplus Jeep, with the rear half of a 1937 Chevy welded as a top, lacked the power to pull his monster across a parking lot, let alone extricate it from a beach of soft sand, but my jeeping buddy and I had a tow rope, a shovel, and plenty of incentive. Ace had two athletic passengers. An hour later he and his pals were back on the highway, happy and grateful, and I was sunburned and flush with a couple of bucks Ace gave me for gas. It finally dawned on me, years later, when my rental car had to be pulled from the sand by "Smith n Tobey—Off Road Recovery Specialists" that being rescued from the tenacious sands of Pyramid Lake is a rite of passage in which the lake claims you and initiates you into the community of the place.

Fifty-seven years after rescuing Ace, serendipity bestowed its favors. Reading through the papers of the Pyramid Lake Paiute Council's attorney Robert Leland, I came across a copy of a two-page handwritten letter from novelist Robert Pirsig to Albert Aleck, the council chair.

Dear Mr. Aleck

I read your article and saw your picture in the NCAI bulletin here at the University of Chicago and suddenly remembered that you were the person who pulled my car out of the sand by Pyramid Lake back in 1953 when my wife and I were working in Reno. I remember that if you hadn't taken time off from watering your stock (or whatever it was you were doing) we would have lost our jobs that we had to get back to.

I am sorry to hear of all the trouble the Paiutes are having with the government. There is nothing I personally can do about it now, but I wanted to write this letter anyway to let you know that I haven't forgotten your help and am working toward a way in which I may eventually may [sic] be able to repay it.

Ford Crestline being pulled from sand on the east side of Pyramid Lake by the author's Jeep modified with the rear half of a 1937 Chevy sedan top, ca. 1953. Photograph by the author.

I think most of the trouble stems from a deep belief on the part of the white people that the Indian way of life is inferior and should be destroyed for the benefit of the Indians. I think that as long as this belief persists you are going to get the same sort of run-around from the government that you are now getting. What I am doing now at the University of Chicago is trying to establish avenues of thinking that will enable, first scholars, then government officials and then the rest of the people to realize that the Indians' way of living *with* nature instead of against it is actually superior and makes everyone a lot more relaxed and happy in the end.

All this takes time, of course, but I am working as fast as I can and think eventually, may get somewhere. In the meantime, I hope you and the tribe will be able to hold off pressure that might cause you to lose the beautiful lake and land to people who are too greedy to understand them.

If you can hold out for a few more years I think things are going to improve.

Yours very truly,

Robert M. Pirsig

This letter, written in the early 1960s while the future author of *Zen and the Art of Motorcycle Maintenance* was struggling with graduate studies and about to be hospitalized and treated for schizophrenia, not only supports my theory that there is an initiation ritual that whites must go through at the lake—getting a car stuck in the sand—but also gives evidence there was a new generation of white college students who saw the civil rights movement, environmental protection, and the "quality" of life as closely linked. Nothing happens at Pyramid Lake without a reason, Pirsig and I are saying, nor in a library, where he saw Aleck's photograph and where much later I found his letter. Time means little at the lake. Sixty years have passed since Ace's and Pirsig's ceremonial entrapments and fifteen since my own. We all became wiser for the experience.

PYRAMID LAKE: SHANGRI-LA? OR SAUDI ARABIA?

Many of us began to wise up on New Year's Day 1954 when the first of four articles by A. J. Liebling on the history of the Pyramid Lake Reservation and Senator Patrick McCarran's thirty-year crusade to destroy it appeared in the *New Yorker*. Liebling's dispatches contain as good a history of Pyramid Lake and its residents in the early 1950s as we are likely to get, but his focus is mostly on McCarran and his legislative efforts to prevent the removal of various white squatters from the reservation and not on the Kuyuidokado, except as they appear at Harry and Joan Drackert's guest ranch. For this reason, and because Liebling's visits to the lake also produced the first version of the story Arthur Miller called "The Misfits," I will return to Liebling's vision of the lake in other chapters. Suffice to say, as Martha Knack and Omer Stewart do in their valuable history of the Pyramid Lake Reservation, the decade of the 1950s was difficult, as the tribe had to fight McCarran, the squatters, the BIA, the Truckee-Carson Irrigation District, and a number of aggressive missionaries who wanted to convert the heathens.

It is worth noting at this point that the Pyramid Lake Paiutes were hardly alone in their struggles to survive in the 1950s. Indians all over the United States were being stripped of land and sovereignty by proponents of big engineering projects and modernization. An eloquent depiction of one of these cases is Edmund Wilson's *Apologies to the Iroquois* that chronicles the unconscionable appropriation of Tuscarora lands in New York State by New York City commissioner Robert Moses. Moses sought to build a dam, which would flood the Indians' property, for power generation. Despite Indian protests, the dam was completed in 1961. Another Iroquois tribe, the Seneca, also lost land to dam projects. If large and well-organized Indian tribes like the Iroquois were powerless in the face of these onslaughts, what chance did the Kuyuidokado have?

Early in the 1960s the Pyramid Lake Paiute Tribal Council, encouraged by the Kennedy administration's revitalized BIA, began soliciting proposals for recreational development at the lake. Tempting plans were dangled like a "Purple Pearl Wing Woolly Worm" fly, a favorite lure with cutthroat trout fishermen, before the cash-starved council, but the Kuyuidokado kept their eyes on the only catch that really mattered, water to preserve the lake, its fish, and its people. Some of the development proposals were utopian, some were grandiose, all depended on saving the lake by increasing the amount of water it received from the Truckee River, an outcome that seemed unlikely as long as the Bureau of Reclamation and Nevada's congressional delegation favored the farmers in the Newlands Irrigation Project.

The harbinger of future development appeared in the late 1950s when powerboat owners began holding races at the lake. This story is also documented in the Robert Leland Papers in the Special Collections of the University of Nevada, Reno. The Reno-Sparks Chamber of Commerce approached the Pyramid Lake Tribal Council in January 1959 with a proposal for boat-launching facilities at Sutcliffe. Chairman Aleck saw benefits, but other members were skeptical. Nonetheless, a motion to promote recreation and grant leases was approved by a vote of ten to zero. On August 28 the tribe entered into a contract with the Washoe County Fair and Recreation Board, allowing it to "occupy certain land and lake areas" from September 15 to October 15, 1959, for recreational purposes. The fair board, on behalf of the Reno Regatta Association, agreed to install two "firmly anchored" concrete ramps, a twenty-two-foot road to the ramps, a sixteen-thousand-square-foot parking lot, and sanitation facilities. Hydroplane races took place October 11 and were attended by more than ten thousand spectators, based on an estimate of six to eight thousand vehicles in addition to those who came on a special Southern Pacific train paid for by Harold's Club. Unfortunately, the fair board had not made good on the planned additional launching ramps, or the parking lot, or the sanitation facilities.

Between heats the audience could spend fifty cents on a thirty-two-page program that included a brief sketch of the Pyramid Lake Paiutes. The author, Reno silver-shop owner Nick Jackson, claimed to be qualified to write about them because he had "spent a good part of his life on the fringes of the reservation," knew their customs and language, was "very active with the Navajo Indians in communications work in the Marine Corps," and was a "registered" archaeologist and representative of the "Smithsonian Institute [*sic*]." Jackson tells the boat-racing fans that in the years following the Donner Party (1846–47), "hundreds of White settlers were to dread the name Paiute. . . . In the late 1860s after a devastating battle during which Captain Ormsby's Virginia City Militia was annihilated, the Paiutes retired to the Pyramid Lake Reservation." Neither his biography nor his history shows much regard for the truth, but, reassured that the Indians, if any were to be seen, were comfortably "retired" to their reservation, the visitors could dump their cans and bottles, enjoy the race, and go home sunburned and happy.

The tribe was left holding three bags—one full of trash, another full of complaints about the traffic jam, and an empty bag that was supposed to hold 15 percent of the concession profits. Needless to say, the tribal council and its attorney were angry. Because the lease was made with the understanding the Regatta Association planned to hold races in October for the next three years, the tribe had some leverage. They could say no to next year's race. Reno hotel and casino owner Charles Mapes, association chairman, was concerned enough to send the tribe a check for $500 in lieu of its share of the concession profits. The Lion's Club, which had handled the food and drinks, said it lost money. But the bribe was small considering that the tribe expected the county fair board to put in $5,000 worth of improvements in the boat facilities over the next three years.

The first two ramps were finally installed by May 20, 1960—in the wrong place. The board ignored the tribe's complaint, and then on August 15 a windstorm washed out both "firmly anchored" ramps. The tribe hired an engineer who estimated that the ramps could be repaired for about $350 and a breakwater installed to prevent future wind damage for about $650. When the board stonewalled, the tribe asked for $5,000 to make its own repairs and improvements. With the races scheduled for the end of October, time was running out. Mapes, busily hosting John Huston, Arthur Miller, and Marilyn Monroe at his hotel while they filmed *The Misfits*, kited into action. In an angry letter to the Washoe County Fair and Recreation Board that begins, "This letter is not to be misconstrued as any criticism of the Fair and Recreation Board or the Pyramid Lake Indian Council," Mapes threatened, "Unless this deadlock is broken by this coming Friday, September 16th, 1960, the Reno Regatta Association will have but one alternative left, and that is to cancel the races planned to be held October 29 and 30. . . . One word of warning—if we should have to do this, in my opinion Reno would be losing one of its greatest tourist attractions for all time."

Temporary repairs were made and the races took place. The county and the tribe continued to skirmish like Major Ormsby and Numaga. The Regatta Association sputtered into 1961. A meeting July 6, in the optimistically named Bonanza Room of the Mapes Hotel, brought together representatives of the regatta, the county, and the tribe. The sticking points again were who would pay for the launching facilities and whether the county's lease, which provided for free access to the facilities they planned, would discourage private investors from developing a more luxurious recreational complex. The potential conflict between public and private development was an expressed concern of tribal councilman Levi Frazier. He and others were also mistrustful of the county because of its failure to keep its promises in the past. Frazier's deepest fear was that the public would get the idea that the developed area was county land and the tribe would not be able to collect for parking and picnicking there. The meeting ended with approval of the county's vague plan, with details to be worked out.

The 1961 races took place as scheduled, complete with a program that contained a glossary of hydroplane boating lingo. "Sticky water" is "calm or flat water which prevents efficient planing attitude of the hull." "Angle of Attack: Refers to the way the hull rides through the water and the direction of the air striking the various surfaces. Too great an 'angle of attack' will cause 'kiting' . . . when the hull 'noses up' and becomes airborne." The argot of hydroplaning can be used to explain why the 1961 race was the last. The lake was often "sticky," failing to provide waves to break the water's surface. The tribe was, with good reason, often sticky and difficult in negotiations. The "angle of attack" by the county recreation planners and the Regatta Association was often too great, and they went "nose up," with dreams of glory and profits that were not meant to be.

The development proposals following these early efforts highlight the clash between public and private ideas of recreation. In July 1961 two Washoe County commissioners, a regional planner, and the Fish and Game commissioner met with the tribe's attorney and partners from a private development company to iron out their differences. The boat launching and fishing area at Sutcliffe was not being maintained, litter was accumulating, and the tribe lacked the money to hire and train a staff to supervise the area and collect fishing and boating fees. A private company from Arizona, Pyramid Lake Enterprises, sought to lease six miles of shoreline and planned to build a hotel, a motel, a trailer park, and a marina with food and drink concessions. They also sought approval for slot machines. Neon signs were not mentioned, but clearly implied. The tribe would receive rent and a percentage of the revenues.

The county, on the other hand, proposed cleaning up about a mile of beach at Sutcliffe, improving the boat-launching facilities, installing ten picnic tables and some toilets, and maintaining access roads and parking on about fifty acres of reservation land. It would not charge for these amenities, allowing the Indians to collect permit fees directly. Pyramid Lake Enterprises strongly objected to any competition to their proposed development and expressed concern that the county would expand its facilities and unfairly compete with a for-profit business, even after being reminded that the agreement between the Fish and Game Commission and the tribe required public access. It is clear from the minutes of several meetings that the private developers were seeking a monopoly on all recreation at the lake, including the stocking of fish. The company succeeded in convincing the tribe to cancel its agreement with the county, but went bankrupt a few months later. The trash problem at Sutcliffe was mitigated temporarily by a cleanup by volunteers from Reno, Sparks, and Stead Air Force Base; the search for a reliable developer continues to the present.

At about the same time, Mapes proposed an extensive resort complex, but failed to submit specific plans and budgets. The tribal council wanted to raise more revenue for the tribe through fishing, boating, and other recreational opportunities at the lake, but some members were concerned about overdevelopment. This was not a concern of Secretary of Interior Stewart Udall, who was encouraging recreation and tourism on Indian reservations throughout the West to reduce unemployment. The BIA commissioned not one but two studies of the potential of the Pyramid Lake Paiute Reservation for development, examples of what might be called "the significance of the 'new frontier' in Native American history."

" 'We Need to Be Shown': A Study of the Talents, Work Potential, and

Aspirations of the Pyramid Lake Indians" was completed in 1962 by William Gomberg, a professor in the Wharton School of Finance at the University of Pennsylvania, and Joy Leland, an anthropologist and wife of the tribe's attorney. Gomberg and Leland focused on the managerial and entrepreneurial potential of the Kuyuidokado, to whom they administered a battery of aptitude and personality tests to determine if tribal members were ready to run their own recreation and tourist-related businesses. The authors' conclusions were candid and somewhat pessimistic. From their interviews and tests, Gomberg and Leland concluded that the Pyramid Lake Paiutes did not like to give orders to other people and lacked self-confidence, although one-third said they would like to learn to be managers. The fact that there were fewer than two hundred employable adults on the reservation in 1962 further limited the size of any potential recreational development designed primarily to alleviate Indian unemployment.

An appendix to the Gomberg-Leland report offers an ironic and revealing insight into academic and business attitudes toward Native Americans and other "underdeveloped" people. The document is a personal letter to Gomberg from Thomas C. Barger, president and chief executive officer (CEO) of the Arabian American Oil Company, Dhahran, Saudi Arabia, in which "Tom" tells "Bill" how he taught Arabs how to be entrepreneurs. Tom Barger, as Robert Vitalis adroitly explains in *America's Kingdom: Mythmaking on the Saudi Oil Frontier*, began his ARAMCO career as a geologist who referred to Saudi and other workers as "coolies" and helped to establish American-style Jim Crow segregation in the oil fields until workers organized in the 1950s and '60s and partially succeeded in challenging American control. Educated Saudis sometimes described themselves as American Indians, selling their land for a handful of beads as the Natives of Manhattan reputedly did. Late in his career Barger regretted his prejudices and tried to make amends, but in light of Vitalis's research there is no question that American racism is part of the nation's imperial footprints throughout the world.

Barger begins his letter by observing that his company benefited from a quiet period of "acquaintanceship" from 1935 to 1945. On-the-job training, with one American to seven Saudis, went on for the next fifteen years. "Then followed organized studies by our practical business people aided by anthropologists (we still have two on our staff) of [sic] psychologists and a host of consultants including Arnold Toynbee." Barger shows he was paying attention to the consultants (two of whom were Solon T. Kimball, whose research focused on the Navajo, rural communities, and race, and Thomas F. O'Dea, a specialist in the sociology of religion) when he poses some questions: "Do they [Paiutes] value success in terms of money and power, or do they acquire social prestige through other means? Who would rate higher according to their value system: J. Paul Getty, or St. Francis of Assisi?" In the next paragraph Barger makes a revealing comment that justifies his reputation as an able agent of American business interests abroad and explains some of the problems currently plaguing the Middle East.

> We have raised hell with the [Saudi] society, whether for good or bad is still moot, but one thing we've tried to do (at least for the last thirteen years) is to avoid enslaving our employees. Over the intense opposition of some of the newly educated Saudis, we have always opted for lines of action in respect to personal affairs that put responsibility on the employee, and except where he obviously needed protection (e.g. food rations during the war), we have tried to avoid forcing him to do what we thought was good for him. By and large, they have responded very well.

They seemed happy to be exploited until they protested unequal pay and segregated housing.

Barger concludes his letter by advising Gomberg to find two or three good men who know the business they are supposed to teach and teaching "them by making the Paiutes *want* to do it." It is unclear whether any members of the Pyramid Lake Tribal Council ever read this report, but they were acquiring a better knowledge of white men's ways through almost daily contact with their attorney and BIA officials. They learned when to applaud a Getty, when to laud a St. Francis, and when to choose their own heroes.

The second study, "Economic Development Plan for Pyramid Lake Indian Reservation," by William L. K. Schwartz and David P. Fogel for a Washington, DC, firm with a customarily bland name, International Development Services (IDS), was submitted to the BIA in August 1963. It called Pyramid Lake "one of the last great undeveloped bodies of water in the United States," and like most of the proposals submitted by developers it was tinged with utopian sentiments. The IDS plan was rejected and rewritten, apparently because it was insufficiently ambitious in the view of E. Reeseman Fryer, who had been promoted, after Myer's resignation, to assistant commissioner of the BIA. Fryer outlined his plan to the Pyramid Lake Tribal Council in March 1963. He envisioned a two-hundred-slip marina, a motel, restaurant, and trailer park, providing forty-seven jobs and an annual payroll of $126,000. (This works out to $2,680 per job, about half the national average yearly wage in 1963.)

The IDS report was based on a site visit and interviews with state and BIA

officials, but no input from the tribe except from its attorney Robert Leland. The
IDS plan reflected Leland's caution more than the BIA's enthusiasm. The plan
called attention to the need for Truckee River water to maintain the lake and
took notice of the Newlands Reclamation Project's waste of water. Although the
report included a map showing considerable commercial and residential development on both sides of the lake, including beachfront residences extending
from near the Truckee River delta to within a mile of the pyramid, its authors
clearly laid out alternatives to "maximum development." Income for the tribe
had to be weighed against "scenic and aesthetic" factors and the "ever growing
need for unspoiled recreational areas." Some of the pros and cons of gambling
on the reservation were also mentioned, an indication that some in the BIA
favored casinos as part of the Pyramid Lake development plan, while many of
the tribal members opposed it.

In June 1963 the BIA office in Phoenix received a proposal that laid bare the
paradox of commercial development versus traditional values. After comparing
his plans to resort hotel developments at Lake Louise in Alberta and the Yel-
lowstone Park Lodge, the author, award-winning architect Wayne R. Williams
of Los Angeles, proceeds without a hint of irony: "As there is an Indian tradition existing on the Reservation, the Indian motive will be real and genuine and
one that will be based on the existing (though somewhat dormant) cultural
background of the Northern Paiute Tribe. A Center, which is thus a genuine
recreation in a true setting will be far more meaningful than a fake KonTiki
South Sea village."

Williams's plans were grandiose, if a bit confused about Paiute culture and
the politics of gambling in Nevada.

> The Hotel, in addition to the various classes of accommodations, would offer
> a gourmet type of restaurant, barber and beauty shop, tobbaconist, newsstand,
> Sauna room and Health Club, as well as a gift shop. The latter should be geared
> towards a revival of the Paiute Tribe's former excellence in the execution of petro-
> glyphs, their long tradition of basketry and possibly still existing production and
> sale of rabbit skin blankets. . . . The possibility of introducing not only a cock-
> tail bar in the Hotel, but possibly a Casino and Night Club should be thoroughly
> investigated. This, after all, would not be entirely foreign to the Paiute, whose love
> for dance and music, as well as for a broad range of gambling games are only too
> well known to the ethnologists.

Although Williams's proposal is comically inappropriate for many reasons,
subsequent projects put forward by Hawaiian builder Q. C. Lum, a New Mexico

consortium made up of savings and loan bankers and oilmen, a San Francisco–based corporation calling itself "City of America," and Reno's own sovereign of economic growth, Norman Biltz, all projected thousands of acres of hotels, casinos, vacation and retirement villages, churches, schools, medical facilities, shopping malls, museums, and golf courses—surrounded by plantings of Lombardy poplars, tall pines, sycamores, river willows, and "canopy trees." The Lum proposal was vigorously advocated by Fryer of the BIA, who advised the Pyramid Lake Tribal Council to sign Lum's contract without waiting for competing offers. When the council smelled a rat and refused, Lum's associate threatened them, telling the council "that Lum had bought a lot of property around Elko for a lot less money than he planned to spend around Pyramid Lake and that it was just as good as Pyramid Lake except there was no lake." Chutzpah meets Coo-yu-ee Pah.

By the mid-1960s the Pyramid Lake Paiutes had learned useful lessons about the ways in which developers, bureaucrats, and lawyers thought about the lake. The outsiders knew that the Indians wanted to preserve their land, but they failed to see the difference between utopian visions and simple respect. The development proposals all sketched a future of idyllic harmony with nature. The tribal council knew the utopia was "no place" and that they were, for better or worse, stuck at the terminus of a river managed by upstream users. When, in 1964, the tribal council submitted its ten-year goals for the Pyramid Lake Reservation, its top priorities were as follows: restoration of fishery, housing construction for residents at Nixon, and lake-based recreational development. The goals were clear. Without the cui-ui there would be no Kuyuidokado, without water no fish. Recreational facilities for revenue were desirable but, in the long run, impossible without practical steps to restore water to the lake. Without achieving the first goal, recreation would wreck creation. In 1967 and 1968, the lake fell to its lowest recorded level, but three events occurred that offered some hope.

THREE

The Lake and Its Totem

Disputes between the Pyramid Lake Paiutes and their rivals for water from the Truckee River continued to fester. Federal and state agencies created to manage Indian affairs, water resources, and fish and wildlife frequently found themselves in conflict with each other as well as with Indians, farmers, businessmen, and municipal authorities, all claiming their rights were not being protected. During President Nixon's administration the Department of the Interior, home to all the major government bureaus involved, attempted to find a solution to the Pyramid Lake problem. During President Reagan's tenure of office, the road to settlement shifted to the US Senate and remained there into the administration of George H. W. Bush. The passage of the Truckee–Carson–Pyramid Lake Water Settlement Act in 1990 was the culmination of more than a century of rancor. The legislation did not solve all the problems, but it created a process for achieving peace.

More important, and overlooked in the accounts of the settlement act that I have read, was the acknowledgment of the complex interrelationship of water rights, human rights, states' rights, and the rights of endangered species.

When the federal government passed laws in the 1960s to prevent the extinction of endangered species, including the cui-ui and the Lahontan cutthroat trout, it trumped the plans of governors, farmers, and dam builders. Laws that recognized the cui-ui as the emblem of a people's heritage found acceptance in a nation that was beginning to understand that humans are part of nature. As Freeman House puts it in his poetic account of fish restoration in the Pacific Northwest, *Totem Salmon,* "Somewhere beyond our modern notions of religion and regulation but partaking of both, human engagement with salmon—and the rest of the natural world—has been marked by behavior that is respectful, participatory, and ceremonial."

Three important examples of the intertwining of rights are examined in this chapter. First, as the proceedings of the Pyramid Lake Task Force (1969–71) reveal, institutionalized racism persisted in the civil rights era. As critics of the task force report pointed out, there was more at stake in preserving Pyramid Lake than protecting sportfishing. The Paiutes were also endangered. In the aftermath of the Vietnam War, the idea of destroying a village in order to save it made little sense. Second, when Nevada senator Paul Laxalt launched his effort to resolve the conflict between the Kuyuidokado and the Newlands Reclamation Project farmers, he understood the issues primarily in economic terms. Both the irrigators and the Indians had a lot to lose financially. But they knew that they had even more to lose if the rights they firmly believed were theirs were not acknowledged and protected. Third, as the 1988–90 negotiations leading to the settlement show, other parties to the dispute were redefining their goals. City managers and power company administrators claimed water rights, endangered-fish management planners required new kinds of public-private cooperation, and many Native Americans saw themselves as part of the postcolonial world. Though they could never recover the freedom and authority they possessed before the conquest of the Americas, they could, as tribal council chairman Joe Ely put it, use a kind of "judo approach"—that is, use knowledge of their opponents' strengths to cause them to lose their balance.

The final episode, the US Senate hearings on the settlement act, gains additional significance because of the Bureau of Reclamation oral history project that provides countless insights into the ways the participants thought about the issues involved. For the practicing historian, there is a lovely irony in seeing the story of Pyramid Lake beginning and continuing in oral testimony.

WATER RIGHTS AND CIVIL RIGHTS

In February 1967 Secretary of the Interior Stewart Udall issued the first regulations for the Newlands Reclamation Project, requiring farmers to conserve water and improve project efficiency. The new operating criteria and procedures (OCAP) also required better management of the water used in electrical power generation. A few months later the cui-ui were placed on the first list ("Class of '67") of endangered species sanctioned by the Endangered Species Preservation Act of 1966. The operating procedures and the listing of an endangered species provided the basis for a series of legal actions by the tribe to secure more water for the lake. In 1968 the tribe filed a suit for water for the endangered cui-ui based on the 1967 OCAP. The suit became known as *Pyramid Lake Tribe of Paiute Indians v. Walter J. Hickel, Secretary of the Interior* and was the third event that shifted the tribe's energies from recreational development to water rights.

Meanwhile, Native Americans were asserting themselves, echoing, as historian Paul Rosier writes, "the pro-independence, pro-development discourse of decolonization activists abroad." The National Indian Youth Council (NIYC) was organized in 1961. One of the founders, Mel Thom, a Walker River Paiute, felt that Indians were in a cold war with the federal and state governments. According to historian Bradley Shreve, Thom was a brilliant organizer and articulate spokesman for the young radicals. Known to some as Mao Tse Thom, the NIYC chairman testified before Congress on the ineffectiveness of federal antipoverty programs administered from Washington. Thom joined with anthropologist Jack Forbes in an effort to create schools for Indians that would help restore Native cultures, but internal conflicts and interference by government and foundation officials limited their success. Young Indian activists compared the struggle for fishing rights in the Pacific Northwest to the war in Vietnam. Ironically or cynically, non-Indian officers and enlisted men referred to the jungles of Southeast Asia as "Indian Country." As the split between antiwar Indian youth and the older generation in control of the National Congress of American Indians widened, the NCAI asked Secretary of Defense Robert McNamara to send a Native American dance troupe from fifteen reservations to perform for military personnel in Vietnam. Authorities in the Pentagon refused to sponsor the trip because, they explained, they sent only famous entertainers.

The following year, 1968, the American Indian Movement (AIM) emerged, and a year later its members and supporters occupied Alcatraz Island in San Francisco Bay. The nineteen-month occupation was justified under an 1868 treaty that made unused federal lands (the prison had closed in 1963) available to Indian claims. In November 1972 almost a thousand Indians traveled to Washington, DC, to press their demands for, among other things, renegotiation of treaties, review of treaty violations, restoration of 110 million acres of land, and economic development. Thwarted, they seized the Department of Interior building and trashed BIA offices. A few months later a group of activists associated with AIM occupied Wounded Knee, South Dakota. For a little more than two months, armed Indians faced US military and law enforcement officers. Thanks in part to the presence of a large contingent of foreign journalists, the occupation ended peacefully, but there had been two fatalities during the encounter, and bitterness and violence followed in succeeding years. Wounded Knee revealed serious divisions within AIM and left it weakened by mass arrests by the Federal Bureau of Investigation (FBI). Rosier thinks the American public lost interest in the cause of Native Americans as their attention turned to the Watergate scandal.

In Nevada the political climate was changing fast and threatening the lake. In July 1968, after thirteen years of sometimes rancorous negotiations, the

California-Nevada Interstate Compact Commission agreed on a plan for sharing the development of the water resources of the Tahoe Basin. Needless to say,
no Indians were consulted and water for Pyramid Lake was not included in the
plans. While the commission waited for the state legislatures to ratify the compact, Richard Nixon won the presidency and a new administration took office.
The compact commissioners expected prompt congressional approval, but protests began to be heard, and Nixon's mercurial secretary of the interior, Walter
J. Hickel, saw an opportunity to calm the turbulent waters. Wally Hickel considered himself something of an expert on water for the arid West. As governor
of Alaska he had promoted a plan to bring water from his state to California in
a two-thousand-mile undersea pipeline, despite the cost and the skepticism of
engineers and fellow politicians. By opposing the California-Nevada compact
that favored rapid development of housing and recreation at Lake Tahoe, Hickel
was credited by *Time* with "saving Pyramid Lake," but the reporter had not yet
seen the plan hatched by Hickel and Governors Reagan and Laxalt on their July
6, 1969, cruise around Tahoe on casino owner Bill Harrah's yacht.

In what was essentially an elaborate public relations effort to quiet growing
sympathy for the Indians' cause, Hickel created the Pyramid Lake Task Force,
with federal representation, identified as the Washington Supervisory Group,
from the Department of the Interior, the Bureau of Reclamation, the BIA, and
the Bureau of Outdoor Recreation. The State of Nevada's delegation consisted
of a past member of the Nevada Indian Affairs Commission, the director of the
state Fish and Game Commission, the chairman of the Pyramid Lake Paiute
Tribal Council, the state engineer, and men from the Sierra Pacific Power Company (SPPCO), the Upper Carson River Water Users, and the Truckee Carson
Irrigation District. California seemed satisfied to be represented by the chairman of the Alpine County Board of Supervisors and the assistant director of
the state's Department of Water Resources. The task force was a dog-and-pony
show. Fourteen other attendees, including two reporters, the tribe's attorney, and Tom Trelease from Nevada Fish and Game, are listed in the minutes.
Trelease's crucial role in saving the lake will be examined in chapter 5.

The task force minutes from its first meeting on October 16, 1969, to its
twenty-sixth, December 14, 1971, available in the Pyramid Lake Water Papers
in the Special Collections of the University of Nevada, Reno, Library, tell an all
too familiar story of bureaucratic rivalries, political ambitions, cultural misunderstandings, and just plain human stupidity.

Charles Renda, regional solicitor, Department of the Interior, chaired the
meeting from the beginning (he was elected a few minutes into the first session

without opposition on a motion of the assistant commissioner of the Bureau of Reclamation) after he and his chief, Raymond C. Coulter, the deputy solicitor from Washington, had assured the group that they were only "supervisory" in the sense that Secretary Hickel "had a deep personal interest in the Pyramid Lake problem" and wanted the task force to have direct access to him. Coulter then asked the task force "to give their impression of their purposes and objectives." This opened the door for James Vidovich, tribal council chairman, to submit a letter that was read aloud by Renda. The minutes summarized the tribe's concerns: "Mr. Vidovich said that the Nevada group for the most part consisted of those interests which were in competition for water which should go to Pyramid Lake and that the State of Nevada did not necessarily represent the interests of the Pyramid Lake Indians. Mr. Renda said that the individual members were not necessarily bound by the vote of the group."

The Kuyuidokado saw that the deck was stacked. The unit rule was in effect, meaning that a majority of task force members from each state would determine the state's position on issues, silencing the minority. Renda's disingenuous response was a clear signal to the rest of the committee that their job was to make Hickel look good and get the Paiutes to shut up. When Vidovich asked about a letter the tribe had sent to the secretary requesting that their attorney, Bob Leland, represent them on the task force, Roland Westergard, the Nevada state engineer, objected, saying that the governor had made the appointments and the Nevada task force group would "have to consider the matter." As the minutes of the following meetings and his public statements reveal, Westergard seems to have enjoyed playing the heavy in this theater of the absurd. His contempt for the Indians and disregard for the plight of the lake were ill-concealed. Next, Renda created a committee to draft task force objectives. The committee consisted of Westergard, the California Water Resources official, and Renda himself. The statement is Orwellian: "to investigate the water availability and needs of the Tahoe, Truckee and Carson basins and to recommend ways and means to use and distribute such waters in such a manner as will, as closely as possible, provide sufficient water to preserve Pyramid Lake and to satisfy the beneficial needs of other users."

Preserving a miniaturized lake without preserving the people who lived there was the unstated goal. Leland, called upon to explain what the Indians "really desired," hedged a bit, suggesting that they may have "rights which could return the lake to its condition prior to the building of Derby Dam," but that they might be "realistic and would probably accept a condition which would stabilize the lake at its present level."

Leland, who had guided the tribe through ten years of assaults by developers, would soon be replaced as the tribe's attorney. Nevertheless, he and Chairman Vidovich hung in for a few more meetings. At the third meeting Renda reported that Nevada governor Mike O'Callaghan, who had just succeeded Paul Laxalt, agreed to name Leland as the tribe's representative and would eliminate the unit rule in voting. Having to deal with a liberal Democrat after Governor Laxalt must have been a shock to the task force enforcers, but Renda immediately ruled that because the tribe had not made up its mind about representation by its attorney, neither Vidovich nor Leland could vote, and he moved on to reports from committees that had been set up to study various solutions to the water problems, including reducing the waste of water by the Newlands Reclamation Project, weather modification, and the importation of water from the Pacific Northwest. The subcommittee report stated, in part:

> The committee believes that *an eventual import of water from the Pacific Northwest is the only firm, permanent, and happy solution to the problem of stabilizing or even increasing the level of Pyramid Lake* [emphasis in the original]. Any permanent solution using only the existing water resources of the Truckee and Carson River Basins alone would at best deny any future growth in the area due to limited water supplies, and at worst it could also require the taking of water away from present beneficial uses with consequent adverse effects on the economy of the entire area and the livelihood of its residents.

The preliminary conclusion was that, although all three of these possibilities for increasing water to Pyramid Lake would be expensive, they were worth further study. The snow- and rainmaking scheme led to a contract with the Desert Research Institute for a five-year study of cloud seeding in the Truckee River basin. The results were, as in every case of weather modification, inconclusive, but the study contributed to a better understanding of the ecology of the area. The task force committee's enthusiastic endorsement of water importation was clearly a sop to Secretary Hickel, but he was soon replaced by Rogers Morton. In the final report in December 1971, the committee ditched "the only firm, permanent, and happy solution" by concluding that "the feasibility of this project was not within the scope of the Task Force." The final report was about fifty pages in a plastic spiral binding. Its basic conclusions were that there was "no outstanding water right to maintain Pyramid Lake at its present or any other level," that to maintain the lake at its present level (3,794 feet above sea level) would require an average of 135,000 additional acre-feet of water annually (for a total of 385,000), and that only 95,150 acre-feet per year could be saved by better water management (for a total of 345,150 acre-feet); hence, the lake would continue to drop by about 20 feet a century, stabilizing in the year 2580 at an elevation of 3,753 feet above sea level. These estimates make about as much sense as the report as a whole.

There was no dissent from the report except a feeble gesture by the assistant area director of the BIA, who wanted a sentence added to the letter of transmittal to the effect that, although he supported the findings and recommendations of the task force, "he considers the out-of-basin imports nebulous and feels that more water should be developed for Pyramid Lake within the Basin." James Wood of the TCID objected, and a compromise sentence reading, "One member felt that additional water for Pyramid Lake should be developed from some of the in-basin sources not recommended by the Task Force as a whole," was suggested, but even this innocuous line was omitted. In its place a prominent single-sentence paragraph reads: "After due consideration, it was concluded that other in-basin potential water sources are impractical and not feasible at this time." It took almost twenty more years to make them feasible.

The conclusions in the letter of transmittal to Secretary Morton and Governors Reagan and O'Callaghan seem benign, but omit any consideration of the environmental and economic effects on the Paiutes, endangered fish, pelicans, or even the white squatters. Moreover, lurking at the end of the report, in the very last appendix, is a graph prepared by engineering consultants from Clyde-Criddle-Woodward, Inc., in Salt Lake City, illustrating the possibilities of "stabilizing" the lake at 3,692 feet in the year 2550 with an annual average inflow of 300,000, or at 3,645 in 2430, with an inflow of 250,000. Many in the task force and in the Truckee and Carson River basins favored no increase, accepting a dead Pyramid Lake by 2430. This was the solution, I might say "the final solution," offered by Clyde-Criddle-Woodward, for which they were paid $122,000 by the Bureau of Reclamation. Indian activist Vine Deloria Jr. rightly compared this recommendation to that of the US Army officer in Vietnam who advocated destroying a village in order to save it.

Outrage and criticism from allies of the Pyramid Lake Paiutes were again swift and effective. Editor Alvin M. Josephy Jr. published an eloquent piece in the *American Heritage Magazine* that reviewed the history of the reclamation project and the chicanery of both federal and state politicians that was keeping the Indians poor and powerless. He stopped short of addressing the racism that motivated most of white America at this time, but this was made clear in the impassioned pleas for justice made by BIA attorney William Veeder to Congress and the secretary of the interior in 1969 and 1972. Veeder's obstreperousness—he was not afraid to use the word *genocide* in describing the Pyramid Lake Task Force report—caused Rogers Morton to attempt to transfer the BIA lawyer to Phoenix. A second wave of editorials across the nation defending Veeder saved his job and brought more attention to the lake.

SIGNS OF PROGRESS? Yes, but in 1964, the year President Lyndon B. Johnson signed the Civil Rights Act barring racial and gender discrimination and specifically prohibiting discrimination by federal agencies, the Nevada Fish and Game Commission published a calendar with a cover photograph of "the Squaw Mother and the Basket." Five years later an ad in *Nevada Highways* for DEL Chemical Corporation of Menomonee Falls (Wisconsin), Honolulu, and Reno-Sparks announced, "We're as western as the cigar-store indian" [*sic*]. The ad was illustrated with a carved wooden figure holding a chemical retort. The ad shows appalling ignorance of the history and purpose of cigar-store Indians, whose seventeenth-century origins in England and popularity in the United States during the period of active extermination of Indian nations yoke the carvings to conquest and colonization. They were called "Black Boys" and "Virginie Men," before they became "Pocahontas," "Squaw," "Buck," "Brave," and "Captain Jack," the latter referring to the Modoc leader who was hanged by the US Army at Fort Klamath at the climax of the Modoc War in 1873.

Folklorist Rayna Green has placed the cigar-store Indian and the squaw in the wider context of demeaning images of Indians in popular literature, advertising, jokes, and songs. Images of Indian princesses and squaws vex Green because both are the creations of white fantasies. The princess is idealized because, in numerous stories and songs, she saves the life of a white man and then either sacrifices her life or leaves her tribe. "Squaws," Green notes, "are shamed for their relationships with white men, and the males who share their beds—the 'squaw men'—or 'bucks,' if they are Indian—share their shame. . . . [T]hey are 'fat,' and unlike their Princess sisters, dark and possessed of cruder, more 'Indian' features." Lustful or comic, the image behind the name "Squaw and Her Basket" is pejorative.

Paremiographer Wolfgang Mieder provides grimmer evidence of anti-Indian prejudice in a scholarly article on the proverb "The only good Indian is a dead Indian." The phrase is usually attributed to General Phil Sheridan. Mieder found an earlier example in an 1868 speech in Congress by James Michael Cavanaugh of Montana, who intoned: "I have never in my life seen a good Indian (and I have seen thousands) except when I have seen a dead Indian." The phrase was often repeated, with slight variations, by commissioners of Indian Affairs, US

Army officers, and Theodore Roosevelt in a book published before he became president. The relevance of Mieder's research to the Pyramid Lake Paiutes comes from an interview in 1969 with a fifty-year-old woman who had grown up in Carson City in the 1920s. She told an interviewer that she frequently heard the phrase when residents of the state capital were talking about Indians on nearby reservations.

But the Pyramid Lake Paiutes were alive and kicking, as were hundreds of thousands of other Indians, when members of the American Indian Movement and supporters occupied Alcatraz in the fall of 1969. The impact of this protest against centuries of persecution and discrimination of Indians was enormous. No wonder the *Nevada State Journal* reported on January 7, 1970, that the "Squaw's" basket had disappeared. A photograph purported to show that the basket part of the tufa formation was missing, but the unfamiliar angle of the photo probably accounts for the "disappearance." A week later a BIA official assured readers of the *Reno Evening Gazette* that the basket was still in place. This bit of what was probably some reporter's attempt at humor also reflects growing public unease as Indians refused to vanish. The BIA had reason to be concerned. A few months after the basket mysteriously vanished and reappeared, Jane Fonda entered the reservation with a group of about two hundred supporters to pour bottled water into the lake in protest over the Bureau of Reclamation's diversion of Truckee River water to the Newlands Project. In her autobiography, *My Life So Far*, Fonda proudly declares that this brief demonstration became the first item in her FBI file. Fonda pioneered the era of Hollywood stars shining in reservation skies. Three years later Marlon Brando endorsed the Kuyuidokado's cause on Dick Cavett's evening television talk show.

According to his autobiography, Brando's interest in Native American rights began in his youth and first manifested itself in January 1964 when he joined a delegation in Washington, DC, that lobbied for Native American rights. In May he participated in a fishing-rights protest by the Puyallup Tribe in northwestern Washington State and was arrested for illegal fishing, but quickly released. He supported the Indian occupation of Alcatraz that began November 20, 1969, and quixotically used the Motion Picture Academy Awards ceremony of March 27, 1973, to protest Hollywood's depiction of Indians as savages. Brando's refusal to attend the awards ceremony and accept an Oscar for his performance in *The Godfather* is one of the best-remembered incidents in his volatile career. He outraged or embarrassed almost everyone in the movie industry and many outside it by sending an unknown actress, Sasheen Littlefeather, to read the protest speech he had written, but he received the attention he sought. Less than three months later, on June 12, he appeared with representatives from the Lummi, Northern Cheyenne, and Paiute Tribes on the Cavett show, where they discussed political, environmental, and health problems on reservations. Brando's biographers dismiss the Cavett appearance as another disaster because Brando, clad in a blue denim jacket accented by a red scarf, mumbled, preened for the cameras, and rambled on about racial injustice, but the real villain of the evening was the obsequious Dick Cavett, who flattered Brando and patronized the Indians. He was especially dismissive of Mervin Wright, the Pyramid Lake Tribal Council chair, cutting him off in midsentence and ignoring him for the more exotically costumed (therefore telegenic) Lummi, Sam Cagey. (The whole program is viewable on YouTube.)

For reasons not entirely explained either in his autobiography or by his biographers, Brando missed the occupation of Wounded Knee, but went on to attend the trial of Dennis Banks and Russell Means in St. Paul in January 1974, ultimately joining them in a sweat-lodge ceremony. In February of the following year, he joined Menominee protesters in Gresham, Wisconsin, where he was shot at, robbed, and otherwise harassed by both local vigilantes and Menominee who were skeptical of Brando's sincerity. Brando continued to provide financial support and hospitality to Banks, Leonard Peltier, and other AIM leaders, but his involvement weakened by the end of the 1970s, just when the Kuyuidokado could have used his support.

The decade of the 1970s witnessed some important gains for the Pyramid Lake Tribe and a brief respite from the relentless effort by Paul Laxalt and others to drive the Kuyuidokado from the lake. Democrat Mike O'Callaghan, remembered by some as Senator Harry Reid's high school history teacher and boxing coach, was elected governor of Nevada. Attitudes in Carson City toward Native Americans swung from ill-concealed hostility to unembarrassed benevolence. As reported November 16, 1971, by the *Sacramento Bee*, O'Callaghan told the two thousand delegates attending the twenty-eighth annual meeting of the National Congress of American Indians that "Indians must find ways to preserve their heritage, yet must also fight for their rightful place in society.... The white man today is jealous of the Indian and mimics him in hopes of capturing some of the color of Indian life for his own life." The delegates must have responded with smiles on hearing that the governor had discovered the "Wannabees." A few months later, while holding hearings in Nixon on water waste by the Newlands Reclamation Project, Senator Ted Kennedy was made an honorary member of the Pyramid Lake Paiute Tribe for his efforts on their behalf.

The first glimmer of hope for increased water allocations for Pyramid Lake came in 1973 when *Pyramid Lake Paiute Tribe of Indians v. Walter J. Hickel* and *Pyramid Lake Paiute Tribe of Indians v. Rogers C. B. Morton* were settled by Judge Gerhard Gesell of the US District Court in Washington, DC, in his landmark decision ordering the Bureau of Reclamation and the secretary of the interior to deliver to Pyramid Lake all Truckee River water in excess of valid Newlands Reclamation Project water rights. The Gesell opinion also contained new operating criteria for the Newlands irrigators that would lead to a reduction in water diversions at Derby Dam from approximately 187,000 acre-feet to 108,000 acre-feet per year by 1988. Needless to say, the TCID and other water users fought this decision tooth and nail, and some of the issues are still unresolved despite the passage in 1990 of the Truckee-Carson–Pyramid Lake Water Settlement Act. Editorial opinion in the *Reno Evening Gazette* in April 1973 expressed outrage that the Pyramid Lake Tribe was asking for water to preserve the lake at the expense of population growth in Reno. Moreover, the Indians had the temerity to make powerful friends in Washington, the editor fumed. "Pyramid Lake is well worth saving, we'd nearly all agree, and should be preserved if possible. But when it comes right down to cases, people's fundamental necessities must take precedence over nature. . . . Indian rights can't be expected to win the day forevermore over men's irresistible urge to make practical use of valuable natural resources." Among the fundamental necessities in Reno were golf courses, lawns, and unmetered water supply.

A small step forward came in 1974, when the tribe assumed full management of all the fish hatcheries and the state Department of Fish and Game stopped stocking the lake. The following year Marble Bluff Dam and Pyramid Lake Fishway at the mouth of the Truckee near Nixon were opened to facilitate spawning runs by cui-ui and Lahontan cutthroat trout. Getting this dam and fish passage to work well took another twenty-five years. This sad story is told by two Bureau of Reclamation employees, Rick Christensen and Brent Mefford, in a paper they presented at the bureau's centennial history symposium in 2002, "A Struggle of Needs: A History of Bureau of Reclamation Fish Passage Projects on the Truckee River, Nevada." After reviewing the early history of water diversion from the Truckee and the ineffective fish ladders installed at Derby Dam in 1905 and 1913, the authors explain how the falling level of the lake caused the river to cut a steeper gradient, preventing LCT and cui-ui from spawning.

The Marble Bluff Dam and Pyramid Lake Fishway constructed in 1975 were designed to control the gradient and provide a fishway from the lake to the river upstream from the dam, a little more than four miles. The dam also had a fish-trap/lift system that was supposed to attract the spawning fish and lift them up to be released into the river. "Neither of the original Marble Bluff Dam fish passage facilities functioned as intended," Christensen and Mefford write. "During the first years of fishway operation, the ladder baffle design and head drop were found to be a poor match for cui-ui behavior and swimming strength. The cui-ui displayed a strong bottom oriented behavior in the fishway that was contrary to passing over a weir and the 8 ft/s flow velocity was found to be too high for many cui-ui. Cui-ui attempting to move up the fishway at times crowded so densely that many fish were smothered."

Imagine that! The fish were too weak or lazy to appreciate good engineering. The authors admit that the fish-trap/lift system was too slow, resulting in "fish over-crowding, delays, and mortality." During the 1993 spawning run, for example, 4,000 cui-ui died from overcrowding and mechanical failures. Greater losses were prevented by netting and transporting the fish upstream. Improvements to the entrance ladder by Fish and Wildlife personnel reduced fish mortality in 1994, and in 1998 the Bureau of Reclamation replaced the old system with a hydraulic fish lock, "a water elevator which operates similar to a boat lock," and made other improvements. This did not solve all the problems created by water diversion, however. The flood of 1997 scoured the river channel downstream from Marble Bluff, lowering the river by several feet, thus denying the fish access to the fish lock. This problem was "solved" by building a small rock ramp three hundred yards downstream "to imitate a natural riffle so as not to block fish passage to the dam." In 1998 the new lock moved 3,500 fish at a time, and a total of 400,000 cui-ui made it upstream alive.

On May 2, 2011, Tim Loux of the US Fish and Wildlife Service (USFWS) gave me a tour of the Marble Bluff facility and reported that in the wet year 2005, 1.3 million cui-ui made the passage. This is a success story, but most of the LCT and cui-ui in the lake are still hatchery plantings. Cui-ui mortality upstream is very high. There are still obstacles at Numana Dam and, of course, Derby. It is the long-term goal of the Pyramid Lake Paiute Tribe and the Fish and Wildlife scientists to see fish spawning up the Truckee as far as Reno.

Improved relations with the US Fish and Wildlife Service and the Bureau of Reclamation may have helped the tribe in its legal conflicts with the state. In 1976 the State of Nevada filed a civil suit asserting its ownership of Pyramid Lake and its fisheries. The action was dismissed in October 1977 by the US District Court. Two months later a team of biologists representing the US Fish and Wildlife Service, the Pyramid Lake Tribe, and the Nevada Department of Fish and Game (this agency's name was changed to Department of Wildlife in 1979, reflecting the shift toward a broader definition of environmental management) published "A Cui-ui Recovery Plan" that began the effort to study and manage the totemic fish. Ten years later enough information had been gathered for Chester C. Buchanan of the USFWS and Thomas A. Strekal of the Bureau of Reclamation to offer a plan, "Simulated Water Management and Evaluation Procedures for Cui-ui (*Chasmistes cujus*)," that took into account the new requirements of water management on the Truckee.

The plan is a model of science in the service of policy, modest in its assertions, based on a detailed analysis of hydrographic and biological data, clear in its presentation of four alternative fish-flow regimes, and alert to the complexities and unknowns of cui-ui life history. The dedication of state and federal scientists to providing the best-possible solutions for a seemingly hopeless cause affirms the value of public institutions created by elected representatives. By the end of the decade, two new tribally managed hatcheries, one for Lahontan cutthroat trout and one for cui-ui, had opened with the cooperation of the US Fish and Wildlife Service and the Bureau of Reclamation. The system was working, but obstacles remained.

The next round in the endless, epic fight between indigenous fish and invasive legumes (alfalfa, an import from the Middle East by way of Spain, means "fresh fodder" in Arabic) opened in 1981 with Ronald Reagan in the White House and Paul Laxalt in the Senate. The Pyramid Lake Tribal Council initiated a series of suits based on the new laws protecting endangered species and regulating pollution. The environmental movement was gaining ground, and the tribe argued that it was the natural steward of the lake. The tribe scored a major victory when it won, on December 22, 1982, the *Carson-Truckee Conservation District v. Secretary of the Interior* suit (filed in 1976), which dealt with the purpose and use of Stampede Reservoir. Stampede Dam is located on the Little Truckee River (a tributary of the Truckee), about twenty-five miles west of Reno. It was completed in 1970 as part of the Bureau of Reclamation's Washoe Project to provide more water to farmers. Rejecting this contention, the court decided that water in the reservoir could be used only to protect endangered fish. This was a major turning point. The Kuyuidokado had been saved by its totem when the courts began enforcing the Endangered Species Act.

Recognizing this, the tribe asserted its demands for more water for restoration of the lake in terms of cultural heritage in addition to the economics of fishing and tourism. Nevertheless, six months later the tribe suffered a defeat when the Supreme Court upheld the Orr Ditch Decree and denied the Kuyuidokado additional water. In August 1983, however, US District Court judge Bruce Thompson ruled in favor of the federal government's authority to

Kuyuidokado men fishing for cui-ui at Pyramid Lake with pelicans in background. Photograph by Gus Bundy, ca. 1966. Courtesy Gus Bundy Collection, Special Collections, University of Nevada, Reno, Libraries.

issue operating criteria and procedures and control the Newlands Project. His decision was upheld the following year by the Ninth District Court of Appeals. Thompson apparently reconsidered his earlier decision giving each farmer in the Newlands Project ownership of his share of irrigation water.

Abundant rain fell from 1981 to 1986, while the legal situation remained muddy. What emerged was Senator Paul Laxalt's revival of the California-Nevada water compact. Thwarted in the early 1970s by public opinion and opposition from President Nixon's solicitor general Erwin Griswold, Laxalt decided to make the passage of a comprehensive water settlement his crowning achievement and introduced S. 1558, "To Settle Certain Claims Affecting the Pyramid Lake Paiute Indian Tribe of Nevada, and for Other Purposes." Those final three words spelled trouble for the Kuyuidokado. Laxalt wanted water for reclamation project irrigators and almost no one else. He lined up the Nevada congressional delegation, Senator Chic Hecht and Representatives Barbara Vucanovich and Harry Reid. All but Reid were Republicans, but the chance to end years of lawsuits had bipartisan appeal. Even the Pyramid Lake Paiute Tribal Council was willing to negotiate, but the draft of S. 1558 was essentially the same old California-Nevada compact, with no water for the lake.

Hearings were held by various committees, most important on October 2, 1985, by the Senate Select Committee on Indian Affairs and, on October 21, by the Subcommittee on Public Lands, Reserved Water, and Resource Conservation of the Senate Committee on Energy and Natural Resources. Sixty-five-year-old Wilfred Shaw, chairman of the Tribal Council, testified eloquently:

> Pyramid Lake is the heart and soul of the Pyramid Lake Paiute Tribe and the Pyramid Lake Indian Reservation. The Truckee River is our lifeblood. The lake, which is about the same size as its sister, Lake Tahoe, and its fish are the source of our sustenance and livelihood, spiritual, physical, and financial. We call ourselves "cui-ui dakado," cui-ui eaters. The cui-ui is not only an endangered species, it is the sole remaining member of its genus. It is found only in Pyramid Lake. The lake is also an unbelievably fertile habitat for the Lahonton [sic] cutthroat trout.

Shaw shifted, regrettably, to a litany of complaints and a tone of victimhood. Contrast his approach to that of Joe Ely. "In his brief to the U.S. Supreme Court," Shaw reminded the Senate committee, "Solicitor General Rex Lee stated that the Federal Government did not know of any other situation in which the interests of an Indian tribe had been so badly represented in litigation by the U.S. Justice Department."

> The tribe therefore believes that Pyramid Lake and its endangered and threatened fish are an especially worthy subject of Congress' concern and assistance. ... The language and structure of the bill seems to be unnecessarily complex and difficult to decipher. That is even more true of the compact which the Pyramid Lake Tribe has opposed for 15 years. But we have struggled to understand and to be fair, and as I said before, we are firmly committed to the settlement process, which we believe should continue no matter what happens here today and at the House hearings tomorrow.

The reference to Lee's opposition to the Laxalt bill was meant to remind the committee members, who included Barry Goldwater and Daniel Inouye, that the Reagan administration was not presenting a united front. Lee's courageous stand precipitated his resignation, but he had made it clear to his fellow Republicans that Laxalt's legislation would be challenged on legal and ethical grounds. Lee, known as a brilliant and highly principled constitutional lawyer, was a cousin of Morris and Stewart Udall and had clerked for Supreme Court justice Byron White. Whatever his reasons for supporting the Pyramid Lake Tribe, his stand was crucial in defeating S. 1558 by forcing Laxalt to resort to attaching his original state compact to the 1987 appropriations bill. Faced with growing opposition in the Senate, including fellow Republican Mark Hatfield of Oregon, the Bounding Basque of Nevada politics tried yet another strategy, a fifty-million-dollar compensation package for the tribe. The Pyramid Lake Council rejected the bribe and was joined in opposition to the bill by the chief executive officer of Sierra Pacific Power and by the head of the Nevada Department of Conservation and Natural Resources. Laxalt retired from the Senate.

This story of the negotiations is well told in Professor Leah J. Wilds's *Water Politics in Northern Nevada,* but there is more in the published congressional hearings and oral histories of the participants than she is interested in telling. As Shaw's testimony indicates, part of Laxalt's strategy had been obfuscation. The senator never intended to compromise with the Indians on water, but let them continue to think that the settlement process could work. His tactic resulted in dissent within the tribe. At the October 2 hearings of the Committee on Indian Affairs, Alvin James and three other tribal members testified. They were labeled "dissidents" by the tribal council, which had spent long hours in negotiations, but still had faith in the process. The dissident position was stated most fully by James, who represented the Ad Hoc Committee to Preserve Indian Water Rights. James began his statement with the announcement that a petition calling for a tribal referendum on the bill was under way. This tactic was essentially a no-confidence vote against the council. He then accused the council and attorney Michael Thorpe of failing to carry out the demands of the Pyramid Lake people. Specifically, James objected to S. 1558 because it did not uphold the 1982 Supreme Court decision that mandated water in Stampede Reservoir for the protection of the endangered fish. He was also critical of Donald Hodel (the last of Reagan's three Interior Department secretaries) for failing to oversee the TCID and issue operating criteria and procedures, as Stewart Udall had.

"Giving complete control to TCID over Derby Dam is like letting the coyote guard the chicken coop," James told the committee, and pointed out that "the TCID testified in court and on appeals on the issue of its intention to ignore the Secretary's OCAP." James concluded by revealing the deceit in the bill regarding the endangered fish. The bill failed to mention the cui-ui, but promised water for "endangered species" until they were no longer listed as endangered. The ambiguity masked the intent to continue lowering the level of the lake until everything in it was extinct and could therefore be removed from the endangered species list.

The first casualty was not a fish, but tribal council chairman Shaw, who had a fatal heart attack shortly after the hearings. His supporters blamed the dissidents

for adding stress. They, in turn, seized the opportunity to redefine the negotiations and select a new chairman and a new attorney.

FROM RECLAMATION TO RECREATION

The story from this point on exists mainly in the transcripts of the oral history
project begun in 1994 by the US Bureau of Reclamation (USBR) after the signing of Public Law (PL) 101-618, the Truckee-Carson–Pyramid Lake Water Settlement Act in 1990. More than a hundred interviews with persons involved in the
process of crafting that legislation were conducted over more than a decade by
Donald B. Seney, an experienced oral historian who was professor of government at California State University, Sacramento. It is rare in my experience as
a historian to have such a timely and extensive record of an event that, while
important to Truckee and Carson River water users, is not of national importance. A clue to the USBR's motives can be found on its website:

> The research design for the Newlands Project in the area of Fallon, Nevada,
> intends for Reclamation to take an all-around look at a functioning Reclamation
> project within a community. This project was chosen because it is a small proj-
> ect with a wide diversity of issues—including legal, water rights, environmental,
> Native American water rights, and even ground water issues. . . . Reclamation
> employees, politicians, water users, Indians from two bands of Paiutes, environ-
> mentalists, Fish and Wildlife Service employees, and many other categories of
> interviewees will provide a pool of 75 to 150 people who will give Reclamation a
> broad perspective on what its project means to the area.

The Bureau of Reclamation, like many other federal and state agencies created in the Progressive Era, or earlier, when conservation meant management
of the environment for settlement and agricultural production, was finding its
institutional culture and its purpose challenged by urbanization, the environmental movement, and the legislation of the 1960s and 1970s. The Endangered
Species Acts and the creation of the Environmental Protection Agency (EPA)
changed the rules of the game. The oral history project is a kind of soul-search-
ing, revealing the human side of what is often seen as a faceless bureaucracy.
Career federal and state employees in scientific and technical fields are, in my
opinion, much maligned. There are obvious ironies. For more than a hundred
years the Kuyuidokado had been abused by government agencies created to
promote the public good. Now, thanks to one of those agencies, the tribe may
benefit from an in-house history project that provides rich documentation of the
ways in which our political institutions operate. The tribe's story is legitimized

by its old nemesis. In allowing the major participants in the Truckee-Carson–Pyramid Lake Settlement Act negotiations to candidly express their opinions, the USBR compiled an account of the transformation of its own agency culture and helped to tell the story of one of the major water-management laws in American history. These ironies are just more examples of the strange twists of the Pyramid Lake story.

Even stranger are the events of the years 1986–90 as related in the oral histories of tribal council members Joe Ely, Norman Harry, and Mervin Wright Jr. and tribal attorney Robert Pelcyger. Because Ely is by all accounts the key figure in the negotiations during these years, I will begin with him. Asked by Seney to give a brief biography, Ely relates that he was born in Reno on July 3, 1957. His father was a Winnebago from Nebraska, his mother a Pyramid Lake Paiute, a descendant of Numaga and a distant relative of Sarah Winnemucca. He says little about his childhood except that he grew up on a ranch, went to school in Nixon, and moved to Reno for high school, but married and started a family before graduating. He worked on nearby ranches and received some training as a police officer before moving back to the Pyramid Lake Reservation in the early 1980s, where he helped to compile a Paiute glossary for the high school, which was beginning Paiute-language lessons. On the completion of that project, he worked briefly in the tribe's planning office, where he learned more about irrigation, flood control, and soil erosion. As he grew more aware of the problems confronting the tribe, he decided to run for the council and was elected in December 1982. By 1985 he was council chairman and leading the negotiations with Laxalt.

Significantly, for someone whose relationship with the reservation was limited to his boyhood until he returned to enter tribal politics, Joe Ely's answer to Seney's question about the "cultural perspective of the Tribe toward the water and toward the fish" was a panegyric on the cui-ui. It is also a coming-of-age narrative worth quoting at length.

> But from our standpoint, there were several things that were important. One is that the lake is extremely important from the standpoint that it was there, it existed just for its own existence and from the fact that anyone could go out and use it. But it was also important because once a year we had the cui-ui run, and that was the time that everybody talked about. I don't know what you would equate that to today, but there are particular times of the year where people get together and that is the part of the year that they look forward to.
>
> Well, part of the year that we looked forward to was the running of the cui-ui, and people would look for certain things to say, well it looks like spring is here,

the flowers are starting to bloom, and the water is running down the river, and now the cui-ui should be coming up pretty quick, and everyone would watch, and then you'd hear news, and you'd ask people "Are the cui-ui running?" My dad would come home, or my uncle would come over and say, "Somebody caught some cui-ui last night," so you knew that the run is on. And you had to get your act together, because it lasted only a few weeks. . . .

And so people would go down to the mouth of the river and fish, and there'd be various fishermen along the lake and the river would come in and all along the two sides of the Delta there would be fishermen. Some of them would be using fishing poles and some would just be using a line. Some would use the parachute cord with the big treble hook at the end of it and swing it out like a rope and throw it out there and then just jerk it back in and roll it around in their hands and jerk it back in and roll it around their hands. I remember that because I remember that in those days a lot of the men wore khaki pants and wore Fedora-type hats, and you'd see the khaki pants and the Fedora-type hats and the work shirts rolled up, and they'd all be wet because the water would be halfway up their thighs as they were wading out in the water trying to catch cui-ui, and they'd just drag them in and they would throw one on the shore.

The shoreline was full of old women who would be in little groups and they would filet the fish and clean them and put them in gunny sacks or plastic bags and get them ready to transport back to the house. It would just be a festive time, very festive, and people would get together, and those who didn't get along— because not everybody got along, but they'd get along during that time and they would have their group that they'd be with, and they'd be talking, and you'd get tired of fishing and put down your pole and go by the fire and warm up and then go back out there.

Sometimes there were fires and sometimes there weren't, and the old ladies would be gossiping or whatever it is they do, and it would just be a real joyous time. It would last for about two or three weeks and then it was gone. And during that period you ate a lot of cui-ui and you saved as much as you could. And so that was always a big event. So that was the big encounter with the lake. That was the big significance of the lake.

Ely's oral history narrative is fascinating and important for both its content and its style. Ely's memory is almost photographic. Compare his description with Gus Bundy's 1966 photograph of men in khaki pants and fedoras casting lines into the delta, shown earlier. The atavistic power of the cui-ui to revive the preconquest culture of the Kuyuidokado is captured in Ely's boyhood memories. Harmony, abundance, community—these were the promise of the cui-ui. It was a memory worth fighting for. We need look no further to explain why Joe

Ely sized up Paul Laxalt and knew the senator was no match for the cui-ui if its story was well told. In this telling, Ely manages to make what is essentially the death of Kuyuidokado culture "a real joyous time." He refuses to be a victim, recalling instead the few weeks during which the annual cycles of life of cui-ui and Kuyuidokado were restored and how the restoration included the initiation of youth through the rituals of gossip around a warming campfire and instruction on fishing techniques. Commenting on the ways the elderly men dressed and how some people did not "get along" acknowledges assimilation to white styles, culture change, and intratribal conflict, but the spawning run of the cui-ui was a panacea and an inoculation of hope in the future.

Ely took stock of the situation after council chairman Shaw's death and seized the initiative. He saw that the council had not paid attention to the concerns of the citizens of the reservation; he knew that once they had voted to continue negotiations, the council and its chairman would have a mandate to confront Laxalt with a united front, and he knew that Laxalt's vanity made him vulnerable. The senator wanted a settlement as his legacy. He could be manipulated. When, at their first meeting, Laxalt wagged his finger in Ely's face and growled, "We're going to get this compact passed. Do you understand me?" he gave Ely the incentive to run for chairman against Mervin Wright Sr., who was appointed by the council after Shaw's death. Ely was elected by fewer than ten votes. With the congressional elections looming in November 1986, Ely and Pelcyger consulted with the lobbying firm of Wexler, Reynolds, Harrison, and Schule. Anne Wexler was a well-placed Democratic operative, having served as President Carter's assistant for public outreach. Nancy Clark Reynolds was a Republican, a close friend of the Reagans, and a serious student of Indian art. The strategy that emerged, as remembered by Ely in his interview a decade later, had three prongs: attack Laxalt's integrity, promote the importance of the lake and explain how the compact would destroy it, and use Laxalt's obsession with the passage of the compact to cause him to make tactical mistakes, or, as Ely put it, "We sort of took this 'judo' approach."

When not opposed by stubborn Indians, the senator was an affable man who had many friends in Congress on both sides of the aisle, so the assault on his character depended on exposing the lengths to which he would go to pass a compact, even a compact without content. Facing opposition from California senator Alan Cranston in the Senate Judiciary Committee and from Senator Daniel Inouye in the Indian Affairs Committee, Laxalt used his position on the Senate Appropriations Committee to insert, without hearings or consulting any of his colleagues, a single line in the 1987 appropriations bill that said: "The California and Nevada Interstate Compact is hereby ratified." This was the slip that Pelcyger and Ely needed to go to Senator Mark Hatfield, chairman of the Appropriations Committee and professed friend of Laxalt. After they explained the importance of the lake and how the compact would destroy it and how Laxalt was trying to sneak the compact through Congress, Hatfield expressed dismay. He met with Ely privately, and they knelt on Hatfield's Senate office floor and prayed. Having raised doubts about Laxalt's integrity, Ely sprang the trap and offered to support passage of a compact with Laxalt's name on it, if everything in the compact that harmed the lake was taken out and a fifty-million-dollar appropriation for restoring water for fisheries was included. "You've got a deal," the senator replied.

If the bill passed, the lake would not be harmed; if it failed, which Ely hoped would be the case, negotiations could begin with a new set of politicians. Almost immediately, the CEO of Sierra Pacific Power and the chief of the Nevada Department of Conservation and Natural Resources opposed the legislation, and Laxalt, as Professor Wilds notes, "then withdrew the ratification provision from the appropriations bill." Some say it was the wind, but the ghost of Major Ormsby sighed from his grave.

The Kuyuidokado had gotten their money's worth—eighty thousand dollars by Ely's estimate—from their lawyer and lobbyists, but how were they going to pay the bill? Once again chance played a role—Jerry Garcia went into a diabetic coma, and Deadheads scrambled to raise money for his hospital expenses. A benefit concert was planned for Boreal Ridge, a resort near Lake Tahoe, but the wealthy neighbors did not want a bunch of hippies and drug users hanging around, so the promoters, a young woman and her boyfriend, needed a new venue. Ely does not explain how he met them, but when they offered to pay ten thousand dollars and 10 percent of the gate, the chairman saw a gift horse disguised as totally clueless rich kids.

Ely asked how many people they expected at the concert, and they estimated more than sixty thousand. Because they were charging fifteen dollars for advance tickets and twenty at the show, the promoters promised the tribe at least sixty-five thousand dollars. Ely took the offer to the council, got their approval, and came back with a counteroffer. He asked for sixty-five thousand dollars without a percentage, backed up by a bond. The boy was nervous, Ely remembers, but the girl was confident and the deal was done. A site was selected in the sand dunes on the east side of the lake between Nixon and Stone Mother. Flyers were printed announcing "Ranch Rock 86," Sunday, September 7, 1986, with the bands Kingfish, Mickey and the Daylites, Problem Child, and Zero, with John Cipollina and musicians associated with Garcia and the Grateful Dead.

The event was jinxed. First the concert was postponed for a week on short notice, and the crowd that eventually arrived was about fourteen thousand, hardly more than the number of hired security guards, Ely remembered with a laugh. The final mistake was to set up two ticket booths on Route 447. When fans came to each gate, they claimed they had given their tickets at the other entrance. Ely was annoyed when he discovered that the promoters were allowing his political opponents time to speak to the audience, but he had the last laugh when the promoters had to call in their bond. He may have laughed louder if he was still around when the band played Greg Douglass's "All Worth the Price You Pay."

Two months after the concert, Harry Reid moved out of the House and into the Senate by winning the 1986 senatorial election. Junior senator Reid arrived in Washington in January 1987 ready to confront northern Nevada's water wars, but with little understanding of what would be involved. Reid's first move was to assign his legislative director, Wayne Mehl, an experienced Senate staffer, to the problem. As Leah Wilds explains, Mehl quickly understood that California, Nevada, the federal government, and the Pyramid Lake Paiute Tribe were the major players. Mehl began setting up meetings between them and devoted a large portion of his time over the next four years to the negotiation process. Untainted by the previous acrimony, he gained the confidence of all the parties except the delusional TCID. Reid's state director, Mary Conelly, was also an important member of the team that achieved the settlement, as was Patricia Zell, Democratic staff director and chief counsel of the Senate Committee on Indian Affairs.

As Thomas Jensen, staff attorney for the Senate Committee on Water and Power, commented in his oral history, Senator Reid "took a risk that no other western politician had ever done in the history of the country." Reid stood up to irrigation interests when he realized that water for power, cities, recreation, and the environment had become more important than it was for agriculture, especially water-wasting crops in marginal lands. Amazingly, and perhaps with some shaman's help, nature again cooperated. A drought cycle began in October 1986 that lasted eight years, adding to the urgency of finding a solution to the water problems. In his oral history Joe Ely attributed the drought to Providence. The executive editor of the *Reno Gazette-Journal* was less specific in attribution, but he urged readers to "say a word of thanks to the drought of 1988. It appears to be the only condition forceful and unrelenting enough to shake loose the community and its many factions from the bonds of lethargy and self-indulgence."

The intense negotiation started to pay off, beginning with the Preliminary Settlement Agreement between the Pyramid Lake Tribe and the Sierra Pacific Power Company on May 23, 1989. The tribe, which had been given control of Stampede Reservoir in 1982, had storage space; the power company had water. By storing excess water, SPPCO had insurance against drought years; in return, it allowed the tribe to have more water for the spring fish runs in average years. This "fish credit water" was managed by the USFWS in cooperation with the Pyramid Lake Paiute Tribe and would continue even after the endangered cui-ui and threatened Lahontan cutthroat trout were removed from the list. Joe Gremban, president of SPPCO, had grown tired of Laxalt's megalomania and worked smoothly with Joe Ely. The provisions of the Primary Settlement Agreement became an integral part of PL 101-618.

Moreover, attitudes were changing in Truckee Meadows. The *Reno Gazette-Journal* began paying more attention to water issues beginning in March 1987 with a lengthy analysis, headlined "Water: Supply, Demand on Crash Course," that included SPPCO's dire prediction that demand for water in the metropolitan area would exceed the supply by 2002 unless new sources were found. The power company was already making plans to import water from nearby Warm Springs Valley and from the Honey Lake Valley on the California-Nevada border, north of Reno. In August of the following year, reporter Doug McMillan put together a six-part series, "Facing the Truth About Water," that covered the history, science, and politics of the water war—a prize-worthy effort that must have helped citizens of Reno and Sparks become more willing to discuss water conservation, even water meters, although they would continue to resist installing meters until the SPPCO arranged to pay for them and put them in over a fifteen-year period.

Meanwhile, hearings continued in Washington on S. 1554, the Senate version of the Truckee-Carson–Pyramid Lake Water Rights Settlement Act. Senator Bill Bradley of New Jersey, who had been instrumental in defeating the Laxalt compact, became the point man for the legislation. At the February 6, 1990, hearings before the Subcommittee on Water and Power that he chaired, Bradley thanked Ely for his testimony and added, "Someday I want to see Pyramid Lake." What he thought if he ever did see the lake would be interesting to know, but the slick promotional package created by Wexler, Reynolds, Harrison, and Schule to drum up opposition to Laxalt proves that you can learn to love a place without actually being there. There was little political benefit for Bradley in supporting the Paiutes' cause, but he went beyond the call of duty, and, according to Wilds, his subcommittee staff counsel, Tom Jensen, played a vital role in crafting the final bill.

Twenty-nine individuals made statements before the committee. It is one of the most comprehensive representations of opinions on the management of the Truckee River in one place. Bradley's opening statement linked justice for the Pyramid Lake Tribe with habitat preservation for migrating birds and better treatment for the Fallon Paiute-Shoshone Tribe that had withdrawn from the negotiations along with the TCID because it, too, was dependent on water from the Newlands Reclamation Project. Neither Senator Alan Cranston (D-CA) nor Senator Pete Wilson (R-CA) were members of Bradley's Subcommittee on Water and Power, but both spoke in support of the negotiations because Reid's bill promised better management of the Truckee and recognized the importance of environmental protection. Cranston brought up a hitherto overlooked problem, water for snowmaking. He was probably referring to the millions of gallons of water that ski resorts require for making snow to extend their winter sports season, as he mentions the allocation of water to California in the Tahoe Basin. It is an important point inasmuch as water for recreation can be as wasteful as water for irrigation. In the final version of the bill, this issue was, like so many other details, left to future negotiations that would create an operating agreement. In a Solomonic dividing of Lake Tahoe's water, the settlement act gave California 23,000 acre-feet and Nevada 11,000, all to be used within the Tahoe Basin. Water released into the Truckee was counted separately.

Bradley, as chair of the subcommittee, was not impartial. He bantered with Joe Ely, whose testimony I have discussed and quoted in this and the preceding chapter, and called him a "real leader." When Dell Steve of the Fallon-Shoshone Tribe, which had allied itself with the TCID, tried to explain his objections to the Reid bill, Bradley cut him off and urged him to summarize quickly. Bradley was even curter with Ted de Braga, president of the Truckee-Carson Irrigation District, and Lyman McConnell, TCIDproject manager. McConnell told the committee that he did not think that more water was "the only solution to the problem with the cui-ui." Bradley interrupted in midsentence and asked, "What is the answer then, if it isn't more water?" McConnell answered that he was not sure, but added that the TCID had asked to be part of the US Fish and Wildlife Service's cui-ui restoration and management planning and been rejected. The subtext here was the old rivalry between the Bureau of Reclamation engineers and biologists from other agencies. As I show in chapter 5, USBR officials saw nothing wrong with breeding all cui-ui in hatcheries and allowing Pyramid Lake to continue desiccating.

Bradley taunted de Braga and Nevada state senator Virgil Getto by asking if they felt it was worth drying up Winnemucca Lake to create "a green oasis in Churchill County." "I am curious," Bradley continued, "whether you feel a sense of loss, or whether you feel that this is something that has evolved the way it was intended to, or whether you believe that there were mistakes made along the way." De Braga, dodging the existential question, was as quick to blame the federal government as the Indians were. He acknowledged that there was insufficient water in the watersheds to satisfy all users, "but somewhere along the line somebody made some mistakes and enticed my family there. The Federal Government has a trust responsibility for the water users on the project."

Newlands Project farmers were now in the endangered position of Indians. This admission was all Bradley could hope for. De Braga and the TCID walked out of the negotiation shortly after this hearing, rightly assessing that their cause was lost in Congress and that they would be better off in the courts, despite the cost in legal fees. The reaction of the more radical members of the TCID was to rally in Carson City and hang Senator Reid in effigy. This was a huge tactical error. Reid's response was to add a section to the bill mandating recoupment of water that had in the past been diverted from Pyramid Lake to the TCID above the amount to which it was entitled. The amendment also gave the secretary of the interior authority to force the TCID to improve the efficiency of the irrigation system. Recoupment of 1,057,000 acre-feet of illegally diverted water, plus "interest in-kind," remains one of the most contentious unsettled issues. Perhaps, as the remaining acres of the Newlands Project dwindle to a few hobby farms and fewer acres are planted in water-wasting alfalfa and melons, recoupment can begin.

Reid's bill, expediently attached to a bill sponsored by Senator Daniel Inouye settling the water claims of the Fallon-Shoshone Tribe, passed the Senate in October 1990 and was signed by President George H. W. Bush on November 11, the holiday once known as Armistice Day. Scholars have tried for the past twenty-five years to decide whether the settlement act (PL 101-618) brought peace or merely a truce. A full-page ad in the November 27, 1990, *Reno Gazette-Journal,* paid for by Westpac Utilities, a subsidiary of the Sierra Pacific Power Company, highlighted the many benefits of the settlement act. The ad explained that the legislation guaranteed that 90 percent of the Truckee's water belonged to Nevada, that endangered species in the Stillwater Wildlife Refuge and

Pyramid Lake would receive additional water, and that, with the installation of water meters, residents of the Truckee Meadows would pay only for the water they used. The meters would be installed over the next ten to fifteen years, paid for by future development. The ad also thanked dozens of conservation organizations, labor unions, business associations, and the Pyramid Lake Paiute Tribe for their support "with time, effort, and resources."

The ink on the ad was not dry before the happy supporters of the settlement were fighting again over interpretation and implementation of the law. It took eighteen years for the Bureau of Reclamation to comply with the settlement act and promulgate a Truckee River Operating Agreement. TROA is a management plan that calls for procedures that will comply with the intent of the settlement act to protect the environment, provide more water for Pyramid Lake, and render a mechanism for continuing negotiations. When a federal court amends the Orr Ditch Decree to incorporate the operating agreement, the Pyramid Lake Paiute Tribe will be able to access the money it was awarded in the settlement. These funds, forty million dollars for economic development and twenty-five million dollars to develop the tribe's fisheries, have been deposited and are accruing interest.

If you listen closely in the silence of the lake, you can hear the wheels of justice grinding slowly. On May 11, 2011, a federal judge reversed the state engineer's ruling that permitted the transfer of water rights from agricultural lands to wetlands at Carson Lake, calling it a form of irrigation. This may seem a technicality, since the settlement act specifically called for water for wetlands, but the US government and the Pyramid Lake Paiute Tribe needed to clarify the meaning of "irrigation" or risk ceding control of unused irrigation water to the TCID. Thanks also to a 1983 change in federal Indian policy and 1987 amendments to the Clean Water Act, the Pyramid Lake Paiute Tribe, contracting with the Limnological Research Group of the University of California, Davis, has developed its own water-quality standards and Water Quality Control Plan. The laws require the Environmental Protection Agency to treat all Indian tribes in a manner similar to states. This gives the tribe some legal basis for controlling regional pollution.

The rapid growth of the Reno area in the 1970s, its uneven development in the 1990s, and its partial rebirth in the early twenty-first century created new water problems stemming from pollution. Fortunately for the lake, scientists have the ability to, as the tribe's website observes, measure and appraise physical and chemical parameters, including "evaluation of nutrient and particulate matter, phytoplankton and zooplankton ecology, algal growth bioassays and nutrient limitation measurement of surficial composition, paleoliminology, measurement of primary productivity and algal biomass, internal and external loading of nutrients, development of nutrient budgets for carbon, nitrogen and phosphorus, estimates of sedimentation rates, evaluating susceptibility of the Lake to anoxia, primary productivity and dissolved oxygen modeling, modeling of total dissolved solids concentration, nonpoint source management and assessment, and Lake and watershed management."

I quote this technical material to remind myself of how much has changed since 1944, when the Kuyuidokado could not even hire their own lawyer. Nor could I have dreamed when I left Nevada in 1959 that the children of the Indians I knew would be managing their fish hatcheries, participating at regional and state levels in water-resource planning, and encouraging scientific research on the ecology of the lake. Recently, I asked Michelle McCauley, then working with the intertribal Higher Education Program coordinator of the Center for Student Cultural Diversity at the University of Nevada, Reno (another position I could not have imagined in 1959), about the state of Kuyuidokado cultural awareness. She responded by mentioning the growing interest in studying Numic language, customs, and traditional dances. "I think," she wrote, "the tribe passes out cui-ui to tribal members that request it throughout the year because the fish is considered endangered and no one is allowed to just fish for them. However, most of our tribal people have become accustomed to non-traditional foods because they simply taste better and don't take much preparation."

This seems to be a candid comment on current realities. McCauley, who won first place in Women's Fancy Dance at the 2011 and 2012 Sacred Visions Pow-wows, puts the cui-ui on the plate and not the flagpole, but honors tradition in other ways. Her remark does not signal an ironic end to a noble battle for self-preservation. Rather, in fighting to preserve the cui-ui, the Indians of Pyramid Lake have won the right to make their own choices, a right that would not have been possible without the survival of the iconic fish. It is a fish story worth telling again and again.

FOUR

Railroads, Ranches, and Dudes

Within any place as large as Pyramid Lake and the reservation that surrounds it, there are countless smaller places. Although these spaces may
be surveyed, mapped, and photographed for political, economic, scientific, or
personal purposes, given names and boundaries, they exist primarily in the
minds of individuals who are experiencing them in the present or who have
memories of the place from past contact. The depth of the experience and the
extent to which the place is understood depend on the mental and visual acuity of the observer, the observer's prior experience with places, the reasons the
observer is at the place, and similar variables.

How do individuals come to value certain places, and how do places affect
individuals who inhabit them? These are questions raised in this chapter as I
shift from the perspectives of the Native population to those of some of the
trespassers, myself included. Although it is impossible to learn what most of
the early settlers knew or felt about their claims around the lake, we have some
enlightening records from the dude ranchers of the twentieth century, newspaper stories, and fragments from memory. Together they provide some idea of
what the Kuyuidokado were up against.

BIG CANYON

The history of white trespass on the Pyramid Lake Paiute Reservation is as complex a story as the Paiutes' own. Because there was no map of the reservation
until 1868, the boundaries of its approximately 475,000 acres (more than 112,000
of which is covered by the lake) were vague, and some of the squatters, who were
given the more official-sounding name of entrymen, may have thought they
were claiming public land. More often, the settlers simply occupied portions
of the reservation and held it by force. According to Martha Knack and Omer
Stewart, the first white trespasser on the reservation was Joseph Fellnagle, who,
in 1861, claimed 120 acres, which he expanded to more than 360 acres by 1890.
Other records refer to his brother Herman, so there may have been two farms.

Within a few years, the Fellnagles had several white neighbors, some of whom they may not have welcomed. On the Fourth of July 1867, a man known only as Gates conspired with two other men to murder a Paiute farmer called Truckee John. Given the date, the killing may have been fueled by whiskey-drenched nationalism. Whereas his coconspirators disappeared, Gates expanded his illegal claim by annexing the land that had been worked by Truckee John. Seventy years later this rich river bottomland at the south end of the reservation was known as the Hill Ranch and claimed by J. A. Ceresola, one of the five farmers who Senator Pat McCarran contended should be given the land that their "ancestors" had "homesteaded" before the creation of the reservation.

Large chunks of tribal land were lost to the railroads, the Central Pacific Railroad and its successor, the Southern Pacific. The CPRR, building east from Sacramento, reached the reservation in July 1868, where the company tried to take 10-mile-square alternate sections of land (6,400 acres). The commissioner of the General Land Office ruled that the checkerboard land claim would be unmanageable on reservation land and confined the CPRR to strips of land along its right-of-way. The resulting confusion, as Knack and Stewart explain, was a wedge that whites exploited as they squatted on the reservation. By 1890 the CPRR had 773 acres of Paiute land for roadbed and maintenance buildings. The State of Nevada claimed 421 acres for roads, schools, and other public uses. The Indian agent reported that fully 80 percent of the 2,000 tillable acres on the reservation were in the hands of white farmers.

Most of their claims were along the Truckee from Wadsworth, where the CPRR had laid out a township, down the river to Nixon, but a few were on the western side of the lake. In the mid- to late 1860s, a cattleman named Mullen claimed land, as did S. D. "Doc" Woods, who also operated a stage relay station. His neighbors were Numaga and Captain Jim, who lived near a creek that supplied freshwater and served as spawning grounds for cui-ui. About 1871 J. W. Whitehead and his brothers kicked them out of what would later be called Hardscrabble Canyon. By the 1880s at least two other squatters had arrived: James Sutcliffe set up a stage stop (Woods seems to have disappeared) that he later expanded into a guest ranch, and a family named Symonds claimed 40 acres in a well-watered canyon a few miles north of Sutcliffe.

The railroad struck again. The Central Pacific was in the process of becoming the Southern Pacific Railroad and was in fierce competition with the Western Pacific and Northern Pacific Railroads for access to Oregon. When a lumber baron from Minnesota acquired a large tract of forest near Susanville, California, the SPRR set out to build a spur from Fernley through the Pyramid Lake

Reservation to Lassen County. An agreement signed by Joseph D. Oliver, BIA agent and superintendent of the Nevada Indian School on the Pyramid Lake Reservation, and a representative of the CPRR on February 12, 1914, gave the railroad 1,217 acres for its roadbed, which was to extend 100 feet on either side of the center line of the tracks. The tribe was to receive $5,620.71 for its loss of rangeland. The right-of-way followed the entire western side of the lake, more or less the route of the old military and post road between Fort Bidwell and Fort Churchill, coming within a few hundred feet of the shore in some places, providing wonderful views of the lake. The August 27, 1931, diary entry of my mother, Katharine "Kay" Mergen, provides an example: "Sun like a red agate— setting in heavy bank of smoke—moon on Pyramid gorgeous." The SP's Fernley & Lassen spur, as the route was called, was completed October 1, 1914. Several trains ran daily over its tracks until after World War II, but by 1970 trucking had replaced rail, and the Fernley & Lassen Railroad was closed and the rails removed for scrap. Typically, the BIA had to be prodded by the tribe's attorney to have the 1,200 acres and the abandoned buildings and water towers returned to the Kuyuidokado.

Many of the SP's buildings, such as the section foreman's house at Big Canyon, a few miles north of Sutcliffe, were removed by 1970 and exist only in snapshots and memory. My first memory of Big Canyon and Pyramid Lake, more than seventy years ago, was when I was three years old and placed in the care of my grandparents by my mother, who had just divorced my father. My grandfather Andy Norrid, almost seventy, was nearing retirement and his own uncertain future. For more than fifty years he had railroaded from Texas to Mexico to Colorado and Nevada, most of those years as a section foreman for the Southern Pacific Railroad. He was foreman of the last all-Chinese section gang on the SPRR, near Susanville, California, when the stock market crashed in 1929. He and about two dozen men, some of whom had labored for the Central Pacific before it became the SP, were laid off. After my grandfather spent a few years in temporary jobs, the railroad assigned him to Big Canyon. This section of the Fernley & Lassen was his last job. The Big Canyon section foreman's house was a little bungalow painted Maria Theresa Yellow, like all the SP properties of that time, and surrounded by a white fence four boards high. The house faced the lake, and I remember standing on its steps, looking past the cottonwood and willow trees at the shimmering blue surface of the lake and the bruise-colored hills beyond.

In 1940 Andy Norrid and his gandy dancers (section hands) were working northwest of the lake at a section that some SP executive or surveyor had whimsically named Zenobia. Probably the namer knew Chaucer's *Canterbury Tales.* The monk's tale gives a condensed version of the life of al-Zabbā' bin Amr ibn al-Ẓarib ibn Ḥassān ibn Adhīnat ibn al-Samīda', known to English speakers as Zenobia, queen of the Palmyrene Empire of Syria in AD 269. Her armies drove out the Romans, and she ruled over Egypt until 274, when she was defeated and taken prisoner by troops of the Roman emperor Aurelian. According to legend, she was taken to Rome in golden chains. In some accounts, she is beheaded; in others, she gets a villa in Tivoli, where she becomes a noted philosopher. In my story Zenobia is a black Labrador. My grandfather found her running lost in the desert and brought her to Big Canyon as a companion for me. I could not get my three-year-old tongue around "Zenobia," so she became Zoby.

Zoby's fate was less verse-worthy than her namesake's. My grandfather retired, and we—my mother, my grandparents, and I—all moved to Wadsworth at the south end of the reservation, where my mom taught in the high school for a couple of years and coached basketball. I gave up my imaginary friends for real ones, but I lost Zoby. Later I learned that Zoby could not adjust to captivity and city life. Wadsworth had a population of maybe two hundred citizens, some of whom had chickens that Zoby loved to chase and kill. My grandfather did the neighborly thing and took his shotgun, a shovel, and Zoby for a one-way trip into the desert. The winds of history had blown a part of my family onto the Kuyuidokado's land, and the same winds blew us off. We took nothing away from Pyramid Lake, but evidence of our sojourn remains—an unmarked grave, lost toys, smooth stones skipped into the lake.

Fortunately, the war was ending, GIs were swelling enrollment at the University of Nevada, and Professor Al Higginbotham asked my mother to come back to teach journalism. For the next fifteen years we were just thirty-five miles from Pyramid Lake. We visited as often as we could. My mother knew a lot of people on the reservation.

One of Kay Mergen's destinations in the years 1945 to 1959 was the Symonds ranch, then occupied solely by their granddaughter Loretta Filler Whittey, known to me as Letty Filler. The spellings of her names vary in the legal and newspaper accounts from Whitty to Whittey to Whitte to Whittier and from Fuller to Feller to Filler, and even "Whittyfiller." My memories of Letty are distorted by time and a child's indifference to adults who ignore them. I remember her as squat, with gray hair cut as short as a boy's. I cannot recall her dressed in anything but blue chambray shirts and denim overalls. She claimed seventy-six

Letty Filler and Kay Mergen at Pyramid Lake, ca. 1950. Photograph by the author.

acres, but had no open-range grazing rights and was constantly petitioning the tribal council for grazing privileges for her cattle. They were never granted. She received a small salary as "postmistress" from 1937 to 1959.

Letty rolled her own cigarettes, and she and my mother sat smoking and drinking the afternoon away while I played in the yard with my soldiers and Matchbox cars. Sometimes we would all walk to Thunderbolt Bay, and my mother and I would wade in the shallow water and throw flat stones, making them skip across the surface of the lake. Once Letty brought a cat, a huge scruffy tom, rowed out a few yards, and tossed him overboard to watch him swim. Unfazed, puss stroked his way to shore, shook himself, and strolled back to the house. Letty roared with delight. Later, she mischievously asked my mother if I was old enough to see a picture of "a bird's-eye view of a cat's rear end." It took me a few seconds to see what she saw in a large question mark scrawled on a piece of letter paper.

My memories of Letty conform to A. J. Liebling's description of her in his 1954 *New Yorker* articles, "The Mustang Buzzers." In those pieces, Pyramid Lake Guest Ranch manager Harry Drackert tells Liebling that Letty had been married to a hobo named Joe. "Joe had been thrown off a freight train in front of the ranch house one day, and Letty and her mother carried him into the house and soothed his lacerations and reduced his contusions." Joe was a big, strong guy, Drackert recalled. "He once picked up a two-hundred-pound ranch dinner bell with one hand and set it on a table." Letty's talent was riflery. "She can shoot a running antelope's eye out at a thousand yards," Drackert assured Liebling. Joe's only complaint was that Letty could not rope. When Joe left Letty for a younger woman, Drackert was surprised because she could not rope either.

Letty had her brushes with "society," notably in 1942 when she was recognized in Lillian Borghi's "Arts and Artists" feature in the *Reno Evening Gazette* for having donated a rare lithograph of Fort Churchill that had been purchased by her grandfather Charles Symonds, probably in the 1860s, when he was a stage driver between Fort Bidwell in the far northeastern corner of California and Silver City, Nevada. The Symonds ranch was a stop on the route. The lithograph took on additional importance when the Sagebrush Chapter of the Daughters of the American Revolution sought to use it as a model for their planned restoration of the fort. When they discovered how much the restoration would cost, they settled for spraying a preservative on the crumbling adobe walls and having the property designated a state park.

On one of our visits to Letty's, I was forced to play with her nephew, a boy a little older than I who convinced me, through not too subtle taunts and other intimidations, to set up my cast-iron army in an ash heap and throw rocks at it to simulate the explosive puffs of artillery shells. The effect was mesmerizing. My throwing arm and aim allowed most of the brittle troops to escape unharmed, but Whittey threw like Roger Clemens and before the sun set and the shadows lengthened, my relatively expensive preplastic army lay in fragments.

Letty's crumbling abode was raided by novelist Saul Bellow, who stayed at the Pyramid Lake Guest Ranch in the fall of 1956. In 1972 Bellow, apparently responding to an inquiry, recalled that he "spent many months at Pyramid Lake," where he met "several elderly women who lived at [sic] mountain sides and in lonely canyons. . . . One of the old girls, now dead, was my landlady. From her I rented a shack built of old railroad ties. It was at the water's edge and I dream sometimes of going back for a look. But I am told that the Lake has become a tourist attraction and I'm afraid of returning to cherished memories and finding only Disneyland." Bellow's misapprehension about the lake becoming a tourist attraction in the early 1970s reveals a lack of understanding of the Paiute struggles in the water wars and perhaps much else, but each sojourner crafted his own fantasy about the place.

Bellow came away with a story, "Leaving the Yellow House," published in

Esquire in January 1958, just three months after Miller's short story "The Misfits." Curiously, for a writer who was criticized for shallow portrayals of women in his novels, Bellow's Pyramid Lake story is told from the point of view of Harriet Simmons Waggoner. "Hattie," a seventy-two-year-old (Letty was only fifty-three at the time, but hard living aged her looks), lives alone in a house a few miles from the guest ranch, near the north end of the lake. Bellow describes Hattie as a delusional alcoholic, "big and cheerful, puffy, comic, boastful, with a big round back and stiff, rather long legs." Bellow's Hattie is an easterner by birth, a not quite Main Line Philadelphian, but a finishing-school graduate, whose husband left her more than twenty years ago. She subsequently lived with a cowboy, whom she finally chased off, and then with a woman who died and willed Hattie the house.

The reader pieces together most of Hattie's story from her movie-like memories as she tries unsuccessfully to cope with poverty, a broken arm, and the realization that she is unable to take care of herself. Her neighbors Jerry and Helen Rolfe, the guest-ranch manager, Pace, and his wife, and Pace's bartender wrangler, Darly, are her only friends and drinking buddies. They are, like the lake, which Bellow calls Sego Desert Lake, fictional creations, but there are recognizable models. The Paces, minor characters in the story, are clearly Harry and Joan Drackert. Brother Louis, "an old actor who had a church for the Indians," to whom Hattie briefly considers leaving her property, is obviously Brother David, former silent-screen star Gareth Hughes. Bellow had daily contact with the Drackerts, and he probably heard about Brother David. Letty is unmistakably the inspiration for Hattie. Not, however, the Letty I remember. By making her an eastern transplant, Bellow falls back on familiar stereotypes of empty-headed women fatally attracted to men with claims to be cowboys. He missed the real story. The Letty I remember was, like my mother, neither addled nor fearful. The lake had been Letty's home for fifty years, and she was as much Paiute in her outlook on life as she was white, although neither she nor any Kuyuidokado would acknowledge it. Forty acres of desert, a few hundred feet of beach, a chance to make a living, and the tranquillity of the lake were all she wanted.

Bellow does better with his descriptions of the lake:

> The weather was hot, the clouds were heavy and calm in a large sky. The horizon was so huge that in it the lake must have seemed like a saucer of milk. *Some milk!* Hattie thought. Two thousand feet down in the middle, so deep no corpse could ever be recovered. A body, they said, went around with the currents. And there were rocks like eyeteeth, and hot springs, and colorless fish at the bottom which

were never caught. Now that the white pelicans were nesting they patrolled the rocks for snakes and other egg thieves. They were so big and flew so slow you might imagine they were angels.

Then he ruins the mood by writing that Hattie no longer visited the lake-shore, saving her strength to go to Pace's bar for a drink. Hattie maybe, Letty never. As for the exaggerated depth of the lake and the colorless, uncatchable fish, these are excusable, parts of the lake's Native and white mythologies. We all want to believe they are true. And the pelicans *are* the far-fetched angels of the improbable lake, nesting on a desert island in a saucer of milk fit for a swimming cat.

My final visit to Letty's occurred about the time of Bellow's sojourn at the lake. There were signs of Letty's decline. A dead horse turned from a bloated, fly-covered, stinking corpse to a skeleton over one summer, Letty unable or unwilling to have it removed. The yard and garden dried up, as Bellow describes it. By 1961 my mother left Reno, and Letty vanished from my consciousness, as she ultimately did from the lake. She died in April 1965, ending a century of Symondses at the lake. Attorney Robert Leland wrote to one of her brothers, indicating the tribe's interest in buying Letty's ranch. There is no reply in the files. Her yellow house, halfway between Jigger Bob Canyon and my grandfa-ther's section house at Big Canyon, is gone, too. Some cottonwoods remain. One final onomastic puzzle abides. A small legal notice in the *Reno Gazette-Journal*, April 13, 1965, concerns the estate of Loretta V. Whittey, also known as Lettie R. E. Whittey. The real Letty ignored the summons.

Bellow's Hattie lets her life unspool like a reel of film. She drinks bourbon, reflects on her past, and debates with herself about what to do with the yellow house. I cannot imagine Letty, her nose pinched by the stench of a dead horse outside her bedroom window, worrying much about what will happen to her house. More likely, she spent her final years wondering how far her cat could swim and whether my mother was bringing good scotch (not bourbon). I can only speculate on what she thought of the desert lake, but I know her day began with the sunrise over the Lake Range and ended with the sunset behind the Vir-ginia Mountains and between those two still moments the water, the sagebrush, and the hills moved in a great migration propelled by light and wind. No need to go anywhere, as the earth came to her.

Mullen, Woods, Whitehead, Sutcliffe, Symonds, and the Southern Pacific Railroad—these were thorns in the west side of the reservation, while the so-called river ranches clung like burrs in a horse's tail in the twenty-mile strip of river bottom that forms the southern panhandle of the Indian lands. Over the years the names of the squatters changed, as the original trespassers sold their claims to people who either did not know or, more likely, did not care that title to the land was in dispute. Some of the more conscientious Indian agents sought help from the US Army, which was supposed to protect Indians and whites. A troop tried to evict Mullen and Woods in 1869–70, but the interlopers simply hid out until the army went away.

Fishing trespass, as Professor Martha Knack has clearly shown, was more damaging to the tribe's economy than ranching. As I recount in chapter 1, the Kuyuidokado quickly learned that miners, railroaders, and city folk were hungry for fresh fish, and, lacking other resources, they caught and sold Lahontan cutthroat trout in large numbers. In 1877 US marshal Ash and his deputies exchanged gunfire with fish poachers at the lake, but this skirmish did nothing to stop the piscine slaughter.

On January 18, 1879, the *Reno Evening Gazette* announced that Lieutenant Oscar J. Brown and twenty-five cavalry from Fort Halleck (near Elko) would evict white fishermen from the lake, but seventy-five poachers in forty-five boats still managed to take more than seventy-three thousand pounds of fish worth seven thousand dollars that month. Just over a year later the Griswold Trout Cannery opened in Wadsworth. Griswold's exploitation of the lake's fish was obviously successful, as he was celebrated in the *Gazette* seventeen years later as one of Wadsworth's leading businessmen, with retail stores and a home in San Francisco. Five thousand dollars' worth of fish was shipped in 1883 and 1886, despite an attempt in 1884 by US troops to prevent non-Indians from commercial fishing. Samuel Houghton, in his pioneering book *A Trace of Desert Waters: The Great Basin Story,* cites a *Daily Nevada State Journal* article dated November 22, 1889, stating that Indian agent W. D. C. Gibson had bought and shipped twenty-three thousand pounds of trout from Pyramid and Mud (Winnemucca) Lakes in the preceding eight weeks. Another hundred tons were shipped in a six-month period in 1888–89. As late as 1912 the enterprising C. S. Crosby was shipping ten to fifteen tons of fish a week.

Even if Derby Dam had not been built and water for Lahontan cutthroat trout and cui-ui spawning reduced to a trickle, it is likely that Pyramid Lake would have been overfished within a few more years. Without doubt the Newlands Reclamation Project speeded up the annihilation of the fish. The last spawning of the Lahontan cutthroat was 1938; by the early 1940s, the trout was thought to have gone extinct. Subsequently, LCT were found in some other lakes and streams in the Great Basin, and the restocking of Pyramid Lake began about 1970. The fish is currently listed as "threatened," to allow regulated sportfishing. The cui-ui, a tougher, longer-lived fish, is also close to extinction, but good management techniques and a sufficient supply of water in the spring spawning season may restore their number to satisfy Kuyuidokado needs.

Efforts by whites to expel the Indians, or at least terminate their reservation, continued, as did countermeasures by the Indians to eject the whites. For 150 years Nevada's senators, representatives, and state legislators made almost annual efforts to turn the clock back to before the creation of the Pyramid Lake Reservation. Thanks to Indian resistance, constitutional checks and balances, bureaucratic inefficiency, political rivalries, changing economies, public concern, and plain luck, their efforts failed. Senators Stewart, Oddie, Pittman, McCarran, and Laxalt must often have felt as if they were punching an inflatable bop bag that kept bouncing back. The Paiutes felt the punches, but their center of gravity was the lake and land around it, and long before Gandhi or Martin Luther King Jr., they employed the power of passive resistance.

The state continued tightening the screws on Indian fishing. "In 1911," Martha Knack writes, "all large fish species, except cui-ui which Anglos did not regard highly, were declared to be game fish, thus placing them under state management. On the grounds there was need to conserve game fish for the benefit of the 'general public' (which meant non-Indian sportsmen), the legislature attempted to force compliance with Anglo ideas of proper fishery management. Therefore, they declared that no one could, at any time, possess more than ten game fish or ten pounds of fish on any one day for his own use or for sale." This restriction also applied to shippers and restaurants, which were limited to ten fish from a single fisherman. In 1914 Charles Crosby tested the law by buying ten fish each from several Paiute fishermen. He was arrested, tried, convicted, and fined, despite his attorney's argument that the fish had been caught in federal, not state, waters. When, the following year, the state supreme court upheld the conviction, and the state's right to regulate fishing on the reservation, the opinion was written by Justice Pat McCarran. At this time the Indian agent was the notorious J. D. Oliver, who not only cooperated with state law enforcement but encouraged poaching by non-Indians and the harvesting of spawn by Nevada Fish and Game officials.

The latter action was too much for the tribe, which refused to cooperate with state or federal fish-planting efforts until the Marble Bluff Dam was made accessible to spawning fish and the river had sufficient water. Oliver was replaced, and the new agent closed the reservation to all nonresident fishermen in 1920, an action that cost him his job. By May 1922, yet another superintendent of the Reno Indian Agency made an effort to collect fees for fishing and boating permits for visitors to the lake. Knack says the permits were admittedly unenforceable. In the midst of this power struggle, Johnny Skimmerhorn, a Paiute, caught a forty-one-pound Lahontan cutthroat trout, a record that is likely to stand forever.

FROM THE WILLOWS TO THE
PYRAMID LAKE GUEST RANCH

News of the excellent fishing helped James Sutcliffe expand his guest ranch, the Willows, and attracted some big-name sportfishermen such as Herbert Hoover and novelist Zane Grey, but when Sutcliffe's wife died in 1926, the old settler leased, and then sold, the place to A. J. and Sarah Olds, ranchers from just outside the reservation. The couple made some improvements and then in 1931 sold to John Albert Marshall, who renamed the ranch the "Desert Inn" and put out the first of several fancy brochures. Recreational development was coming, whether the rightful stewards of the lake were ready or not.

Marshall soon discovered that he had two major obstacles to overcome before he could make money from tourism: poorly maintained roads and open hostility from Reno businessmen who wanted all out-of-state revenue to stay in the "Biggest Little City." He got some help from the *Nevada State Journal,* which on March 21, 1932, carried a story headlined "Reno Invited to Help Boost Pyramid Lake," concerning Marshall's letter to the Nevada State Automobile Association, in which he complained about the "concerted effort and action among various interests in Reno to give Pyramid lake a black eye." The next day the *Journal* followed up with an editorial, "Give Them a Chance," urging members of a US Senate committee to make good on their promises to do something for the reservation. "They were a quiet, peaceful race of Indian," the editor writes, "and made little trouble for the white man as compared with other Indian tribes." Adjacent to the editorial is a column by former governor James G. Scrugham, praising the beauty of the lake and urging improvement of the road to it.

Nevada Fish and Game car with catch of Lahontan cutthroat trout, ca. 1948. Courtesy Special Collections, University of Nevada, Reno, Libraries.

Marshall had a flair for promotion, as judged by his flyers that extolled "the Hidden mystery-land of the Piutes" and "a desert paradise on the shores of Pyramid Lake," but he had little regard for facts. The text and a small pyramid-shaped map announced:

RE-DISCOVERED!

PYRAMID LAKE

. . . the "Happy Hunting Ground" of the Piute Indians . . . jealously guarded against the white man since the invasion of Kit Carson just ninety years ago . . . **now for the first time open to the sports-loving public.**

A recreation land with more to recommend it than any other desert country you have ever visited . . . including Egypt itself. No desert in the world offers the varied attractions nor compels such instantaneous appeal.

Among the attractions was the lake itself, a "crater of a dead volcano, with deep, bottomless, underground passages," fossil remains of "the Camelops, the three-toed horse, and a peculiar species of lion," mummies said to antedate those of Egypt, a sea serpent, the "Kwi-We" fish that "professors tell us is left over from pre-historic times," sunbathing, boating and fishing, hunting, hiking, horseback riding, motor tours, and, "if you must golf," there was a course in Reno, only an hour away. This and a subsequent flyer revive Dan De Quille's fabulist impressions of the lake. The cartoonlike map resembles a panel of "Ripley's Believe-It-or-Not!" Pyramid Lake is advertised as a Barnum's Museum of natural wonders, but the real oddities were the people attracted to the ranch and the surrounding desert. Among his guests in 1932, Marshall listed Mrs. William Randolph Hearst (Millicent, who left Hearst in 1926, but never divorced him), "Pop" Warner and his "Stanford University Football Coaching Staff," the Doles of Hawaii, the Oscar Steens of Shanghai, and two fairly successful artists, Clarence Mattei, primarily a portraitist, and Ferdinand Burgdorff, one of the Taos–Santa Fe painters of Native Americans. In 1934 Clark Gable fished with Marshall. The Desert Inn should have made Marshall a fortune, but he was ready to sell by 1934 and finally, in 1936, found buyers, for sixty-seven thousand dollars, with zanier ideas than his.

The new owners were the Kitselmans—rich, flamboyant, and ill-fated, a Nevada family saga of the twentieth century. The story begins with Leslie Curtis, who had arrived in Reno in 1909, an aspiring young journalist and playwright. She claimed to be related to Samuel Clemens. Her humorous stories and poems, collected in *Reno Reveries,* helped spread the image of Reno as an exciting and naughty town. She followed her own story line, as Alicia Barber notes in her superb history, *Reno's Big Gamble,* by marrying Alva LaSalle Kitselman in 1911, after his Reno divorce. Kitselman was a wealthy steel manufacturer from Muncie, Indiana. Leslie and Alva had three children: Marjorie, who, in 1938, was married to aviator Floyd Hanson, who rounded up wild horses by airplane; Donald, whose role in the Pyramid Lake story is limited to his marriage in 1944 to a local low-budget western movie actress known as Reno Browne; and Alva LaSalle Jr., known as Beau.

Beau had been proclaimed a child prodigy, but in 1936, age twenty-two, he was having a hard time settling down. He published his own version of Laozi's *Dao De Jing* as *Tao Teh King* (The Way of Peace) rather than the traditional translation *The Classic of the Way/Path and the Power/Virtue* in the same year he moved to the lake. Some of the passages from Laozi (Old Master) are identical to James Legge's nineteenth-century translation, but others seem to be Beau's creations. Taoist philosophy, like the Bible, is enigmatic. His decision to translate the title as "The Way of Peace" suggests discordance in his own life. Numerous passages admonish the believer to humble himself and become one with others, but the Laozi also recognizes that "the sage does not act from any wish to be benevolent; he deals with people according to their nature." This advice seems to have shaped Beau's management style, as revealed in "The Resort Employee's Bible," cited below. His mother's style was more refined. As reported by Gladys Rowley, on May 1, 1941, Leslie Curtis Kitselman entertained thirty-six of the top editors, business managers, and reporters from the Reno daily newspapers. If she hoped they would respond with favorable publicity, she was rewarded when, on May 6, Rowley wrote a glowing column on the lake and mentioned Pyramid Lake Guest Ranch and its beautiful lilacs.

In April 1942 Beau asked the tribal council for permission to build stairs to the dome of an unspecified rock, where he planned to mount a telescope. No action was taken. Indians at Sutcliffe had probably reported on his whims. He could also be a cheapskate. On August 14, 1942, Avery Winnemucca, a member of the Pyramid Lake Tribal Council, called attention to the fact that Kitselman had launched his boat before paying the $300 he had, in 1940, agreed to pay for an annual boating permit. Five months later he still had not paid. By this time he had signed ownership of the ranch over to his mother and sister, but he was still in residence.

Beau apparently hoped to combine his interests in Taoism, yoga, and astronomy with a high-end resort. Beau seems to have had a role in managing the guest ranch and considered himself the sole owner. He oversaw renovation of the rooms and the installation of electricity. We know a little about Beau's behavior thanks to the material Mary Cutlip Bean deposited with the Special Collections in the University of Nevada, Reno, Library. Bean's parents, Mary Bernice (Bernie) Hood and Wayne Gordon Cutlip, worked for Kitselman at the Pyramid Lake Guest Ranch, now dubbed "the Sage," from 1936 to 1943, when the navy, in an agreement with the tribe and the Kitselmans, took over the facilities for the Pyramid Lake Torpedo and Bombing Range. The navy's leases expired in 1946, but it did not clean up the lake until 2004–5, when it finally removed more than thirteen tons of munitions.

After the war the Kitselman family, without Beau's consent, leased the twenty-five-acre ranch to Harry Drackert. Beau went on to study mathematics and psychology, but nothing ever seemed to hold his attention very long. The Bean Papers contain a nine-page handwritten pamphlet, probably written by Beau, titled "The Way Things Are; or, The Resort Employee's Bible with Special Reference to the Pyramid Lake Guest Ranch," with directions such as "Be invisible," "Never argue with the manager in public," "No gossiping," and "Create an employee's council." Apparently, Beau thought his wit could overcome employee discontent. When Bernice Cutlip filed a claim for $46.76 in wages, Beau gave her a check, October 9, 1936, for $25,000, signed Mozundar

Karamchoud Gandhi. Was he thinking of himself as the Mahatma? Was his spelling of Mohandas Karamchand Gandhi merely eccentric or another weak attempt at humor? Or was he also thinking of A. K. Mozumdar and his New Thought movement that likely appealed to young Beau? "If man thinks and acts," Mozumdar wrote, "is not the thinker and actor God?"

In June 1956 the *Nevada State Journal* announced that A. L. (Beau) Kitselman, Reno psychotherapist and director of the Institute of Integration, 30 East Sixtieth Street, New York City, would lecture on "Bridey Murphy, Former Lives and Other Mysteries," at the Reno Chamber of Commerce. Kitselman is described as "a writer and lecturer in the field of lay psychotherapy—which, he says, is a method of self-improvement and non-medical healing which may be safely used by the average person at home. He is the author," the story continues, "of 'E-Therapy,' 'The Upstairs Mind,' 'Insight—Cause and Effect,' 'The Second Silence,' 'Integrative Concepts,' and 'Academic Death.'" Only *E-Therapy* seems to have been published.

The best-selling book *The Search for Bridey Murphy*, by Morey Bernstein, appealed to readers who believed in reincarnation. Bridey was the invention of a Colorado woman who, under Bernstein's hypnosis, relived an earlier life. Kitselman indicated he would play tapes of his own patients recalling past lives. E-therapy as created by Kitselman in 1953 was not, of course, today's online therapy, but a variant of Dianetics, a way of understanding how the mind works. Kitselman was seeking to build a community of believers at Pyramid Lake, even though he had lost control of the guest ranch. On July 16, 1957, the "Personals" in the *Reno Evening Gazette* carried the following: "A matter of Life and Death! Is there something inside of you which can throw off your incurable disease? Would you like to have it activated and pay for results only? Inquire at Pyramid Lake Guest Ranch."

The words echo the "invitation" at the beginning of Beau's book *E-Therapy:* "Would you like to improve your conduct? Is there a habit you'd like to get rid of? . . . Would you like to lose the feeling of insecurity? Make an end of doubt and perplexity? Lose all sense of fear, hatred, and grief?" The ninety-six handwritten pages of *E-Therapy* promise results in just a few hours of therapy with an "observer" who coaches the afflicted "transient" to locate his or her "E"—the transforming power within each individual. Kitselman acknowledges Emerson, Whitman, Socrates, Laozi, Ayn Rand, and Aldous Huxley as his forerunners in E-therapy and adds mystics and science fiction writers such as George Gurdjieff, Edwin Abbott, and A. E. van Vogt. Like Scientologists, Beau believed in perpetual reinvention of self—there is no past, there is no future, there is only now. This was Beau Kitselman's last desperate effort to find what he sought at Pyramid Lake, a place struggling to escape its own bloody past.

Beau's flirtations with the paranormal and with non-Western religion and philosophies would later extend to travels in South Asia and the study of Sanskrit. At the time of his death, he was translating "ancient physics studies," according to an e-mail posted on a website by his daughter Suzette in 2006. She repudiates a claim that her father's work on "insight therapy" was part of L. Ron Hubbard's Scientology or that her father and mother were involved with the Huna cult in Hawaii. For whatever reason, Beau Kitselman's name is dragged around the Internet on sites that link to UFO abductions, Hawaiian shamanism, the "Philadelphia Experiment" (an unverified attempt by the US Navy to use electromagnetic radiation to make a destroyer invisible to enemy radar), and other hoaxes. He was fifty years ahead of his time; he would have been right at home at Burning Man.

Kitselman retained an interest in the development of Pyramid Lake long after he left Sutcliffe to live in La Jolla, California. Sometime in the late 1960s, at the end of the decade of utopian-resort development schemes described in chapter 2, Beau sent letters "to all voting Indians who live on our reservation." This document and a follow-up letter are in the papers of Margaret Wheat in the University of Nevada's Special Collections. His undated letter is addressed to "KUYÚY TIKÚTA NÚUMU (Kwee-wee eating Paiutes)" and begins: "We are at war. We must fight for our water, we must fight for our land, and we must do it now. . . . We must protect our water and our land from TAIBOOS (whites) in Washington, Sacramento, Carson City, Reno, and Los Angeles. They are getting ready to finish us. We cannot waste any more time. We must not talk against each other, we must not let our feelings be hurt, and we must do what needs to be done without delay." Having uttered his war cry, Kitselman tries to establish his credentials: "These words were written by a KUYÚY TIKÚTA NÁNA (Kwee-wee eating man) who was born a TAÍBOO (white) but was adopted by ATSAYAYÁ (who was also known as Doctor Sam, or Bob Kane). This man has talked with many people to find out what must be done, and will tell it here in numbered paragraphs. On the extra page enclosed you can say whether you agree or not, and what you say will help the Council do what needs doing."

Kitselman makes twelve points. He asserts that no white person should own land or water rights on the reservation, that the tribe should stop paying Bob Leland thirty thousand dollars a year and hire Beau's friend Jim Hagerstrom and his associate Bill Russler for fifteen thousand. His friends have assured him that using federal claims money, the tribe can develop commercial farming, cattle raising, fishing, canning and freezing facilities, and hotel and resort businesses. Checks would go three times a month to every member of the tribe. Beau would be finance-and-projects planner. He invites the recipients to comment, but concludes: "It is an old Indian rule that silence is agreement. If you *don't* send in the extra page, we will know that you agree to all of this."

On February 2, 1970, Kitselman wrote to a woman in Nixon, reporting on the outcome of his effort. Twenty-five of the 134 Kuyuidokado contacted made comments, most quite hostile. Six accepted some points, but not others. Kitselman received no replies from 109, assumed they all agreed with him, and declared his proposal approved by a large majority. He received a rude shock when he attended a meeting in Nixon and was told by the council chair that there was no rule of assent by silence. When Beau argued that it was an old Indian custom, he reports that a young woman near him said, "Times have changed." His letter rambles on in defense of his plan, but concludes, "I can live without it [the lake]. Can you?" He signs himself Bo, not Beau, Kitselman, TÚT-SIU ATSAYAYÁ, which translates as "Small Red (or Red-Headed) Person." This was his farewell to the lake.

HARRY DRACKERT, the manager of the Pyramid Lake Guest Ranch from the mid-1940s to the mid-1950s, was a well-known character in the Reno area before World War II because of his fame as a champion rodeo rider, horse trainer, and ladies' man. When he was shot in the abdomen by his best friend, Jack Warner, in an argument over a divorcée, Harriette Henningsen, the December 24, 1937, *Nevada State Journal* gave the incident front-page coverage, placing a large photo of the femme fatale between stories of labor violence at Ford Motors and a clash between the US Navy and Japanese fishing boats off the coast of California. A smaller photo of Drackert above the caption "Near Death" ran beside the lede.

The story is rich in detail, as befits one of the Biggest Little City's most colorful citizens, but it missed one important detail: Drackert was shot on his thirty-third birthday. In the reporter's account, Drackert accosted Warner and Henningsen drinking in a downtown bar about midnight and threatened them. His "best friend" immediately asked the police to send a guard to Henningsen's apartment. As Warner was driving her there, Drackert cut him off with his car and forced him to stop. Warner told the cops that as Drackert approached, Warner asked him to stop, and when he did not, Warner shot him with a .22 rifle that he kept in the back of his vehicle. Ms. Henningsen, who had divorced Arthur P. Henningsen, "Shanghai, China, merchant," a year earlier, "was not detained by the police, who declared she was innocent of any blame in the affair." Chivalry toward women was the code of the West in those days. The police, Wagner, and Harry seemed to have held Harriette blameless. To heighten the drama, the reporter said the doctors gave Harry "one chance in a thousand to live."

What's a guy supposed to do when his gal two-times him with his best friend on his birthday? He gets drunk, gets in a fight, and moves on. Apparently, no charges were pressed; Warner and Henningsen disappear from the newspapers, and Harry recovered and continued to attract unwanted attention. In June 1939 a man named H. Robert Wolfe accused Drackert of "inducing" him to leave Hollywood and become a riding instructor at Harry's dude ranch. The charges were dropped. On October 17, 1940, the *Reno Evening Gazette* reported Drackert's arrest by "Indian Agents" for shooting four ducks at Pyramid Lake without tribal permission, for failure to have federal duck stamps in his license, and for failing "to plug the magazine of his repeating shotgun." Harry paid the fines (ten dollars for lack of a duck stamp and ten dollars for his unplugged shotgun). That he was not fined for violating reservation laws suggests that the offense against the tribe was considered too trivial to punish.

Two years later Drackert won the saddle-bronc competition at the Reno Labor Day Rodeo. He spent the war years working in shipyards in the Bay Area and returned to Reno and managed the Mount Rose Guest Ranch. Soon, he took over the Sage and changed the name to the Pyramid Lake Guest Ranch.

Beau sued his mother, sister, Drackert, and several other persons in 1947 in a futile attempt to regain the property. It was an ugly family fight in which Beau blamed his mental problems on excessive yoga and grief over his father's death. It was a bad start for Drackert's new career, but Harry had survived rougher rides. Harry met an even more beautiful divorcée, Joan Abry of Talbot County, Maryland, a Powers model, licensed pilot, and champion skeet shooter, and married her. They were hosts to some of the most important literary figures of the century, one of whom spent three months with them almost unnoticed.

Thanks to a discovery by historian Dennis Dworkin, we now know that the influential Trinidadian journalist and political activist C. L. R. James stayed at the Pyramid Lake ranch in 1948 while awaiting a divorce from his first wife, because their earlier Mexican divorce was not recognized in the United States. Racial prejudice prevented James from finding suitable accommodations in Reno, and he needed work. His attorney, Charlotte Hunter, called Drackert, who agreed to give James something to do. For the next few weeks James, the brilliant socialist theorist and student of cricket, washed dishes, raked leaves, and watered the garden at the guest ranch. Although he was writing constantly to his not yet legal wife, Constance Webb, in New York, he says little about

Pyramid Lake and its social problems. He did, Dworkin tells us, feel renewed by the natural beauty and physical labor, and he was bemused by Drackert's attractiveness to women. For reasons unknown, Harry terminated James's employment, but let him stay on as a guest. James finished writing a book on Hegel, but, sensitive to racial feelings among the guests, he kept to himself, enriched, we hope, by the solitude and silence of the lake.

Harry and Joan left the Pyramid Lake ranch in the late 1950s, after continuing disputes with the Kitselmans, and moved to Reno, where they operated restaurants and other guest ranches until Harry's death in 1990. Joan died a year later. The Pyramid Lake ranch burned to the ground in March 1969. The cause may have been arson. An epoch ended, but Harry and Joan, cowboy and naiad, have been immortalized by the writers who came to the lake—A. J. Liebling, Basil Woon, Arthur Miller—to whom I shall return in later chapters.

There were, from snippets in the newspapers, other squatters who may have led lives as colorful as Harry and Joan Drackert, but they did not leave their papers and photographs to libraries. About the time the Sutcliffes departed, the Vanderbilts and the Wests arrived. On October 17, 1928, the *Reno Evening Gazette* alerted its readers to the arrival of Mr. and Mrs. Cornelius Vanderbilt Jr., who had just built "a new stone house" at Pyramid Lake. This Mrs. Vanderbilt was Mary Weir Logan, the second of seven wives of Cornelius IV. She left him in 1931. He blamed the cartoonist Peter Arno for alienating her affections and

Postcard of lodgers at Pyramid Lake Guest Ranch, ca. 1955. Courtesy Special Collections, University of Nevada, Reno, Libraries.

chased Arno around the country with an unloaded gun, according to a story in the *Nevada State Journal*. A few months later the *Journal* reported that the junior Vanderbilt was back in Reno to give a talk on his world travels and "the 'dude' ranch business." A clue to his approach to the dude business may be found in an ad in the *Journal*, November 30, 1931, which reads:

RIDE ? ROPE ? PLAY
on a Real Ranch!
You cannot dream yourself into a character;
You must hammer and forge yourself into one.
                                                    —Thoreau

LAZY ME GUEST RANCH

Thoreau had a lot to say about dreams, but I doubt that the sage of Walden would have approved of the association with "Lazy Me."

Other members of the Vanderbilt family paved the way for yogis at the Sage. On September 11, 1930, the *Reno Evening Gazette* ran a story about Winfield J. Nicholls's (a.k.a. Mortimer K. Hargis) divorce from his wife, the daughter of Mrs. W. K. Vanderbilt. Both Nicholls and his wife had been members of Dr. Pierre Bernard's (a.k.a. "Oom the Omnipotent") yoga colony in Nyack, New York. The *Gazette* played up the story with the headline "MEMBERS OF CULT ARE FIGURES IN RENO DIVORCE TRIAL."

Pyramid Lake residents untainted by scandal are harder to document. The earliest notice I have found for the Wests is a classified ad for German shepherds from the Lewanno Kennels in Big Canyon in the *Reno Evening Gazette*, December 12, 1925. The name of the kennel suggests that the Wests were breeding descendants of Filax of Lewanno, who once rivaled Rin Tin Tin as a World War I canine hero. Additional details of this property are provided in writer Basil Woon's rambling and somewhat unreliable book *None of the Comfort of Home, but Oh, Those Cowboys: The Saga of the Nevada Dude Ranches*. The dogs, he writes, were Belgian, not German, police dogs, and Mrs. West was Mae Lovina Barnum, part of the extended family of showman and great American humbug P. T. Barnum. Six months later a brief item in the society pages of the *Nevada State Journal* announced that "Mr. and Mrs. Hiram Dana West have issued a large number of invitations to Reno people to attend a housewarming party to be held today [June 13, 1926] at their new ranch home on the Circle S Ranch, near Pyramid Lake. The affair will be very unique and elaborate."

Two years later a *Gazette* headline reported that "Wests' Dogs Win Prizes" at a San Francisco dog show. A few months later a cryptic notice appeared in the same paper: "The Circle S Ranch of Big Canyon is the private home of Mr. and Mrs. Dana West, and is in no way connected with the Dude Ranch owned by Mr. Neil West at Sutcliffe" (although he was her brother-in-law). "Please address mail accordingly. Maie R. B. West." Three years later, December 6, 1930, the *Gazette* published an obit for Hyrum [*sic*] "Hi" West, a well-known rancher who conducted a riding stable in Reno. According to the story, he had purchased the Big Canyon ranch five years earlier. His widow was Mrs. Mae B. West. *Maybe,* but not *the* Mae West. No wonder the poor woman wanted her mail addressed correctly. Neither of the Reno newspapers seemed able to agree on the spelling of her name or her husband's.

The mystery deepens when, on June 19, 1934, the *Reno Evening Gazette* announced that Mrs. Anna Roosevelt Dall, only daughter of President Franklin D. Roosevelt and his wife, Eleanor, was establishing residence in Nevada in order to obtain a divorce. According to the page 2 story, Anna Dall was taken on a tour of Lake Tahoe and then brought to Reno by "Mr. and Mrs. H. P. Dana, friends of the Roosevelt family." "The Danas have a ranch near Pyramid Lake," the story continued, "and Mrs. Dall will probably spend some of her spare time at Pyramid in addition to viewing the Sierra Nevada mountain [*sic*] district from various points." A brief item in the *New York Times,* June 23, 1934, disclosed that Anna Roosevelt Dall "has given up her lease on the bungalow Cal-Vada . . . and has moved to the desert ranch of William Sheppard Dana, near Pyramid Lake." An entry in my mother's diary for July 23, 1934, confirms that Anna and her children "Sistie" (Anna Eleanor) and "Buzzie" (Curtis) were at Sutcliffe, as was her mother, Eleanor. Anna Roosevelt Dall departed from Nevada a week later, her six-week residence completed and her divorce granted in Minden, but who were the Danas who may be somehow related to the Wests? I happily leave this to some industrious future historian. Suffice to say that many famous and infamous Americans passed through Sutcliffe and benefited from their moments at Pyramid Lake.

The squatter stories become even more complicated. In November 1939 the *Nevada State Journal* published a notice of a deed filed. The executor of the estate of the late Maie R. B. West deeded her property to Francesca Frazier Blackmer of Big Canyon Ranch. Blackmer appears in the press earlier, in a February 23, 1936, *Journal* article on millionaires moving to Nevada to avoid income taxes. The story references a Mrs. Frances Beverly Blackmer, formerly Frances P. Frazier, who had built a $200,000 house at Big Canyon ranch. (This would be more than $3 million in 2013 dollars.) By August, when the house was threatened by wildfire, the *Journal* upped the house's value to $250,000. The mansion was apparently saved by the firefighting efforts of the "boys" from the CCC camp and some SP section hands. The Bean manuscripts and a little Googling turn up additional information.

Francesca Blackmer owned River Ranch north of Hardscrabble in 1936 where Bernie and Wayne Cutlip were caretakers. In an article in *Science* in 1938, the eminent anthropologist A. L. Kroeber acknowledges the financial support of Mr. Beverly Blackmer in the excavation of "Lodi Man," a prehistoric burial near Sacramento. After this, nothing, except a passing mention of Hardscrabble, "better known as Hi West's T-H, one of the first dude ranches in the state, now in ruins," in an article in the *Journal*, March 6, 1955. Another article just five months later stated that the Matley brothers owned Hardscrabble and that bandleader Harry Richman recently sold Big Canyon Ranch.

Woon tries to sort out all the ranches and their owners, but at times adds to the confusion. He confirms that Hardscrabble Ranch began as a squatter's homestead in 1864, the questionable claim of John Wesley Whitehead. The land was briefly owned by P. F. Flanigan, a local politician and would-be cattle baron who went broke in the post–World War I depression. In the 1920s a rancher named Neill West (not Hi) bought a ranch called Red Rock and the brand T-H from a Tom Hill and then expanded his holding by buying the adjoining Hard-scrabble land and renaming it the T-H. In 1926 it became, according to Woon, the first of many dude ranches in northern Nevada. West paid the tribe $1.25 an acre for 563.47 acres, pursuant to the congressional act of 1924. When Neill West died in the early 1950s, his widow sold the ranch to the Matley brothers, local ranchers, who sold it in turn to Al Peigh, a local sportsman, who dreamed of building a sailing marina at Pyramid Lake.

Robert Leland, the tribe's attorney, apparently bought, or put money down on, Peigh's property, which he estimated at 1,300 acres. According to the minutes of the Pyramid Lake Tribal Council Development Committee on October 21, 1969, Leland had interested a Los Angeles development enterprise, Great Western Cities, in financing a resort on the property over which the tribe would eventually take control. A representative of Great Western Cities attended the meeting and expressed a desire for a ninety-nine-year lease. Several members of the tribal council were angry that Leland had bypassed the council and negoti-ated directly with the development committee. Leland resigned as tribal attor-ney, and the house of cards collapsed. The era of utopian resorts was over for the immediate future. In the cui-ui recovery plan of 1977, the property on Hard-scrabble Creek is still referred to as the Peigh Ranch, but by then it was a family home in the hands of a man named Jack Horgan and his sons.

On December 31, 1984, the *Reno Gazette-Journal* reported that the Crosby Lodge and 21 acres at Sutcliffe, owned by thirty-seven-year-old Fred Crosby (great-grandson of the fish-shipping Crosby of 1912), were for sale for $1.8 million. Fred Crosby's father-in-law, Herb Capurro, owned the Sutcliffe Inn and Letty's place. In 2010 Crosby and Thomas Bobella, who leased the Marina and RV Park, were in a dispute with the tribe over payments for permits to sell fuel and beer and to operate slot machines. In the spirit of the times, Bobella accused the Paiutes of "commercial terrorism." Who owned what and where? What name were they using? It is no wonder the Paiutes could not evict the squatters—they were always on the move.

An oral history interview with Phyllis Walsh and a brief history by Carrie M. Townley, both in the Special Collections of the University of Nevada, Reno, bring to light yet another squatter family on the Truckee River north of Wadsworth, the Thomases. Walsh, who was a companion of Helen Marye Thomas at the S Bar S Ranch from Thomas's divorce in 1938 to her death in 1970, recalled that Thomas's mother bought their property in 1939 from Joe and Maria Gardella, a parcel in dispute since the Central Pacific land grab. The Thomases were wealthy from mining and investments and laid claim to being old Virginia aristocrats. After purchasing land that, Townley writes, "slipped through" government regulations and was a "legal" patent, Helen hired architect Dale Frederick, who had designed a ranch house for Clark Gable and Carole Lombard in the San Fernando Valley, to plan buildings that would provide suitable accommodations for her notable guests—Bill and Patty (Ziegfeld) Stephenson, Mrs. Otto Preminger, Dame Judith Anderson, Hedy Lamarr, Sophie Tucker, Tallulah Bankhead, Salvador Dalí, and local politicians such as Pat McCarran, Charles Russell, and Rex Bell. Helen Marye Thomas's 120-acre Xanadu was named Staige Stop Ranch (hence the brand S-S), a pun on a family name and a belief that a stage stop had existed near her land. That it was very near is unlikely, as her claim was five miles north of Wadsworth.

Shortly before her death, Thomas gave the property to the University of Nevada for an agricultural experiment station. Apparently, no thought was given to restoring the land to the Pyramid Lake Tribe. The attitude of whites on reservation land is revealingly summed up by the loyal Phyllis Walsh: "[The Indians] had become so imbued with the idea that they were there first, and therefore their land was stolen away unjustly. This, in some cases, sadly enough, is correct."

FIVE

Squatters and Sportsmen

It is important to see the differences between the white squatters on the west side of the reservation, who lived by wrangling livestock and dudes and who ponied up when given a chance to buy reservation land, and those in the thin strip of reservation along the banks of the Truckee River between Wadsworth and Nixon, who reneged on the chance to buy. The men, who took from the Paiutes the best bottomland along the river, thwarted the BIA's goal of turning hunters and gatherers into subsistence gardeners. Left with mostly arid benchland, the Kuyuidokado were expected to divert water from the river for crops, not for spawning fish. The Indians had to build earthen dams and dig irrigation ditches as well as learn farming. They were forced to destroy the river and the life it sustained to receive the BIA's dubious benefaction of seeds, plows, wagons, and agricultural advice. The squatters, and farmers all along the banks of the Truckee from Reno to Wadsworth, also contributed to the demise of spawning fish by cutting trees that shaded and cooled the water, by polluting the river with cattle manure, by altering stream flow with silt from roads and irrigation ditches, and by destroying native vegetation and wildlife habitat by introducing alien plant and animal species. Some of these devastating changes would have occurred eventually without the land grab, but the rapid ecological change from 1860 to 1900 was catastrophic for the Native economy and culture. It is all the more shameful that this era of the Pyramid Lake story is largely unrecorded.

The second phase of the environmental disaster that affected the Kuyuido-kado, the extinction of the Pyramid Lake strain of LCT and near extinction of the cui-ui, was, as seen in the previous chapters, directly linked to the market for edible fish and the demand for water in irrigation agriculture. Ultimately, both fish and water management would be improved for maximum financial return, but initially fish management seemed easier and cheaper than good water management. As this chapter reveals, federal and state governments and private entrepreneurs began, in the 1870s, stocking streams and lakes with fish taken from other locations or raised in hatcheries, just as the Pyramid Lake fish bonanza was beginning. Little wonder that fish were thought to be an easily renewable resource. The cycle of breeding, planting, and catching appeared to be as perfect as the hydrologic cycle. Both are far more complex than first assumed, as scientists are still learning how to cope with drought and long-term impacts of invasive species. Neither cycle is purely a matter of science; each is also tangled in politics. The story of the restoration of LCT to Pyramid Lake and the efforts to save the cui-ui forms the second half of this chapter, but it is part of the larger story of both the agricultural and the piscatorial economy of the lake.

"ENTRYMEN"

Back at the ranches on the Truckee River, the squatter problems evolved from murder (Truckee John, 1867) to politics, which, to revise von Clausewitz's famous observation, may be the continuation of murder by other means. The beginnings of the Newlands Reclamation Project and the diverting of water to farms near Fallon in 1905 opened a new phase of the struggle to oust non-Indians from the reservation. Because farmers assumed that water rights came with the land and because water was becoming even more valuable due to increased demands from upstream landowners, power companies, and municipalities, and because the Indian policy of both Democrats and Republicans was termination of reservations, squatters and squatter wannabes were already celebrating. A brief visit to Lake Tahoe by Richard Ballinger, the secretary of the interior, set off a frenzy of speculation. "Part of the Pyramid Indian Reservation to Be Opened for Settlement Soon," proclaimed a banner headline on the front page of the *Reno Evening Gazette,* October 12, 1909. Smaller headlines announced a new reclamation project that would turn Pyramid Lake into a huge reservoir to irrigate arid reservation land. A few paragraphs are worth quoting for the breathless excitement that such a possibility raised and for the attitude expressed about Indians:

> There is something doing on a large scale in connection with Pyramid Lake Indian reservation, but just what it is cannot be learned at this hour. Profound mystery surrounds every act of those immediately connected with the big scheme. . . .
>
> In talking with one who is informed upon the subject, but who cannot be quoted, a Gazette representative learned that not only is the promulgation of this vast enterprise assured and a part of the great scheme of the conservation of the waters of this state and reclamation of its arid lands by the federal government but that this particular dam and water ways system is to be one of the most complete in the country, involving a vast outlay of money by the department. . . .
>
> Of the 640,000 acres embraced in this great reservation over 300,000 is taken

up by Pyramid Lake, a beautiful sheet of clear mountain water which makes this reservation one of the most picturesque of all of Uncle Sam's similar domains. . . .

At the left of the road [to the lake] may be seen the burial places of the Indians where piles of stone alone mark the spots where the bodies of some of their number, wrapped in the skin of their pet war horse, was [sic] interred. . . .

The reservation is an oasis in a desert. Surrounded on all sides by vast areas of sage brush and lands [sic] this verdant spot, where exists the activity of the government work, is made more beautiful by contrast in its extent of greenery.

The article concludes with praise for the good job that the superintendent, Lorenzo Creel, is doing. Creel may have regretted talking to the *Gazette,* since his name comes up several times in the story in ways that imply he is the anonymous source for the new reclamation project and the opening to settlement of Indian lands. He might have mentioned his efforts to get a better dam and fish ladder on the reservation and his hope that more of the unclaimed land could be irrigated, which wishful thinking turned into the purple prose of the article. Notice that the reporter exaggerates the size of the reservation and almost triples the size of the lake in his desire to make the story important. His praise for the beauty of the lake ill conceals his longing to possess the oasis. Although he mentions the Indian school being built at Nixon, the good Indians are all dead, wrapped in the skins of their "pet" war horses.

Creel succeeded in getting the BIA to take action against the squatters, and the Indian Agency began an investigation, sending an agent named S. F. O'Fallon in 1910 and another, Washington J. Endicott, in 1920. O'Fallon was able to reconstruct some of the transfers of the trespassers' lands from one claimant to another because there were still people living who remembered them. On the Truckee River between Wadsworth and Nixon, a squatter named Jesse Howell had claimed 120 acres in 1865, sold it to E. H. Short, who sold it to Domenico Ceresola in 1901. What was called the Hamilton Ranch had been stolen from the Indians in 1864 or 1865 by William Goetz. The property changed hands many times and belonged to Elias Olinghouse, a teamster turned rancher, in 1910. In 1915 it was the property of J. A. Ceresola, evidence that the sale of the disputed properties continued in the face of BIA efforts to achieve some kind of settlement with the tribe. By 1913 state senator S. P. Flanigan apparently "owned" the Constantina, Hardscrabble, Big Canyon, and Milk Ranches on the reservation, since he denies in the New Year's Day *Reno Evening Gazette* that he is about to sell these and "minor properties" to an English syndicate for a million dollars. A Pyramid Lake real estate bubble was growing. It is doubtful that Flanigan got a million for his illegitimate properties, but the SPRR named a little town on its spur up the west side of the lake for him.

Fearing that federal courts might be sympathetic to the Indians, Senator Key Pittman, a Democrat, introduced a bill in 1921 allowing white farmers to buy up to 640 acres of reservation land each for $1.25 an acre (the nineteenth-century homestead price), if they had settled "in good faith," meaning, as Knack and Stewart point out, that they trespassed simply to have a family farm. The families were now quite different from those who had settled in the 1860s and 1870s. Some of the reservation pastures and grazing lands had passed through several hands before becoming, about 1915, the empire of five or six families of Italian immigrants. American immigration history makes clear that the shift in immigrant origins from northern Europe to southern brought social tensions and required adjustments in attitudes. As Wilbur Shepperson vividly recounts in *Restless Strangers: Nevada's Immigrants and Their Interpreters,* Nevada's stories of ethnic conflict are as full of mistrust, discrimination, and sorrow as any other state in the country, but the fate of the Pyramid Lake *paisans* took a unique turn when Senator Pat McCarran took up their cause.

After the Department of the Interior sent yet another inspector, C. R. Trowbridge, to assess the value of the Indian properties, it supported Pittman's bill, a revised version of which passed in 1924, but because it required some resurveys, there was legal uncertainty. The owners of the Mullen, Hardscrabble, Sutcliffe, and Bonham Ranches on the west side of the lake took advantage of the opportunity and promptly bought their disputed property from the government. Some of the squatters in Wadsworth and on the river made partial payment; others ignored the law. During the next seven years, the agricultural depression deepened, the stock market crashed, and the Great Depression began. Now the delinquent farmers claimed they were too poor to pay anything. Their pitiful stories reached the sympathetic ears of Senator McCarran. The Ceresola, Garaventa, and Depaoli families had legally purchased land in the Newlands irrigation district but had also acquired disputed titles to squatter lands on the reservation as well—the ranches known as Hamilton, Hill, Home, Hoover, and Olinghouse. McCarran's affection may have been waning in 1943, as he was trying for a fourth time (out of nine attempts) to get his bill passed that would give the disputed land to the squatters, when he wrote to a lackey in Reno that a political rival had lost a lot of votes by opposing McCarran's bill. "He will carry Nixon, but the Waps will give him the Tommy-hawk." The senator was an equal opportunity bigot.

McCarran introduced Senate Bill 840, "to authorize the Secretary of the Interior to issue patents for certain lands to certain settlers in the Pyramid Lake Indian Reservation, Nevada." Hearings were held April 12 and 13 and May 3 and 17, 1937, before the Committee on Indian Affairs. What the senator proposed was to give the delinquent squatters title to the pilfered land for free. Needless to say, this proposal seemed a bit extreme even for McCarran's fellow Democrats, and it was strongly opposed by Indian commissioner John Collier, who had the backing of the acting secretary of the interior, Charles West, and the Indian Rights Association. The 134 pages of testimony and debate between McCarran, Collier, and others provide, as A. J. Liebling amusingly recounts in a four-part article in the *New Yorker* in January 1955, a kind of theater of the absurd, with McCarran bloviating and posturing in the halls of Congress, while squatters, sojourners, and survivors went on with their daily lives on the reservation.

As Liebling observes, only four of the thirteen committee members bothered to attend, but they were important players—Elmer Thomas (D-OK) was chairman; Burton K. Wheeler (D-MT) had been cosponsor of the Indian Reorganization Act of 1934 that reversed the policy of termination of reservations and assimilation of tribes into Anglo culture; Lynn Frazier (R-ND), a supporter of tribal councils; and Dennis Chavez (D-NM), whose state had a large and diverse Native American population that provided useful lessons in solving land disputes. Note that McCarran himself was not a member of the Committee on Indian Affairs, but was rapidly establishing himself as a spokesman for western interests, so his request to speak on behalf of a special interest bill (five farmers) was honored. Little did his colleagues realize that McCarran, failing to succeed with S. 840, would be back to this committee and others in every session of Congress until his death in 1954, trying to make the squatters legal.

Faced with opposition from the Interior Department, based on the fact that the entrymen had been given time to buy the disputed land after the congressional act of 1924 but had failed to do so, McCarran chose to ignore the facts and present an alternative history in which the Indians become the interlopers because the first settlers arrived before the reservation was created by "merely an Executive order." He also ignored the Indian Reorganization Act in 1934, which prohibited Indians from selling their reservation land. Eliding the seventy years between the land grab by the Fellnagles, Gates, Mullens, and others and the pretext by the Garaventas, Ceresolas, and Depaolis that they could not afford to pay any amount to keep the disputed property, McCarran pleaded: "We only ask now that they be permitted to have the lands on which their families have been reared, on which they have married and given in marriage, and on which they have buried their dead, if you please. That is the story of these settlers. There is a continuous chain, with never an hour of abandonment, never a time in which those settlers were not citizens of that community."

The senator, looking and sounding more and more like political boss Edward Arnold haranguing Jimmy Stewart in *Mr. Smith Goes to Washington,* denounced the Kuyuidokado as "fishermen." "They are nomadic. They are a rambling tribe." The absurdity of rambling fishermen escaped comment by the Senate committee, but Liebling points it out, adding that because the Indians had occupied the area for several thousand years, he would like "to hear the Senator's definition of permanent resident."

Although no tribal representatives appeared at the 1937 hearings, the objections to McCarran's bill by the Pyramid Lake Tribal Council appear indirectly in the senator's angry response to a story in the *Reno Evening Gazette,* February 4, that summarized a letter sent by the council to Indian commissioner John Collier and to McCarran. In the *Gazette* article, council chair Dewey Sampson turns McCarran's family-values rhetoric back on him, making the case for "our young men who are starting to have families and who do not have good river bottom land and have to live with their folks and use the small acres that are not enough for so many people." McCarran's three-thousand-word response is mostly a rehash of his usual contentions that the squatters were farming the Truckee River lands before the reservation was created, but he vastly overstates the size of the reservation, perhaps to make the Indians seem greedy. "The total area of the reservation is 822,000 acres," he asserts. "The Indian population is approximately 500 persons. The amount of land of the same class and quality as that in the controversy, which could have been put under irrigation by the Indians, is in the neighborhood of 6,000 acres. The amount of land actually cultivated by the Indians between 1859 and 1937 is something less than 2,000 acres."

Aside from more than doubling the amount of land on the reservation, McCarran underestimates the population, overstates the amount of irrigable land, and, without a hint of irony, uses the earlier date for the creation of the reservation, the date he previously rejected, to make it seem that the Indians were lazy and took seventy-eight years to cultivate only two thousand acres. Here we see McCarran trying out the "big lie" technique that would serve him well in the 1940s and early '50s when he joined Joe McCarthy in hunting subversives. Collier does his best to refute the senator's most egregious lies, but Liebling is right to note that Collier seems a little pallid in comparison to McCarran's florid performance. Nevertheless, Liebling misses the subtlety of Collier's strategy. Collier knows that Congress can do whatever it wants, so he is careful to show deference to McCarran, but he also works hard to keep Thomas, Wheeler, and Chavez on his side. He has the backing of Harold Ickes, his boss at the Interior Department, and he has the Indian Reorganization Act, a law that largely reflects his goals to protect what is left of Indian land and culture and give Indians the tools they will need to become and remain self-sufficient in the future.

Collier begins his testimony by pointing out the obvious but ignores the assumption of the 1924 act that authorized the squatters to buy reservation land—that in legitimizing the purchase, it legitimized Indian ownership. Collier elicits Chavez's support by comparing the situation at Pyramid Lake to a similar one in New Mexico, where Indian protests over trespass were ignored by the BIA in the nineteenth and early twentieth centuries. When the Supreme Court found for the Indians in the case, they excepted the settlers who had farmed in the belief that they were on government, not Indian, land. Collier then presents evidence that the Pyramid Lake squatters were given due notice in the 1860s that they were in violation and ordered to remove themselves. That was too much for Senator Wheeler, who, like McCarran, invoked the myth of the frontiersman. "'Due notice served,'" he blurted out, "—that is a joke. How in the name of Heaven is a fellow who goes out and takes up a piece of land out on the side of a mountain to know anything about whether an order has been written down here in any one of these departments!" Shortly after this exchange, Thomas adjourned the session.

The next day the hearings began with Collier summarizing his position and regretting that Alida Bowler, superintendent of the Nevada Indian Agency, was no longer in Washington to present more details of the tribe's case. McCarran immediately objected to including her written testimony in the record and expressed his dislike of Bowler on several occasions during the hearings.

Bowler's career is worth a brief review. She had undergraduate and graduate degrees in psychology from the University of Illinois. After refugee work during World War I, she became California secretary of the American Indian Defense Association at the time Collier was its director. In the early 1930s she conducted research in association with the University of Chicago on crime rates among recent immigrants, demonstrating that the foreign-born committed fewer crimes than native-born Americans. She also found evidence of police brutality against immigrants. Her studies were used to defeat a bill introduced in 1930 to restrict Mexican immigration as a way to reduce crime. For a brief period she was director of the Delinquency Unit of the US Children's Bureau and published a booklet, *Institutional Treatment of Delinquent Boys,* in 1935. Just before Collier asked her to join him at the BIA, she had been public relations director for the Los Angeles Police Department. Bowler must have been accustomed to political heat, but McCarran succeeded in driving her from the Nevada Indian Agency in 1939, and she left the BIA in 1942, rejoining in 1948 before finally retiring in 1952. Her career and the good work she did for the Pyramid Lake Indians and other Nevada tribes deserve a fuller treatment than Liebling or I can provide.

In the last few pages of his *New Yorker* articles on the lake and the McCarran machinations, Liebling describes a visit with Bowler at her home in Glendale, California, comparing her to women he remembered from the Federal Theater and Federal Writers' Projects, or women like Eleanor Roosevelt and Frances Perkins. Bowler is more in the mold of the now largely forgotten but terrifically important women social scientists of her generation, such as anthropologist Hortense Powdermaker, urban sociologist Frances Donovan, and *Middletown* coauthor Helen Merrell Lynd. Bowler shared their concern for making the emerging academic fields of psychology, sociology, and anthropology relevant. Her range of experiences—with Romanian refugees, American Indians, Mexican immigrants, and juvenile delinquents—is almost as great as Powdermaker's, and Bowler's outrage at injustice was certainly equal to Collier's. And she was appreciated. As a Paiute tells Liebling over a 7-Up at Drackert's bar: "It was really she who started us to fight." No surprise, then, to find, in the tribal roll of 1960, a Paiute child named Alida.

After McCarran's outburst against Bowler on the second day of the hearings, the senator introduced more documents that he alleged supported the claims of the squatters, and he sparred orally with Collier and members of the committee. Chairman Thomas overruled McCarran's objection to including Bowler's testimony, even though it contained a bombshell. Bowler inserted a telegram she had received from a member of the Nevada Assembly, L. K. Gregory, who claimed that some of the squatters had authorized him to offer the Indians $32,000 for their land in the event that McCarran could not get the land for free. This assertion was denied in a sworn affidavit by Frank L. Garaventa submitted to the hearings by McCarran when they resumed a month later in May. The senator's attempt at damage control by attacking the character of Gregory and Bowler apparently did not achieve his desired end. He dropped his insistence that the squatters were too poor to pay and offered to amend his bill to have them pay for the land, including some interest.

May 17, 1937, the final day of hearings, began with a statement by McCarran that the "settlers" were willing to pay whatever Congress approved rather than have to face further controversy. McCarran's concessions and the two weeks between the opening and closing of the hearings gave Collier confidence and time to assemble new material in support of expelling the squatters. Feeling he now had the committee with him, Collier played his Lincoln card, introducing previously unknown documents from the secretary of the interior to the president on April 28, 1864, recommending approval of the two tracts of land set aside for the Indians in 1859, and Lincoln's response: "Let the reservation be excepted from public survey."

Collier was audacious in introducing these documents, since McCarran dismissed them as referring only to a section of forest unconnected to the Pyramid Lake Reservation. Yet Lincoln's message was ambiguous, and the strategy of ignoring some dates and privileging others that McCarran had been using was turned back on him. Collier continued by introducing more documents that supported the contention that the squatters had all been notified of their trespass. He brought up the murder of Truckee John and debunked the claim of unbroken ownership from the first squatters of the 1860s to the Ceresolas and Garaventas. Interior's assessments of the value of the squatter properties in 1910, 1920, and 1924 were entered into the record to refute the squatters' claims of poverty. On July 22, 1937, the Senate passed an amended version of McCarran's S. 840 that required the Ceresolas, Garaventas, and Depaolis to pay a total of $21,728.70 within a year. Political rivalries prevented the bill from passing in the House. Roosevelt would never have signed it had it somehow slipped through. It was clearly in violation of the spirit, if not the letter, of the Indian Reorganization Act that promised an Indian New Deal.

The efficacy of the IRA, whose preamble declares it to be "an Act to conserve and develop Indian lands and resources; to extend to Indians the right to form businesses and other organizations," and grant other rights such as home rule, has been the subject of debate among historians and political scientists for almost eighty years. The IRA permitted greater tribal autonomy, but continued federal paternalism. Professor Elmer Rusco provides a thorough overview of the thinking behind various reform efforts and the legislative history of the act. He disputes the conclusion of some scholars that the act was essentially a conservative response to maintain the status quo, but follows Vine Deloria in finding that "self-government wasn't wrong, just inadequate." Rusco's own research on the formation of the Pyramid Lake Paiute Tribal Council, 1934–36, shows that neither conservative nor liberal critics of the IRA are totally correct. Like the labor unions that organized with the slogan "Roosevelt wants you to join," the Kuyuidokado and other tribes were reassured that Collier and the Roosevelt administration were in support of tribal self-government and would not let their efforts fail as past efforts had.

Historian Wilcomb Washburn, reassessing the IRA on its fiftieth anniversary, dismisses criticisms that Collier was ignorant of traditional family and band governance and that by insisting on tribal constitutions, he forced white ideas of politics on Indians and turned their reservation councils into "puppets." "Collier chose the tribe [rather than larger or smaller organizational structures] because that was the way Whites saw Indians," Washburn writes, "and he could use the term to convey a favorable historical and romantic image to justify the preservation of Indian cultures and group organizations to a potentially unsympathetic Congress." Although it is true that the act did not favor traditional leaders, medicine men, and shamans, it recognized that the old ways were gone forever. With the annihilation in some areas of as much as 90 percent of the Native population and the subsequent reduction of their lands to a few reservations, it would be impossible to restore Indian life to some fading memory of an ideal. Moreover, forms of government always change in response to new social, economic, or environmental conditions. Indian life was never sealed like a fly in amber. To assume otherwise is an insult to those who survive into the twenty-first century, ready and willing to use whatever tools it takes to improve their lives and the lives of their children.

HATCHERY FISH

The Kuyuidokado knew that the IRA was not going to solve all their problems. As the previous chapters show, they had to survive Dillon Myer and the BIA's outrageous interference with their legal representation in the 1950s before things really began to turn around. While the tribe's struggles with the federal government were going badly, their relations with at least one Nevada state agency improved. In May 1950 the tribe signed a ten-year agreement with the Nevada Fish and Game Commission to stock the lake with Lahontan cutthroat trout found in other lakes and streams in the Great Basin, and sportfishing slowly returned, despite the initial pessimism of Thomas Trelease, the chief of fisheries. In a letter to Harry Drackert at the Pyramid Lake Guest Ranch, dated January 18, 1955, Trelease enclosed an article he had published in *Field and Stream* in February 1952, titled "Death of a Lake."

Trelease begins his lacustrine obituary with the story of Johnny Skimmerhorn's forty-one-pound LCT. Trelease assures his readers that no one will ever catch as big a fish again in Pyramid Lake because of "greed and lack of foresight."

The cause of the extinction of the LCT in Pyramid Lake, Trelease explains, was not overfishing, or the much-maligned pelican. "The trout killer's name was Derby Dam." It took real courage for a state employee to openly accuse his federal colleagues in the Bureau of Reclamation of mismanagement and poor construction of the fish ladder at the dam. Little had changed in the ensuing three years, but Trelease was a bit more upbeat in his letter to Drackert, recounting the success with planting kokanee salmon and the survival of rainbow trout in the lake. With the support of local sportsmen, a stocking program could go forward. In 1954, 76,718 hatchery rainbows and 220,848 kokanee (a landlocked salmon) were planted. Trelease concludes his letter with a prediction and a warning: "As you can see from the above statements we have gone to considerable expense and work to bring back Pyramid's fishing. We, as you can realize, would not do this if we didn't feel that it would pay us dividends. Here in the Commission we feel very strongly that Pyramid Lake will be one of the best fishing areas in the State of Nevada within the next few years. Of course, we could always be wrong and could have misinterpreted some of the data we've acquired. However, I do not believe this is the case."

Trelease is an unsung hero of Nevada conservation. Born in 1919, he came to Sparks with his family in his teens and began making bicycle trips to Pyramid Lake in the mid-1930s and soon realized that the lake and its fish were in danger. There was insufficient water for the fish to spawn. In 1939, unsure of where to turn, he wrote to the Izaak Walton League, an organization founded in Chicago in 1922 devoted to promoting sportfishing and clean water. Trelease laid out the problems the Pyramid Lake Paiutes were facing, emphasizing the failure of federal and state agencies and especially the BIA to protect the lake. Officials at the league passed his letter on to John Collier, who was trying to revive Native economies. Collier faced opposition from the US Fish and Wildlife Service that felt the lake was a lost cause, but within a few years the federal government had opened a hatchery in Carson City. After World War II, when Trelease returned from the navy, the Nevada Fish and Game Commission began working closely with the tribe and by 1947 had won its confidence and begun restocking the lake.

Before the hatchery programs were operational, Trelease, who had learned to fly in a program at the University of Nevada before the war, flew with Warren Toby, game warden for the Pyramid Lake Tribe, to Summit Lake, 120 miles north of Nixon, where he had discovered a strain of LCT. With Toby's help, he convinced tribal elders there to allow him to restock Pyramid Lake with the Summit Lake fish. Later researchers found that there are two distinct varieties of *Oncorhynchus clarki henshawi*, stream dwellers and lake dwellers, and some variation by watershed. Stream dwellers usually weigh less than a pound, whereas their lake-dwelling relatives have been known to grow to more than four feet in length and weigh more than forty pounds. While the prospect of restoring these monsters for sportfishing was one goal of Trelease's work, he was also interested in saving the cui-ui, also endangered by low water flow into the lake and poorly constructed fishways. Moreover, the cui-ui was found only in Pyramid Lake. There were no related stocks in isolated lakes and streams. Trelease, Professor Ira La Rivers of the University of Nevada, and Richard Miller, an ichthyologist with the Foresta Institute, worked tirelessly to have the cui-ui placed on the first federal endangered species list in 1967.

The fish-planting agreement between the tribe and the commission was renewed in 1960, and Fish and Game began stocking cutbows, a hybrid of rainbow and cutthroat trout. In 1974 Pyramid Lake Tribal Enterprises took over all hatchery operations and stocking of the lake from the Nevada Department of Wildlife, successor to the Fish and Game Commission. The following year the LCT was reclassified as "threatened" to allow sportfishing.

Although raising LCT and cui-ui in hatcheries and planting other, nonnative, fish species in Pyramid Lake has obviously saved the endangered species and provided revenue to the tribe from sportfishing, it has come with costs. Considerable evidence, scientific and anecdotal, exists that hatchery fish are not as robust as members of their species who can spawn naturally. Biologists speculate that the current strain of LCT in Pyramid Lake will never reach the size their close relatives reached before the 1930s. The story of fish management at Pyramid Lake is a microcosm of the story of *An Entirely Synthetic Fish: How Rainbow Trout Beguiled America and Overran the World*, as told by ecologist and journalist Andres Halverson. A brief digression will put the Pyramid Lake story in a larger context.

The leading authority on trout, Robert J. Behnke, thinks that the "Lahontan cutthroat trout may have been the first trout artificially propagated in North America." He notes that a private hatchery operated on the Truckee River as early as 1868 and that the wonderfully named Ornithological and Piscatorial Acclimatizing Society of California, which sought to import game birds and fish from other states and countries, obtained LCT eggs and shipped them to New Zealand in 1875. It is not known whether the hatchlings survived to greet their American cousins the rainbows eight years later, but it has become clear that both these hardy fish are good travelers.

The extracting and hatching of eggs from female fish was begun in France in 1843 and expanded commercially in Germany. Brown trout from Germany and

Scotland were transplanted to streams and lakes in the eastern United States in the late 1870s, about the same time that the US Fish Commission (USFC) began shipping hatchery-raised rainbows to almost every state in the Union and many foreign countries. The native range of the fish that came to be known as the rainbow was limited to the coastal waters of the Pacific—from Baja California to the Kamchatka Peninsula—and to the rivers of California, Oregon, Washington, Canada, and Alaska, where they spawned. Their synthetic descendants, inbred and crossbred, are now found throughout the world. The reason for their success, Halverson argues, is that Spencer Baird, secretary of the Smithsonian and commissioner of the USFC, gave away trout eggs and fry to any state, country, or private fish farm, of which there were more than two hundred in 1870, that would take them. There was also a widespread feeling that many game fish were declining and that the West in particular was lacking in birds and fish. Some observers even linked the extinction of fish with the extermination of the Indian. Halverson quotes a writer for the magazine *Forest and Stream* in 1886: "The brook trout must go. It is sad to contemplate the extinction of the 'anglers' pride' in public waters, but the stern fact remains that in this utilitarian age its days are numbered and its fate irrevocably sealed. As the red man disappears before the tread of the white men, the 'living arrow' of the mountain streams goes with him."

Not so the rainbow. In addition to their hardiness, the rainbow possessed another characteristic Halverson deems significant: they matched the skills of "gentlemen" sportfishermen. Brown trout were too hard to catch, cutthroats were too easy, but rainbows were "just right." As fishing in the twentieth century evolved from subsistence to recreation, the sport anglers who founded organizations such as Trout Unlimited demanded a reliable product for the rivers and ponds they fished. As Halverson archly puts it, "Sportsmen were 'paying customers' and fish were now called a 'hatchery product.'" New terms such as *return to creel*, meaning the percentage of stocked fish that were caught, entered the language of fish management. Studies indicate that between 1991 and 2006, the number of Americans who fish declined from 21 percent to 13 percent of the population, and they are divided into fierce advocates of artificial lures versus live bait, streams versus lakes, dinner versus catch and release, but they are all politically active, and Pyramid Lake has benefited from the commitment of those favoring lures, lakes, and catch and release.

Fish management is, of course, another way of colonizing the frontier, analogous to silviculture in the Forest Service. Historian Frieda Knobloch argues persuasively that agriculture—trees, food crops, grasses, and weeds—was part of the colonizing force, as native trees and plants were destroyed and replaced by imports. Deforestation is the lesser part of the process; reforestation is more significant because it involves reclassifying species, hybridization, fire control, experiments in forest-product laboratories, and a host of management practices that reshape the landscape, redefine what is natural, and create bureaucracies to administer the enterprise. Unable to dislodge the Paiutes from Pyramid Lake, white poachers and irrigators succeeded in nearly exterminating the cui-ui and the LCT, that is, depiscation, and then claimed the right to restore fish to the lake by planting hatchery-raised species, repiscation, all in the name of sustainable aquaculture.

The "Cui-ui Recovery Plan," prepared in 1977 by a team of federal and state wildlife biologists led by Earl Pyle and including Tom Trelease, with John Frazier representing the tribe, was essentially a proposal for research and experimentation in habitat restoration. Its goals were ambitious—"to restore the Cui-ui to non-endangered status" and "to maintain a self-sustaining population at optimum level in Pyramid Lake"—given the uncertainty of sufficient water. The thirty-page report outlined a host of actions, including operating the Marble Bluff Fishway and the Numana Dam; the restoration of the Truckee River canopy; the construction and operation of spawning channels, nursery ponds, and hatchery facilities to produce two million fry annually; and the acquisition of the white-owned ranch on Hardscrabble Creek to ensure hatchery water supply. The plan also called for a public education program and for the training of "tribal members in fish cultural techniques."

The budget for the plan was almost three million dollars over fiscal years 1977 to 1980, including five hundred thousand dollars to purchase the Peigh Ranch on Hardscrabble Creek. The project required the cooperation of several state and federal bureaucracies whose comment letters reveal some of the problems any such plan encounters. Personal and institutional rivalries are foremost. The vice president for administration of the Desert Research Institute found the US Fish and Wildlife Service "presumptuous" in claiming that its personnel had developed techniques for artificially spawning, hatching, and rearing cui-ui when the techniques they were using were developed by David L. Koch, a PhD candidate at the University of Nevada, who worked with the tribe in the late 1960s and early 1970s. The commentator also suggested acknowledging Koch's publications in the report. When it opened two years later, the cui-ui hatchery was named in Koch's memory.

The snarkiest comments came, as might be expected, from the regional director of the Bureau of Reclamation in Sacramento, B. E. Martin. His letter clearly illuminates the wide gap in attitudes toward the natural environment between engineers and biologists. The bureau was obviously beginning to feel the winds of change blowing from Washington, a change well documented by Wendy Nelson Espeland in her study of the Yavapai resistance to the flooding of their land by the proposed Orme Dam on the Salt River in Arizona in 1981. Environmental protection was challenging the big dams and reclamation projects of the past seventy years. Its foot soldiers in the Truckee Carson Irrigation District had been fighting the Pyramid Lake Tribe for most of that time, and the bureau was in no mood to surrender.

Citing the 1956 Washoe Project Act that had authorized several reservoirs primarily for agricultural use, but conveniently ignoring the Gesell decision, Martin avers that his agency lacks the authority "to spend further nonreimbursable funds for fishery purposes." He then questions the source of USFWS authority. If it is the Endangered Species Act of 1973, he continues, that and the sources of funding should be made clear. The letter then gets nastier. Despite the fact that the cui-ui plan is all about habitat restoration, the reclamation official suggests that an environmental assessment be included, knowing full well that it would slow the recovery efforts by many months, if not years. In the concluding paragraphs of the three-page letter, Martin asserts the bureau's authority over biological and cultural issues with naked arrogance: "The recovery plan seems to regard artificial propagation as strictly a contingency measure. If it can be made to work, however, it may be the most economical and perhaps the only politically possible expedient if natural propagation must take place in the Truckee River. The competition for the use of that stream for a multitude of purposes is increasing every day, as you know. If the Cui-ui can be succored (pun intended) through the use of hatcheries, it would seem wise to retain that option."

Having rejected restoration of the Truckee River for spawning fish, the Bureau of Reclamation regional director attempts to appease his biologist colleagues by offering them more opportunities for habitat management. The West is big enough for two big government bureaucracies if they stay out of each other's way. "What are the possibilities of establishing the Pyramid Lake Cui-ui in other watersheds as well? Perhaps it could thrive in the Klamath Lake system which supports the short-nose sucker or in Utah Lake which has the June sucker. At any rate it seems the recovery plan ought to include the consideration of alternative and additional habitats."

Finally, the territorial Mr. Martin plays victim. His agency has been unfairly maligned.

> We note that the Bureau of Reclamation receives prominent mention in the last paragraph on page 2 wherein the demise of the cutthroat trout and the near-extinction of the Cui-ui are attributed to the works of our agency. Would it be asking too much to request that you mention us also in Item 1 on page 5 where you describe the fishway completed in 1976 as a key step toward restoration of the cui-ui? We built the fishway too, you know. Incidentally the proper name of the fishway is the Pyramid Lake Fishway—not the Marble Bluff Fishway as appears in a few places in the recovery plan.

The words *politically possible expedient* leap up like a spawning trout. Martin's veiled threat pits the TCID and its friends in Congress against the tribe, and while you're at it, he implies, why don't you just move the damned fish to another lake and take the Indians with you? Understandably angry that his agency is accused of exterminating a fish unique in the world, he manages to sound a conciliatory note by claiming the new fishway (Marble Bluff, which required twenty-five years of constant rebuilding before operating successfully) as a part of the solution to the problem Derby Dam created. The rivalry between the USFWS and the Bureau of Reclamation continues on their websites where, in 2012, the biologists state that they operate the Marble Bluff Fish Passage Facility in partnership with the Reclamation Bureau and the Pyramid Lake Paiute Tribe, while Reclamation claims that it operates the Marble Bluff Dam and that the Fish and Wildlife Service is responsible for the "Pyramid Lake Fishway."

A decade after the recovery plan was initiated, USFWS compiled its research and cui-ui management experience in *Life History and Status of the Endangered Cui-ui of Pyramid Lake, Nevada,* authored by G. Gary Scoppettone, Mark Coleman, and Gary Wedemeyer. This report is evidence of the success of the recovery effort. The biologists now had a much clearer picture of the spawning habits of the endangered fish, its diet, the age structure of the population, and the effects of the Marble Bluff Dam and Fishway. Female cui-ui begin laying eggs at about six years of age and may live and continue to spawn for thirty years. Spawning is triggered by the increase of freshwater into the lake in the spring as snow melts in the Sierra Nevada and feeds the Truckee River. The study found no evidence that the cui-ui had spawned in the river from the 1930s until the completion of the fishway in 1976, although the hardy fish attempted to do so on several occasions, which allowed the Indians to catch a few and maintain their cultural traditions.

Cui-ui being tagged and measured at Marble Bluff Fish Passage Facility. Courtesy US Fish and Wildlife Service.

Historically, the cui-ui usually spawned in the lower twenty miles of the river, spending a few days to a few weeks before returning to the lake. The fertilized larvae also migrate back to the lake after a few weeks, usually traveling at night. By 1982 an estimated 187,000 cui-ui, about half of them females, gathered in the prespawning aggregation at the mouth of the Truckee. With females laying between 24,000 and 196,000 eggs each, recovery began despite high mortality (90 percent) of the larvae due to temperature changes, pollution, and predation. By 1996 there were more than 1 million cui-ui estimated to be in the lake, but most of them were planted from hatcheries. For true recovery, the river needed reliable spring flows.

The degradation of the river, the cutting of the cottonwoods and other shade trees that cooled its water, and chemical pollution from upstream sources all took their toll. The *Life History* report compiled data on the effect of water temperature, speed of the river's flow, and the availability of midges, copepods, algae, and other foods consumed by the cui-ui. All this information was utilized by Chester Buchanan and Tom Strekal in their 1988 management plan, *Simulated*

Water Management and Evaluation Procedures for Cui-ui, which illustrates how well the system works when agencies cooperate. Buchanan and Strekal integrate hydrologic and biological data and propose four fish-flow regimes depending on lake elevation, the size of the spawning population, temperatures, hatchery production, and the availability of water in Stampede Reservoir. The regimes can be adjusted as conditions change during the January through April inflow. The elegance of the *Simulated Water Management* plan lies in its balance of hydrological realities with biological goals and its explicit admission of unknowns. The plan allows for constant feedback and modification.

Lahontan cutthroat trout are a different kettle of fish. While the tribe would not exist if there were no cui-ui, it and the cui-ui could not survive without the sport fish and the thousands of trout fishermen and -women who pay to fish in the lake. Gary Horton, in his estimable *Truckee River Chronology,* to which every historian of the watershed is indebted, cites a pamphlet sponsored by the USFWS, the Bureau of Land Management (BLM), the US Forest Service, the Nevada Division of Wildlife, and Trout Unlimited that declared the LCT extirpated from Lake Tahoe in 1939 and from Pyramid by 1944. Horton and others distinguish between the Pyramid Lake cutthroat trout and the Lahontan variety, though both are designated *O. clarki henshawi.* When Tom Trelease began stocking Pyramid Lake with LCT from Summit and Walker Lakes, some purists were offended.

According to reporter Tom Knudson, a USFWS biologist, Don Duff discovered LCT in streams on Pilot Peak near the Utah-Nevada border in the mid-1970s. The species was confirmed by Robert Behnke of Colorado State University. Later, DNA analysis of museum specimens of LCT led biologists to assert that the Pilot Peak fish were the closest relatives of the extinct Pyramid Lake LCT. How the Nevada fish ended up in Utah is unknown, but the best guess is that some early sportfishing enthusiast transported stolen fish by rail to stock the streams of the Beehive State. The discovery also suggested that the original strain might be restored, using these rambling survivors for hatchery production. Knudson credits Bryce Nielson, a biologist with the Utah Division of Wildlife Resources, with creating the first LCT hatchery, a private enterprise, near Pilot Peak.

In 1995 he shipped LCT eggs to the USFWS Lahontan National Fish Hatchery in Gardnerville, about fifteen miles south of Carson City, Nevada. This facility had been authorized as part of the Washoe Project in 1956 and had been raising LCT from various Nevada lakes and streams since 1967. Joining the Lahontan hatchery in an effort to save endangered fish were the David Koch Cui-ui

Hatchery in Sutcliffe in 1973, the David Dunn Hatchery in Sutcliffe in 1976, and the Numana Hatchery, eight miles north of Wadsworth, in 1982. The Dunn and Numana Hatcheries raise LCT only. Since the inception of these facilities, more than two million LCT have been planted in the lake. The current goal is to replace hatchery fish with spawning fish that, with the aid of the Marble Bluff Fish Passage Facility and riverbank restoration, will be able to make their way up the Truckee River. If the fish succeed and their offspring make their way safely back to the lake to feed and grow, sportfishermen may celebrate the replacement of five- to ten-pound hatchery-raised fish by twenty- to twenty-five-pound spawners. Early indications have been good.

By the late 1980s the state and federal agencies involved in fish management, the Pyramid Lake Tribe, and nongovernment sportfishing and conservation organizations had brought Truckee River and Pyramid Lake fishing to national attention. John Roush's 1987 book, *Enjoying Fishing Lake Tahoe, the Truckee River, and Pyramid Lake,* was one sign of renewed interest. Roush is a big-game hunter and sportsman-conservationist. According to his website, he has a doctorate in business administration and has written several books on the history of hunting. Roush presents himself as an experienced guide and a debunker of myths. "The key to successfully fishing Lake Tahoe or Pyramid Lake is knowledge of the terrain—submerged terrain. . . . You can often get a hint of the submerged ridges from observing the shoreward ridges. . . . Needless to say an underwater ridge that affords the proper hideouts and depth is one of the best places to fish." At Pyramid Lake, "one must exercise caution in wading the southern portion of the lake for sand cave-ins have brought about drownings." For anglers unable to make long casts, he recommends trolling and fishing from a boat. Roush revives legends of the lake's monster, only to reveal that the twenty-five-foot creature swimming in the lake was "a school of minnows banded together in an attempt to discourage attacks by larger fish." Roush is scornful of the continued diversion of water to the Newlands irrigation project that "serves only a handful of hay farmers and melon growers."

In 1988 Doug McMillian devoted one part of his magnificent *Reno Gazette-Journal* six-part series on the water wars to fishing. *Fin and Feathers* magazine, McMillian wrote, ranked Pyramid Lake as the third-best fishery in the country, and the forty-thousand-member Federation of Fly Fishers named the lake the nation's best trophy-trout fishing spot. McMillian credits Nevada's first chief of fisheries, Tom Trelease, with collecting and transplanting cutthroat trout from other rivers in the state to Pyramid in the late 1940s and early 1950s, thereby saving the lake's sportfishing. Although the reintroduced Lahontan cutthroats were placed on the endangered list by the USFWS in 1970, the hatchery programs were supplying enough fish that they were upgraded to threatened in 1975, allowing sportfishing to resume. Thousands of trout fishermen with rod, creel, and step-ladders were about to displace the hay farmers and melon growers.

Such was the scene described by *Sports Illustrated* writer Clive Gammon in 1989. In what journalists call a "think piece," Gammon, a fishing writer born in Wales, laments the inevitable decline of the lake and ponders its future. His opening paragraphs set the tone:

> Throughout the night, because of the glow from the neon lights of Reno, 30 miles to the south, there has been no true darkness in the sky over Pyramid Lake. Not until 6:30 A.M. does the first finger of sunlight come over the Nightingale Mountains to the east. Then in the dim light of dawn on the strange and legendary lake of the Paiute Indian Reservation, the first-time visitor is witness to a seemingly inexplicable sight.
>
> On the western shore fly-fishermen are working in a style that shows them to be expert in the ways of Stillwater trout fishing. They are throwing the long, heavy lines that anglers call shooting heads. They barely pause between stripping in one cast and sending the next one flying out over the flat surface. While this in itself is not remarkable, the visitor blinks in disbelief because it appears that all these anglers are standing on the water. The sight is made stranger still by the chest-high waders all of them are wearing.
>
> Not until the sun rises above the distant mountains and the efforts of one of the fishermen are finally rewarded is the mystery solved. As the fish thrashes, the angler steps down into the water. It suddenly becomes clear that he had been standing atop a stepladder.

The purpose of the ladders, Gammon finally learns, is to get the fisherman closer to the deep water where the trout lurk and to allow the anglers to fish without keeping their arms raised, as they must if they are standing in deep water. When the fisherman steps off the ladder, he is chest-deep. He walks backward toward the shore, letting the trout run and tire before reeling it in step by step. Gammon is duly impressed. An angler tells Gammon that he has been fishing in Pyramid Lake for thirty years and is still fascinated by its rapid changes of mood. His own mood is good, having just landed a twelve-pound trout, lessening the stress he feels as a customer-service agent at Reno Airport. He tells Gammon that the lake can be dead calm one minute and then turn choppy with three-foot swells. In the formula of fisherman talk, he begins to elaborate. The Paiutes tell of Water Babies in the lake, crying at night. Maybe they make the waves. "Pyramid Lake does not give up its dead," says the angler. "A Navy plane went in last year, and they never found the crew, only a piece of wing and part of the motor."

This story smacks of what folklorists call disaster lore—improbable stories of mishap told by someone who claims he was present at the event or heard about it from a friend who was. For centuries, Pyramid has been the subject of such stories. Water Babies inhabit its depths, it is bottomless, and it conceals a monster. One of the earliest stories about the lake, from the *San Francisco Daily Evening Bulletin,* July 25, 1860, reported that three duck hunters from Downieville had seen an eight-foot alligator in Pyramid Lake. In 1952 the *Nevada State Journal* reported that two railroad workers at the lake saw a thirty- to forty-foot fish swimming at sixty miles an hour. Joan Drackert and four guests observed something strange one evening. Joan dismissed it as a school of fish or a flight of birds above the still lake. Another resident at Sutcliffe shrugged off the phenomenon as windblown tumbleweeds. In the early 1950s Harold's Club ran one of its Nevada history ads featuring the Pyramid Lake Sea Monster, claiming that an engineer named Spence investigated the legend in 1869 and concluded that the monster was a mass of copper-colored worms. A member of the state assembly, alert to PR possibilities, introduced a bill in 1959 that prohibited the hunting, molesting, or capturing of the Pyramid Lake Sea Monster.

Gammon goes on to tell the history of the lake from Frémont to the negotiations in progress. Gammon concludes his piece by noticing that the sky above the lake, which had been clear all day, was streaked by contrails. "The artificial haze seems symbolic of the pressures on Pyramid Lake. 'Ever think there'll be a 40-pounder caught here again?'" he asks the airline employee. "'Hey give them time, they took 10,000 years to get that weight before.'" Gammon wonders if the lake has ten thousand years of life left. It is a melancholy thought, but a realistic one. Subsequent discussions of fishing in the lake have recognized the fragility of the environment, but hoped for the best outcome.

Lou Cannon, journalist and chronicler of the Reagan administration, brought the LCT restocking efforts to the attention of readers of the *Washington Post* in 1998. Accompanying the secretary of the interior, Bruce Babbitt, to Pyramid Lake, Cannon retells the history of the lake's destruction and recent efforts at recovery. Cannon concludes his report by linking the recovery of trout fishing to Reno's declining economy. With the value of the entire downtown of Reno worth less than one Las Vegas casino, "restoration of the native fishery could be significant to the Reno area." The implication in Cannon's story of decline and revival is that the lake, long ignored by most Nevadans, is vital to its future as values change and economic priorities are reordered.

This is a theme that novelist, environmentalist, and fly-fisherman David James Duncan highlights in "Lake of the Stone Mother: One Fly-Fisherman's Impressions of a Land-Locked Great Basin Drainage," an essay that appeared in 1994 in a collection sponsored by the Nature Conservancy on "the last great places." Duncan gives Pyramid Lake its place among Terry Tempest Williams's Moab Slough, Utah; Rick Bass's Texas Hill Country; Bill McKibben's Adirondacks; Carl Hiaasen's Florida Keys; Peter Matthiessen's Peconic Bay, New York; and Barbara Kingsolver's Horse Lick Creek, Kentucky. It is stellar company for author and place, but Duncan fails to convey why the lake is a great place. Perhaps he assumes his readers will know that the Nature Conservancy is involved in the restoration of the lower Truckee River, buying abandoned ranches, including Pat McCarran's, and land once occupied by the Mustang Ranch bordello that bordered the river. The ironies involved in the acquisition of these lands would make a better story than the one he tells.

Duncan dutifully begins with Frémont's arrival and his naming of the lake, which outrages Duncan because it ignores the Paiutes' own name. "Resident Paiutes had long ago named it after a little tufa-rock formation just behind Frémont's grand pyramid, a formation called Tupepeaha, which translates 'Stone Mother.' Unprepossessing though she was, the Stone Mother's legend was the Paiute people's origin myth—their three-dimensional Book of Genesis, if you will—and for centuries the tribe has told stories and sung songs that gave her real presence in their lives. It was her tears that had created the lake and its life-giving bounty (and when you taste the water, sure enough, it's salty)."

He attributes this information to Joe Ely, the tribe's former chairman, who has used the Stone Mother story in many interviews to make his point about the tribe's deep feeling for the place, but never, to my knowledge, has Ely claimed that Stone Mother made her appearance before the 1930s. Duncan's knowledge of Pyramid Lake appears to be limited to a one-day, first-time visit in April 1993, in the company of a friend, a Nature Conservancy official, and Paul Wagner, the tribe's fisheries biologist at the time. Apparently at a loss for words to describe the lake, he tries to be amusing by mimicking Frémont, dubbing it "Aluminum Stepladder Lake." Arriving at Warrior Point to fish, after his second beer, he tries "skimboarding" on cow pies along the beach. While admitting that his idea of fly-fishing is standing in a stream in Oregon, he takes the expected cheap shot at federal agencies—"Bureau of Wreck the Nation"—and misplaces the heyday of commercial trout fishing in the lake by several decades. Nor does he leave the lake any wiser than when he arrived. "Will the big cutthroats ever again climb the Truckee to Lake Tahoe and beyond?" he asks, though climbing beyond

Tahoe would require more than a leap of faith. "Will the guardians and users of this small inland sea and river one day yearn to see their trout set the same beautiful example [as the salmon of the Northwest]? I don't pretend to know."

He must have been skimboarding when Ely and Wagner explained the fundamental goals of the long fight for water for the lake and its cui-ui and how the hatcheries were just part of the plan for the partial restoration of river spawning. Duncan's essay means well, but the point it unwittingly makes is that the full importance of Pyramid Lake in the history of conquest, settlement, conservation, and management is linear, not cyclical. Time's arrow, like a projectile shot from a hunter's bow, moves forward. The lake's condition in 2044 will never be what it was in 1844.

One of the best fishing books on the lake is *Terry Barron's No Nonsense Guide to Fly Fishing Pyramid Lake: A Quick, Clear Understanding of the Nation's Top Lahontan Cutthroat Trout Fishery*. It is both a practical text and a paean to the lake and its spiritual meanings. Perhaps this is not unusual in fishing books. I am not a fisherman, but when I discovered Barron's guide, I came to understand better their passion. Barron, a Reno native, first visited the lake in 1963, returning after military service in the 1970s to begin his quest to understand the lake and to correct the bad information about it.

In his preface, Barron insists on respect for the lake. Litterers should be harshly punished and catch-and-release anglers (the only kind he respects) must know how to handle fish properly. "If you need to keep fish, abide by the slot and creel limits set by the Pyramid Lake Paiute Tribe, who own and manage the lake." (The limit in the mid-1990s was two fish per day; only one could be more than twenty-four inches, and neither could be less than sixteen inches. Taking fish between nineteen and twenty-four inches was banned in order to preserve the spawning stock.) "Improved spawning techniques," Barron writes, "and abundant snow pack notwithstanding, it is the angler's responsibility to help the fishery. To kill a large fish, in this day and age of catch and release, is largely an ego driven urge that should be discouraged. I have taken about 6 fish in over 28 years of fishing Pyramid Lake. I admit they are very tasty."

Referring to books by Ira LaRivers and Sessions Wheeler, Barron explains that historically, there were several spawning runs and that the Indians had separate names for winter and spring trout. Barron provides fascinating information on the variety of fish in the lake and the aquatic insects and crustacea they feed on. Tui chub, a carp that can grow as large as sixteen inches, make up 90 percent of an LCT's diet. Based on his knowledge, Barron recommends and illustrates more than a dozen flies to be used when fishing in Pyramid Lake.

Fishing is not the only recreational activity on the lake: the tribe has encouraged other environmentally low-impact activities such as swimming, picnicking, and photography. Beginning in 1988, they allowed the Friends of Pyramid Lake, a volunteer support group founded in 1980 by a state assemblyman, to sponsor an annual triathlon. Kayakers have also discovered the lake, and at least one guidebook, by Michael Jeneid, has been published. Jeneid combines kayaking with bird-watching and gives advice on paddling near the delta and which beaches are best for hauling out and exploring on foot. In his travels around the lake, he has seen a wide variety of hawks, falcons, and cormorants. And, of course, there are the white pelicans, whose iconic status was recognized in 1913 when President Wilson took Anaho, a large island in Pyramid Lake, away from the Paiutes and made it a wildlife refuge for pelican breeding. It was returned to the tribe in the water-rights settlement of 1990.

PELICANS

Pelicans have been sharing the bounty of fish at Pyramid Lake with humans for thousands of years, combining some characteristics of squatters and sportsmen. The first naturalist to comment on the pelicans of Pyramid Lake was a seventeen-year-old from Illinois, Robert Ridgway, who had been recommended to geologist Clarence King by Spencer Fullerton Baird, pioneering ornithologist and ichthyologist, assistant secretary of the Smithsonian, and, as noted, the person responsible for spreading nonnative fish throughout the nation. King was assembling his scientific staff for his 1867–69 survey of the fortieth parallel and, only twenty-five years old himself, had no objection to adding a teenage birdman. Ridgway fulfilled his early promise. He was a keen observer and excellent illustrator. He served as curator of ornithology at the Smithsonian for fifty years and published major monographs on birds and the first important book on the standardization of color in biology, *A Nomenclature of Color for Naturalists,* in 1886.

Ridgway was camped on the Big Bend of the Truckee (Wadsworth), July 24–August 18, 1867, with short stays near Pyramid Lake August 10–16, December 9–19, and again May 17–June 6, 1868. Thus, he was able to observe a full annual cycle of migration and breeding of the 128 species of birds he observed on the reservation. In August 1867 and again in May 1868, Ridgway visited Anaho, which he called simply "the main island," and the pyramid, which he and a companion climbed with some difficulty, finding only a great blue heron and a pair of peregrine falcons.

Pelecanus erythrorhynchus, the American white pelican, was called "Bahns" or

"Bah'nus" by the Paiutes, according to Ridgway, but other sources offer alternative names, as seen below. "These melancholy-looking birds," as Ridgway characterized them, were beautiful in flight, often flying single file from the center of the lake to their fishing grounds near the delta. "In their flight, the line preserved the utmost order and method; the leader being invariably the first to beat or extend his wings, each one of the line following in succession."

The second birdman of Anaho was a taxidermist from the Public Museum of Milwaukee, Owen J. Gromme. His article "A Sojourn Among the Wild Fowl of Pyramid Lake, Nevada" appeared in the *Year Book of the Public Museum of the City of Milwaukee, 1930* and was an account of fieldwork conducted in June and July 1927. It focused on the white pelicans of Anaho Island. That Gromme was identified as a taxidermist rather than an ornithologist does not demean his credentials as a scientist. In this period, as Melissa Milgrom shows in her enjoyable book *Still Life: Adventures in Taxidermy,* museums took enormous pride in the scientific accuracy of their natural history dioramas. Men like Carl Akeley combined the skills and knowledge of a biologist, artist, and chemist and were as widely admired in their day as recent popularizers of science such as Carl Sagan, Jared Diamond, and Elizabeth Kolbert are in ours.

Gromme was born in Fond du Lac, Wisconsin, in 1896, and died in Milwaukee in 1991, after a forty-three-year career with the Milwaukee Public Museum, one of the premier natural history museums in the United States. Gromme, who claimed he dropped out of high school but who received five honorary doctorates, was a pioneer wildlife artist. His *Birds of Wisconsin* is still considered the definitive work, and his paintings and prints sell for thousands of dollars. He was an active conservationist and an associate of Aldo Leopold, and he helped to establish the International Crane Foundation. He was, in the parlance of the day, "a good museum man," someone with a solid background in science, art, writing, photography, bookkeeping, hunting, and taxidermy.

Gromme begins his article with a general description of the lake and his arrival by train at Sutcliffe, where his party engaged the services of Sam Kay, a Paiute who operated boats and a landing there. They made their camp on the southwest side of the island, a mile from the nearest rookery so as not to disturb the nesting birds. Their first task was to clear the area of rattlesnakes, many of which were "placed in a box for future shipment." Anaho's notorious serpents were earning their own place in science. Much of the preparation for the group's study of bird life involved selecting sites for setting up motion-picture cameras and building blinds, or "hide-ups." "Of the several necessary factors to be considered when placing a blind," he writes, "the angle of the sun is probably the

Pelicans at Pyramid Lake. Photograph by Jack Oakes, Nevada Highway Department. Courtesy Special Collections, University of Nevada, Reno, Libraries.

most important. This is particularly true at Pyramid Lake, where the reflected glare on the white tufa, added to the distorting heat waves, makes photography inadvisable between the hours of ten and three." The forty photographs that illustrate Gromme's article attest to his skill as a photographer. Close-ups of the birds probe their regurgitation of food for their young. Gromme elucidates: "The inside of the mouths of all the young examined were contaminated in the roof and pouch with wriggling masses of maggot-like parasites which covered their entire membrane surface. . . . When suddenly disturbed or frightened the young in excitement will generally disgorge a vile mass of worm-infested, sinking fish."

Not a pretty sight and the odor must have been awful, but in the air, Gromme assures his readers, "the pelican is one of the most remarkable birds in the world." The roar of their wings sounded like a windstorm. "Frequently," he notes, "a flock would be flying straight as a string in single file when the lead bird would suddenly bank upward as if surmounting some invisible obstacle or air pocket and, once over the barrier, he would glide down to the former plane. Each bird in turn, upon approach to this place, would do likewise and a peculiar wave-like effect was produced. Ordinarily birds returning from the fishing grounds were flying low over the water and, as seen from the heights above silhouetted against the cobalt blue waters of the lake, resembled a white string." Earlier, he notes that the birds "indulged in these extraordinary aerial maneuvers apparently for the sheer love of power in the air."

Although pelicans were his chief concern, Gromme observed California Great Blue Herons, vultures, falcons, Rock Wrens, American Mergansers, California Gulls, Farallon Cormorants, Canada Geese, Western Grebes, Western Willett, Black-necked Stilts, Killdeer, Brewer's Blackbirds, Yellow-Head blackbirds, Say's Phoebes, Arkansas Kingbirds, and Mourning Doves. (I follow his capitalizations.) He visited the cormorant nests at the "Pinnacles" ("Needles") at the north end of the lake. Gromme's bird count is far short of the 128 bird species identified by Ridgway in 1867 and a fraction of the hundreds of species found in Fred Ryser's 1985 book, *Birds of the Great Basin*, but Gromme was at the lake for only six weeks. It was enough time to give him a good sense of the pelicans' fishing techniques and hatching ceremonies, but he could have learned more from observing the interaction of birds and the Paiutes.

The white pelicans, like the Kuyuidokado, made their home at Pyramid Lake, but roamed with the seasons. The spring runs of cui-ui and other fish joined birds and humans in a common pursuit, and their fishing techniques were remarkably similar. Both pelican and Paiute fish in shallow water near the shore, forming a semicircle and driving the fish toward the beach, where they can be speared or beaked. Curiously, the pelican apparently does not figure in Paiute mythology. In Catherine Fowler and Joy Leland's invaluable article on Native biological taxonomies, "Some Northern Paiute Native Categories," many edible birds are listed—geese, ducks, sage hen, mud hen, and mountain quail—but the Numa word Fowler and Leland give for pelican, *páanos•a,* is modified in their word list by *noho,* meaning "egg." Paiutes apparently saw the bird primarily as a source of omelets. Anaho Island appears on a map of Pyramid Lake in Israel Russell's *Geological History of Lake Lahontan,* published in 1885. This is the earliest appearance of the name "Anaho" I have found. Some sources give the island's Paiute name as "Panossa nnobi," or "Pelican's House." Different ethnographers use different transcriptions of Numic, but *egg* and *house* might be the same phoneme, and the *naho* in *Anaho* might be evidence that the original Paiute name survives, slightly abbreviated. On the other hand, I heard Ralph Burns of the tribal museum say that Anaho's Paiute name is "Pasakatudu," or "Dry Sitting." Powell's 1873 glossary dubs the island in Pyramid Lake "Pa'-u-vi-ku-ti-ri." No translation is offered.

The American white pelican is impressive in size and shape. Weighing between ten and twenty pounds, and with a wingspan of eight to ten feet, its only rival in size in North America is the California condor. The number of American white pelicans declined in the mid-twentieth century because of DDT spraying. Habitat loss was also a factor. By 1980 the population in North America was estimated at one hundred thousand. An average of forty-five hundred breeding pairs nested on Anaho in the 1980s and '90s. Scoppettone and his colleagues counted 427 cui-ui lost to pelicans in 1982. The war between the pelicans on the island rookery and the spawning fish is far older than that between the Indians and the farmers. Yet few seem to take the pelican seriously.

Easily recognized by its more than foot-long beak with a flexible throat sac, the pelican understandably inspired a Tennessee newspaper editor, poet, humorist, and amateur ornithologist to write, in 1910, a ditty that almost everyone has heard, but few can quote correctly. The version I learned from my mother goes like this:

> A wondrous bird is the pelican,
> His beak can hold more than his belly can,
>> He can hold in his beak
>> Enough food for a week
> But I'm damned if I know how the hell he can!

This may not be Dixon Lanier Merritt's original version, but it is the one I remember.

BY THE 1950s the American white pelican had joined the LCT and the cui-ui on the path to extinction. DDT and other chemicals sprayed on lawns and agricultural fields eventually turned up in lakes and streams where the birds fed, causing their eggs to break before the chicks were ready to hatch. Wetlands and coastal nesting areas were destroyed by urban development. If you look again at Gus Bundy's photograph in chapter 3 of elderly Paiute men harvesting cui-ui with nearby pelicans floating watchfully for their chance to feed, you are witnessing an apocalypse, the revelation of the consequence of habitat loss for three intertwined ways of life. Recognition of their common fate was slow in coming, but as each endangered creature received the attention of judges and environmentalists, the other two benefited. The failure of the Depaolis, Garaventas, and

Ceresolas to make full payments on their claims on reservation land when they had the chance culminated in the 1940s and 1950s in the return of their "ranches" to the Pyramid Lake Paiute Tribe. The backlash against indiscriminate spraying of pesticides contributed to the recovery of the pelicans in the 1960s and 1970s, and the cui-ui was, as noted before, on the 1967 list of endangered species.

But those were just the first steps in the effort to prevent the extinctions of the Kuyuidokado, the pelican, and the cui-ui. For the tribe the favorable court decisions beginning in 1973 and the federal water-settlement act of 1990 encouraged the restoration of their Pyramid Lake habitat. For the waterfowl, habitat recovery was a matter of private and public efforts to replace lost nesting places with newly created and well-managed wetlands. For the cui-ui and the LCT, recovery required hatcheries and comprehensive plans based on years of research that will continue far into the future. Given a chance, the ecosystem of Pyramid Lake might function as it once did, as a safe haven for fish and bird and man. If it means managing the lake like an aquarium and welcoming sportsmen and an occasional gawker, so much the better; the lake is spacious, a liquid sky.

SIX

Pyramid Lake Observed

Add to the survivors, squatters, and sportsmen at Pyramid Lake the so-journers—visitors who do not remain long, but who are more than casual tourists on fishing or camping trips. Whether they are drawn back to the lake or visit only once, the sojourners preserve their impressions in words and pictures. Their purpose may be capricious or sagacious. Sojourners are often scientists, artists, or writers, or some combination of these.

It may seem odd that it took twenty-three years for the federal government to follow up on the observation of the lake by Frémont in 1844, until we remember that the federal government first had to fight a war against Mexico in order to claim the land on which the lake was located and then fight a civil war to determine, in part, how the newly acquired land would be settled. Pyramid Lake was just far enough off the overland gold rush routes and the immigrant trails to be bypassed in the 1850s. But the Comstock silver mining rush of 1859 hastened the end of the lake's privacy. Pyramid Lake was espied, beheld, and scrutinized, observation's menacing synonyms. The result was usually useful knowledge, sometimes even deep understanding. It took a century, but the lake became a place in the American consciousness. The process began with a photograph.

TIMOTHY O'SULLIVAN

In 1867, twenty-three years after Frémont's arrival at the lake, the flamboyant twenty-five-year-old geologist Clarence King began a survey of the fortieth parallel. Whether King knew that Frémont's pyramid is just over a mile south of that line of latitude is unknown, but the pyramid came to be a kind of benchmark, a point from which both physical and psychological landscapes could be mapped. What King, whom Henry Adams considered his best friend, would have thought about the pyramid if he had seen it can be only speculation, but a passage in his 1872 book, *Mountaineering in the Sierra Nevada*, provides a clue. Standing on the eastern slope of Mount Whitney, above Owens Lake, King praised the sublime snow-covered peaks behind him, but:

Upon the other hand, reaching out to horizons faint and remote, lay plains clouded with the ashen hues of death; stark, wind-swept floors of white, and hill-ranges, rigidly formal, monotonously low, all lying under an unfeeling brilliance of light, which for all its strange, unclouded clearness, has yet a vague half-dark-ness, a suggestion of black and shade more truly pathetic than fading twilight. No greenness soothes, no shadow cools the glare. Owen's [sic] Lake, an oval of acrid water, lies dense blue upon the brown sage-plain, looking like a plate of hot metal. Traced in ancient beach-lines, here and there upon hill and plain, relics of ancient lakeshore outline the memory of a cooler past,—a period of life and verdure when the stony chains were green islands among basins of wide, watery expanse. . . . [L]ooking from this summit with all desire to see everything, the one overmastering feeling is desolation, desolation!

Desolation? Maybe King glimpsed the future. The environmental similarities between Owens Lake, "a plate of hot metal" to King, and Pyramid Lake, "a sea of molten silver" to an anonymous reporter in 1860, are striking. Within sixty years, Owens was dust and Pyramid Lake was sinking. King may have confused topo-graphic elevation with mental loftiness, but for him altitude mattered; water did not. To secure his place in history, King was compelled to climb the peaks that Frémont had hurried past. The fortieth parallel survey had been conceived by King as a civilian enterprise on the scale of the Lewis and Clark expedition, but it was financed by the secretary of war. Clearly, the work King planned—a topo-graphical, geological, biological, and ornithological survey of the Great Basin from the Sierra Nevada to the Wasatch in Utah—benefited both military and civilian interests. In July 1867 King set up a base camp at Glendale, southeast of what would become Reno. Directing members of his party to survey in all directions, he moved down the Truckee, camping near Wadsworth and sending a geologist, an ornithologist, and the photographer Timothy O'Sullivan on to Pyramid Lake, where O'Sullivan took photographs of some of the Paiutes living there (see the first figure in chapter 1) and of the lake, including the pyramid.

Timothy O'Sullivan was in his late twenties. A New Yorker, he had gone to work for photographer Mathew Brady as a teenager. He served briefly with the Union army, photographically copying maps, but it was as a civilian working with Brady and, later, with photographer Alexander Gardner that he made his memorable photographs of many of the most famous battle sites of the war and was present at Lee's surrender. He was part of several western surveys, begin-ning with King in 1867 and ending with Wheeler in 1874, but his personal life was tinged with tragedy. He settled in Washington, DC, but struggled to make a living. His only child was stillborn, and he and his wife contracted tuberculosis. She died in 1881, he a year later.

O'Sullivan's crisp albumen prints, roughly nine by twelve inches, remain the standard against which all subsequent photographs of the pyramid and the lake must be judged. Rising above the surface of the lake several hundred yards from the shore, it is, in O'Sullivan's composition, the head of a parade of monoliths following the pyramid into the lake. His perspective both enhances and diminishes the pyramid, a paradox that later photographers either deliberately avoided or lost as the lake receded until, in 1967, the pyramid ceased for a few years to be an island.

O'Sullivan's photographs of the pyramid complicate Frémont's impression. No longer a towering symbol of a new political empire, the pyramid, in O'Sullivan's composition, is a specimen of geologic history. Both concepts— metaphorical monument and Pleistocene benchmark—of the pyramid are heroic, but O'Sullivan's is a shrine to geologic science, to the evolution of the earth, shaped by volcanoes, earthquakes, glaciers, water, and wind.

Several of O'Sullivan's photographs from the fortieth parallel survey were

Pyramid and tufa domes, Pyramid Lake, Nevada. Photograph by Timothy O'Sullivan, 1867. Courtesy Library of Congress, LC-USZ62-22284.

reproduced as engravings in an article attributed to John Sampson (possibly O'Sullivan's pseudonym) in *Harper's New Monthly Magazine* in September 1869. The article, "Photographs from the High Rockies," describes the travels of King's crew as they journey from California to Utah, so their brief visit to Pyramid Lake is told in a little more than one page, but illustrated by three engravings. The first illustration is of the *Nettie,* a two-masted twenty-five-foot boat that the men borrowed from Indian agent Parker and navigated downstream to the lake. Sailing on, they finally arrived at the "principal pyramid," where the writer notes: "In color the pyramidal mounds vary with the varying light. At some moments they convey the impression of a rich, warm, brown tint; at others the hue is a cool gray that more nearly resembles the color which a close examination will prove to be the true one."

The accompanying illustration reproduces O'Sullivan's photograph but turns the flat, calm water of the lake in the photograph into churning whitecaps breaking on the pyramid and adjacent rocks. The moods of the lake in the two representations could hardly be more different. Timeless serenity versus volatile turbulence, this was, and remains, the visual experience of the lake. The third engraving shows a member of the survey crew seated in a large field of watermelon-size pieces of white tufa, inspiring the writer to note that tufa "greatly resembles a vegetable growth of great size." O'Sullivan's Pyramid Lake photographs are enigmatic. What was the lake communicating to the young New Yorker with his memories of war and massacre? The photographs of the boat, the pyramid and giant rocks, and the illusory plants tell of a voyage of discovery from the sublime to the xenogenetic, life-forms of alien origin.

DAN DE QUILLE (WILLIAM WRIGHT)

William Wright, a native of Ohio, was one of the thousands of young men who flocked to California in search of gold in the 1850s. Failing to strike it rich there or in the silver mines of Nevada, the thirty-year-old aspiring writer was hired by the editor of the *Territorial Enterprise,* Virginia City's notorious newspaper. In 1863 he was joined by Samuel Clemens. They soon became friends and roommates and encouraged each other in the development of a distinctive humor that punctured social conventions, mocked pretense, and often depended on lurid exaggerations. Both men adopted the pen names by which they are known today while working at the *Enterprise.* Clemens left after a year; Wright remained with the paper until it ceased publication in 1893 and stayed in Virginia City until shortly before his death in 1898.

Reporters began writing about Pyramid Lake as a place of beauty and possible mineral riches in the 1850s. A reporter for the *San Francisco Daily Evening Bulletin* riding with the troops in June 1860 combined these interests in his description of the lake as "a sea of molten silver." A short item in the same paper just two months later recounts the adventures of a man from Marysville, California, and thirty companions who spent several weeks prospecting in the hills near the lake. A few of them braved "the fury of a mimic ocean" by paddling canoes to Anaho in a thunderstorm. Implicitly confirming Sarah Winnemucca's charges against the Indian agents, the reporter comments that "the Indians might remain there unmolested, if troops were on the spot, and an agent possessed of intelligence and humanity."

Eight years later, agent H. G. Parker possessed a yacht, if not intelligence. In an unsigned item possibly written by De Quille, the *Territorial Enterprise* reported that the agent was having a twenty-five-foot vessel built in Carson City for pleasure sailing on Pyramid Lake. On June 26, 1868, the *Enterprise* elaborated on the possibilities of using the agent's "fairy yacht" to explore "a beautiful place of summer resort." The writer predicted that "it will become very popular with excursion parties as soon as it can be reached by rail and its attractions become known." He recommends visiting the Indians' farms and workshops and going fishing, provided the tourists "do not encroach upon the rights of the Indians, which, we understand, are very jealously guarded by the sub-agent."

A long piece in the *Daily Evening Bulletin,* July 31, 1878 (an abbreviated version appeared in the *New York Times,* August 14), extolled the "weird, but picturesque" grandeur of the lake. "Pyramid Lake is 40 miles long and 15 miles wide and of immense, but unknown depth," writes the reporter. In a fascinating reshaping of Frémont's pyramid, the author says, "It rises from the water as light and graceful as a summer-house and of a shape frequently used in that style of building—or like an elongated Prussian helmet. The spike very perfect." A sentence like this should send you immediately to a photograph of the pyramid and then to a book on shingle-style summer homes. Our scribe was something of an architectural visionary, since the great pyramid-shaped summer houses designed by the architectural firm of McKim, Mead, and White did not appear until the 1880s. He may have been thinking of those colossal piles of stone that H. H. Richardson called Romanesque.

The travel writer moves on to describe Goat Island, which he also labels "Rattlesnake Island," "Anaho" not being in common use until the 1890s. The snakes, he learns from an old-timer camped on the island, were brought over in 1872 when he and some friends rowed to the island with two kegs of whiskey and a pound of crackers to live on for a week. The next topic in this Cook's Tour of the lake is a discussion of its origins. Again, the reporter has followed the geological reports and knows that Pyramid Lake was once part of a vast inland sea, but lacking climatological records he is left wondering where the other lakes went. He notes that both Pyramid and Winnemucca Lakes (he does not call it Mud Lake) are evaporating faster than the Truckee can replenish them, because of water diversions for agriculture. This observation was made almost thirty years before the construction of Derby Dam.

Commercial fishing on both lakes draws his attention and the comment that "a few white-sailed fishing boats floated lazily, looking as if they had strayed off with a fragment of the Bay of Naples." Warming up to his subject, he plagiarizes a line from Mark Twain's description of Lake Tahoe: "Over a white sandy bottom, we seemed to be suspended in mid air. The color is a beautiful blue." In conclusion he muses: "I cannot but wonder that Tahoe, which has nothing but what may be seen in hundreds of places on any handsome lake, must be visited by every tourist who completes his list, while Pyramid Lake, which is unique and unapproachable—unlike anything in any country in half a dozen respects—should lie neglected and unknown without a house on its banks where a traveler could rest his bones or stay his hunger."

These excerpts set the scene for Dan De Quille, who must have visited Pyramid Lake many times in his more than thirty years of residence in Virginia City. In chapter 9 I will discuss his beautiful story "Pahnenit: Prince of the Land of Lakes," a fantasy based on Paiute mythology. The Indians fascinated and bemused him. In his 1877 history of the Comstock, *The Big Bonanza*, he devotes more than thirty pages to what he calls "the Red Proprietors" in recognition of their former occupancy of the land on which the Comstock mines are located. He comments favorably on Captain Truckee and Chief Winnemucca. He retells some Paiute folktales, and then, in a reversal all too characteristic of those sympathetic to the plight of the "red men," he attempts a series of humorous sketches that show the Paiutes to be degraded, gullible, and misguided.

In De Quille's May 16, 1886, article in the *New York Sun*, titled "Strange Lakes in Nevada," he steps away from his comic persona and becomes the cicerone of Coo-yu-ee-pah. After introducing the lake by location and size, De Quille ventures comparisons between the lakes of the Great Basin and those of Asia. He rattles off the names of what are several Mongolian and central Asian lakes—Kosso-gal, Suyomac Kolynan, Karagai, Kerril-bach-Noor—a tribute to the influence of nineteenth-century geological expeditions on American frontier journalists with inquiring minds. He is certainly correct in pointing out the similarities between the Great Basin and the Taklamakan Desert of western

China. Lop Nuur, a seasonally dry lake at the eastern edge of that desert, is Winnemucca Lake on a grander scale. Lakes in other parts of central Asia are also on arid high plateaus, surrounded by treeless mountains, and lack outlets. De Quille's point is to demystify the setting by citing the topographic similarities of various parts of the earth, but he ends up exoticising the place and its inhabitants. Focusing on the Needles, the tufa spires at the north end of Pyramid Lake, De Quille exclaims: "At a distance they look like monster mushrooms or eggs standing on stems—eggs such as might have been produced by the roe, that bird of ancient times, one wing of which, according to Ibu-El-Wardee [sic], was 10,000 fathoms long."

Ibn al-Wardi was a fourteenth-century Arab who wrote a history of the world, including things strange. De Quille's reference to al-Wardi and the roe bird shows that interest in the Islamic world was growing in late-nineteenth-century America as biblical scholars uncovered the roots of Christianity in the mythologies of the ancient Middle East. Since the lake and its environs have always drawn comparisons to the geography of Judea, it is not surprising to find De Quille explaining that Pyramid Lake is larger than the Dead Sea and "much larger than the Sea of Galilee," a fact that did not bother director George Stevens when he filmed *The Greatest Story Ever Told* at Pyramid Lake almost eighty years later.

De Quille's paragraph on Frémont's pyramid is very similar to the anonymous *Daily Evening Bulletin* reporter in 1878, suggesting that De Quille was either the author of that piece or indulging in the old journalistic practice of plagiarism. Moving on to an unnamed island populated by goats and rattlesnakes, De Quille calls it "a Juan Fernandez without Crusoe," implying that the hermit of 1878 had departed.

Correcting earlier accounts that indicated that the Paiutes were unable to reach the island, De Quille says they "fearlessly navigate" the lake on tule rafts and gives a detailed description of their construction. "They are so buoyant," he writes, "that it is impossible to sink them; indeed, a California man has a patent for a life raft made of tules." De Quille next describes Indian methods of spearing and netting fish and driving ducks. His description of Mud/Winnemucca Lake is similar to the one given in 1878, but more sanguine about its future. He then describes the fish of Pyramid Lake—"ordinary trout, salmon trout, silver trout, chubs, and suckers"—and a fish unknown to the rest of the world, called by the Paiutes "coo-ee-wan." De Quille is repulsed by the cui-ui, although he finds it tastes like sturgeon.

De Quille next describes a cane, the one used to make arrow shafts and from which the women gathered sweet juice. He thinks that this might be cultivated commercially. In conclusion De Quille relates the Paiute stories about mastodons with whom the Indians were at war. "To this day," he writes, "when there is a heavy storm, and big black waves are seen rising and sinking out toward the centre of the lake, the Paiutes say it is the backs of the great beasts that were driven into the lake in olden time." This part of De Quille's article was picked up and reprinted in the *Galveston Daily News* in Texas in June 1886.

The lake was beginning to attract national notice. A trickle of tourists might turn into a stream. Two years later the *Atchison (KS) Daily Champion* picked up a story from the *Territorial Enterprise* of a visit to Pyramid Lake by "Miss Julia Hyde" of Atchison. Hyde was no slouch in matching De Quille's enthusiasm for the lake's beauty.

> I think I have never in my life seen a more glorious sunset than that I witnessed here on the evening of my arrival. The western sky was a mass of purple, vermillion and gold, resembling painted and gilded towers. From the deep blue of the lake rose the sun tipped pyramids of the lower world, as though towering to meet those of the more ethereal realms above, while between all the air seemed filled with a quivering golden haze. All in this wild and treeless region seemed a dazzling picture done in vermilion, blue and gold.

Hyde's fondness for vermilion, a pigment often made from cinnabar, a common mineral in Nevada, aside, her discovery of the sublime in a Pyramid Lake sunset speaks volumes about late-nineteenth-century American aesthetics. For her and other Americans, the frontier was a meteorological experience. Like geology, atmospherics linked the scientific and the divine.

ISRAEL COOK RUSSELL AND HAROLD W. FAIRBANKS

Much of what we know about Pyramid Lake's progenitor, Lake Lahontan, comes from the prodigious efforts of Israel Russell to survey, map, and explain the geologic origins of the Great Basin and its lakes. Russell was born in upstate New York in 1852 and obtained bachelor of science and civil engineering degrees from the University of the City of New York (now New York University) in 1872. He did postgraduate work in the School of Mines at Columbia University, where he taught geology. In 1880 he became a member of the US Geological Survey (USGS) and spent the better part of 1881 and 1882 in Nevada. He sojourned at Pyramid Lake in August and September 1882.

Russell published the results of his fieldwork first in 1883 in a short report titled *Sketch of the Geological History of Lake Lahontan, a Quaternary Lake of Northwestern Nevada,* and two years later in a USGS monograph, *Geological History of Lake Lahontan, a Quaternary Lake of Northwestern Nevada.* Although Russell's work for the USGS was clearly part of the federal government's subsidy of mining interests, and his report focused on the potential wealth of the "Great American Desert," he retained a jot of transcendental ideas advocated by Ralph Waldo Emerson and Henry David Thoreau. Although I doubt that he was a precursor of the modern environmental movement, as Patrick Sylvester claims in his thesis on Russell, he had a kind of Ruskinian aesthetic sensibility. In his introduction Russell provides a glimpse of the Great Basin:

> The bare mountains reveal their structures almost at a glance, and show distinctly the many varying tints of their naked rocks. Their richness of color is sometimes marvelous, especially when they are composed of the purple trachytes, the deep-colored rhyolites, and the many-hued volcanic tuffs so common in western Nevada. Not unfrequently a range of volcanic mountains will exhibit as many brilliant tints as are assumed by the New England hills in autumn. On the desert valleys the scenery is monotonous in the extreme, yet has a desolate grandeur of its own, and at times, especially at sunrise and at sunset, great richness of color. At mid-day in summer the heat becomes intense, and the mirage gives strange delusive shapes to the landscape, and offers false promises of water and shade where the experienced traveler knows there is nothing but glaring plain. When the sun is high in the cloudless heavens and one is far out on the desert at a distance from rocks and trees, there is a lack of shadow and an absence of relief in the landscape that makes the distance deceptive—the mountains appearing near at hand instead of leagues away—and cause one to fancy that there is no single source of light, but that the distant ranges and the desert surfaces are self-luminous. The glare of the noonday sun conceals rather than reveals grandeur of this rugged land, but in the early morning and near sunset the slanting light brings out mountain range after mountain range in bold relief, and reveals a world of sublimity. As the sun sinks behind the western peaks and the shades of evening grow deeper and deeper on the mountains, every ravine and canyon becomes a fathomless abyss of purple haze, shrouding the bases of gorgeous towers and battlements that seem incrusted with a mosaic more brilliant and intricate than the work of the Venetian artists. As light fades and the twilight deepens, the mountains lose their detail and become sharply outlined silhouettes, drawn in the deepest and richest purple against a brilliant sky.

All right, maybe more than a glimpse. This long paragraph presents the basins and ranges of Nevada as seen through a giant kaleidoscope. The lack of shadows and relief is disorienting, the surfaces self-luminous. It is like being in the sun at the moment of creation. What could be more sublime?

Although Russell's description of Pyramid Lake is brief and factual—the lake 30 miles long, 10 miles wide at the north end, and 361 feet deep, and the pyramid is 289 feet, "as determined by sights with an engineer's level"—his choice of illustrations (if they were his choice) reveals a knowledge of the aesthetics of mid-nineteenth-century photography. The most striking illustration is an engraving of Frémont's pyramid as seen through a circle or iris diaphragm of an eye. The pyramid is centered like a triangular pupil with a small boat floating in the water at its base like a mote. Behind the pyramid the setting sun's rays fan out into rows of stratocumulus clouds above dark mountains. Lacking only an eye, the lake's pyramid resembles the Great Seal of the United States on the back of a dollar bill. *Novus ordo seclorum,* the new order of the ages was now geologic, evolutionary time. Another engraving is a panorama of the Needles under a cumulonimbus. A thunderstorm in the background seems to alarm two men in a rowboat in the foreground. In the text Russell comments on the beauty of the north end of the lake:

> In the northern part of the lake the water becomes wonderfully clear, and at some distance from land of a deep blue color. On looking down into the waters from the neighboring hills the color appears almost black, or black tinged with deep blue. Near shore, especially where the bottom is of white sand, the water presents a clear greenish-blue tint, as is the case on nearly all lake shores where the bottom is light colored. When thrown into breakers by strong winds it exhibits a play of colors that is only rivaled in beauty by the surf of the ocean.

The sands at the Needles are oolitic, Russell writes, meaning that they are spherical (egg-shaped) grains about the size of granulated sugar that have been rounded smooth by the action of waves. At Pyramid Lake they are probably calcium carbonate like the tufa. Russell goes on to describe the pelican rookery on Anaho, estimating that there are six to eight hundred nesting birds. He includes a photograph of a mushroom-shaped tufa on the island. Russell's attention to the changing colors begins to establish the most remarkable feature of the lake, the quintessence of Pyramid Lake, upon which almost every visitor comments.

HAROLD WELLMAN FAIRBANKS was a New Yorker who worked his way west in the late nineteenth century, graduating from the University of Michigan with a bachelor of science degree in 1890 and earning a PhD from the University of California in 1896. He became one of California's leading geographers and educators, publishing geography textbooks for elementary and secondary students and general works on conservation and the geology and geography of California, the West, South America, and Europe. He was active in the nature study movement of the period, which emphasized field trips as well as classroom instruction. I do not know exactly when or for how long he sojourned at Pyramid Lake, but his brief article in the March 1901 issue of the influential journal *Popular Science Monthly* indicates that he spent at least several days studying its geology on both sides of the lake and at the north end.

The article is illustrated with eight excellent photographs of the pyramid, the terraces of Lake Lahontan, and several tufa formations, including the Mushroom Rocks on Anaho and the Needles on the north shore. Fairbanks goes into considerable detail on the formation and appearance of the tufa formations. He knows that tufa deposits are formed only underwater and are revealed as the level of the lake declines.

> Some of the forms are merely encrusting, and apparently structureless. Others show beautiful dendritic and interlacing figures, lapping over each other like the successive branches of some organic growth. The great deposits in Pyramid Lake have been built up in the form of towers, domes and pinnacles. . . . This group of tufa domes and crags [at the north end of the lake] is by far the most interesting of any about the lake. Exceedingly picturesque in the effect as one rows among them, gliding over the quiet waters, from whose clear depths rise these fantastic forms. Some are low and rounded, their mammillary or botryoidal surfaces made up of an aggregation of domes.

Fairbanks was probably just employing the flowery prose of magazine journalism, but the images he evokes of breast-shaped domes and globular tufa resembling bunches of grapes contribute to both the sensual and the sensuous appeal of the lake, a scene of houris and flowing wine at an oasis in the Arabian Desert. The geographer enjoys a bath in the hot springs, but becomes melancholy as he muses, "Rising and falling with the different seasons, the lake seems to have slight hold on life."

Pyramid Lake, for all its resilience, evokes, in many writers, a tragic sense of life, in the sense the phrase was used by Spanish philosopher Miguel de Unamuno. From Fairbanks's perspective as a geographer, the lake was the dying remnant of a vanished lacustrine ecosystem. Lahontan was always volatile, growing and shrinking with climate changes over hundreds of thousands of years, reaching its last maximum extent about 12,500 years ago at the end of the last ice age. As the climate warmed, the dozens of watersheds became separate lakes, then dry lakebeds, until a century ago only Winnemucca, Walker, and Pyramid Lakes remained, and Winnemucca was already doomed. Russell understood the atmospheric and geologic forces at work, but he had no answer as to why such a beautiful place as Pyramid Lake would ultimately die. That was irrational. The Great Basin and its fragile lakes exemplify Unamuno's paradox: "Everything vital is anti-rational . . . and everything rational is anti-vital." A life-giving lake in the desert seems to defy explanation; the rules of science destroy its enigmatic allure.

GILBERT NATCHES

Gilbert Natches, Sarah Winnemucca's nephew, was born near Lovelock in the 1880s and lived most of his life at Pyramid Lake. According to the brief biography by Pete Bandurraga in the *Nevada Historical Society Quarterly,* Natches suffered a crippling fall from a horse or a train as a child and as a consequence spent many hours with his mother and grandmother learning about Paiute life before the white invasion. This made him a valuable informant for anthropologists, including Omer Stewart and A. L. Kroeber. Kroeber arranged an exhibition of Natches's paintings at the University of California in October 1914. Natches continued to paint until his death in 1942, but Bandurraga could find only four examples of Natches's art, some small drawings the artist had given his friend John T. Reid, which are now located in the Nevada Historical Society.

My only contributions to solving the mysteries surrounding Natches's life are a discovery of three articles in the *Reno Evening Gazette* that mention him and a 1922 report by the "farmer in charge" at the Pyramid Lake Reservation. The most important is a story on May 9, 1907, of two accidents on the Nevada-California-Oregon (Fernley & Lassen) Railroad. Under a subheadline reading "Yesterday a Day of Misfortune on N-C-O Road—Indian Run Down and Injured," the paper explains that after the wreck of a southbound passenger train was cleared up, another train coming into Reno struck and nearly killed "Gilbert Natchez [sic], an Indian." "He was found lying on the track near the Evans' field about 12 o'clock last night," the story continues, "with one leg terribly mangled. He was taken to the county hospital and although he was very weak and exhausted from loss of blood, it is stated that he will recover." Since he was in his early twenties at this time, it was not a childhood accident that left him lame. Natches appears next, July 19, 1915, on page 1 in an article about drunk and disorderly prisoners being released or put to work on a chain gang. Natches was released after pleading guilty. His name appears a third time in 1932 on a list of fifty-seven registered voters in the Nixon precinct.

In 1922 the BIA farm agent mentioned in the first chapter described Natche [*sic*] as "a Cripple, single, has a ranch next to [Joe] Morgan. Most of the place is in Alfalfa, 14 acres. He also has about an acre of wheat and barley and ¾ acre of truck and orchard. Trees have some cherries on this year but he says they have never given a good crop owing to frost. He has 4 horses, and lives in 2 room house. Walks with a crutch but does most of his own work. About 35 years old." Fourteen acres of alfalfa and a few cherry trees soon reduced him to penury. By the 1930s, Bandurraga tells us, he was making appeals to the BIA and Senator McCarran for increases in his welfare payments.

None of the five Natches paintings I have seen suggests a tragic life. For an apparently self-taught artist, his skill is remarkable. In the black-and-white reproduction in the *Quarterly,* he presents a panorama of the lake from the Truckee delta. Anaho rises darker than the surrounding lake and sky in the middle of the scene, the foreground dominated by tule and willows cut and bundled. Several reed dwellings are also present. The upper half of the painting is sky filled with fluffy cumulus. The scene may depict a temporary fishing or hunting camp. As Bandurraga observes, "The over-all effect is pleasant and peaceful, putting the viewer into the land, but not too close to the major features."

Pyramid Lake. Painting by Gilbert Natches, ca. 1915, ca. 8″ × 10″. Courtesy Nevada Historical Society.

Another painting is of Pyramid Lake from the eastern shore, the lake light blue, the sky a featureless blue-gray. The perspective seems skewed. Anaho, visible to the left of the pyramid, seems too small compared to the tufa formation, especially since it is shown in its full length. Given Gilbert Natches's importance as one of the first artists to represent the lake, as well as being a member of one of the Kuyuidokado's distinguished families, we need a better inventory of his work and more thorough analysis of his techniques by an art historian. My thoughts on this painting are that Natches depicts the lake as it might have been before Frémont. The overturned basket, "wono," is farther from the shore than either the 1845 engraving that was part of Frémont's report or O'Sullivan's 1867 photograph. Moreover, by eliminating the tufa formations near the pyramid that show in other photographs and paintings and by juxtaposing wono and Anaho, Natches isolates the landmarks that are prominent in some of the Kuyuidokado legends. The pyramid and the island are presented not as part of the landscape, but as portraits of the living spirit world inhabited by the Numa. Stone Mother appeared only in the last years of Natches's difficult life, and it is unlikely he ever painted her. A loss for us all.

WALTER VAN TILBURG CLARK

Walter Van Tilburg Clark, who grew up in Reno in the 1920s when his father was president of the University of Nevada, reflected, in his novels, as Fairbanks had in his description of a dying Lake Lahontan, Unamuno's tragic sense of life. The Spanish philosopher's assertions that we humans are quite insignificant in the cosmos and the struggle of the artist to show that feeling triumphs over reason are clearly the themes of Clark's 1945 novel, *The City of Trembling Leaves*. In his novels and short stories he sums up the experiences and concerns of the provincial intellectual in the chaotic period of American history leading up to and following World War II.

One of Clark's earliest attempts to express his feelings about Pyramid Lake is a sonnet published in an obscure California literary magazine in 1932, when he was twenty-three years old. The poem places the lake in the contexts of divine and geological creation, setting "God's dark chaotic mind" against the sudden appearance of Pyramid Lake with its "clean sky" and "sapphire nakedness." The Creator is astonished by the beauty and order that have emerged from the forces he set in motion. Sapphires—which can be blue, purple, green, yellow, even black—are said to symbolize mental clarity and clear perception. It is a perfect symbol for the elusive but gem-like lake.

Pyramid Lake figures prominently in three sections of *The City of Trembling*

Leaves. Often described as a coming-of-age novel about a young man who aspires to become a composer and his best friend, a painter, the book is also about the meanings of place. The young protagonists, Tim Hazard and Lawrence Black, are assumed to be Clark and his good friend the painter Robert Cole Caples, who arrived in Reno from New York City in 1924 at the age of sixteen, a year older than Clark. *The City of Trembling Leaves* begins with a physical description of Reno about 1920, but within forty-five pages of an almost seven-hundred-page novel the narrator takes us to Pyramid Lake when two families go picnicking at the north end. Clark frames the afternoon's events, which include the first meeting of Tim and Lawrence, with portentous comments on the lake and its meanings to the boys and their adult lives.

He imagines what the lake was like in its "childhood," filling the water and skies with creatures from geologic periods that have nothing to do with Pleistocene Lake Lahontan. He gleefully populates the land with the mesohippus of forty million years ago and the pterodactyls from the Cretaceous, two hundred million years ago. "If this childhood seems to you somewhat confused or fabulous, so much the better. So is the life of all children, and, besides, Pyramid has long since ceased to keep even its millenniums straight." Clark's lake is a backdrop for childhood imagination, where "the white Needles shone in the sun like temples and minarets." Later, when Tim meets Lawrence, the aspiring artist is sculpting clay figures inspired by a tortoise he found crawling in the desert. The tortoise, carrying its castle wherever it goes, and visibly prehistoric in appearance, inspires the boys to perform a ceremony by placing the living creature and their replicas in the bowl of an overturned tufa dome. Clark's narrator observes: "They squatted there, washed the clay and sand from their hands, and felt that the affair of the turtles was ceremoniously completed. 'It'd be fun if we found those turtles again, some time a long time from now,' Timmy said. He felt that such a discovery would somehow circumvent the chanciness of life."

The boys spend the remainder of the day creating a walled city of sand and clay, but "the building of this Utopia" proves impossible because of the quality of the sand. Clark, like the religious seekers described in the next chapter and the developers in chapter 2, responded to the utopian potential of Pyramid Lake by walling out the chaos of the real world. Clark ends the chapter "About a Totem Tortoise and a City of Sand" with a description of the lake that mirrors Caples's many lake and desert scenes. "The mountains across the lake glowed softly," Clark writes, "their canyons and ravines, and the fluting of the escarpments toward the north, a smoky amethyst. The still water was opalesque, and brokenly reflected both the mountains and the sky."

A few chapters later, a slightly older Tim remembers "the ceremony of joy as practiced by the wild birds of Pyramid Lake." He evokes the atmospherics of an approaching thunderstorm, with the setting sun thrusting "long, low beams between" the clouds, causing the "shadows to change shape slowly, like smoke in the still air, so that in one instant a peak flamed upon the east, and then it dimmed out and after a minute was black against the sky, while a ravine below it was suddenly disclosed as by searchlights." And, he recalls, the light of the sky extended so far that it ceased to measure distance and began to measure time.

Time passes and Tim finishes school, struggles with his musical career, falls in and out of love. With one of his loves, he hikes in the Sierra Nevada to a point where he can see "an illusory sliver of Pyramid Lake." He looks back at Lake Tahoe, where the mountains "seemed very near and final on the sky," but rejects its charms. "It was the pale, burning and shadowed east that led the mind out." Lawrence moves to California to study art and returns to Reno with a wife, Helen, a wealthy easterner. Lawrence insists on a camping trip to Pyramid Lake. For a week the two men maintain a kind of monastic silence, walking the beaches by the pyramid, swimming, meditating on life and art.

Helen joins them, and it becomes clear that she is unhappy with Lawrence because of his refusal to do more commercial art and make money. One morning while Lawrence is sketching "down by the squaw rock," Tim and Helen swim to the pyramid and sit on the wide ledge at its base, feeling small and insignificant. Helen asks Tim if Lawrence would still brood over his work if she supported him. Tim's answer is that Lawrence would not act any differently. This seems to be the answer she expected, if not the one she wanted. Helen has the wit to seal the moment with a Tim and Lawrence ritual. She suggests climbing the pyramid. "So they climbed." Clark avers, "The wind was coming up, and when they stopped to rest and gaze down at the surface of the water, they could hear it playing a score of soft, hollow tones around them. On the top it struck them cool and strong, coming out of the north-west. The lake was rippling finely before it, in long curves. From that height Lawrence and his shadow were one dark point upon the beach, but when they waved and he replied, the shadow also raised an arm."

For the remainder of the novel, Tim and Lawrence continue to anguish over their respective loves and creative failures. Tim realizes a measure of peace with the completion of his symphony, *The City of Trembling Leaves,* and Lawrence with his painting, *The Promised Land,* an insider joke for those who know that Clark has Tim write a comic ballad called *The Sweet Promised Land of Nevada.*

Clark's use of the lake to explore the meaning of friendship and artistic integrity is not all Sturm und Drang. Clark's humor is subtle, but his use of a character he calls "Professor Clark" and "Master Footnote" as his omniscient narrator clearly has a comic effect. For Clark and many others, Pyramid Lake is a place for slumbering, dreaming, imagining what has been and what might be. It is also a cosmic joke on those seeking meaning. Lawrence and Tim are mere shadows on the land.

POETS

To conclude this chapter on Pyramid Lake observed, I consider three poems by three writers who tried to capture the primary meaning of the lake as each understood it. I quote each poem in full because they are not easily accessible and because I want the reader to join me in thinking about the poems, not simply my interpretations.

Katharine Norrid Mergen wrote her poem "Pyramid Lake" in the late 1940s. The state's landscape was about to become a symbol and a preview of the next war's devastation. The lake for her is beautiful, but "harsh and poignant," a place where only the strong can endure. Using Frémont, military officer, as a symbol of the invader who sees only what he wants to see, she sets the obvious appeal of the lake's colors against the invisible and terrifying power of its silence. It is what is not apparent that challenges her.

Fremont must have halted sharp
The day he topped the last dry hill
And looked upon a lake
Spread in a desert valley.

Was it a day of clouds
With waters shading jade to agate gray?
Or was there sunshine then
With the sky echoed in deeper blue?
Was the surface calm and cool as turquoise
Or were there sharp-edged waves awash?

Fremont must have seen the mountains
On the further shore reflected—
Lavender shadows offered back in purple
From the surface of the lake.
Perhaps he came at sunset

When cerise and tawdry gold
Were muted and transfigured in reflection
With mystery and magnificence.

And Fremont saw gray pyramids of stone
Raise conic tips above the lake
To make the name inevitable:
"Pyramids," he murmured, "Lake of Pyramids,"

Yet there is more than this.
The agelessness of Egypt hovers there
In bare, dun soil and ochre-tinted rock
Without the grace of plant or tree
To cushion man against the earth.
There silence, like a voice
Still as conscience, bugle-keen
Calls to depths primordial
Where man might face a god
Or challenge giants in the earth.

So Fremont passed along
And after him came others.
But few have stayed to know
The beauty, harsh and poignant;
Or listen for a muted challenge
Since silence only terrifies
The small, godfearing soul.

I never discussed this poem with my mother, but I know that she was pleased to be included in the Nevada Federation of Women's Clubs' 1950 anthology. She believed in the importance of women's community and professional work and in the power of poetry. The sentiment in her "Pyramid Lake" is almost a response to Clark's affirmative belief in the power of a place or an idea about a place to create harmony from the noise of history. Significantly, both poets find analogies between the lake and gemstones. Prospecting for truth and beauty, poets mine the lake. Kay Mergen poses a series of questions about what Fré-mont saw besides the pyramid, which allows her, like so many other observers, to employ a thesaurus of colors, but it is the silence of the place, not the "sap-phire nakedness," that gives her the strength to "face a god / Or challenge giants in the earth."

At the time she wrote this poem, my mother had recently converted to Roman Catholicism after being raised by an agnostic father and a Methodist mother. She was attracted to the church by its intellectuals, Thomas Merton in particular. To the extent that this poem reflects her spiritual quest, it is obvious that she does not expect any easy or immediate answers to life's big questions, from the lake or from an artist's depiction of it. The lake is water and sky, "without the grace of plant or tree," a minimalist creation inviting rediscovery with every visit. No wonder "small, godfearing souls" are terrified. Mergen's use of "poignant" in reference to the lake does not mean sadness or regret, but means penetrating and eloquent. The lake, she is saying, invites persons to stay and listen to their "conscience," as the Kuyuidokado have for centuries.

Harold Witt came to Nevada during World War II, when he was assigned to a camp for conscientious objectors at Galena Creek. Witt's "Pyramid" was probably written in the 1950s when Basil Woon and A. J. Liebling were bringing attention to the threats to the lake. Witt sees the lake as a holy place, divinely inspired if not actually created by a deity.

> The desert cries with gulls, the dry is wet—
> in violence like this, disciples might
> toss and toss until toward their boat
> a raying savior walked through wests of light.
> Then radiance of aftermath might lap
> shores like these, pelicans resurrect
> and, where swans slide too, farfetchedly flap
> beaks, wings, webs, applauding their own éclat.
> Beside weird shapes of tufa where they slept,
> snakes might unwind and faintly castanet,
> cui-uis leap through lavenders of quiet,
> the purple pyramid turn to burning red—
>
> Marvelous loaves, and water into wine,
> infinities of fin where none had swum—
> miracles as likely as this shine
> and shadow-shattered coming of the night
> to such a lake, a place where nature seems
> —raying with changing ranges, windrow-lined—
> symbolic splendor, suspending disbelief,
> we walk the Christ-calmed mirrors of that deep.

The poet sees the lake at sunset and thinks of the story of Jesus walking on the Sea of Galilee to test the faith of his apostles. Next, the poet notices the birds, snakes, and fish at the lake. In Christian mythology pelicans symbolize Christ's sacrifice. Swans are normally associated with gracefulness and beauty, but in Witt's imagination they join the pelicans in the farfetching flap of beaks, wings, and webbed feet. The birds are immodestly applauding their own brilliant show. Rattlesnakes on Anaho provide music for this comic "swan lake" performance by shaking their castanets, and the cui-ui leap in grand jetés. Witt next thinks of the miracle of the loaves and fishes and compares the improbability of that event to the miracle of the lake with its dramatic atmospheric effects. The poet's response to the synergy of the religious and natural wonders allows him to participate in the miracle of creation.

Witt's and Kay Mergen's poems of Christian pilgrimage are complicated by Robert Hume's powerful poem "Late Spawning at Pyramid Lake." Bob Hume was one of my favorite professors during my undergraduate years at the University of Nevada. He offered gentle criticism and wise advice. His affinity with the lake was similar to Walter Clark's and Harold Fairbanks's—the "tragic sense of life"—the failure of utopian dreams amid the constant changes in life over which we have no control.

Impassioned among these rocks, land-
ward flail the redhorse suckers, dying
heedless that yesterday's stream is flowing
barely enough to trouble the sand.

Aware not of death, aware but of lust's demand
that rushes them to the topmost rocks to spill
their blood and milt in the ultimate lunacy
of assertion, senseless also that will
to live is will to die, they throb to order,
phalanxed a hundred deep for punctual murder
by the sun, beating his sword across dry land.

Fly, white gulls, snatch up this agony
of renewal, doomed but to redden the sand.
My words are salt, my heart an infinite stoning
on a bloodied door. Is there no atoning
for love, my love? Reach me your hand.

Here the Truckee River's diminished flow is "barely enough to trouble the sand" of the delta. The fish, driven by instinct to spawn upstream, are thwarted and die. The inspired use of the technical term *milt,* meaning the seminal fluid of male fish, echoes the repeated "wills" of to live and to die. I am puzzled by Hume's decision to identify the fish as a "redhorse sucker," not as cui-ui. The species are related but belong to different genera. Perhaps because Hume was an easterner, he called all suckers redhorse. The poet is only partially interested in the environmental disaster caused by water diversion. Cui-ui would fit the meter, but the name sounds too exotic, too specific to a place, when the poet's intent is to be universal. Humans, he says, are also subject to "lust's demand" and destroy themselves for what they think they love. His Darwinian answer to religion's promise of an afterlife is not without its own kind of existential salvation that comes when individuals extend the hand of love in atonement.

Poetry can be rooted in a place without being provincial. In these three poems Pyramid Lake functions as a compass rose, orienting the reader to one or more of its thirty-two points, each a unique perspective and a personal discovery. Each visitor-reader finds the thing she or he seeks, be it knowledge, beauty, salvation, courage, or forgiveness. A compass rose also points to the winds and to the stars. Regrettably, none of these poets finds a place for the Kuyuidokado in their poems. Nor was it necessary that they do so, as the Numa had their own poets.

One of the favorite Ghost Dance songs of the Paiutes, according to ethnographer James Mooney, was "Nüvä' ka Ro'räni," translated as "The snow lies there." The phrase was chanted four times, followed by "The Milky Way lies there" sung twice. Mooney, who visited western Nevada during a cold, snowy January, compared this song of "patriotic home love" to the "lyrics of singing birds and leafy trees and still waters" of people of "more favored regions." He was also aware that in Paiute mythology, "the Milky Way is the road of the dead to the spirit world." The milky water of Pyramid Lake, as Saul Bellow described it, and the Milky Way of the Paiutes invite eschatological meditation. They are both uncharted routes to places beyond our immediate consciousness.

SEVEN

Pyramid Lake, Mustangers, and *The Misfits*

The place of Pyramid Lake in reporter A. J. Liebling's 1954 *New Yorker* articles, "The Mustang Buzzers," and playwright Arthur Miller's 1957 *Esquire* short story and 1960 novel and film script, "The Misfits," is, like the lake, both transparent and opaque. Liebling is quite clear about the origins of his story about two cowboys and a pilot who round up wild horses and sell them for pet food. He met the trio at Drackert's guest ranch in 1953. Liebling's three caballeros are Hugh Marchbanks, a Jack Mormon cowboy; Bill Garaventa, a local rancher who flies a Piper Cub; and Levi Frazier, a Pyramid Lake Paiute and champion roper. (Basil Woon claimed that Marchbanks had simplified his name from Marjoribanks, a prominent English family.) Miller gives his wranglers fictional names: Gay Langland, Guido Racanelli, and Perce Howland. In his autobiography Miller identifies Langland as a cowboy named Will Bingham, but leaves the inspirations for the other two mustangers unnamed. Guido, based on his ethnicity and role as pilot, is obviously Garaventa. Perce is obviously not based on Levi Frazier. Liebling has his wife deliver some of the lines about cruelty to animals that Miller gives to the character Roslyn. In Liebling's story the roundup captures six horses—two stallions, a mare, and three yearlings; Miller's herd consists of a stallion, three mares, and a colt. Liebling and his cowboys find their paltry catch funny, for Miller and his "misfits'" five horses are pitiful and tragic. Miller's story involves numerous American myths: freedom on the western frontier, salvation through love, and the importance of work in defining self. Both stories are about the meaning of place. The deeper influences of the lake and its surroundings on Liebling and Miller, however, remain opaque. This chapter attempts to bring some clarity.

Because Miller's version of the mustangers' story is better known and more complex, I begin with him. With the first production of *Death of a Salesman* in 1949, Arthur Miller became America's leading playwright. At his death in 2005, he was one of the most eminent literary figures writing in English. In 1956 he divorced his first wife to marry Marilyn Monroe, who had emerged as "America's sex goddess," an actress whose persona was more important than her performances. Their unlikely union was both celebrated and derided in the media as a version of "Beauty and the Beast." Their marriage lasted less than five years, and by 1962 Monroe was dead.

Married to Monroe and living in England, Miller wrote a short story, "The Misfits," about three men hunting wild horses, called mustangs, to capture and sell for pet food. A version appeared in *Esquire* in October 1957, with a longer rendering published in 1967 in a collection of stories, *I Don't Need You Anymore.* According to Miller, the story was based on a chance meeting with some cowboys while Miller was residing at Pyramid Lake for six weeks in order to obtain a divorce. Thirty years later in his autobiography, *Timebends: A Life,* he recalled the mustang hunters, "whose intact sense of life's sacredness suggests a meaning for existence." Miller's own beliefs had been shaken by the House Un-American Activities Committee investigations and the nuclear threats posed by the Cold War. He was moved to write "a story about the indifference I had been feeling not only in Nevada but in the world now. We were being stunned by our powerlessness to control our lives, and Nevada was simply the perfection of our common loss." Miller's life had continued out of control as Marilyn's drug addictions worsened, and the couple separated.

In 1959 producer Frank E. Taylor interested John Huston in directing a movie version of "The Misfits." Miller seized the chance to rewrite the story as a gift to his wife, enlarging the character of Roslyn, a divorcée who accompanies the cowboys on their roundup. He worked with Huston on the shooting scripts and expanded his story into a novel. Clark Gable, rising young star Montgomery Clift, and durable character actor Eli Wallach were cast as the three mustangers. Thelma Ritter, a respected character actress, played Roslyn's middle-aged friend Isabelle. Filmed in the small town of Dayton, Nevada, in Reno, and at Pyramid Lake (the tribal council received a "donation" from the producer) during the summer of 1960, the movie was released in 1961 and received mixed reviews. Gable's death from a heart attack soon after the film's opening generated some additional attention. *The Misfits* is valued primarily by fans of Gable and Monroe because it marked their final performances. Miller and Huston were only halfway through their careers, and *The Misfits* is eclipsed by much of their other work. The movie continues to hold interest for historians of Hollywood, however. Gail Levin's documentary *Making "The Misfits"* premiered October 2, 2002, on public television, and the summer 2002 issue of *Film Quarterly* contains an article on the photographs taken by photographers from Magnum, the international photo agency, who had unlimited access to the actors and crew. The shoot seems to have been a madcap affair, with Magnum's photographers following the antics of the Hollywood stars while locals, extras, and wranglers performed their "aw-shucks" western put-on.

In *Timebends* Miller describes one of the Pyramid Lake cowboys who inspired the character Gay Langland, played by Gable. "The older of the two, Will Bingham, a rodeo roper in his early forties, had left a wife and six-year-old daughter whom he occasionally stopped to visit in a small town in the north of the state. He had a lone, self-sufficient life that he seemed to think inevitable if not ideal, but the guilt of having left his child was always with him. The sensitivity of some of these brawny Western men was somehow reassuring, something I did not recall reading about, except for hints of it in Frank Norris's forgotten masterpiece, *McTeague*."

Miller says little else about real mustangers except that he once visited a shack in the desert where he found stacks of *Playboy* and western story magazines. It surprised him that men who had lived on horseback for years looked to the movies for their models and could imagine no finer fate than to be picked up for a film role. The movie cowboy was the real one, they the imitations. The final triumph of art, at least this kind of art, was to make a man feel less real as a person than as an image.

These observations are acute and their implications potentially profound. They also tell us something about Miller, whose own sense of guilt over leaving his wife and children, and his movie-based knowledge of the West, made him particularly susceptible to similar feelings and perceptions in others. He was also disoriented by his surroundings. He found Pyramid Lake "uninhabited" and "enigmatic," and Nevada in general "easy to define, hard to grasp." "I had moved into the unknown, physically as well as spiritually, and the color of the unknown is darkness until it opens into the light." Elsewhere in *Timebends* he writes, "Nevada thus became a mirror to me, but one in which nothing was reflected but a vast sky."

Given Miller's limited encounter with the historical West and the intimidation he felt from its natural environment, it is not surprising that his story is largely interior and limited to a single day. Both versions of the short story begin on the morning of the roundup and end at dawn of the following day, with the men waiting for the five captured horses to be picked up. During those twenty-four hours the characters of the men are revealed through their talk and Miller's reflections.

Miller describes Gay Langland as forty-six, separated but not divorced from his unfaithful wife. He has two children whom he has not seen in years. He is a man who "when there is something to be done in a place he stayed there, and when there was nothing to be done he went from it." He has been living with Roslyn, a fortyish, educated divorcée from the East, who pays him to do odd jobs. He is an amiable drifter who needs the companionship of other men more than he needs the love of a woman.

Perce Howland is twenty-two years old. He has been on the rodeo circuit for six years and has known Gay for five weeks, but has become familiar enough with Roslyn that she has called him "cute" and kissed him on the back of the neck. Miller also tells us that Perce saw his father killed by a Brahma bull in a rodeo many years ago and that he does not " 'feel comfortable takin' these horses for chicken feed.' " Guido Racanelli is about fifty, his pronunciation "unaccountably eastern," a World War II veteran who "had bombed Germany." He is still brooding over the death of his wife and unborn child seven years earlier and is obsessed by thoughts of his own death in his deteriorating airplane. He and Gay have been catching wild horses for many years, using Guido's plane to chase the herds out of the mountains onto dry lakebeds, where they pursue them in a flatbed truck and lasso them with ropes tied to heavy truck tires to keep them from running away. "The whole method," Miller writes, "—the truck, the tires, the ropes, and the plane—was Guido's invention, and once again he felt the joy of having thought of it all."

Roslyn, lacking a last name, never appears in the short story. We learn about her through the thoughts of Gay and Perce. Near the end of the story when Gay tells Perce that Roslyn will drive them north in search of larger herds of mustangs, the younger cowboy is surprised, but Gay assures him that she has stopped complaining about killing wild horses because she has seen how small and miserable they are. She will "razz them about all the work they had done for a few dollars, saying that they were too dumb to figure in their labor time and other hidden expenses," and she will "feel sorry for the colt," but she knows what is in the can she feeds her dog.

Stripped to its essence, Miller's story is about men on the margins of society, but exploiting niches in the larger economy—providing sexual pleasure for wealthy women and pet food for indulgent cat and dog owners. Miller's characters perpetuate the myth of the western frontier where the strong survive, while conceding that modern technology—airplanes and trucks—makes their work possible. For Miller, both wild horses and cowboys are misfits in contemporary America, not only because the frontier is closed, but also because they are archetypes of an impossible ideal of freedom. One of the oldest American myths is that freedom is found in the struggle to bring civilization to the wilderness.

British critic Dennis Welland compares Miller's "Misfits" to Herman Melville's *Moby Dick,* William Faulkner's *Bear,* and Ernest Hemingway's *Old Man and the Sea,* in which hunters find freedom in the chase, only to lose it in the capture.

In an early draft of the script of the movie version of "The Misfits," Miller explicitly references the myth of the virgin land when his characters have a campfire discussion about the power of the land. Perce tells Gay, Roslyn, and Guido that his great-grandfather was so overwhelmed by the beauty of the California land he settled that it was a year before he could tell a lie. The trio laughs at his Mark Twainesque humor, but Perce somberly concludes that his family's ranch was like the Garden of Eden. Gay counters with the observation that it probably did not stay that way, and Perce agrees. When Roslyn wonders why, Guido, paraphrasing Psalm 51:5, declares man to be born in sin.

Guido, the man who brought the (flying) machine to the Xeriscape garden, is as hopelessly romantic as his cowboy friends, however. He shares their belief that Roslyn's love will restore meaning to his life. Roslyn's beauty is only part of her power over men. What they sense is her deeper awareness of the human condition, specifically the inherent instability of life, the necessity to change, to accept loss. All the characters are displaced persons who cannot return to their homes because those places have changed or existed only in their imaginations. Roslyn is their utopian dream, an Eve who is nowhere and everywhere. In the first draft of the script, Miller has Roslyn tell Perce that she does not belong to anybody, but in the novel her response is, "I don't know where I belong." In the context of her conversation with Perce, her remark suggests that Miller wants her to be seen as the spirit of the place, more than an object of sexual desire. The men all see Roslyn as more in touch with her surroundings than they are, though they have lived in the desert all their lives.

The myth that there is a single perfect place where each individual belongs is cleverly debunked by the designers of the movie's opening credits. The screen is filled with mismatched pieces of a jigsaw puzzle, a motif repeated on the book's title page. The illusion that there must be a missing piece that solves the puzzle may be an allusion to Orson Welles's *Citizen Kane,* another movie that explores the myth of salvation by love. Kane, disappointed in love, retreats to Xanadu, where his second wife fills her empty life by doing jigsaw puzzles. Roslyn, with the help of Guido and Gay, finds the missing pieces of her puzzle in the vastness of space. In the film Roslyn looks at the moon in the night sky and calls: "Hello. Helloooooo! Can you see us? . . . We're here!" Then, gesturing toward the heavens, she whispers, "Help!"

The following evening, camped in the desert before the roundup, Guido tells Roslyn, "That star is so far away that by the time its light hits the earth, it might not even be up there anymore," then adds didactically, "In other words, we can only see what something was, never what it is now." Roslyn expresses admiration for his knowledge, but Gay, jealous, scoffs. In the final scene of both book and movie, however, as Gay and Roslyn drive away from the roundup to their uncertain futures, Gay confidently announces that they will "just head for that big star straight on. The highway's under it; take us right home." By adding yet another American myth, that of the open and endless road, Miller suggests that home and place are relative to space and time.

It is clear from his autobiography, short story, and script that Miller, though impressed by the deserts, mountains, horizons, and sky of the western Great Basin, lacked the vocabulary to express his awe, falling back on clichés such as "moonscape" and "enigmatic" to describe the desert. Moreover, he was accustomed to working in the limited space of the theater. The spectacle captured on film reduced the impact of words and even gesture. In a telling passage in *Timebends* he writes:

> Right off, on the first day of shooting on a Reno street, I had trouble with the literalness of the camera, whose acknowledged middle name is "merely." For me the streets of Reno might be feeling, but the camera made them a thing; even commonplace things that I had known from my Nevada time nearly four years earlier took on a theatrical self-consciousness as soon as the camera turned on them. In part to avoid this, Huston decided on using black and white rather than color, but to me it was still there. The camera had its own kind of consciousness; in the lens the Garden of Eden itself would become ever so slightly too perfect.

Leaving aside the questions of whether Eden can be more perfect than Judeo-Christian mythology depicts it, and whether Huston filmed in black and white because his producer would not pay for color, Miller means that while he found personal symbols in the Nevada landscape, metaphors for loneliness, rootlessness, and longing, they did not translate well into visual images. Miller's experience of the place was that of a six-week sojourner, carried from airport to cabin to rodeo to courthouse by car, his view limited for the most part to what was visible through the windshield.

The book opens with a description of the neon sign that arches above the main street announcing, "Welcome to Reno, the Biggest Little City in the World." Then the point of view switches to the interior of an automobile:

We see through our windshield almost to the end of Main Street, a dozen blocks away. . . . [A] woman steps up to the side window of our vehicle. She is carrying a three-month-old baby on her arm, and a suitcase. . . . "Am I headed right for the courthouse, Mister?" She is thin, and her polka-dot dress is too large. . . . The few people on the sidewalks are almost all women, and women who are alone. Many of them are strolling with the preoccupied air of the dis- connected, the tourist, the divorcee who has not yet memorized the town. . . . Two young Indian men in dungarees stand on a corner watching us pass by; their faces are like the faces of the blind, which one cannot look at too long.

In the movie this perspective is abbreviated as we follow the point of view of Guido (Eli Wallach) driving his tow truck to an apartment house where Mrs. Roslyn Tabor (Marilyn Monroe) is preparing to go to the courthouse to receive her divorce. She has asked him to provide an estimate for repairs to her car, damaged in a collision. He then gives Roslyn and Isabelle, the woman who will "witness" that Roslyn has not left the state during the six weeks necessary to establish Nevada residency, a ride to the courthouse. Isabelle's left arm is in a sling, the result, she tells Guido, of too boisterously celebrating with her pre- vious boarder. That both Miller and Bellow give their elderly women charac- ters broken arms may be a coincidence, but it probably symbolizes for them the absurd and prodigal nature of the uncivilized frontier.

The movie begins and ends in the cab of a truck, and a considerable part of the film takes place in and around cars. Whether this framing device was Mil- ler's or Huston's, it works brilliantly, giving parts of this movie about the West of the 1950s a semiurban, claustrophobic atmosphere that heightens the impact of the final scenes of the roundup, which takes place in the dazzling expanse of a sunbaked alkali flat.

Much of the visual style of *The Misfits* is clearly Huston's and that of his direc- tor of photography, Russell Metty. Huston had been making movies for twenty years, most of them based on literary works and many of them notable for their sense of place. His first directorial effort was Dashiell Hammett's *Maltese Falcon* in 1941, in which the fog-shrouded streets and steep hills of San Francisco play a major role. During World War II he filmed *The Battle of San Pietro* for the army, providing Americans with a vivid sense of Italian geography. In 1948 he created a palpable Mexico in his treatment of B. Traven's novel *The Treasure of the Sierra Madre* and made a hurricane as memorable an actor as Humphrey Bogart and Lauren Bacall in his filming of Maxwell Anderson's play *Key Largo*. In 1960 his panoramas of the West Texas plains and sky in *The Unforgiven* rivaled the best of John Ford's westerns.

Huston quickly establishes the backgrounds and emotional states of Roslyn, Isabelle, Gay, and Guido in four brief scenes that depend as much on visual clues as on dialogue. After the driving scene, Huston has Roslyn accosted by her ex-husband (Kevin McCarthy) on the steps of the courthouse, where she dismisses his pleas for reconciliation: "You aren't there, Raymond. If I'm going to be alone, I want to be alone by myself." In the next scene we see Gay putting a woman (Marietta Peabody FitzGerald Tree, one of Huston's lovers, who would later become a delegate to the UN Human Rights Commission) on the train to St. Louis. She is like the Roslyn of the short stories, closer to Gay's age and rich enough to support him. The third scene is of Roslyn and Isabelle on the bridge over the Truckee River, where Isabelle tells Roslyn the folk belief that a divorcée who throws her ring into the river will never divorce again. They laugh and go into a casino bar for a drink where, in the final Reno scene, they meet Gay and Guido, and Roslyn quickly decides to rent a station wagon so they can explore the countryside and see Guido's unfinished house, which he offers to Roslyn.

Huston wasted little time in getting the characters out of the city and into the desert, where he and Miller invented scenes. In the first draft of the script, Miller wrote a page of instructions for a scene in which Roslyn is riding and reading a homemaking magazine with articles for women who live alone. She talks to her horse and some desert birds and breathes the aroma of sagebrush on a spring morning. As in all Miller's descriptions of the desert, the sky is cloudless. In the final cut of the movie, all this is reduced to a brief scene of Monroe's buttocks bouncing in the saddle. The abrupt cutting of the scene is as jarring as her riding style and suggests that Huston, who had little patience with Monroe's emotional problems, decided to have some fun with his temperamental star. In a scene in which Guido and Isabelle visit Gay and Roslyn, who have been living in Guido's unfinished desert house for a few weeks, Roslyn shows Guido a closet Gay has built, only to reveal pinup photos of herself inside the door. Prominently displayed is the famous *Playboy* centerfold of the young Marilyn Monroe.

Breaking the frame of the fictional story to draw attention to the off-screen personas of actors has always been a Hollywood publicity device, of course, and Huston's inclusion of the Monroe nude photographs never fails to elicit a knowing laugh from audiences. Miller's treatment of this scene in the book suggests his complicity. Huston, in his autobiography, *John Huston: An Open Book,* reports that Monroe constantly humiliated Miller on and off the set during the filming. One scene in the movie not in the book or any version of the script that I have seen shows Roslyn and Gay on a beach at Pyramid Lake frolicking with Gay's dog. The scene establishes their idyllic romance and allows the audience to see Monroe in a bikini. The myth of Marilyn Monroe is cleverly exploited by Huston to be the element that breaks up the male bonding of the mustangers. She is both Eve and the serpent in their Eden.

Guido's jealousy festers, and he tries to tempt Gay away from domestic life by telling him that he has spotted a small herd of wild horses in some nearby canyons. Roslyn, believing that the horses are to be sold for riding, begs to go with them, and they leave the house to attend a rodeo, where they hope to hire a second roper for the hunt. At the rodeo they encounter Perce Howland (Montgomery Clift), who agrees to the hunt if they will pay his entry fees to the rodeo, where he will ride bucking horses and Brahma bulls.

The quintet (Isabelle is included) go to a crowded bar and stand next to an old man whose grandson has a paddleball, a popular toy of the 1950s consisting of a wooden paddle and a small rubber ball attached to a foot-long strand of rubber. The geezer bets Roslyn that she cannot hit the ball ten times without a miss, and she begins what is for some the most memorable scene in the movie. For a minute and a half Roslyn paddles the ball with increasing intensity as cheering cowboys place bets. The camera shifts from Roslyn's face to her derriere, gyrating wildly to the beat of the ball on the paddle. The camera cuts to the faces of Gay, Guido, and Perce expressing various degrees of lust. The tethered ball strains to pull free as the mustangs will later strain against their ropes, but at the moment we feel only the machinelike action of the paddle striking the ball. Monroe's body + the paddleball = sex machine. As Norman Mailer puts it in *Marilyn: A Biography:* "[Monroe] is not sensual here, but sensuous, and by a meaning of the word which can go to the root—she seems to possess no clear outline on the screen. She is not so much a woman as a mood, a cloud of drifting senses in the form of Marilyn Monroe—no, never has she been more luminous."

The drape of her memorable polka-dot dress may have inspired Mailer's image. As the paddleball count nears a hundred, a cowboy tries to grab her, and Gay scuffles with several men. The bartender restores order, and, as the friends count their winnings, an elderly lady (Estelle Winwood) approaches them for a contribution to put a fence around a church graveyard. In the changing West, even the dead have their frontiers fenced in. At almost the same moment Isabelle announces that she is leaving to visit her ex-husband and his wife. The three men and Roslyn go to the rodeo arena, where Perce is thrown from both a horse and a bull and sustains a broken nose and probably a mild concussion. Roslyn is horrified by the violence of the rodeo, and after they go to a bar she cradles Perce's head in her lap. Drunk, they drive to Guido's house, where each of the men reveals the cause of his sorrows. These scenes are energized by the creative tension between Huston's interest in male bonding and Miller's in dysfunctional families.

Perce tells Roslyn about his father, killed by a deer hunter (a change from the short story), perhaps not accidentally, since his mother soon remarries and his stepfather takes over the ranch and offers Perce wages. The indignity of working for others for wages is more important in the movie than in the short story and shows Huston's influence. Men in Huston's movies are largely defined by what they do and how they do it. In two drafts of the script, Miller attempted to link this work ethic to the definition of misfit. As Gay, Guido, and Perce banter over the meaning of the word, Guido asserts that a misfit is a man who will not take a job unless it is fun. The myths of work for salvation or character building or material comfort are debunked, because work for pure fun makes a man a suspect and misfit in American society. Guido's guilt over his inability to save his wife when she miscarried their child compounded by his memories of bombing civilians during World War II have left him incapable of joy in any occupation. Gay's estrangement from his children and his refusal to let anyone influence his decisions make him unable to love selflessly. Roslyn finally realizes that the purpose of the roundup is to sell the horses for pet food, and she denounces the men as killers. Gay compares the corruption of his work to her own career as a nightclub dancer. The fun of work has been spoiled.

The final act is set on an alkali flat near Pyramid Lake, where the roundup will take place. Guido takes off in his plane to chase the mustangs onto the dry lakebed, and Gay, Roslyn, and Perce look at the scene. In the novel Miller writes:

The silence is absolute. There is no wind.
Roslyn: "It's . . . like a dream!"
   Set between mountain ranges the lake bed stretches about twenty-five miles wide and as long as the eye can see. Not a blade of grass or stone mars its absolutely flat surface, from which heat waves rise. In the distance it glistens like ice.

Miller's atmospherics are important because he wants the place to seem totally alien, an impossible combination of heat and cold. The silence is broken by the appearance of Guido's plane, driving the mustangs. When the exhausted horses stop in the lakebed, Guido lands near the truck and joins Roslyn in the cab. With Gay and Perce positioned in the back of the truck to lasso the horses, he begins a second chase of the misfit horses. Each horse is roped and tied to a heavy truck tire. To prevent the horses from choking, each one is roped again, retied, and hobbled. When Gay battles the stallion, Roslyn tries to pull him away, but he shoves her to the ground. The struggle with the horses over, a weeping Roslyn offers the men money to release the animals. Gay is insulted and reacts angrily, Perce with guilt. That night Perce frees the horses, but Gay arrives in time to catch the rope trailing from the stallion's neck. The mythical battle between man and beast ensues, ending with the stallion's recapture.

South African writer J. M. Coetzee's commentary on "why the horse-capturing sequences of *The Misfits* are so disturbing" is worth noting here. The horses, stuntmen, cameramen, and actors are all real, Coetzee observes, and the horses make no distinction between the screenplay and the life they are living. "They are or are not, depending on one's point of view, the misfits, who have never heard of the closing of the frontier but are at this moment experiencing it in the flesh in the most traumatizing way." In other words, the myth of the West is reality for those performing it and when it is replayed endlessly on the screen. It is an irony beyond any that Miller and Huston intended.

The roundup is twenty minutes of harrowing action with dozens of changes of point of view and rapid cutting between close-ups and long shots. According to James Goode, who was present throughout the shooting and whose *The Making of "The Misfits"* was published in 1986, Miller wrote twenty-eight scenes for Gay's fight with the stallion. Neither he nor Huston could decide how to end the movie, and they fought almost as violently as Gay and the horse. When they finally agreed that Gay would release the stallion and announce to the others that "it's all finished," with the further explanation that "I don't like nobody makin' up my mind for me, that's all," Miller has Gay and Roslyn drive off together into the night following a star to "find [their] way back in the dark." The ending is falsely hopeful, given Guido's astronomy lesson. The starlight leads to the past. Moreover, the movie ends as it began, in the cab of a truck. The cycle of hope and disappointment is eternal. This works well for Miller's tragedy of domestic life, but it also works for Huston's comic battles of the sexes. Roslyn believes that Gay freed the horses because he loves her, and Gay believes that he loves her because she understands his need to make up his own mind. How long will those illusions last? We can almost hear Huston laughing as they drive off into the night.

Or is that laughter coming from the office of A. J. Liebling, whose two-part article "The Mustang Buzzers" in the *New Yorker*, April 3 and 10, 1954, told essentially the same story as "The Misfits," without a search for deeper meaning? Abbott Joseph Liebling, called "Joe" by his friends, first came to Nevada in the summer of 1949 to obtain a divorce in order to marry Lucille Hille Barr Spectorsky, a former model and ex-wife of writer A. C. Spectorsky, who was later the fiction editor of *Playboy*. Liebling was well known for his powerful reporting of the North African campaign and the Normandy invasion during World War II, his penetrating critiques of the press, piquant essays on food, and philosophical articles on boxing. His style of autobiographical journalism prefigured the work of Norman Mailer, Truman Capote, Tom Wolfe, and lesser imitators.

Liebling stayed at Drackert's Pyramid Lake Guest Ranch. Miller spent some time near the lake in 1956, residing at another ranch nearby. Under the tutelage of Lucius Beebe, who had revived Mark Twain's first journalistic venue, the *Territorial Enterprise* in Virginia City, and who was at the height of his career as a popularizer of western history, Liebling fell in love with Nevada and its many characters. As his biographer Raymond Sokolov writes, "Reno was for Liebling what the abbey of Theleme had been for Rabelais, a utopia of innocent sensuality and well-meant corruption devoted to the systematic suspension of puritanical rules." In 1953 Liebling and Lucille returned to Pyramid Lake to research a story about the Paiute Indian Tribe's century-long struggle with the federal government and local ranchers for water rights to maintain Pyramid Lake for fishing. "The Lake of the Cui-ui Eaters," his four-part exposé of the chicanery of Nevada's political leaders in their efforts to deprive the Indians of their water rights, was published in January 1955. He was temporarily distracted from this story, however, by a personable cowboy named Hugh Marchbanks.

Marchbanks explained to the Lieblings that he was a mustanger, who caught wild horses in the desert near the reservation for the pet-food market. In the early 1950s most people knew from western movies and novels that feral horses called mustangs had roamed the country after escaping from Spanish settlers in the Southwest, but few knew that there were still several thousand in the western states, Canada, and Mexico; even fewer knew that these animals were still being hunted by federal range managers, ranchers, and freelance mustangers. These animals were seldom descendants of the Spanish horses, however, but of stock abandoned or lost by settlers who came west after the Civil War. Literate Americans knew from reading the popular Texas writer J. Frank Dobie that *mustang* was a gringo corruption of the Spanish word *mesteña,* one of several terms used to describe stray livestock. Dobie's stories of mustangers, some of them African Americans, supported an image of horses and men living a free, exciting, and dangerous life outside the bonds of civilization, an image proffered by the great landscape designer Frederick Law Olmsted, who, in describing his travels in Texas in 1856, wrote that "the business of entrapping [wild horses] has given rise to a class of men called 'mustangers' composed of runaway vagabonds and outlaws of all nations."

Much of the history is mundane, but vital if we are to see what opportunities Miller, Huston, and Liebling missed in telling their stories of the mustang buzzers. According to historian Anthony Amaral, as early as 1899 a man named Benson opened a cannery and tannery near Pyramid Lake, paying for the meat and hides of wild horses. The meat was processed and shipped to China, Japan, and the Philippines for human consumption. Some of it was labeled wild goat meat and shipped to Boston. Although Benson's enterprise ultimately failed, by the 1920s there were two major markets for wild horse meat: California chicken-feed processors, who continued to consume thousands of pounds each year until the 1970s, and the rapidly expanding pet-food industry, which set up processing plants in Oregon and Wyoming. Amaral also notes that the use of airplanes to chase horses out of remote canyons into corrals was proposed as early as 1912 and was common by the 1930s.

The federal government joined cattlemen and meat processors in mustang hunts because the critters destroyed vegetation in national parks and forests, as well as on rangeland. The passage of the Taylor Grazing Act in 1934, which introduced the concept of carrying capacity, limited the number of livestock permitted to feed on public land and authorized the removal of unclaimed horses. Despite the protests of animal rights advocates, the killing of mustangs was encouraged until 1959, when a federal law was passed making air and motorized roundups illegal on public land if the horses were unbranded. The wording left many obvious loopholes, but the law brought attention to the larger issues of land management and made the mustangers of Huston's movie outlaws as well as misfits.

The 1959 statute was the result of a ten-year effort by Velma Johnston and Marguerite Henry. Johnston, who lived in Reno, began her crusade for more humane treatment of wild horses in the early 1950s, but remained an object of ridicule—she was dubbed "Wild Horse Annie" by the press—until Congress held hearings on the issue. Henry, an established author of children's books, entered the fray in 1953 with *Brighty of the Grand Canyon,* a book about a wild burro whose plight was similar to that of the horses. Later she publicized Johnston's cause in *Mustang: Wild Spirit of the West.* The rescue and protection of mustangs and wild burros became a staple of children's books, and in 1975 it was made the subject of a Disney television program.

Johnston had a considerable talent for public relations, organizing letter-writing campaigns by Bambi-struck schoolchildren and founding the Society for the Protection of Mustangs and Burros. Later she helped create a more militant group called WHOA (Wild Horse Organized Assistance) that sent volunteers into the desert to report illegal roundups. Her Quixotic cause drew support from other Nevada characters, notably Lucius Beebe and Joe Conforte, who called his infamous brothel near Reno the Mustang Ranch. In 1971 Congress strengthened protection for the mustangs and burros by declaring them to be "living symbols of the historic and pioneer spirit of the West" and making it a crime punishable by a two-thousand-dollar fine, a year in prison, or both to hunt or sell them for meat. The law remains controversial and a headache for wildlife managers. In recent years the BLM has spent a large portion of its total budget placating ranchers, whose cattle are in competition with the horses for grass on public lands, by rounding up mustangs and keeping them in pens. If you cannot eat them, you have to feed them.

Liebling immediately saw the larger issues in the mustangers' story. In the first installment of his 1954 "Mustang Buzzers" article, he noted: "The increasingly passionate devotion of the American people to pet dogs has put up the price of horse meat—a Great Dane will eat several pounds of it a day—and consequently mustangs bring four cents a pound on the hoof instead of five dollars a horse, which was the standard price before the First World War, when dogs' and cats' appetites were less discriminating and the horse's hide was the only thing of value."

Moreover, Liebling's cowboys are far from Miller's guilt-ridden, moody, oedipally conflicted wranglers. Marchbanks's partners in mustanging, Garaventa and Frazier, were businessmen. "'I know it's sin and a shame for anybody who likes horses to run them mustangs,' Marchbanks tells Liebling, 'and a dude woman once said to me why didn't I get an honest job stealing cattle, but somebody's going to get that money and it might as well be me.'" Seeing an appreciative audience in Liebling and Lucille, Marchbanks grew expansive: "'I been catching up on my romancing, and I drunk enough Seagram Seven to kill a Mexican, but I come of hard stock. They had to rope my mother up in Idaho and hog-tie and blindfold her so she'd let me nurse.'" Harry Drackert of the Pyramid Lake Guest Ranch confirmed that Marchbanks came to his bar frequently to "initiate" divorcées into mustanging.

After several false starts, the Lieblings, an Italian correspondent for *Tempo* named Lamberti, and their guest ranch host, Harry Drackert, accompany the mustangers on a hunt. In Liebling's version of the roundup, Garaventa chases the horses out of the mountains with his plane toward a V-shaped corral, while Marchbanks, on horseback, cuts off the herd when it tries to turn back. Frazier was not needed. Only six horses, two stallions, three yearlings, and a mare, were captured. When they all meet at the corral, Lucille sees the older stallion and tells the mustangers, "'You ought to let him go.'" When Garaventa protests that he had risked his life and might be killed in the airplane, she replies, "'It would serve you exactly right.'" Liebling archly comments that "she is a great protector of animals, especially cats (for which she often buys horse meat), and she took a highly partisan stand." Later she urges the stallion to jump the fence and confronts Marchbanks: "'And what will happen when the horses are all gone?' my wife asked the partners. She thinks Hugh and Bill are darlings, but she wishes they would find a nicer way of making a living, like being outriders at a race track. 'Then them cats of yours will have to get used to these ten-cent cows, Ma'am,' Hugh answered, in his most courtly fashion. 'But I sort of think the wild horse will last me out.'"

Liebling presents his wife as more than casually interested in the mustangers, so we are not surprised to learn from Sokolov that a couple of years later, Lucille left Liebling and returned to one of the mustang buzzers. Liebling's tone throughout the articles is ironic. His mustangers are having fun and making good money. Garaventa tells him they have captured two hundred horses in a year and averaged thirty-two dollars per horse, a total of sixty-four hundred dollars, considerably "better than wages." Liebling and the cowboys know that they are part of an ever-changing West. As Liebling sees it, Marchbanks and Garaventa "feel ambivalent toward their work—proud because it calls for a lot of skill but defensive because there is a special human sentimentality about horses, and, as horsemen, they aren't immune to it. 'I like *good* horses,' I once heard Hugh rationalize over a can of beer. . . . 'But those wild ones are no good to nobody, suffering out in the cold and so poor they ain't none of them worth breaking.'"

Liebling, unlike Miller, devotes some attention to Pyramid Lake. While driving to the roundup in the Smoke Creek Desert north of the lake, he remarks, "The lake, at our right, was Prussian blue against the naked, snow-tipped djebels on the other shore, and the tufa islets stood up like castles and churches. Pyramid Lake was the Paiutes' Mediterranean, the center of their stone-age world, which continued into the nineteenth-century, and it is still theirs, inside the Reservation's barbed-wire fence."

His use of the Arabic word for "mountain" for the Lake Range, his transformation of the Needles into castles and churches, and his identification of Pyramid Lake with the sea that French historian Fernand Braudel described as the cradle of European civilization all point to Liebling's cosmopolitanism and his desire to be a serious chronicler of history. "The Mustang Buzzers" may be read as a prelude to his more serious political history of the Pyramid Lake Paiutes' struggles with Senator McCarran and the federal government. Some might read

Liebling's description of the lake as an example of "orientalism," a term of oppro-
brium since 1978 when literary scholar Edward Said used it to characterize virtually all Western commentary on Islamic cultures as racist. This would be wrong.
One of Liebling's favorite historians was the fourteenth-century North African
Arab Ibn Khaldûn, who tried to identify the causes of historical events. Like
Liebling, Khaldûn recognized the role of accident and chance in history. When
Liebling took up the cause of the Paiutes in "The Lake of the Cui-ui Eaters," he
developed his insight into the para-doxes that left the Paiutes in a barbed-wire
cage. Miller saw the mustangers as misfits, anachronisms in capitalist America;
Liebling saw both buckaroos and Indians as players in a power struggle as old as
human history. Both were able to use new technologies to survive. In Liebling's
story of Pyramid Lake, good fencing makes good neighborhoods.

Although Liebling's sketch of mustanging is briefer than Miller's, it contains
remarkable similarities, notably the divorcée who wants to free stallions and capture cowboys, the Italian American pilot, and the dude-ranch cowboy who does a
little mustanging on the side. These characters are variations on the gamecocks of
the wilderness described in Constance Rourke's *American Humor: A Study of the
National Character,* and Liebling depicts them as such. He appreciates the comic
performances they put on for him. Miller recasts these characters in a classical
tragedy of divine heroes destroyed by their own myths. Whether Miller borrowed
his characters and action from Liebling, which is possible since he never mentions
seeing an actual roundup, or whether he heard the same stories from the same
cowboys is less important than what he did with the material. Liebling, Miller,
and Huston all drew on characters recognizable in western American literature
from Mark Twain to Zane Grey. Miller calls the American cowboy Will Bingham,
Liebling calls him Hugh Marchbanks; both may be real, both may be composites.

We can only speculate what kind of rollicking comedy *The Misfits* might have
been if Huston had teamed with the witty Liebling instead of the dour Miller,
but Huston's light touch saves the movie from being gloomy. From the opening scene in which the character Roslyn, like the actress Marilyn, struggles to
remember her lines, to the closing, in which Gable and Monroe utter nonsense
straight out of a screwball comedy of the 1930s, Huston manages to debunk the
myths of frontier—freedom, romantic love, and salvation through work—and
celebrate them at the same time. Movies are like stars; their flickering light tells
us where we have been *and* maybe where we are going.

EIGHT

Pyramid Lake Proclaimed

After nearly a century of discovery and description by journalists, scientists, and poets, the observers of chapter 6, a new era of visual and written depiction began. The men and women I call proclaimers moved beyond initial impressions, postcards from an exotic place so to speak, to create a lake that served new purposes. Whether their proclamations were of self-discovery in the atmospherics of the lake or economic development through tourism, of a better understanding of geology and cultural survival or the pleasures of fishing and camping, these writers and artists celebrated the lake with brash claims of its uniqueness and resilience. It was time to proclaim, as Stone Mother did, that the lake was numinous. It was a place with a power to overwhelm human consciousness and inspire an appreciation for all life. No one declared that they knew the secret the lake possessed, but many felt it, none more than the painters and photographers who kept returning to the lake and its environs for a glimpse of the infinite.

ROBERT CAPLES AND THE "ATMOSPHERICS"

Pyramid Lake has attracted a few outstanding painters, but despite the dazzling palette of the lake and surrounding mountains as praised by writers, desert landscapes seem to have less visual appeal to artists and the public than seascapes, urban scenes, and mountain peaks. Lorenzo Latimer (1857–1941), a major California artist and teacher who lived in Reno and founded a school and gallery there, did some Pyramid Lake scenes, but he is best remembered for his landscapes in the Sierra Nevada with forested slopes. Minerva Lockwood Pierce (1883–1972) studied with Latimer and executed some watercolors of the lake with bright bands of light and clouds reflected on the water. The Nevada Art Museum in Reno occasionally displays her work. The interplay of lake, sky, and clouds is a repeated theme in the work of all the visual artists at the lake. The sky and clouds put the lake and surrounding mountains in motion. Pyramid is a terminal lake in two senses of the word. It is the terminus of the Truckee River whose water ceases to flow on reaching the lake. But the lake is not dead. Rather, it is a place where light, clouds, and wind are in constant movement, like passengers arriving and departing in an airport terminal. There are moments when the lake seems lifted into the sky. Paradoxically, this terminal lake is not only an end, but a beginning.

The 1940s and '50s were breezy days for Pyramid Lake art, a period of fine weather for writers such as Clark and Liebling, as we have seen, and for three Nevada artists whom I will call the "atmospherics." Hildegard Herz (1894–1979) is the oldest but remains the least known of the group. Her luminous watercolors capture the moods of the lake as well as any painter I have seen. Two of her watercolors of Pyramid Lake may be viewed on the University of Nevada's Art Collection website. One, from a point on the west side of the lake north of Sutcliffe, places the pyramid in the center. In the foreground a pile of tufa rises from the lower left of the picture to almost the top of the right side. Beyond these rocks the lake is calm and blue. The pyramid and Lake Range are pale beige, the sky grayish-blue streaked with off-white clouds. Jim McCormick concludes in his biographical entry on Herz at the *Online Nevada Encyclopedia* website that "her style of watercolor painting could best be described as traditional with in-focus treatment of objects in the foreground and soft cool washes to describe distant vistas."

The other Herz painting in the university's collection is a view of the lake from the eastern side. In this scene a tufa formation occupies about a third of the 6" × 7½" watercolor on the left (south) side. The viewer's eye travels down several hundred yards of beach to the deep blue water and beyond to the Pah Rah Range south of Mullen Pass. The predominant colors, apart from the lake, are burnt orange, tan, and yellow in the sagebrush blossoms. The sky, about a third of the watercolor, is light blue, streaked with stratocumulus clouds. The piece conveys solitude, silence, mystery, but on a human scale.

Herz was the daughter of one of Reno's most prominent families. Her father established Herz Jewelry in 1885, and she studied art at the University of Nevada under the eccentric but well-trained realist painter Katherine Lewers, graduating in 1919. As a teenager she toured Europe and studied in Dresden. She later studied with Latimer and several University of Nevada art teachers up until her death in 1979. Recent art historians have pointed out the important role women played in the development of American art in the late nineteenth and early twentieth centuries despite the patriarchy of the art world. As Kirsten Swinth observes in *Painting Professionals: Women Artists and the Development of Modern American Art, 1870–1930,* women artists had to prove to male teachers and art dealers that not only could they draw, but they were dedicated professionals. Women artists were often silenced by charges that they were immoral, odd, dabblers, or worse. In Herz's case her focus on the foreground in her Pyramid Lake pictures asserts the immediate realities of life, the daily struggle of desert plants to survive. The distant shore, the shadowed mountains, the clouded sky imply the uncertainty of the future. I am here, Herz is saying, where for a few hours I experience the aura of this space where my easel stands. That is enough.

This is what I mean by "atmospherics," which has two distinct but related meanings. In meteorology atmospherics refers to natural electrical discharges, such as lightning, that disturb radio frequencies, causing static. The other meaning is "actions taken to create a mood." In literature and in painting this takes the form of details added to enhance a mood or impression. Sunlight, moonlight, wind, clouds, and temperature control the physical appearance of the lake. The Kuyuidokado are acutely sensitive to changes in the atmosphere, as are the wisest of the sojourners who came after them.

The contrast in styles among the paintings of Pyramid Lake by Ben Cunningham, Robert Caples, and Hilda Herz is considerable, but they share a mood, an atmosphere. Cunningham (1904–75) grew up in Reno in the years 1907–25 and then moved to San Francisco, where he studied art at what is now the San Francisco Art Institute. In 1934 he was hired by the Public Works of Art Projects, a pioneering program of the New Deal. Cunningham and two dozen other artists were commissioned to paint murals in Coit Tower. Cunningham's contribution depicted outdoor recreation. He continued to work for the PWAP and did a mural on the ceiling of the Reno Post Office that was later obliterated. He moved to New York City in 1944, producing geometric abstract paintings with a limited range of colors.

His large, twenty-nine-by-fifty-six-inch oil on canvas Pyramid Lake is a view of Anaho Island and the pyramid from the western side of the lake. The foreground consists of four rounded hills with dark-green dots and a strip of white beach. The lake darkens from light blue to indigo. A white band at the bottom of the pyramid and the shore of Anaho indicates the drop in the lake's surface. The rest of the pyramid and the island are deep reddish brown. The Lake Range fades from burnt umber to cerise. The Nightingale Mountains beyond Winnemucca Lake can be glimpsed in the upper-right-hand corner of the painting. They are violet. The sky is light blue with a small nondescript cloud and a few cirrus. The atmospherics in this painting are neither present reality nor future dreams, but "eternity." The Lake Range is creased with ravines, giving the mountains the form of a reclining body, Mother Earth.

Robert Cole Caples (1908–79), Walter Clark's friend, frequent visitor to the Drackerts' guest ranch, and creator of a magnificent portfolio of portraits of Nevada Indians, arrived in Reno in 1924. Over the next thirty-five years he moved frequently, studying in California and New York City, but returning for extended periods, developing a distinctive style of landscape painting. His biographer in the *Nevada Historical Society Quarterly* issue on Nevada artists, Marcia Cohn Growdon, points out the influence of Grant Wood and Thomas Hart Benton, but omits the more obvious similarity to Georgia O'Keeffe. "In the 1950s and 1960s," Growdon states, "[Caples] created elegant, haunting land-scapes that portrayed no place in particular, but were precise distillations of the desert, mountains, and dramatic atmospheric effects experienced in the desert. Space is at once telescoped and expanded infinitely. The substance of the moun-tains and the volume of air are sucked out in favor of the essence of mountains and glowing atmospheric effects."

This is true enough of the 1941 pastel on paper *Red Mountain,* used to repre-sent Caples in the *Quarterly,* but less true in his other more abstract landscapes. Nor does this judgment apply to his 1950 watercolor and ink mixed-media piece *Pyramid Lake,* where the multihued lake occupies the bottom quarter of the scene and the lavender mountains of the eastern shore rise like waves toward a turbulent sky. Clark's biographer Jackson Benson quotes a letter from Caples recalling his first view of the lake as "an awestruck teenager." "Such unexpected beauty really hurt. It was like being struck by the sky."

In Caples's watercolor the pyramid almost vanishes between the smoky blue-gray water and the upswept charcoal and sepia peaks of the Lake Range. The mountains seem to be pushing the clouds higher in the sky. Place and time are fluid, mysterious, and even violent. Caples was, by all accounts, a troubled man. Aspiring to perfection, uncompromising in his art, but seeking fame and for-tune, he refused to make money doing portraits, preferring to find his utopia in desert landscapes.

There are two examples of these "good places" in the university's art collec-tion, viewable online. *Landscape—Black Rock Desert,* based on its style, prob-ably dates from the late 1940s. It consists of two calm, horizontal bands, a tita-nium yellow playa at the bottom and an inky blue sky at the top. The center of the mixed-media painting is of a dark reddish-brown mountain with three sharp peaks above that are gray and white cumulonimbus clouds—thunderheads in the making. These clouds provide more motion than is usual in Caples's land-scapes, an emblem of stormy future. The second piece, an untitled oil on canvas, has neither foreground nor background, just continuous, fulvous atmosphere,

Pyramid Lake. Robert Caples, mixed media, 1950, 14½" × 19½". Courtesy Nevada Museum of Art, Gift of Jerry Read.

from which sinuous dark-red mountain ridges and peaks rise like the cliffs in Chinese paintings of Huangshan. What Caples found in the desert and transferred to his desert landscapes were illusions, the deceptive appearance of things, proof that, as Walter Clark observed, Caples and his shadow were one.

In the Drackert Papers I found two pieces of Caples's ephemera. One is a two-page typescript titled "The Indian Speaks at Pyramid Lake," with faux Indian glyphs between the paragraphs. The story told is a version of a Paiute origin myth. A man and a woman meet at the lake and have two sons and two daughters. The children quarrel and fight. Coyote comes to the mother and instructs her to keep one boy and one girl and send the other siblings away. She sends them east, and they become Shoshone. The other two created the Paiutes. The final sentence reads simply: "That is why the Paiutes never harm coyote; no, not even to this day." Why Caples wrote this, and for whom, may never be known, but the second item gives us another glimpse of the importance of the lake for him. It is a five-by-seven-inch card labeled *Indian Symbol Map of Nevada*. The lake is surrounded by symbols of Caples's design—a big fish symbol, Paiute and paleface stick figures, and a stick figure on its side labeled "throw away paleface wife," "Ho Ho." Other symbols for pine nuts, clouds, the sun, and springs are surrounded by an outline of the state. At the top is a "Happy Lightning Snake," a figure that is part of Paiute weather lore. In John Wesley Powell's *Anthropology of the Numa,* Tu-gwu'-kui-zi-ba pa-at-ti-to-gwok is lightning, a red snake. Caples's cartoons and fractured folktale are the products of a mind at ease at the lake, or at least the lake he knew from Drackert's bar. It was a place he felt comfortable while the shadows lengthened and the lake's surface rippled and changed colors like a kaleidoscope.

NEVADA HIGHWAYS AND BASIL WOON

Nevada Highways and Parks, a bimonthly magazine published by the Nevada Department of Highways to encourage tourism, began in January 1936. Like its older and more famous sister publication *Arizona Highways,* it attempted, under various editors, to show the state's natural attractions and promote outdoor recreation. In its early years it avoided publicizing gambling and divorce, but by the 1970s when it was published by the Nevada Commission on Tourism and edited by the colorful C. J. Hadley, it became *Nevada: The Magazine of the Real West* and shilled for the casinos. Currently, *Nevada Magazine* has, in the words of its website, returned to "its tourism roots" and publishes beautifully illustrated articles on the history and culture of the state.

In its third issue, May 1936, *Nevada Highways and Parks* published an article on fishing that included a photo of "Castle Rock" at Pyramid Lake. A little more than two years later, the magazine published an article on recreation that featured several photos of the lake and its tufa formations. The unidentified author begins with observations that were rapidly becoming platitudes: "Unlike Tahoe, however, Pyramid's framework of lofty mountains lacks the crowded pines, but strikingly displays the vivid and varied colors native to the barren hills. Upon visiting Pyramid Lake for the first time one wonders by what rhyme or reason it should be found in such a strange place."

The article exaggerates the size of the lake, its depth, and the height and location of the pyramid, suggesting that the author may not have visited the lake himself. The article identifies "Cathedral Rock" as one of the most noted landmarks along the western shore, but this name does not appear on any maps that I have seen. It may be the same as "Monument Rock," which appears on a 1993 fishing map, or "Castle Rock." The reader is told that "numerous guest ranches have their locale along the shores of this strange body of water" and that "many Hollywood celebrities spend their weekends or vacation periods at Pyramid, which is less than 45 minutes drive from Reno over a hard-surface highway." As noted in the first chapter, a photograph of "the Squaw Woman and Her Basket," a "group of rocks near the northern end of Pyramid Lake . . . is one of many strangely formed rock projections found along the shore and on some islands in this remnant of a prehistoric lake." Strangeness, colorful landscape, and antiquity are the features of the lake that its promoters hope will sell a visit. Such a description neatly elides the Kuyuidokado, squatters, water conflicts, and controversy of any kind.

The narrative reappears in the April 1954 issue under the title "Pyramid: A Strange Desert Lake." The author is even less concerned with facts than her predecessors (I am certain the author was Jane Atwater, because an almost identical essay appeared under her name in the November issue of *Desert Magazine*), asserting that the pyramid is six hundred feet high and the depth of the lake has been sounded to fifteen hundred feet. "Access to the lake is unrestricted," the reader is told, "although the Indian Service exercises control over boating and fishing privileges." The author admits that fishing is not as good as it once was, but that it is still possible to catch a fifteen-pounder. Strangeness, not sportfishing, is again the attraction. "By all laws of nature this arid region should contain no such body of water," the author writes. "Yet there it is, intense turquoise blue, crystal clear, incredibly deep, and petulant in mood. . . . To many persons, upon viewing it for the first time, Pyramid Lake seems a mirage." One of the illustrations for this article is Adrian Atwater's often-reproduced panorama of the lake with the faces of five elderly Paiute men in full feathered war bonnets superimposed in the sky above the pyramid. Their heads still float above a different view of the lake on the Pyramid Lake Paiute Tribe's website.

Mirage and fiction. An article in a 1957 issue of *Nevada Highways and Parks* begins, "Strange . . . beautiful . . . primitive," and goes on to assert that the lake, with its "azure blue water," is little changed since "the time when giant sloths and primitive men wandered along its shorelines." The reader is also told that Frémont reported that Indians came from as far away as central Utah to fish in Pyramid Lake and that the Ghost Dance (1889–90), which inspired the last of the bloody Indian uprisings and climaxed with Custer's defeat at Little Big Horn (1876), was started at Pyramid Lake by a Paiute medicine man. The three major errors in this article—that the lake is little changed in ten thousand years, that the Ghost Dance originated at the lake, and that Custer died fourteen years before Wounded Knee—hardly matter. This article is not really concerned with history; it wants to spread the good news that, despite the lake's declining level, the Nevada Fish and Game Commission is restoring the fisheries.

During the following half century the magazine, under various titles, continued to present the lake as strange, moody, and dying. Whether focusing on pelicans, fish, or solitude, *Nevada Highways and Parks* seldom wavered from the formula it had created in the 1930s. The lake had changed dramatically; public perception had not. By 1970, however, the state was changing. When an article in the winter issue asked "Will it survive?" the editor meant the state, not the lake. Recognizing that environmental pollution and overcrowding threaten the unique beauty of the desert, the attributes that attract many visitors as well as longtime residents, the writer challenges the state's planners to consider quality of life as well as economic development.

Nevada Magazine's July–August 2011 special issue, "Indian Territory," reveals how far the state has come in its relations with its Native citizens. Articles on tribal members working to keep the Paiute language and culture alive, petroglyphs, and powwows emphasize respect for Native customs and places. Another article briefly describes eighteen of the state's reservations and colonies. And Sarah Winnemucca is remembered with a piece reprinted from an earlier issue. Although the article on Pyramid Lake still chooses to use the 1874 date for the creation of the reservation, it makes clear that the Kuyuidokado are living, modern people, not relics of some prehistoric civilization.

WHILE *NEVADA HIGHWAYS* was creating one myth about Pyramid Lake, Basil Woon was creating another. Woon, whom I introduced as the impresario of the 1953 Nevada Day Indian Pageant, was one of several droll characters who entertained northern Nevadans in the 1950s—Lucius Beebe was another—with their antics. Wilbur Shepperson, my entertaining history professor, seems to be the only scholar to take Woon seriously. In his aptly titled book *Mirage-Land: Images of Nevada,* Shepperson sets out to describe how images of Nevada were constructed by various writers from the early explorers to late-twentieth-century social scientists. Early in the book Shepperson presents Woon as one of the image makers whose own lifestyle, writings, and personal aplomb help define a widely held belief about the eccentricity of the state.

Woon was also a pioneer, arriving in Reno for the first time as a seventeen-year-old to see the 1910 Jack Johnson–Jim Jeffries boxing match. He left shortly after to cover the Mexican Revolution for United Press. He became an aviator in World War I and was shot down over France. Remaining in Paris, he was a member of the Lost Generation, and, like another well-known member of that crowd, Woon ended up in Cuba in 1927, where he was a PR man for President Gerardo Machado's government. He left before the military coup that brought in Fulgencio Batista, moving on to a career as a screenwriter for now largely forgotten movies—*While Paris Sleeps* (1932), a violent mystery story starring Victor MacLaglen, and *This Was Paris* (1942), a spy thriller with Ann Dvorak and Robert Morley. While in Hollywood Woon explored the Southwest and returned intermittently to Nevada. During World War II he worked for the BBC in London. Seeking his third divorce, he settled in Reno in the 1950s and lived there off and on until his death in 1974.

One of his first pieces in the *Nevada State Journal,* June 26, 1953, was ostensibly about Harry Drackert and the Pyramid Lake Guest Ranch, but it was also an encomium to the lake, one of many Woon would write over the next three years. Woon praises the lake's beauty and deplores its destruction by irrigation farming. He wonders why the lake is not better known to tourists and residents alike. Inevitably, he adds his choice of colors to the lake's pallet: "In winter the water can be as gray as the North Atlantic. In August it is often emerald green. Just now it alternates between deep Mediterranean blue and topaz." He assumes that his readers will have images of the Mediterranean and the North Atlantic, based on the recent war. This association in his mind of the lake and the war may have led him to garble the legend of Stone Mother, or "Weeping Rock," as he calls it. "It was Stone Mother's tears for her sons lost in war that formed Pyramid Lake," Woon writes, repeating this error a year later when he revisits the lake and a Paiute village he calls Potato Patch, halfway between Nixon and Gerlach.

These articles were the beginning of a seven-part series on the Pyramid Lake area in which Woon explores old mining roads and stage routes, often with Drackert as driver and guide. Most of the pieces are harmless concoctions of self- and tourist promotion, but the June 6, 1954, installment is a passionate defense of the lake and its inhabitants from government termination and consequent rapacious development on Indian lands. Woon has learned that there is support in Congress for the abolition of the Bureau of Indian Affairs and the transfer of responsibility for Indian welfare to the states. If this happens, Woon writes, a movement is developing to have Pyramid Lake declared a national park in order to protect it. Woon is certain that the BIA is doomed, and he has learned that geologists have determined that there is oil under the lake.

Woon was a sympathetic observer of the citizens of the Pyramid Lake Reservation. One of his last *Journal* articles, August 5, 1956, focuses on Nixon, a place long neglected by both journalists and anthropologists. Illustrated with seven photos that evoke those of Depression-era America by the Farm Security Administration photographers, Woon praises the efforts of Tom Trelease to restock the lake with game fish and admires the tribal council members who face the prospect of a dying lake with equanimity. Woon concludes: "The Paiutes have heard about the Washoe Project [a federal plan to build more reservoirs on the Truckee and divert more water from Pyramid Lake] but are philosophic. 'The white man "gave" us our own lake,' they say, 'and now the white man dry it up to make the sagebrush green somewhere else.' Then they shrug."

Woon gives the reader a sense of the place and its people—Abe and Sue, proprietors of the town's only store; Katie Frazier and the other women struggling to make a profit from the Wa-Pa-Shone craft shop; Joseph Hogben, the Buckaroo Priest—whose lives at the lake seemed doomed by the Washoe Project. Woon predicts the lake will be dead by the year 2000. He was wrong, of course, but in 1956 his pessimism was widely shared.

BUCK WHEELER AND PEG WHEAT

Sessions "Buck" Wheeler was born in 1911 on a ranch near Fernley, in the heart of the irrigation project. He grew up in Reno and received a bachelor and master's of science in biology from the University of Nevada. He worked during summers for the US Forest Service in the early years of the New Deal and came of age as a naturalist at a time when Bob Marshall and Aldo Leopold were formulating a new environmental ethic to expand the goals of the conservation movement of the Progressive Era. He taught biology at Reno High School from 1936 to 1966, except for three years (1947–50) when he served as the first director of the newly reorganized Nevada Fish and Game Commission.

Wheeler wrote two books that concern Pyramid Lake. A novel, *Paiute,* was published in 1965, and a history, *The Desert Lake: The Story of Nevada's Pyramid Lake,* in 1967. *Paiute* is the story of the Pyramid Lake war of 1860 framed by a romance between Julian Chadmore, a young New Englander who has fled west to begin a new life after his father was killed by a mob angry at the news that his father was shutting his lumber mill in order to allow his forests time to regrow, and Sarah Martin, daughter of a wealthy rancher in Washoe Valley. Julian's meeting with his old history professor from Boston College George Black, their ultimately successful attempt to strike it rich mining silver, and the developing romance between Julian and Sarah consume the first two-thirds of the book. Wheeler introduces the Indians, whom he calls Paviotso, citing anthropologists from John Wesley Powell to Omer Stewart, through conversations between Julian and the Martins. Sarah's father, Henry, is on good terms with all the local Indians. Julian learns even more after saving Numaga's life from a mob in Virginia City. In gratitude, Numaga works with Julian in the mine, teaches him Paiute, and uses him to help keep casualties to a minimum on both sides in the battles of May 12 and June 2.

Wheeler's sources for the conflict were Myron Angel's 1881 history of Nevada, government documents, and some of Dan De Quille's writings. Curiously, he does not cite Sarah Winnemucca's *Life Among the Piutes,* though his sentiments and some of the details of Paiute life mirror hers. Physically, the lake does not play a large role in the novel, since much of the action takes place in the ravines and arroyos of the Truckee River before it enters the lake. Wheeler acknowledges the importance of Pyramid Lake to the Paiutes by having a Kuyuidokado tell Julian that "when we leave the lake we will perish." This inspires Julian to travel to San Francisco to suggest creating a reservation for the Indians at the lake. Historically, of course, Julian is about a year late with the idea, but Wheeler is allowed poetic license. The Paiutes get their land, Julian gets the girl and a big ranch at Washoe Lake, and Numaga fades into the sunset. It is difficult to capture both a place and a myth about the place in a single book. Wheeler took a second shot.

The Desert Lake was written for a wider audience. It is essentially a picture book with about seventy pages of text. The first twenty pages cover prehistory based on archaeological investigations by the Nevada State Museum. Wheeler's flair for the dramatic, which must have made him a great teacher, leads to this opening sentence: "Approximately four thousand years would pass before the Egyptian King Khufu would build his great pyramid, and the teachings of Christianity were more than seven thousand years distant when man stood on a ledge above the shore of the desert lake."

Wheeler's point is that the indigenous claim to the land is indisputable and that Frémont's comparison of the tufa formation to Cheops is diminished by the antiquity of the lake and its pyramids. Using the Arabic name Khufu rather than the Greek Cheops suggests that Wheeler understood Frémont's desire to compare his discoveries with Napoleon's. By restoring its earlier name, Wheeler disassociates himself from "the Pathfinder's" Eurocentric imperialisms. Wheeler goes on to explain the evidence turned up by Donald Tuohy of the Nevada State Museum during excavations in the late 1950s and early 1960s. There were artifacts from at least three different cultural groups before the Paiutes, who, according to one hypothesis, arrived from the south about six hundred years ago.

Wheeler begins his history chapter with extensive quotations from Frémont's journals. He briefly sketches the creation of the reservation and the battles of 1860. His deft use of the report by Colonel Frederick W. Lander, who made peace with Numaga and preserved the reservation, provides a smooth transition to the tricky issue of "early settlements." Wheeler ignores the Italian American squatter problem that had recently been settled, but he mentions a few of the white ranches on the west side of the lake—the Symonds place and Sutcliffe's—not as contested by the tribe, but as part of the "settlement" history of the lake. His endpaper map conveniently cuts off the ten miles of the reservation that had been in dispute. Wheeler concludes his history lesson with a brief mention of legends about dwarf Indians living on Anaho Island, a monster in the lake, and buried gold stolen from some Chinese miners. He dismisses these stories as examples of the myths that enhance the allure of every lake in the world and then assures his readers that the Pyramid monster is of greater antiquity than the more famous one in Loch Ness.

The concluding chapters, "The Desert Lake Today" and "The Future," are largely about sportfishing and the crisis caused by lack of water. He cites two National Park Service assessments on the unique beauty of the lake and offers his own description:

> Its water has been described as constantly changing from shades of deep blue to green, and actually this does occur. Angle and intensity of the sunlight and suspended inorganic particles are factors, but plankton blooms during a certain time of the year bring the most spectacular transformations. . . . Fishing and water sports currently bring many people to Pyramid, but to those who love the desert lake it is a special place. They know its friendly beauty as the morning sun paints its mountains with pinks and reds, and they feel its strength when storm clouds sweep in from the west and waves break white against tufa domes. And at a certain time of the year [the evening of November 6, 1966], they may see something unusual.

Timeless, yet doomed. Wheeler joins Fairbanks and Woon in predicting the lake's demise. Wheeler's sadness is palpable and with good reason. Citing engineering reports from 1962, he estimates the lake will be too saline to support trout within seventy-five to one hundred years at the current rate of desiccation. Wheeler the scientist accepts the facts as they are presented and assumes that the future of the lake is sealed, but earlier in 1967, the year this book was published, when the lake sank to its lowest recorded level, the secretary of the interior took two actions that started the lake on the path to recovery. Secretary Udall issued the first operating criteria and procedures for the Newlands Reclamation Project that required the irrigators to conserve water and minimize diversions from the Truckee, and he placed the cui-ui on the first list of endangered species, the "Class of '67," as provided by the Endangered Species Preservation Act of 1966.

Wheeler's book appears at the end of a political period in which the lake and its residents were seen as victims. Margaret Wheat's *Survival Arts of the Primitive Paiutes,* published in the same year, marks the beginning of a new generation that saw future survival in the study of local environmental knowledge. As the work of Tom Trelease, David Koch, Gary Scoppettone, Chester Buchanan, Tom Strekal, and others whose efforts, with the cooperation of the Pyramid Lake Paiute Tribe, created successful fish management programs has shown, local knowledge and modern technology must work together.

IF WHEELER WAS THE ALDO LEOPOLD OF NEVADA, Peg Wheat was its Rachel Carson. I recall Peg as a force of nature. I have vivid memories of my mother and Peg at Maya and Dick Miller's place in Washoe Valley, hashing out the political and environmental issues of the 1950s. Peg grew up in Fallon, my mother in Wabuska. Their lives had gone in different directions, but they shared a love of Pyramid Lake and the deserts and mountains of the northern Great Basin. Peg was a geologist who became an ethnographer; my mother was a journalist who became an editor for the Soil Conservation Service. They blazed trails in the early stages of the current environmental movement.

Wheat's *Survival Arts* is the result of more than twenty years of research and patient listening to elderly Paiute women and men who told and showed her how their grandparents understood and made use of the resources of the rivers, lakes, and mountains of northern Nevada. Wheat's book is beautifully illustrated with black-and-white photographs of her collaborators at work making baskets, gathering seeds and nuts, and preparing traps for hunting and nets for fishing. Wheat rewrites the narrative that dominated popular and much scientific opinion for more than a century, that the Great Basin is an empty and sterile desert, its people lacking political organization and arts. Wheat corrects this impression by pointing out that there is not one "Great" Basin, but many small ones, each one a potential marsh or lake when storms came or the climate changed. "In the Great Basin the marshes and playas were intermittent affairs, always at the mercy of dry cycles and shifting dunes and channels. In a half dozen years a marsh could change into a dust bowl, or conversely, a desert flat would be transformed into a luxuriant nesting ground for migratory water birds. Seeded by the wind the margins of the marshes became tangles of cattails and tules that furnished roots for muskrats and man, grew leaves for the houses of blackbirds and man, and produced seeds for ducks and man."

These two sentences encapsulate the food-web and ecological context of the Cattail Eaters, Trout Eaters, and Cui-ui Eaters of the Carson Sink, Walker Lake, and Pyramid Lake Paiutes. To show the interrelations among the tribal bands, Wheat takes her readers through the cycle of a year: the return of ducks and geese in the spring, the spawning of cui-ui and trout in April and May, the reaping and thrashing of Indian rice grass in July and the gathering of buckberries in August, the harvesting of pine nuts in the fall and the accompanying dances and gambling, and finally the rabbit drives of November and the long period when the last of the dried fish and fowl were consumed. Alice Steve; Wuzzie George and her husband, Jim, a shaman; Edna Jones; Nina Dunn; Mable Wright; and Katie Frazier and her husband, Levi, were Wheat's principal sources of information. Wuzzie was born about 1883 and related many things she remembered her grandmother telling her about life before the coming of white men. Indians lived in tule houses for miles along the Carson Slough, but many died from diseases brought by the invaders, and some may have been deliberately poisoned by the army.

Wheat did what every ethnographer, oral historian, and friend should do: she walked and listened as the elderly Indians went about their daily routines of gathering food, making a cattail boat, twisting hemp into cordage, making arrows, tanning hides, fashioning cradle boards from willow branches, and building houses from willows, tules, and cattails. Like Woon's traipsing, Wheat's rambles provide a kinetic sense of place, the body in relation to paths, landmarks, and topography, the body passing through a landscape in time as well as space. Pyramid Lake is not prominent in the story Wheat tells, but she mentions Mable Wright's song about the "beautiful Pyramid Lake, that now was going dry because white people needed so much water elsewhere," and the reader better understands that the identities of each band in its food niche depended on the environmental health of the others.

Wheat's recordings of her friends as they gathered desert plants offer a deep understanding of Paiute attitudes toward nature. On one occasion in 1964 she was with Mable Wright Paulina and Herbert Poncho, two elderly residents of Nixon. Poncho was sixty-eight, Paulina probably older. Paulina began to sing in a mixture of English and Numic about the lake. When Wheat asks her to explain, she answers that it is hard, but it is clear that her song is a lament for a dying Pyramid Lake. The water is going down, there are fewer trout and cui-ui, people go hungry. Rocks that were underwater are now sticking out. The venerable Kuyuidokado woman feels like crying because things are out of their natural order. She then sings in English:

Peg Wheat recording Paiute women gathering sagebrush and other plants for baskets and clothing, ca. 1950s. Courtesy Special Collections, University of Nevada, Reno, Libraries.

My beautiful lake that God made for us is going down. Everything going down. My poor lake. I feel like to cry all the time. I don't eat no fish any more like use to be. What's wrong? What is happening to my lake? Where the water goes to? Which way the water goes to? White people they turn the water to their side. They use it for themselves. They forget about us. They forget about our lake to fill 'em up again. That is why cui ui is so scarce now, big trouts are scarce. Now I am hungry for fish, never get no fish for how many years, and I'm singing away, sitting down on the rock sticking out, singing about this lake which my old timer-people say, old-timer that died off long time ago, they say, "Don't give this lake up. Don't give it up. Hang on to it as long as you live."

Her song continues for several more lines and ends by asking why the people who have put the Indians on welfare do not look into the future. Her song is a true dirge, asking her god to direct her and her tribe toward salvation. Despite the chaos of the present landscape, she has faith that the extinction of the lake can be averted; a path will be found. The 1960s, as I have indicated in earlier chapters, was a crucial time for the lake, and Wheat took an active role by chairing what was called the Pyramid Lake Area Technical Group. Its recommendations for the improvement of reservation schools, housing, health, and ranch management were compiled with the full involvement of the tribal council. The group was optimistic because President Kennedy had recently called for reforming the BIA. Paulina's song was both a warning and an anthem for the lake and its people. Hers was a small voice, but thanks to Wheat, it is not forgotten.

AN ADDENDUM may put the contributions of Wheeler and Wheat in perspective. As I have indicated throughout this book, Paiutes have been the subject of anthropological study since John Wesley Powell and the beginnings of the Bureau of American Ethnology. In the 1920s and '30s, Julian Steward and Omer Stewart made global reputations as students of the Indians of the Great Basin, while Isabel Kelly, Willard Z. Park, and a few others made additional contributions to understanding Paiute religion and legends. As discussed earlier, American anthropology in its early years focused almost exclusively on the reconstruction of Native life before conquest. It was often assumed that once in contact with white religion, technology, and education, Indian cultures would and should rapidly disappear. This is one reason many anthropologists opposed or scoffed at John Collier's efforts to give Native people the choice to preserve some of their cultural practices and to assimilate at their own pace.

Things began to change after World War II, when it became obvious that Indian cultures had not vanished and "the Indian problem" was part of larger national problems of racial discrimination and systemic poverty. The end of Euro-American colonialism also made it more difficult for aspiring anthropologists to locate people to study. The days when an anthropologist could proudly claim to be the authority on his or her "tribe" were over. Anthropologists, not Indians, were in danger of vanishing. Into this simmering cauldron that would boil down to what is now known as "reflexive" anthropology, in which the observer explicitly questions his or her own motives and reasons for studying another culture, stepped a young PhD candidate from Boston University with a nursing background. Pamela Jane Brink spent about nine months in Nixon in 1967 and 1968. Supported by a US Public Health Service grant, her avowed purpose was to study persistence and change in Kuyuidokado medicine, child rearing, religion, education, and related activities.

She did not have a good time, nor was the information she gathered anywhere as complete as she had hoped it would be. After several weeks during which people either avoided her or refused to answer her questions, she finally found five elderly women who cooperated in exchange for rides to Fernley and

Reno for shopping or to the mountains to gather pine nuts and willow. Their daughters and daughters-in-law supplied additional information. Participant observation at tribal council meetings, community sporting events, powwows, and funerals helped fill in some gaps, but the real value of Brink's dissertation is her candid chapter on fieldwork. Beginning with the Department of Anthropology at the University of Nevada, which was unwilling or unable to assist her in making contacts and finding housing on the reservation, she was frustrated by a lack of cooperation. Although she cites Wheat's book, she never mentions meeting Wheat, the one person who might have facilitated her research at Pyramid Lake. Moreover, the chairman of the tribal council claimed never to have received Brink's letters of introduction. When she attempted a house-to-house canvass in Nixon, she was turned away.

Brink admits that her "personality may have had a detrimental effect." She interprets a question asked by a tribal council member, "Why pick on Pyramid Lake anyway?," as antagonistic, but she does not seem to have had a ready answer. She refused to join a women's basketball team because she thought she was "not much of a player," realizing too late that in Paiute culture, it is participation that is important, not the level of skill, as in Anglo-American sports. She also blamed tribal factionalism for her failure to obtain sufficient data when she learned that because she had talked with some women, others would not meet with her. Brink seems to have received no training in fieldwork methods, nor read essential commentaries on participant observation.

When Brink finally made a breakthrough by hanging out at Abe and Sue's store and meeting some of the women struggling to create a Pyramid Lake arts and crafts shop, she began to realize that the citizens of the reservation had more serious problems than she did. Nevertheless, Brink was bemused by what she saw as Paiute ignorance of what an anthropologist was, without realizing that her informants were putting her on. One of the women she got to know introduced her by saying: "This is my friend Pam. She is not a VISTA worker. What are you anyway?"

Brink's final conclusions, that material conditions have changed, but many medical and child-rearing practices resemble those described in the ethnographic reports of the nineteenth century, were unlikely to win her any professional prizes, although she went on to a distinguished teaching career and edited journals in the fields of nursing and cross-cultural research. The value of her fieldwork for understanding living conditions at Pyramid Lake lies in the glimpse it provides of women's lives on the reservation in the 1960s. Neither Wheeler nor Wheat dealt with current issues in their books. Wheat did what she could to help impoverished Indians and attended many tribal council meetings at Pyramid Lake, but she knew that Nixon was a place of economic hardship and bitter internal disputes over development and the future of the reservation. Wheat also knew that only the Kuyuidokado could improve conditions. Brink's work underscores the difficulties the Pyramid Lake Indians faced in the 1960s and provides a context for recent work on life at Pyramid Lake by William Saxe Wihr in 1988 and Justin R. Foley in 2008.

THE AMERICAN ARTIST AND WATER RECLAMATION

The federal government's involvement with the arts neither began nor ended with the New Deal, as many history texts imply. Among recent projects are "Documerica," a photographic documentation of the American environment sponsored by the Environmental Protection Agency in the mid-1970s, and the Bureau of Reclamation's "American Artist and Water Reclamation," a project in the late 1960s in which forty artists completed more than 375 pieces of art, 2 of them watercolors of Pyramid Lake. Some well-known artists such as Norman Rockwell, Peter Hurd, Richard Diebenkorn, and Fritz Scholder contributed to the Bureau of Reclamation art program. A large selection of paintings from this project may be seen on the bureau's website and in the catalog to a traveling exhibition of these paintings in 1972. In his lively introduction to the exhibition catalog, Douglas MacAgy of the Hirshhorn Museum places the reclamation art project in the context of the great government surveys of the West in the nineteenth century when painters such as Thomas Moran and Albert Bierstadt accompanied scientists. The new perspective, of a West dammed and managed, is necessary, MacAgy argues, because the myth of a virgin land persists. An awareness of what needs to be done must be made clear. Only artists, he believes, can help the public understand the vital sense of place.

According to the introduction to its website, the Bureau of Reclamation gave the artists permission to depict a subject in any style, "as long as it pertained to a Reclamation program—the development of the West's water resources for irrigation, hydropower generation, recreation, water conservation, and fish and wildlife enhancement." Needless to say, a lot of dam sites were depicted, as well as reservoirs, irrigation ditches, and even turbines. Fletcher Martin and Billy Morrow Jackson chose Pyramid Lake and produced remarkably similar watercolors.

Fletcher Martin was born in 1904 in Palisade, Colorado, and was largely self-trained. He taught art at universities in Florida, Iowa, Minnesota, and Washington and was a war correspondent for *Life*. His perspective on the lake is similar to O'Sullivan's, foregrounding the tufa pillars leading to the pyramid. The colors of the stones are burnt sienna, chestnut, and tan. The lake, glimpsed behind the rocks, is cornflower blue. In the immediate foreground in his twenty-two-by-twenty-eight-inch painting are clumps of what may be shadscale or salt grass in the sandy beach. The sky is completely occluded by dark-gray clouds with white borders, inserting a cartoonlike atmosphere. It is a pleasing, unpretentious representation of the pyramid.

Billy Morrow Jackson was born in Kansas City, Missouri, in 1926 and received a bachelor of fine arts from Washington University in St. Louis and a master's of fine arts from the University of Illinois, where he taught for many years. He did paintings for NASA's art project. His *Pyramid Lake,* twenty-one by twenty-nine inches, views the lake from about a hundred yards back up the hill from Martin's position. Jackson's painting is three-quarters foreground—gray boulders, light-gray sand, and a swath of pale-green vegetation bordering a pale-blue lake. The top of the pyramid almost touches the border of the paper. The sky is cloudless and almost white. The dark-brown pyramid is nearly featureless, as are the slate-gray Virginia Mountains to the west.

In the lower-right corner of the painting, a figure dressed in a blue shirt and wearing a broad-brimmed hat faces the painter with arms akimbo. This makes Jackson's piece one of the few depictions of the lake with a human presence. Aside from some photos by Gus Bundy and Richard Misrach's *Swimmers, Pyramid Lake Indian Reservation, Nevada,* humans are usually absent in representations of the lake and its pyramid. The face of the figure in Jackson's watercolor is shadowed, making sexual identification impossible, although the figure's hair appears to be at least shoulder length. The figure is wearing trousers, but its legs are partially obscured by a rock. Girlfriend? Indian guide? Water Baby? Wovoka? Letty Filler? Homage to nineteenth-century frontier painters and photographers who sometimes put themselves in a corner of their pictures? The answer may have died with Jackson in 2006. His other contribution to the story of the lake is a very pale-blue watercolor of the spillway at Stampede Dam with a tiny figure at the river's edge.

The significance of these paintings is partially due to the fact that they were funded by the agency that contributed most to the lake's near destruction and current distress. Museums are, of course, full of great art depicting conquerors, murderers, and polluters. Surely, there is room for portraits of their victims as the reclamation art project provides in some measure. But it is difficult to accept the contention of self-styled "ecocritic" Paul Lindholdt, who dismisses the work of all forty artists as "ecopornography," art that "masks sordid agendas with

Pyramid Lake. Watercolor by Fletcher Martin, ca. 1969, 22″ × 28″. Courtesy the American Artist and Water Reclamation, US Bureau of Reclamation.

illusions of beauty and perfection." He shrilly denounces all the paintings that suggest a "technological sublime" in dams and reservoirs.

My point is that his interpretation of the paintings, which he uses merely to denounce a bureaucracy that was caught in the shift in federal policy from promoting irrigation and hydropower to encouraging wildlife conservation and recreation, is overkill and tars all environmentalists with his vitriol-dripping brush. More important, Lindholdt ignores the fact that ecosystems are dynamic, not static, as I have attempted to show in this book. There never was a single pristine, unchanging wilderness. Climate change and fluctuations in species population relentlessly alter landscapes, albeit more slowly than human settlement. MacAgy was correct in observing that the public needs a new perspective on the West that shows what has happened to canyons and deserts under federal administration. Whether they find the results an improvement or a loss should be left up to them. Fletcher Martin's and Billy Morrow Jackson's engaging watercolors of Pyramid Lake meet the USBR's requirement of showing places touched by its projects. Like it or not, Pyramid Lake would cease to exist without the cooperation of the Bureau of Reclamation and other agencies that control the upstream dams, ditches, and reservoirs.

PHOTOGRAPHERS

The lake does not lack photographic souvenirs. After O'Sullivan, a deluge of albumen prints, Kodak snapshots, and digital images followed. If each photo was an acre-foot of water, the lake would probably be a hundred feet higher. In the twentieth century almost every newspaper and magazine article on the lake was illustrated. Postcards of the pyramid and local Indians were for sale in hundreds of gas stations, drugstores, and tourist shops. E. L. Linton recorded life at Wadsworth in 1905, zoologist C. Hart Merriam took photos at Nixon in 1938, anonymous government photographers recorded cattle-grading demonstrations and a cotton mattress project at Nixon in the 1930s and '40s, Ray Curtis and Frank Kinsey of Reno took thousands of photographs of the lake over many years, Harry Drackert took hundreds, and I have taken dozens, but the number of truly great photographers of the lake remains small. Five stand out: Gus Bundy, who lived in Washoe Valley and was active as a photographer from the 1940s through the 1970s; Jonas Dovydenas, who photographed the lake for "Documerica" in 1973; Peter Goin and Robert Dawson, who, working together and separately, have produced a beautiful but grim portfolio of the lake and its ravaged environment; and, last but not least, Richard Misrach, famous for his large-scale photographs of deserts, sky, the Golden Gate Bridge, and the aftermath of Hurricane Katrina.

Gus Bundy, as his biographer Ahmed Essa makes clear in the special art issue of the *Nevada Historical Society Quarterly*, was an enigma to many who knew him. Gus was born in New York City in 1907, where he studied art, painted, and taught. In 1927 he began to travel, first as a seaman, then in the American South. In 1937 he left for Japan, where he met Jeanne, who was Swiss. Expecting their first child, they returned to the United States and settled in Washoe Valley, a place he had visited on his way to Japan.

Bundy's black-and-white photographs of Pyramid Lake capture its many moods, but the images of elderly Paiute men fishing for cui-ui that he took in the mid-1960s are most historically important. (See the first figure in chapter 3.) In one, four men in fedora hats and work clothes stand ankle-deep in the lake, fishing with drag lines. Hundreds of white pelicans watch from about twenty-five yards away. Though the birds may be waiting for a chance to seize a fish, the moment is serene, the pelicans adding their symbolism to the ritual. Since the cui-ui had just been or was about to be declared an endangered species, the occasion may have been a final harvest, or a special heritage allowance that would allow a few fish to be taken and parceled out to the tribe in small amounts, a tribal communion wafer. The day is sunny with a few fair-weather cumulus to the north.

Jonas Dovydenas was born in Lithuania in 1939, but his career as a photographer has been with American magazines such as *National Geographic*. In May 1973 he visited Pyramid Lake under contract with the Environmental Protection Agency. The EPA's "Documerica" program operated from 1972 to 1977 and employed dozens of the country's best photographers, including Danny Lyon, Marc St. Gil, and Charles O'Rear, who did a series on Las Vegas. Dovydenas's photos of Abe and Sue's Grocery in Nixon with Paiute children playing on a pickup truck humanize life on the reservation, while his portrait of Avery Winnemucca sitting in a folding chair at the Sutcliffe marina with a wrecked couch and dog in the background is a study in broken promises. The lake was just beginning to recover from reaching its lowest level in 1967, and the distance from the marina to the lake is dishearteningly long. The dog looks angry; Avery looks bored. Dovydenas's photo of the pyramid is spectacular, an aerial shot from the south that provides a better understanding of O'Sullivan's perspective. (This image and others taken by Dovydenas at Pyramid Lake may be seen on the National Archives and Records Administration website.)

Peter Goin and Robert Dawson are well known to northern Nevadans who care about their environment. The book of photographs *A Doubtful River* with text by Mary Webb provides a vivid survey of the Truckee and its lakes. Goin is especially good at encompassing a host of environmental factors in one scene. His aerial view of Marble Bluff Dam and Fishway reveals both the simplicity of the structure and the complexities it hides. His pyramid after sunset is hardly more than a silhouette of the giant stone, but its shadow cast across the luminous water challenges the viewer to look closely at the textures. In Goin's eye the pyramid is more Edward Weston than Timothy O'Sullivan, an abstract but recognizable shape filling a void.

Dawson's photograph of Stone Mother is one of the best ever taken, the woman's profile clearly etched and the open basket revealing a miniature pyramid inside. Dawson's photos of revelers and campers at the Needles with their piles of trash clearly explain why the Pyramid Lake Tribal Council voted to close the north end of the lake. His black-and-white photos of Nixon are like Dorothea Lange's of Depression-era America. One photo not included in *A Doubtful River* is of Nixon from about a mile away as a storm comes in from the northwest. The scattered houses, the nearly treeless delta, and the mountains on either side of the lake are dwarfed by the roiling black clouds. The fragility of the environment is palpable. (See the first figure in the epilogue.)

Richard Misrach was born in Los Angeles in 1949 and received a bachelor of arts in psychology from the University of California, Berkeley, where he began using a camera to document poverty and work for social change, but his interest soon shifted to the natural environment. In 1983 he visited Pyramid Lake. By that date the lake had risen considerably, as his *Swimmers, Pyramid Lake Indian Reservation, Nevada* reveals. Three tiny figures are in the golden water a few yards from the dark-brown pyramid. Misrach eliminates both the near and the opposite shores. A faint shadow cast toward the east indicates a setting sun. Otherwise, the pyramid is as stolid and lonely as those of Egypt, which Misrach photographed in 1989. These can be seen together on the Museum of Contemporary Photography's website. Misrach returned to the lake in 2004 and took another striking photograph, *Pyramid Lake (at Night)*. In January 2010 the beautiful moonlit scene turned up as a screen saver on Apple's new iPad. The Pyramid Lake Tribal Council was taken by surprise. They had not received the fee they charge for commercial photography on the reservation, but the tribal chairman thought it was good publicity.

ROAD MAPS

Roads, as they appear on maps of northern Nevada and the Pyramid Lake area, are another way of understanding the political and cultural creation and control of a place. Four maps representing three different perspectives on the lake will be examined here. They are fragments of the perspectives of sportfishing, the Bureau of Land Management (and the political and business interests with which the BLM cooperates), and the Pyramid Lake Paiute Tribal Council. The maps also reflect changes in views of the lake since 1973 when court decisions, legislation, fish management, and public opinion began to shift in favor of the preservation of the lake and its resources, aquatic and human.

The 1973 map is the work of Weekend and Wide World Outdoor Publications, a commercial publisher in Oakland, California. The map is 17½ × 22½ inches, with six vertical folds and one horizontal. The scale on the map is 2 miles to 1 inch, allowing for many details of topography. One side has a map of the lake and a few miles surrounding it. It is a guide not to finding the lake, but to enjoying it once you are there. The background is bright yellow. The legend identifies "State highways," "Main travelled roads," and "Secondary roads" by color and line thickness. The contours of the lake are given in feet; each "Resort or Marina" is identified by a black square, although Sutcliffe is the only black square on the map. The boundaries of the reservation are indicated by a broken black line. More than two dozen fishing and boating spots are identified by name, and other sites are identified for swimming, waterskiing, and hiking. The reverse side, titled "Four Seasons of Pyramid Lake," contains about four thousand words of information on the history of the lake and on fishing, hunting, swimming, boating, "family recreation" such as rockhounding and bird-watching, and information on weather, climate, ecology, and environment.

The map was published in the year that US District Court judge Gerhard Gesell issued his opinion on a suit brought by the Pyramid Lake Paiutes against the secretary of the interior, 1968. Gesell's ruling required the secretary to reduce the amount of water going to the Newlands Reclamation Project and increase water to the reservation. The Truckee Carson Irrigation District, which managed the allocation of water from the Truckee River, refused to comply, filing its own suit the following year against the federal government. A decade later, in 1984, the TCID lost, and the secretary of the interior ordered a total reorganization of the river's management. Moreover, the Paiutes began to win their legal actions based on their cultural heritage—fishing, not farming. The cartographers may have been premature in cele-brating the recreational possibilities of Pyramid Lake because many issues remained to be settled, but the bright-yellow map and its visual clutter of text in little white boxes convey a sense of cartoon-like happiness and the varieties of recreational opportunities.

The 1986 BLM map is the product of the bureau's Winnemucca District. It measures 22 by 34 inches, with eight vertical folds and two horizontal, folding to 4½ by 11 inches. The scale is 10 miles to 1½ inches, and the map side covers more than 100 miles north and east of the lake. Although Pyramid Lake and the reservation are prominent on this map, the recreational areas include the Black Rock Desert, several mountain ranges, and parts of the Carson and Humboldt Rivers. The legend identifies "BLM, Forest Service, U.S. Fish & Wildlife, Indian Reservation, 'Other Federal Lands,' and Private Lands" by color coding. Areas closed to off-road vehicles (ORVs) are marked by a red-striped border, emigrant trails by dashes, historical markers by a diamond, rockhounding areas by crossed picks, winter recreation by a snowflake, and wild horse viewing areas by a red silhouette of a horse.

The text side of this map offers information on prehistory and archaeology, history, ecological communities (illustrated by line drawings), ghost towns, and recreation, which includes "sand dunes," "photography," "wild horse and burro viewing," "off-road vehicle driving," and "cross-country skiing," in addition to the fishing, hunting, rockhounding, camping, and hiking of the preceding map. The range of recreational activities was becoming richer. In its introduction the BLM writer approaches poetry: "It's a big, beautiful, quiet sort of country . . .

free from the noise and congestion of urban living, a place where a person can stretch and roam. That's the Winnemucca District of the BLM." There are echoes here of a verse, "Mornin' on the Desert," first published in 1927 in an anthology of poetry sponsored by the Nevada Federation of Women's Clubs and reprinted several times in *Nevada Highways and Parks* as an unofficial state poem. The unknown poet celebrates the individual freedom of the desert:

> Mornin' on the desert, and the wind is blowin' free,
> And it's ours, jest for the breathin', so let's fill up,
> > you and me.
> No more stuffy cities, where you have to pay to breathe,
> Where the helpless human creatures move and throng and
> > strive and seethe.

Enthusiasts for and managers of Nevada's lands have long sought to counter negative images of emptiness, loneliness, and wasteland. From Bertha Raffetto's "Home Means Nevada," which became the official state song in 1933, to Walter Van Tilburg Clark's humorous "The Sweet Promised Land of Nevada," the state's writers have embraced what others found ugly and menacing. The BLM, increasingly sensitive to attacks by Sagebrush Rebels and forced to comply with the multiple-use provisions of the 1976 Federal Land Policy Management Act, responded with a variety of public relations programs, including maps and guides to the proper use of public lands.

Readers of this map are advised to "protect your public lands" by preventing fires and leaving gates as you find them. Visitors are told to protect themselves from hypothermia, heat stroke, giardia in streams, and flash floods. Addresses and telephone numbers for the BLM, the Forest Service, Nevada Parks, county sheriffs, and the Nevada Highway Patrol are listed.

A map produced for the Pyramid Lake Paiute Tribal Council in 1997, like the 1973 tourist map, but unlike the BLM maps, puts the focus on the lake, specifically the "Pyramid Lake Scenic Byway," a creation of the Clinton administration's "National Scenic Byways" initiative. The Pyramid Lake Scenic Byway follows the western shore of the lake for about two-thirds of its length and the eastern side of the lake from Nixon to the pass dividing Pyramid from the dry bed of Winnemucca Lake, where there is a turnoff to the west onto a dirt road leading to the tufa formations of the pyramid and the Stone Mother. This is a small map, just 11 by 17 inches, with three vertical and one horizontal fold that turns it into a shirt-pocket-size 3½ by 7½ inches. The scale of the map is 2 miles to 1 inch, providing ample room for place-names, but this map is both less colorful (tan, brown, blue earth tones) and less cluttered than the 1973 tourist map. The overall effect is calmness, not frenetic activity.

The map's legend identifies five types of roads as well as points of interest along the lakeshore and assures the visitor that he or she can find public restrooms, public showers, gasoline, LP gas, a minimarket, a Laundromat, and RV hookups at the tribe's I-80 smoke shop in Wadsworth and at the Pyramid Lake Marina in Sutcliffe. Tribal headquarters and the tribal museum and visitor center are marked on the map, but not the grocery store and gift shop in Nixon. The obverse of the map has color photos of the pyramid, the Stone Mother, and Anaho Island and aerial views of the lakeshore and the mouth of the Truckee River. The brief text provides an overview of the Paiute people, the natural wonders of the lake, and the recreational opportunities —hunting, fishing, boating, swimming, and scenic views. A subtle reference to the tribe's water conflicts with irrigators appears at the bottom of the map where the Truckee Canal, which diverts water from the lake, is more clearly identifiable than it is on BLM maps. The Numana Fish Hatchery and the Marble Bluff Fish Facility, a dam with fishways and a fish-handling building, are also prominent on the map. Both are managed by members of the Pyramid Lake Paiute Tribe, the Marble Bluff facility in cooperation with the Bureau of Reclamation and the US Fish and Wildlife Service. Both are open to tours. The primary purpose of this map is obviously to attract tourists, but an important secondary message is tribal progress and pride in ownership and management of the lake.

The 2001 BLM map is an update and expansion of the BLM Winnemucca Field Office map of 1986. It differs from the earlier version in some significant ways. It is slightly larger, 24 by 36 inches, and the scale is 1 inch to 5 miles. Side 1 has the northern half of the Winnemucca District, that is, the northwest part of Nevada from approximately the forty-first parallel to the Oregon border. Side 2, the southern portion of the district, now includes Reno in the southwest corner of the map, providing first-time visitors to the state with a recognizable starting point. There is less text on the 2001 map than on the 1986 map, but more information. Side 1 begins with a warning from Smokey Bear about fires, clearly linking BLM and Forest Service land-management problems. This is followed by sections on prehistory and history of the region and longer pieces on safety and visitor etiquette: "Tread Lightly" and "Leave No Trace." The 2001 map makes several additions to the recreational activities. ORVs are now referred to as OHVs (off-highway vehicles), indicating a significant change in recreational vehicles.

Before the 1980s desert adventurers usually drove their four-wheel-drive trucks to the end of paved highways before following old dirt trails. Twenty years later Japanese automakers were successfully marketing four-wheeled ATVs built to drive cross-country in the most rugged hills. ATVs and OHVs are trailered to roadless areas. The Pyramid Lake Tribal Council, recognizing their negative environmental impact, prohibits the use of ATVs and OHVs on the reservation.

The legend of the 2001 map carries eleven symbols, five more than the earlier BLM map. Wild horse viewing is divided into wild horse (black silhouette facing right) and wild burro (dark-blue silhouette facing left), mountain bike trails (silhouette of a bike), hiking trails (stick figure with trekking pole), campgrounds (a tent), rest areas (a picnic table), wildlife viewing (binoculars), rockhounding (crossed picks), historical markers (solid black triangle), and two symbols for gates, "locked" (blue backward slash) and "seasonal" (black backward slash). This meets the needs of a wide range of public-land visitors. The text on cultural artifacts sets forth the regulations on using metal detectors and the limits on harvesting petrified wood—25 pounds per person per day up to 250 pounds, no explosives may be used, and no trading in petrified wood without a license. There are some odd omissions. The town of Wadsworth at the south end of the Pyramid Lake Reservation disappears on the 2001 map, as does the Southern Pacific Railroad spur through the reservation, which appeared on the 1986 map even though it was closed and the tracks removed in 1970. Without an active constituency, some history is inevitably lost.

The quantity and specificity of information on these map symbols suggest that the BLM is both recognizing and reaching out to the growing variety of tourists on its lands. This is supported by the other part of the legend on the 2001 map—the types of landownership and management. This category of information increased from five to thirteen categories with color codes: BLM (light tan), national forests (light green), national forest wilderness (dark green), BLM wilderness (dark tan), wilderness study area (tan with diagonal stripes), national conservation area (dark-green border enclosing dots), instant study area (gray-green), wildlife refuge (teal blue), Indian reservations (salmon), Nevada state lands (light blue), water (dark blue), private lands (white), and Department of Defense (pink). The end of the Cold War may account for the identification of the pink areas as military use instead of the vague "Other Federal Lands" on the 1986 map. The text on this side of the map focuses on recreation and explains some of the technical differences between "Wilderness," "Wilderness Study Area," and "National Conservation Area."

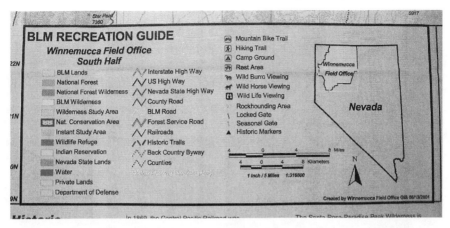

Map legend and portion of BLM Northwestern Recreation Guide, 2001. Courtesy Bureau of Land Management.

Another change in the BLM maps is the identification of eight types of roads on the 2001 map in contrast to two—paved and gravel—on the 1986 map. Now the observant motorist can locate herself on interstate highways, US highways, Nevada state highways, county roads, BLM roads, Forest Service roads, historic trails, and backcountry byways. If the driver breaks a strut or punctures an oil pan, proper blame can be assigned. Such detail would make for a cluttered map if Nevada had more roads, but the apparent plethora of road types on the BLM map legend informs the map's reader that public land is accessible, right to the edge of the roadless wilderness areas.

The story these four maps tell is one of both progress and decline. The progressive story is that of expanding recreational activities. From the focus on fishing and water sports at Pyramid Lake to the inclusion of Paiute heritage, immigrant trails, desert eco- and geosystems, and the search for solitude and quiet, the maps chart the evolution of the idea of the desert. The story of decline, the loss of the very qualities that make the desert unique—emptiness, silence, the fragile ecosystem—is also apparent in these maps, as each printing invites more and more visitors. More important, by identifying old trails, ghost towns, and abandoned mines, the 2001 map helps to correct views of the lake as "pristine," "primitive," even "prehistoric," claims that ignore ten thousand years of human stewardship and a century and a half of mining, logging, commercial fishing, farming, urban development, and tourism within the watershed of the Truckee River and the lakes it joins.

* * *

THE COLORS of the lake and hills are an acknowledgment of the atmosphere that filters light from sun, moon, stars, and neon through a soup of chemicals, bacteria, microorganisms, ash, and sand that we call air. Pyramid Lake's relatively warm, shallow water, trapped between mountain ranges running north to south, with fairly constant winds and mostly sunny days, is a veritable artist's box and scientist's lab of materials from which to make discoveries about nature and the creatures, including humans, who take life from the lake.

NINE

Seekers in the Desert

There are probably more people who dislike deserts than those who love them, but deserts, such as the shrub steppe ecoregion that surrounds Pyramid Lake, continue to attract large numbers of people who feel comfortable in minimalist landscapes. The apparent simplicity of the desert is calming, like a snowscape. Nature appears relaxed, content with a few rocks and plants; fervid minds are cooled. Even though desert weather can be capricious, a challenge to a meteorologist or a shaman, desert lovers will take a dare. Desert lovers are dreamers, their imaginations a kind of screen against the sun.

This chapter continues and elaborates on two topics of this book, human attachment to places and Numa explanations of their history and environment. Despite the cultural differences between white sojourners at the lake and Native residents, both recognize the environmental constraints. Both use the tools available—magic, dreams, technology, storytelling—to understand and mitigate desert harshness. If history were simply chronology, it would be easy to begin the story of mystics and seekers near Pyramid Lake with Wovoka, the Paiute shaman and creator of the 1890 Ghost Dance religion; move on to journalist Dan De Quille's charming fantasy of the origin of the Numa and the lake; and conclude with Idah Meacham Strobridge's evocative essays on Nevada deserts. There would be a progression, but no pattern. My alternate chronology begins with a broad survey of the meanings of deserts in Christian and Euro-American heritage, narrows to focus on specific cases of Wovoka's shamanistic powers and some examples of Paiute cosmology, and concludes with De Quille's attempt to blend what he learned from his Indian neighbors with the fairy tales of Europe learned from books and family storytelling to memorialize Pyramid Lake. The mirages of Strobridge, the visions of Wovoka, and the whimsy of De Quille create a mosaic of the deserts of northwestern Nevada.

DESERT FATHERS AND MOTHERS

To understand the power of the desert over spiritual seekers in the environs of Pyramid Lake, from Wovoka to Beau Kitselman and Brother David, it may help to begin with the lives of the "Desert Fathers," the Christian hermits of the third and fourth centuries CE who fled into the desert west of Cairo to escape the persecutions of the Roman emperor Diocletian and who then rejected the official Christian state of his successor, Constantine. As depicted by the twentieth-century Trappist monk Thomas Merton, the early Christian seekers were drawn to the desert as a refuge from sinful society and as a test of their faith. Dissimilar as they are, the western desert of Egypt and the Great Basin share an arid barrenness that offers environments presumably free of distractions, a place mostly unmapped where mystics, ascetics, and pilgrims could spiritually pioneer, create their own paths to God. The Desert Fathers believed in the individual's ability to do God's will without instruction from church hierarchy; indeed, they insisted on it. "Obviously," Merton writes, "such a path could only be traveled by one who was very alert and very sensitive to the landmarks of a trackless wilderness."

Merton is speaking metaphorically. Just as there are numerous trails across the Black Rock, Smoke Creek, and Carson Deserts that end at springs and lake beds emptied by drought or human greed, there are false steps on the way to self-knowledge, the essential first achievement of the Desert Fathers seeking to apprehend God. "The flight of these men and women to the desert," Merton observes, "was neither purely negative nor purely individualistic. They were not rebels against society. True, they were in a certain sense 'anarchists,' and it will do no harm to think of them in that light." So, the Desert Fathers were seeking to understand what it means to be human away from the annoyance of daily interactions with other humans. This leads Merton to see similarities between them and Indian yogis, Zen Buddhist monks, and American Indians. "If we were to seek their like in twentieth-century America," Merton continues, "we would have to look in strange, out of the way places. . . . We might perhaps find someone like this among the Pueblo Indians or the Navahos: but there the case would be entirely different. You would have simplicity, primitive wisdom: but rooted in a primitive society. With the Desert Fathers, you have the characteristic of a clean break with a conventional, accepted social context in order to swim for one's life into an apparently irrational void."

Merton's search for contemporary examples of desert exile and his stereotype of "primitive" society lead him off the path. He is too focused on human nature and not enough on nature without humans, the desert as real place. The Desert Fathers knew better. Merton translates one of the hermits who wrote, "If a man settles in a certain place and does not bring forth the fruit of that place, the place itself casts him out, as one who has not borne its fruit."

Deserts are good places to be alone because they do not support large populations, but they are inhospitable if you do not learn how to survive in them. The Paiutes understood this very well. Once they had learned to bring forth the fruits of the desert—seeds, nuts, fish, and game—they, too, went on private quests to doctor rocks, sacred mountains, and scattered springs to be closer to the divine. Life in small bands can, I suspect, be as distracting as life in midtown Manhattan, if that is all you know. To know a place well you may start with a guided tour, but at some point you have to go there alone. You even need to get lost. "Getting lost is to sense the 'animus' of nature," proclaims novelist Jim Harrison. "When we are lost," he adds, "we lose our peripheries." Having lost our landmarks, we begin to relocate them. As anthropologist Keith Basso explains in his insightful study, *Wisdom Sits in Places: Landscape and Language Among the Western Apache,* "People, not cultures, sense places, and I have tried to suggest that in Cibecue, as elsewhere, they do so in varying ways." There may be culturally agreed-upon meanings of place, but there are as many subtle variations as there are individuals. For the Paiutes and other first settlers in the Great Basin, seeking God and an earthly home was a single act. Their creator supplied the "fruits" of the place, and they learned to harvest. Self-knowledge learned in solitude was as natural as spearing a fish. The silence and isolation of the desert were confirmation of the creator's faith in "the People."

The Desert Fathers provide many images of the desert: a place of seclusion, of silence, of reflection and renewal. Edward Abbey, popularizer of the desert experience in recent times, found its silence "a suspension of time, a continuous present." As Basso clearly shows, place is more important than time for Apaches. The lessons of history are in the stories places tell. Like written history in European cultures, the stories told by individuals about places on the Fort Apache Reservation are constantly reimagined and revised, as are the stories told by Paiutes on the Pyramid Lake Reservation.

The desert, with its illusion of simplicity and permanence, is a place suitable for a type of religious personality whose faith resides in his or her self-confidence and adaptability, who is not troubled by the paradoxes of the desert— seemingly empty yet abounding with life, presumed silent but reverberating with the sounds of the wind, made up of dust and sand, still somehow *clean.* The seeker in the desert, Christian hermit, Native shaman, or perceptive sojourner, needs visual, aural, olfactory, tactile, and even gustatory acuity to find the unseen order of life that William James says is the fundamental goal of religion.

Joseph Wood Krutch, an astute desert naturalist of mid-twentieth-century America, boldly asked, "What is a desert good for?" and answered, "Contemplation." The desert, he thought, seems to brood and encourages brooding. Krutch thinks the desert speaks in different voices to those prepared to hear. "To the biologist," he writes, "it speaks first of the remarkable flexibility of living things, of the processes of adaptation which are nowhere more remarkable than in the strange devices by which plants and animals have learned to conquer heat and dryness." "To the merely contemplative it speaks of courage and endurance of a special kind." The sea, mountains, valleys, plains "invite action and suggest limitless opportunity," while the desert provokes awe rather than inviting conquest. Tell that to Frederick Newell, the first director of the US Reclamation Service, and to the dreamers of irrigated Edens.

Contemplation may lead to conclusions unwelcome to the desert lover. For some, as historian Elizabeth Raymond has pointed out, pondering the desert may lead to despair. Others attempt to overcome the arduous environment. Whether travelers found the Great Basin dismal or beautiful, Raymond concludes, they were all provoked by it because the desert is a challenge to the prevailing American environmental faith in the beneficence of nature. Deserts do not welcome; they impose limits. The arid, rocky, treeless, yet fragile environment does not need people to be complete. In fact, the presence of humans may have a greater impact on a desert than on any other biosystem. A desert is diminished by people. Krutch is absolutely wrong when he calls the desert "the last frontier" because "it cannot be crossed." It can be crossed *and* crossed out. For those for whom contemplation is painful, the desert is a cacotopia. Seen as wastelands, deserts become dumping places, toxic with mining debris, radiated by nuclear blasts, grotesquely lit in neon, and ritually cluttered by pseudo-countercultural chimeras such as Burning Man—part arts festival, part end-of-summer bacchanal, part corporate marketing scheme, all masquerading as environmentally correct and "spiritual."

The potential for the utopian dreams of Burning Man to become dystopian was candidly stated by Larry Harvey, one of its founders, in an interview May 13, 2012, with *Washington Post* reporter Suzy Khimm. "'If we can create a world that's defined by brilliance at the top and soulful association at the bottom, you command everything in between,' Harvey exclaims. 'After all, isn't that what the Republicans did?'" To which the answer is, yes, as did Beau Kitselman's

E-therapy. Harvey was in Washington to wheedle concessions from the Bureau of Land Management to exceed the Black Rock's permitted crowd limits. Harvey was also blunt about his shift from limited liability corporation to 501(c)3 nonprofit status as a way to benefit financially. Selling tickets at $300 a pop to a crowd of more than sixty thousand, Burning Man officials claim that they are urban planners experimenting on "the blank slate of the Nevada desert." Their otiose philosophy is yet another misreading of the desert.

Burning Man seems to have spawned other breeds of seekers. A group calling itself Symbiosis Gathering advertised on the Internet a meeting at Pyramid Lake on May 17–21, 2012, of various artists and "modern earth-based" spiritual healers. The party was timed to coincide with an eclipse of the sun, allowing the organizers to link their fandango to Wovoka's first vision. The Symbiosians seem to be deeply into "Neo-Tribal dance," and websites linked to this event feature pictures of young California and Oregon yoga instructors and belly dancers. To their credit, the organizers emphasized the cooperation of the Pyramid Lake Tribal Council and urged the eight thousand participants they hope will pay $280 a ticket (and $40 to the tribe for vehicle permits) to refrain from getting intoxicated and naked and to leave behind "that crazy Indian headdress you got at the costume store and wore at the Burn one year!" Burning Man is not the only related event. The Symbiosis Eclipse Festival met on the same beach at the south end of the lake where the ill-fated Ranch Rock concert took place in 1986.

The organizers of the Symbiosis festival and similar gatherings around the world seem to seek out desert settings or beaches, preferably both. These places are liminal, between life (water) and death (sand). The desert also represents a postapocalyptic landscape where a new, more peaceful, organic community can be created—if only for a few days. Erik Davis, a student of countercultural spirituality in California, has described such communities as resembling refugee camps more than Brook Farm or Herland. Referring to a similar gathering in Portugal in 2008, Davis calls it "a postmodern ghost dance, a party at the hot rim of a volcano ready to burst." Given the accelerating pace and increasing magnitude of environmental disasters in the past century both locally and globally, the Neo-Tribal dancers are obviously responding to real problems. The cults that have arisen in the deserts of the world have all sought to bring meaning and order to the perceived chaos and void of their surroundings. Some became religious institutions and suppressed self-expression. Yet periodically, skies grow dark, metaphorically and atmospherically, and dancers begin to move to plangent music in an effort to revitalize themselves and the places where they dwell. Wovoka *would* understand.

There are many reasons for liking or disliking the desert, of course. One reason for distaste I recall from the late 1950s when Professor Charlton Laird of the University of Nevada took one of the first internationally recognized American studies scholars in Japan to visit Pyramid Lake. Laird invited me along. We reached the top of Mullen Pass and collectively gasped our appreciation of the view of the lake. Laird inhaled deeply, slammed on the brakes, leaped from his car, and ran out into the sagebrush, where he tore off some branches. Rushing back, he thrust this garland of the state's flower into our guest's face with some characteristically enthusiastic words about its magnificent fragrance. Our distinguished visitor jerked his head back with an anguished howl. Too late, Laird realized his mistake, apologized, and drove on. Whatever favorable impression the Japanese professor had of Pyramid Lake was tainted forever by the redolence of *Artemisia tridentata*. For me it was a lesson in environmental conditioning. The professor from the land of *hanakotoba* was accustomed to the scents of cherry blossoms (gentleness), white chrysanthemums (truth), and hydrangea (pride), not the pungent odor of sagebrush. He did not know that some Natives use sagebrush in healing ceremonies.

IDAH MEACHAM was a true daughter of the Golden West. Born on her parents' ranch in California in 1855, she grew up in Lassens Meadows, Nevada, between Lovelock and Winnemucca where her father ranched and ran Humboldt House, a hotel near a Central Pacific Railroad stop. Meacham graduated from Mills Seminary (now Mills College) in Oakland, California. In 1884 she married Sam Strobridge, the son of one of her father's mining partners, and they lived on property near her parents, but tragedy struck and she lost three children and her husband to disease and blizzards within five years. Widowed, she took up ranching, mining, bookbinding, and writing, scratching out her living in Nevada until she sold her ranch and moved to Los Angeles in 1901, where she became friends with Mary Austin and Charles Fletcher Lummis, photographer, editor, and Indian-rights advocate.

Idah Strobridge's desert is dominated by mirage and by the men and women who give themselves over to the desert's eternal rhythms. This pairing of atmospheric phenomenon and workplace is both highly original and brilliantly perceptive. A mirage is an illusion created by light passing through cold and warm air, nature's bonanza. The miner's desert is a landscape of dark shafts and pale tailings, nature's borasca. Strobridge, living for many years in the land of the Paiute and only a few miles from Pyramid Lake, goes even deeper into the mystique of the place. Mirage for Strobridge may be Austin's water of imagination and fantasy. "The mirage is," Strobridge writes, "in very truth, a part of the Desert itself—just as the sagebrush, and the coyote, and the little horned toads, and the sand-storms are part. To those who know the Desert-land, the picture would be incomplete without them." She gives examples of the mountains in spring mornings when "the mirage runs riot with its fantastic fashioning."

Strobridge tells an amusing story (humor is notably absent in most desert writing) about a man who built a station on the wagon road to Idaho. He was so successful that a rival appeared and threatened to build a better facility. When the original proprietor returned from getting supplies, he saw to his horror that a new, larger building stood near his. He pulled out his rifle and drove his team toward the offending station, only to see it disappear in the shimmering heat. He had been fooled by a mirage, but he took it well and told the joke on himself to every guest and traveler. When the railroad reached the spot, the railroad men named it "Mirage" and told passengers on their way to California or back to Chicago that they were passing "My-ridge." Strobridge tells this story as though the station and its optical illusion might need different but similar names. Mirage, Helen Carlson tells us in *Nevada Place Names,* was twenty-six miles northeast of Wadsworth.

Strobridge is scornful of those who need to define the desert in words. "Speech is not needed, for they who are elect to love these things understand one another without words; and the Desert speaks to them through its silence." She dismisses "those who flit by in a day and night of car travel, and then talk about 'how lovely' the Desert is, and how 'it appeals' to them. . . . The Desert does not need such lovers. . . . If you love the Desert, and live in it, and lie awake at night under its low-hanging stars, you know you are part of the pulse-beat of the universe, and you feel the swing of the spheres through space, and you hear through the silence the voice of God speaking."

Strobridge adds another set of tracks for seekers in the desert. Hers leads to a place of solitary harmony, which, when she finally left Nevada, she tried to re-create with what she called her "Wickiup" on a breakwater in San Pedro.

SO THE DESERT IS HEALTHFUL, a place of solitude but not loneliness, silent but not empty, starkly beautiful, real and imagined, timeless but subject to seasonal and climatic changes, tragic yet promising. A place to work and a place to play. To this litany, nature writer David Quammen adds cleanliness. According to Quammen, when someone asked Lawrence of Arabia why he liked the desert, he answered, "Because it's clean." But what did he mean? The desert is composed of dirt and dust. Probably he meant spiritually clean. This leads

Quammen to consider what a desert is and how it is defined scientifically. He begins with aridity and mathematical formulas devised by Russian-born German geographer and climatologist Vladimir Köppen. This formula is based on temperature and precipitation. "Any region where *potential evaporation* exceeds actual precipitation, by a certain margin, can be considered a desert." And what creates this condition of extreme temperatures and little precipitation? High pressure in the atmosphere between 30 degrees and 35 degrees north and south of the equator, mountains, and cool ocean currents are the three most important components. Or, in Quammen's vivid simile, "Our planet wears its deserts like a fat woman in a hot red bikini."

As the earth rotates, surface velocity produces winds that cause hot air to rise over the tropical equator until it cools and rains. The air, now dry, flows north and south past the Tropics of Capricorn and Cancer, where it begins to descend. As the pressure of the descending air increases, so do the temperature and dryness. Cool ocean currents along the coasts of southwestern Africa, the west coast of South America, and California also act to deprive the air of moisture. Mountains cause storms to deposit rain and snow on their western sides, leaving their eastern slopes and valleys dry. Finally, the differential in temperature between falling cold air and rising warm air causes winds to blow almost continuously, powerfully, and erratically across the deserts and through its canyons and mountain passes. The Washoe Zephyr and the dust devil are two examples.

In *Where the Lightning Strikes: The Lives of American Indian Sacred Places*, cultural historian Peter Nabokov quotes with approval anthropologist Robert Heizer's observation that "California Indians lived in two worlds at the same time. There was the practical world where they hunted, traveled, loved, fought, and died. And there was the equally real world of the spirits. Trees, animals, springs, caves, streams, and mountains might each contain a life force, spirit or soul and must be treated with caution and respect." Nabokov goes on to warn against the assumption that Native beliefs were unchanging. "Like societies everywhere American Indian cultures and their religious systems are the products of this tug-of-war between historical change and inherited traditions." This will become apparent in the discussion of Wovoka and Brother David.

PAIUTE COSMOLOGY, WEATHER, AND WOVOKA

Two alternative origin stories, some versions of the Water Babies legend, and a few examples of weather lore extend the hypothesis that Pyramid Lake and the surrounding desert are crucially linked, in the minds of those who know the lake well, in an ecosystem very sensitive to small changes in weather, light, and the behavior of wild creatures. That many of these changes occur suddenly, last a fraction of a second, and require supernatural explanations is not surprising. The lake and the desert appear empty. Behind the illusory curtain of light and wind there are wizards shifting shapes. These wizards account for critters partly invisible and varmints unusually loquacious.

Lawrence Daniel Myers's 1987 doctoral dissertation, "Levels of Context: A Symbolic Analysis of Numic Origin Myths," provides the fullest selection of these legends. Myers draws primarily on the stories collected by John Wesley Powell, Robert Lowie, Edward Sapir, Isabel T. Kelly, and Julian Steward. This provides him several variants of dozens of creation myths, animal tales, and explanations of geographic and meteorological phenomena recorded between 1873 and 1930 from Indians born between the 1840s and the 1880s. The most active period of collecting was 1920–30, when many Americans thought the Indians had vanished. Myers argues that the myths provide information on Paiute knowledge of and attitudes toward their physical environment and explain the value system underlying their complex social and political organization.

One interesting variant of the creation story was collected by anthropologist Isabel Kelly in 1930 from a seventy-year-old man, Billy Steve, who had grown up at Pyramid Lake. In his version a large cannibal arrives at a place where Indians are camped and playing the hand game. A woman who had a camp by herself (during her menstrual period) heard the cannibal and ran to warn the gamblers. She hid herself in a hole under sagebrush. The cannibal kills and eats all the Indians except the woman and a baby. After the cannibal leaves, the woman takes the baby and walks toward a mountain in the Stillwater area, where she thinks she will find a man to be her husband, but another cannibal accosts her. She escapes by directing him toward the baby while she hides again in a hole under some sagebrush.

Escaping from the cannibal, she meets a Beaver who is also an Indian. The Beaver hides the woman until the cannibals leave, and then Beaver casts the woman over a mountain, where she stays with Gopher, Beaver's sister. Gopher gives her a lot of roots for food and sends her off on her quest with a warning: "On the road there is a head in a basket, don't touch them!" Of course, she does not obey, and the head and the basket chase her. Fortunately, the woman's uncle, Rat, had "painted" (urinated on) his home. The head and the basket roll into the side of the house and break into a thousand pieces. The woman walks on and finally comes to the house of the man she is seeking. He feeds her, and she sleeps nearer to him each night for five nights. On the fifth night they are "married." The man and the woman have four children: one boy and one girl were Paiutes; the other two were Pit Rivers. The siblings fought. The father sent the Paiute pair to Doyle (a present-day community between Pyramid Lake and Honey Lake). The Pit River pair he sent to Humboldt in Northern California. The man told his wife that he was going "to the other side of the clouds," where people go when they die. The storyteller did not know what happened to the woman.

But Billy Steve was not through with his storytelling. He offered Kelly a different version, called "Coyote Begets Indians." This is a bawdy story. It begins when a pretty girl propositions Coyote, but he cannot catch her. He keeps trying to find her and eventually tracks her to an island in a lake. When he gets to the island, he meets an old woman who tells him the girl is hunting swans. She returns and they have a feast. Coyote notices that the women throw some bones under where they are sitting. He hears crunching. He knows the women have toothed vaginas. He sneaks out and gets a rock that he uses to knock out the girl's vagina dentata. He does the same with her mother. Coyote lives with them while his mother-in-law makes a water jug. When he and his wife leave for his home, he realizes that his children are in the jug that his mother-in-law has forbidden him to open. Of course, he opens it, and all the children but one run away to the west, followed by their mother. Coyote is very sorry. He blesses the remaining boy and goes home alone, knowing that if he had not opened the jug, he would have had all his children at home and "they would have been raised right."

Myers finds support for both his hypotheses in these tales, arguing that they show Paiute knowledge of and respect for fellow creatures and, symbolically, support a social structure that gives women some autonomy while placing authority with male figures. The stories sanction plural marriage and the isolation of menstruating women, and they explain tribal diasporas. He subscribes to the notion that "the removal of the vagina dentata is equated with menstruation itself." He sees cannibalism and vagina dentata as being male and female versions of the same thing, linking the consumption of human flesh to the forming of distinct exogamous groups for marriage. This is all probably right to some degree; it is what I was taught in anthropology a half century ago, but I doubt that it is a full explanation.

Recent interpretations of Western Shoshone cannibal myths, some of which are similar to Paiute tales, posit them as statements of national identity in which the cannibals are identified as white invaders. Richard O. Clemmer, an anthropologist at the University of Denver, is specifically interested in recent changes in these stories as told at fandangos (powwows) held in Ruby Valley.

By focusing on revisions and changes in the stories, Clemmer implicitly exposes one of Myers's principal weaknesses. Neither Myers nor the ethnographers whose data he mines ever fully address the fact that even their oldest informants have been exposed to Christian and other white mythologies, consciously or unconsciously incorporating these influences into earlier Numa legends. Myers's other problem is his assumption that the longer narratives are complete.

These stories are chiefly concerned with food and sex, which are universal human needs. The structure of the stories resembles all the fables with which I am familiar—they begin with something like, "Once upon a time," take their main character through a series of fantastic adventures, and come to "The End." Heroes and heroines break rules and are punished or rewarded, evildoers are defeated or escape, order is restored or created anew. This is not to say that the Paiute tales are simple or childlike. In fact, they seem to me to resemble stories from the Bible, or a movie by Tim Burton. Rolling, talking heads, vaginas with teeth, cannibals that kill with a look, this is the stuff of late-night cable television and comic books. The Paiute legends can also be meant as entertainment, just like David and Goliath, Jack and the Beanstalk, and Pinocchio. Entertainment, of course, carries multiple messages to diverse audiences.

Take the Water Babies, for example. Powell collected a Water Baby legend in the early 1870s. In this version two women are walking along the shores of Pyramid Lake. One of the women leaves her sleeping infant in its cradleboard in some reeds and wanders away. A Pa-o-ha (Water Baby) lurking nearby strangles the baby, eats it, and takes its place in the cradle. The mother returns and begins feeding the infant. The Water Baby bites her breast and the mother tries to throw the Water Baby off, but the creature swallows the whole breast. The woman seeks help, and various members of her camp try cutting and burning the Water Baby without effect. Finally, "a renowned sorcerer" amputates the mother's breast, and the "mermaid" runs back to the lake. In some versions of this legend, Water Babies and mermaids are the same creature, or the mermaid is the creator of the Water Babies—they are the curse she brings down on the lake when she is banished by the tribe.

In 1980, more than a century after Powell's interviews, an enterprising English professor at the University of Nevada, Reno, sent students off to Pyramid Lake to collect stories from willing Indians. Part of the result of this assignment is preserved in the Special Collections of the University of Nevada library. They are the Pa Oha stories of Dewey Sampson, Abe Abraham, Poncho Quintero, and Mel Thom. Sampson, a former tribal council chairman, told one student, Peggy Lear Bowen, about an Indian who was not having any success fishing. In disgust, the fisherman said, "I wish I could catch one of those water babies." In a few minutes he hooked what he hoped was a trout, but it was a Water Baby. Frightened, he threw it back and went home. That night he died. Sampson made the moral of the story plain: "The land and water is sacred. No one should ridicule Nature, or Mother Earth, or go hunting or fishing without first making a prayer to our creator, Me ma nu wu tudu."

Another student, Vina Day, collected three Water Baby stories. Nixon store owner Abe Abraham told her that the Water Babies spoke Paiute, were two to three feet tall, and were "light complected." They were born and raised in the warm springs at the northern end of the lake, and they disappeared when those springs dried up about 1952. Nixon businessman Poncho Quintero's version takes place on the Truckee. A Paiute woman is picking berries by the river. She puts her baby in a cradleboard by a tree. When she hears it cry for food she nurses it, and it bites her breast and cannot be removed. Her village elders send for a medicine man, who sees that her infant has been replaced by a Water Baby. The shaman offers the Water Baby animal blood and it releases its grip on the woman, but her child has been killed by the Water Baby.

Mel Thom's account follows Quintero's, but the human baby is spared when the Water Baby returns to the lake with the mother's breast. About 1952, Thom continues, a white man scoffed at his Indian friend's belief in Water Babies and rode his horse to the lake. The Water Babies grabbed the man and his horse. A search-and-rescue team from Reno failed to find the bodies. The 1950s, it will be recalled, was an especially difficult time for the Kuyuidokado. The BIA limited their autonomy, and the lake level was declining rapidly. It is not surprising that the Water Babies, in the stories told by tribal members, were feeling threatened and fighting back.

The legend continues to fascinate and evolve. On a website called "AOL Travel News," an item titled "The Water Babies of Pyramid Lake" was posted September 24, 2010, by Ron Anderson. His version links the Water Babies to the annual drowning of "an unlucky fisherman." He then speculates that the Paiutes once threw malformed and stillborn babies into the lake, and "the angry spirits of the unfortunate infants . . . take their revenge on lake dwellers." Anderson next relates the story of the doomed romance between a Paiute man and the mermaid he brings back from California that results in a curse on the lake and the creation of the Water Babies. With tongue in cheek he quotes a local Paiute, "If you hear [the laughter of the Water Babies] it's bad news; if you see [them], you're dead."

The Water Baby story is clearly a cautionary tale—an example of what one of

Basso's Apache colleagues calls stories that work like arrows, stories that "make you live right." Another Apache says, "The land is always stalking people. The land makes people live right. The land looks after us." The Water Baby story warns mothers to be vigilant with their babies, fishermen to respect the lake, and, in one version, men to conform to tribal marriage customs. In a more contemporary context, it could be seen as sounding an alarm on the damage done by invasive species and careless tourists.

Pa-o-ha are also creators of Pa-gu-nab (pogonip)—fog or steam—that goes to the ocean and comes back with the west wind. This tidbit of information was collected by Powell and provides an important link between these angry water sprites and the weather. The Paiutes knew that most of their precipitation came over the Sierra Nevada. From trade and travel they also had some knowledge of the ocean that lay beyond the western mountains. Steam rising from the hot springs at Pyramid Lake vanished into the sky. Even though Paiute scientists lacked knowledge of the chemistry of water, they made a logical deduction about the hydrologic cycle—water to vapor rising, back to rain falling from the sky. Something was stirring the atmospheric pot; why not Water Babies? And if their power could be harnessed, weather might be controlled, a dream shared by shamans and some meteorologists. Anthropologist Robert Z. Park, in his 1938 study, *Shamanism in Western North America: A Study in Cultural Relationships*, translates Pa-o-ha as "breath of the water-holes" and says that Water Babies have the power to cause wind, a power that ties them more tightly to the hydrologic cycle.

Paiutes, like the rest of us, have several often-contradictory bits of weather lore. Peg Wheat quotes one of her collaborators to the effect that the porcupine brings storms and that whirlwinds cause headaches. Julian Steward learned that among Owens Valley Paiutes, "flying cobwebs mean rain the next day" and that "a breeze called o-so-ja-pu, 'its breath,' foretells a storm." In addition to learning that lightning is a red snake, Powell discovered that another red snake with a head like a man was the source of roaring thunder. A ring or a snake around the moon foretold rain. Many of these signs are similar to beliefs held by other Indians. Stansbury Hagar writes that the Micmac in Maine attribute thunder to seven flying rattlesnakes shaking their tails as they cross the sky. Some Micmac claim that weather control is achieved by retelling certain legends, talking about the desired weather.

I recall a conversation with Peg Wheat more than fifty years ago, in which she told a story about the Paiute shaman Jim George. Mr. George was proudly displaying his sacred objects, including some miniature baskets that looked to Wheat like a child's toys. "Oh, no," George smiled. "I made these to take to France in the First World War to capture winds and destroy the German soldiers." He assured her that the baskets provided storms on more than one occasion.

At the Pyramid Lake Guest Ranch, a discussion of weather modification led to an experiment. As related by Basil Woon in the March 6, 1955, *Nevada State Journal,* a representative from a rainmaking company in Denver, probably smitten by Joan Drackert, left one of his firm's cloud-seeding machines at the Pyramid Lake Guest Ranch with instructions to start it whenever he phoned. Faced with a request from a construction crew extending the dirt road past Letty's ranch for an inch of rain to settle the dust, Joan fired up the contraption, which, Woon writes, was a small box that looked like an old-fashioned refrigerator. "There was a tiny motor, a blower, a miniature furnace and a hopper which fed small dark crystals into the furnace." " 'Silver iodide, I think that's what the man said it is,' said Joan. 'See, it drops just a few crystals into the fire and they become a kind of heavy ash and the ash gets blown into the air into the clouds and they become too heavy and so—' " Harry, deadpan, finished her sentence: " 'Rain falls in Winnemucca.' " "Everyone roared." An hour later, at 1:30 P.M. on February 13, Woon reports, an inch of rain fell in "the purviews of Pyramid." " 'My old Chief Rain-in-Face,' said Harry, proudly. Nobody laughed. 'Oh, well, I just lit the thing,' said Joan, nonchalantly."

Woon's playful account of weather modification accomplishes three things. It depicts his friends Harry and Joan Drackert as sorcerers of an enchanted place, it highlights the lake and the state's dependence on water, and it recasts the myth of the eternal, unchanging desert. Woon presents the joking between Harry and Joan as a kind of screwball comedy, but in the context of the article, which describes Geiger counters and uranium prospecting on the reservation, and the building of new roads, most readers knew that major environmental changes were about to take place, twenty years before the Desert Research Institute began its rainmaking experiments as part of the Pyramid Lake Task Force. Despite the lack of any conclusive evidence of the efficacy of cloud seeding to produce rain, Nevada and other western states have spent millions of dollars on rainmaking with essentially the same equipment Joan Drackert used in 1955. None of the efforts to make rain had any effect on cycles of drought and flooding. The Corps of Engineers began a number of river-changing projects under the Flood Control Act of 1954, but too late to prevent the worst flooding in recorded history in December 1955. No new Indian messiah arose to resist the degradation of the Truckee and Pyramid Lake, but the following decade witnessed the beginnings of a new national environmental awareness. Wovoka's prayers were answered at last.

LESS THAN ONE HUNDRED MILES from Pyramid Lake, Wovoka, the Paiute "messiah," also called Quoitze Ow, Jack Wilson, and other names, revived the Ghost Dance, a set of songs and dances that portended the return of deceased ancestors and the removal, by some unspecified natural cataclysm, of all white people from the continent. As Wovoka's message spread eastward, it lost its peaceful vision and became a rallying point for angry Plains Indians and an excuse for military action by the US Army, ending in the massacre of more than three hundred Indian men, women, and children at Wounded Knee, South Dakota, December 29, 1890. The military force lost, in the account compiled by James Mooney, a total of forty-nine.

Mooney's book *The Ghost-Dance Religion and the Sioux Outbreak of 1890* was the first full account of this religious movement. Because Mooney was, briefly, a sojourner in the deserts southeast of Pyramid Lake and because his description of the place is rich in detail relevant to the story of desert seekers, he deserves some space here. He was born in Indiana in 1861, became a schoolteacher and newspaper reporter, and then, pursuing his dream of studying Indians, went to Washington, DC, in 1885, seeking a job with John Wesley Powell's newly established Bureau of American Ethnology. Powell gave him a position, which he held until his death in 1921. Mooney was also a passionate advocate of Irish culture and nationalism, views that made him somewhat sympathetic to the Indians' cause.

In the wake of Wounded Knee, Powell sent Mooney to interview the prophet Wovoka and put the revitalization movement into a larger context. Mooney arrived in Wabuska and set out in a wagon accompanied by an unnamed driver, Wovoka's uncle Charlie Sheep, and a young white storekeeper, Edward A. Dyer, to find Wovoka.

It was New Year's day of 1892, and there was deep snow on the ground, a very unusual thing in this part of the country, and due in this instance, as Charley assured us, to the direct agency of Jack Wilson. It is hard to imagine anything more monotonously unattractive than a sage prairie under ordinary circumstances unless it is the same prairie when covered by a heavy fall of snow, under which the smallest clumps of sagebrush look like prairie-dog mounds, while the larger ones can hardly be distinguished at a short distance from wikiups. However the mountains were bright in front of us, the sky was blue overhead, and the road was good under foot.

Mooney's wonderfully playful sentence that moves him from the unattractive sage prairie to the fantasy of snow-covered wikiups in a fairyland of bright
mountains and blue skies is worthy of W. B. Yeats—Celtic tomfoolery in the
Nevada wilderness. In this enchanted setting, Wovoka mysteriously appears.
Mooney and the messiah meet, talk briefly, and agree to get together that evening after Wovoka has finished his rabbit hunt. Mooney and his party journey
on but get lost in the evening darkness. They stumble around, cold and hungry.
Mooney complains, "To add to our difficulty, the snow was cut in every direction by cattle trails, which seemed to be Indian trails, and kept us doubling and
circling to no purpose, while in the uncertain gloom every large clump of sagebrush took on the appearance of a wikiup, only to disappoint us on a nearer
approach." Paiute and cow trails are indistinguishable, the Indians' *karnee* (their
wikiups) mirror the brush, people and land are wild and untamed, yet Mooney
and his companions arrive at Wovoka's, guided by the sparks from his sagebrush
fire. Reversals of expectations follow rapidly. Mooney is entranced. Wovoka is
an impressive man. Mooney gets his information, and he feels he has become a
blood brother. Now he can reveal the deeper meanings of the Ghost Dance and
the true nature of Wovoka.

> The physical environment was favorable to the development of such a character.
> His native valley, from which he has never wandered, is a narrow strip of level
> sage prairie some 30 miles in length, walled in by the giant sierras, their sides
> torn and gashed by volcanic convulsions and dark with gloomy forests of pine,
> their towering summits white with everlasting snows, and roofed over by a cloud-
> less sky whose blue infinitude the mind instinctively seeks to penetrate to far-off
> worlds beyond. Away to the south the view is closed in by the sacred mountains
> of the Paiute, where their Father gave them the first fire and taught them their
> few simple arts before leaving for his home in the upper regions of the Sun-land.
> Like the valley of Rasselas, it seems apart from the great world to be the home of
> a dreamer.

Mooney struggles to explain Wovoka by his physical environment. His reference, Samuel Johnson's *History of Rasselas, Prince of Abissinia* (1759), is a philosophical inquiry into the meaning of human happiness in the form of an adventure novel. In the story, Rasselas grows bored with his perfect life in his father's
happy valley and escapes with his sister, her attendant, and his poet-friend to see
the world and search for true happiness. After a while they realize the futility
of their quest and return to his father's utopia. Mooney seems to be comparing
Rasselas's dreams with Wovoka's. In Mooney's view, the Paiutes have escaped

the worst of white conquest and should be happy to live under the protection of benevolent white ranchers in Smith and Mason Valleys. Yet Mooney appears to believe that those valleys, scarred by volcanic eruptions but healed by the infinite sky, are responsible for Wovoka's power to challenge the status quo.

The impressionable ethnographer also learned that on New Year's Day 1889, during an eclipse of the sun, Wovoka, about thirty-one years old, apparently suffered "cataleptic seizures," or perhaps a high fever, from which he emerged with a vision of the future. There are many versions of Wovoka's dream, but Mooney contends that "the great underlying principle of the Ghost Dance doctrine is that the time will come when the whole Indian race, living and dead, will be reunited upon a regenerated earth, to live a life of aboriginal happiness, forever free from death, disease, and misery." To make this happen, Wovoka, the Indian messiah, instructed believers to live good and peaceful lives, abstain from alcohol and other white men's vices, and perform a dance and sing songs for five days. These dances, which allowed for great variation among tribes, were to be repeated at regular intervals.

Mooney immediately saw the similarity of the Ghost Dance to other dreams of paradise lost. "The doctrine of the Hindu avatar, the Hebrew messiah, the Christian millennium and . . . the Indian Ghost dance are essentially the same, and . . . have their origin in a hope and longing common to all humanity." In the case of the Paiute messiah, restoration of the earth included all creatures, encouraging historian Louis Warren to reevaluate the Ghost Dance as a part of the growing conservation movement of the late nineteenth century. By including the return of the buffalo and forbidding the killing of horses in funeral rites, Wovoka and prophets from other tribes were sending a clear message that conservation measures were needed to save people and place.

Wovoka, whose powers as a shaman and controller of weather remain in dispute, was, Michael Hittman demonstrates, a successful promoter of the status conferred on him by Mooney. Growing old and without skills other than his imagination, Wovoka needed to charge for photographs and interviews. As historian Frank Goodyear explains in his study of the Lakota chief Red Cloud, Native Americans embraced photography as a way to communicate. Photography was a medium for bridging the gap between cultures. For Wovoka it was another way of managing his image. Through photographs he became a personality in a world beyond Mason Valley.

Movie cowboy star and showman Tim McCoy recalled appearances by Wovoka in which he worked his audiences for donations. "Billy Graham had

nothing on him, to say nothing of Amy [*sic*] Semple McPherson." McCoy's analogy is a bit of a stretch, but a brief sketch by Omer Stewart of the Pyramid Lake
shaman Joe Green provides some insight into the complex lives of Paiute Desert Fathers. Stewart was surprised to discover that Green, a respected shaman
healer, was also a deacon in the Episcopal Church who seldom missed a Sunday
service, despite spending Saturday evenings in Native American Church peyote
rituals. Green told Stewart that he liked the Christian hymns, the peyote songs,
and his shamanistic prayers equally. Stewart wisely concludes that Green was
"living testimony to . . . religious harmony." Stewart fails to mention that the first
recorded Episcopal marriage on the reservation was between Joe Green and
Bessie Winnemucca, on August 9, 1898. That Green and Wovoka took different
paths to harmony would not surprise any desert seeker.

"PAHNENIT, PRINCE OF THE LAND OF LAKES"

It is unknown whether Dan De Quille paid Wovoka for the story "Pahnenit,
Prince of the Land of Lakes," but De Quille attributes the story to him. De
Quille probably wrote the piece in 1893–94, before the publication of Mooney's
monograph, but Wovoka had been the subject of articles in local newspapers
since 1889. When De Quille's story begins, western Nevada is covered with
interconnected lakes. Tamogoowah (the Creator) breathes on the ground and
creates all life, and those life-forms were free to change into whatever species
they liked. There were also evil giants who lived in the active volcanoes and
either killed the people or changed them into birds. Wungee, a boy living on
an island in what is now Pyramid Lake, comes of age and begins to explore his
surroundings. He sees that he is not like the black pygmies who live near him,
which causes him to wonder who his parents were.

One day while staring at his reflection in the lake, he sees another face beside
his, but before he can act the face disappears. He realizes that the face is not a
reflection, but a creature that lives in the water. Later he sees an old woman carrying a bundle of wood, but she also disappears before he can talk with her. That
night he has a dream in which he is told to speak to the woman when he sees
her again. The next day he sees the old woman, but she transforms herself into a
bush. He implores her to answer, and she does, instructing him to take a green
stone that she gives him and, when he sees the beautiful face in the lake again, to
throw the stone out into the lake and return to her.

He does all this and soon sees a tall young girl wearing "a clinging robe of
some ethereal material that took in the shifting light as many hues of green, blue,
gold and purple as did the waters of the lake when dancing in the sun." Wungee

immediately proposes and the maiden consents, if they are married by "Mother Bush." The bush changes into an old woman who tells Wungee that he can marry Thel, the Spirit of the Waters, as long as the green stone remains in the lake. If it is removed, Thel will return to her underwater home. The old woman also gives him a crystal with a few drops of pure water inside and instructs him to keep it with him at all times or he will lose his wife. She sends him on a quest to find Hela, the Spirit of the Air, and provides him with two more gifts—a magic bow and single arrow with which he can kill anything except rabbits, and a thong with five knots that he can untie whenever he is in danger and needs her help. She tells the newlyweds that she is Thea, Queen of the Cedars.

Thel wants to start looking for the Spirit of the Air immediately, but Wungee delays because they need to gather provisions for their journey. As a test of the Cedar Queen's powers, he unties a knot. She appears and he orders supplies, which she quickly provides. They travel for many days, finally exhausting their provisions. When Wungee fails to find any game, Thel waves her hand over a stream and a school of large fish appears. Wungee starts to net them all, but Thel stops him, saying, "One is enough." Before they can continue their search for Hela, the Queen of the Cedars appears and tells Wungee that he is Pahnenit, Prince of the Land of Lakes, and that his father had been chief of a tribe of noble people who incurred the jealously of the giants who turned them into rabbits. Wungee escaped because his mother had left him by a tree away from their village. Thea explains that she has found a way to break the spell the giants cast on Pahnenit's people; he must marry four sisters—Thel, Spirit of the Waters; Hela, Spirit of the Air; Ela, Spirit of the Earth; and Mae, Spirit of Fire.

With a clearer idea of the goal, but no idea how to achieve it, Pahnenit travels east until he comes to a large sea. He is stumped, but Thel uses her power over water creatures and causes a pelican to become large enough to carry them both on his back. After a few hours of flight they discover that the giants have sent eagles to attack them. A terrific aerial battle ensues, with Pahnenit shooting the attackers with arrows and Thel conjuring flocks of birds for counterattacks. They win and arrive on Hela's island. At night they are attacked by demons but, sheltered by a cedar tree, remain unharmed. In the morning they ascend a mountain and find the conch shell that the Cedar Queen instructed him to blow three times to summon the Queen of the Air, but the shell is too large for his mouth. Again Thel uses her powers and brings a giant frog who easily sounds the notes. Hela steps forward, and Pahnenit is about to take her hand when the frog claims her. No problem. Thel quickly shrinks him back to frog size, and Pahnenit acquires a second wife.

Not a moment too soon. The forces of evil have set a fire that surrounds them, but now Pahnenit has the Queen of the Air to save him. She creates a rainstorm and provides a flying chariot for their escape. They fly to the garden of earth. Pahnenit picks a white flower and discovers it is Ela, Spirit of the Earth. The foursome settle down and enjoy paradise until they discover Thel has been kidnapped by the giants. Pahnenit is forced to untie the second of his magic knots and seek help from Thea, who admonishes him for falling asleep and allowing the giants to steal the water-filled crystal. To rescue Thel he must find and marry Mae, Spirit of Fire. Thanks to the powers of his two remaining wives, he flies to the land of fire and proceeds to enter a burning cavern. Inside he finds another lovely garden and a tall red-haired beauty who becomes his fourth wife. She gives him a poisoned red fruit to dip his arrows in for the coming fight against the giants. He dispatches his first giant as he and Ela emerge from the flaming cave, and, mirabile dictu, he finds the missing crystal under the giant's tongue.

Reunited with Thel, Pahnenit and his four wives return to Mae's cave and its delightful garden, but not to rest. Mae wants them to recover a magic torch the giants stole from her. The restoration of the torch will weaken the giants' power. Over the next few days a great battle rages between the giants and their wizards who constantly change shape and the Spirits of Water, Air, Earth, and Fire. The fight creates all sorts of bad weather and disasters. Prince Pahnenit gets off a few good shots with his bow. Together they drive the enemy into hiding, but they cannot lift the spell from the people turned into rabbits. Once again Pahnenit unties a knot, and the Cedar Queen leads them into the bowels of the earth in pursuit of the evildoers. They succeed in capturing Kievah-Kosoac, leader of the wizards, forcing him to surrender his medicine bag.

In the final chapter the spirit sisters finish up their work by creating Lake Tahoe, banishing the wizards to the hot springs in the desert, and returning to the land of the lakes, where they discover the lakes are shrinking because of all the upheavals caused by the war with the giants. Pahnenit unties another knot, hoping that Thea can change the rabbits back into his people. She tells him that thanks to her visit to the father of all rabbits, the one you can see in the moon when it is full, his people will be freed. This happens during the next full moon, and Pahnenit becomes the most powerful shaman as well as prince. The dark dwarves are sent to the mountains, where they become the Washoe Tribe! Everything seems to be going well, but Thel seems unhappy. Pahnenit suddenly realizes that due to the shrinking of the lake, the green stone that prevents Thel from returning to the water is about to be exposed. He searches for it frantically without success, forcing him to untie the last knot. Cedar Queen shows him where the stone is and at his request places it under the great pyramid in the deepest part of the lake. Thel is pleased that he loves her so much. The Cedar Queen forgives him for using his last knot when he was not in danger, but makes him promise that his people will never move away. Pahnenit's descendants include "Chief Winnemucca, and all the royal family of Winnemucca."

De Quille's little fantasy is certainly in the spirit of Dr. Johnson's *Rasselas.* "Pahnenit" is a philosophical fairy tale critical of the giants, who may or may not represent the white invaders, but obviously are the forces of wanton destruction of Native life. "Pahnenit' is also an environmental lesson, the Spirits of Cedar, Water, Air, Earth, and Fire, the physical environment that Wungee and all humans must learn to respect if they hope to survive. De Quille values the authentic Paiute myths and legends that he must have known, but incorporates them into an adventure story that borrows from the *Odyssey, Sinbad the Sailor, The Golden Bough,* and East Asian and Mayan rabbit-in-the-moon stories. Like Rasselas, Pahnenit wanders from his "happy valley" in search of knowledge, only to return, having learned that home is the best place. Dan De Quille is the most humane of all Nevada's Desert Fathers, and the Queen of the Cedars is the most wonderful Desert Mother, at least until Roslyn in "The Misfits."

THE PATHS IN THE DESERTS of the earth are now well trodden. The "desert challenge," as historian Richard G. Lillard called it, is an endless succession of deep insights and unanswerable questions. Those in recent times who sought in the desert an understanding of their lives and the world they live in must, like James Mooney, be able to tell sagebrush from a wikiup or, like Idah Strobridge, a hotel from a mirage. Today, Pyramid Lake dazzles the desert seeker and sustains the Kuyuidokado. It exists to remind the surrounding desert that it was once, paradoxically, an ocean bed and to remind us that what we think we find at Pyramid Lake may be equally illusory.

TEN

Pyramid Lake as Theater

The sky forms a proscenium arch over Pyramid Lake, framing the ever-changing scenes of atmospheric drama and acts of human nobility and cupidity. Little wonder that the lake attracts histrionics, from the entrance of Kit Carson and J. C. Frémont with a howitzer in tow to the exit of an environmental artist plowing circles in a playa. The lake served as a backdrop for the religious ceremonies of the Kuyuidokado for centuries, and continues to do so, but the coming of Christian missionaries moved religious spectacles indoors. "In 1890," Lorraine Wadsworth explains, "the Paiutes of Pyramid Lake were assigned to the Episcopal Church." The federal government assigned various denominations to reservations. The first Episcopal services were conducted in 1894 in a building at Nixon loaned by the BIA. Two years later mass was held in a small frame church called St. Mary's. Another Episcopal church, St. Michael's, was built at Wadsworth.

The ritual of the Mass is, like Elizabethan drama, usually divided into five parts (acts): a gathering with hymn singing, a sermon, an offering of prayers, an exchange of greetings by the congregation, communion with sacred bread and wine, and dismissal with a prayer of thanksgiving. Since five is a symbolic number in Paiute culture, this ritual may have been especially appealing. Photographs of St. Mary's in Wadsworth's book show a spare interior with about eight rows of pews seating 150, a simple raised altar about the size of an upright piano, but no pulpit. This church was built of stone and concrete blocks in 1917, after the first structure burned down. Gothic-style arched windows with stained glass illuminate the interior. St. Mary's introduced the Kuyuidokado to the spatial conventions of Euro-American theaters as well as churches. How that space was used depended on the performer and the audience.

BROTHER DAVID

Why Brother David, born William John Hughes in Wales in 1894, and known to theater and movie audiences as Gareth Hughes, chose the Paiutes of the

Pyramid Lake Reservation for his religious mission remains a mystery. He took the name David, he told me, because the biblical David was a musician and author of many of the psalms. Hughes's presence at the lake coincided with the sojourns of Liebling, Miller, and Bellow, and he appears as "Brother Louis" in Bellow's short story "Leaving Yellow House." Liebling appreciated Rabelaisian characters and took time out from his investigation of the conflict between Senator Pat McCarran and the Pyramid Lake Tribe to have tea with Brother David in Nixon. Liebling was curious about a man who had "held in his arms the pulsating forms of the most beautiful women in the world's history"—Theda Bara, Pola Negri, Viola Dana, Nazimova—but he was intimidated, he wrote, by Brother David's cassock. Liebling records that they shared a pot of Lapsang, and Hughes "spouted Shakespeare in a musical Welsh voice and warned me of the machinations of the Mormon Church, which, he said was laboring to convert the Indians and exploit the untapped mineral resources on all the reservations." Brother David was at one time a thespian, then an Episcopalian, finally, perhaps, a Jansenist, and always uninhibited.

Brother David's early career has been tantalizingly described on websites by his acolyte Stephen Lyons of Cwmcaddon, Wales. According to Lyons, Hughes left home in 1910 and became an actor, touring England and Wales, playing boyish roles in Shakespeare's plays and popular melodramas. In 1914, not yet twenty years old, he arrived in New York and soon became part of James O'Neill's touring company, famous for its production of *The Count of Monte Cristo*. James's son Eugene was just beginning his career as a playwright, and Gareth Hughes's association with the O'Neills may have helped him get good roles in New York and in Hollywood. In 1916 Hughes played Ariel in a Broadway production of *The Tempest*. Hughes appeared in more than fifty movies between 1915 and 1931, notably in the 1919 version of the comic novel *Mrs. Wiggs of the Cabbage Patch* and in James Barrie's *Sentimental Tommy* in 1921. He apparently made a considerable amount of money, counted Isadora Duncan, Lionel Barrymore, Jack Dempsey, and Sally Rand among his acquaintances, and lived the good life in the 1920s, but his career did not survive the coming of sound and he lost most of his fortune in the stock market crash of 1929. His farewell to the stage occurred in 1937 when he was director of religious and Shakespearean dramas for the Federal Theater Project in Los Angeles.

Experiencing a spiritual crisis, Gareth Hughes reinvented himself as Brother David and in the 1940s convinced the Episcopal bishop of Nevada, William Fisher Lewis, to allow him to minister to the Paiutes at Pyramid Lake. Although there had been an Episcopalian presence on the reservation since the 1890s,

Brother David with (*left to right*) Margelina, Harry, and Ramona Jim, ca. 1952.
Courtesy Special Collections, University of Nevada, Reno, Libraries.

little progress had been made in converting the small band of cui-ui eaters.
Initially, things went well for Brother David. The Indians accepted him, and,
according to Lyons, "the Bishop of Nevada wrote of him, 'he is the only white
man I have ever known who seems to win immediately the unreserved affection
of the Paiute people. He is the most effective teacher of the simple essentials of
the Catholic faith I have ever known.'"

Within a few years, however, Bishop Lewis began to suspect that the essentials of Brother David's faith might be based more on Shakespeare than on
the Book of Common Prayer. Brother David designed his own vestments and
invented his own forms of communion for his Native flock. He and Lewis
clashed on several issues, and the bishop dismissed him from the Paiute mission. "I feel like I've been goosed by the Holy Ghost," he remarked to friends.
Defrocked, but not discouraged, Brother David sailed for the land of Rabelais,
got himself ordained a Jansenist priest, and returned to preach to the Paiutes,
unfettered by the Episcopal hierarchy. At least that is the story I heard in the
1950s.

Historian John Marschall tells a different version in his online biography of Hughes. According to Marschall, Hughes was gay and had been involved in various Hollywood scandals in the 1920s. He entered, about 1940, the Episcopal monastery of the Society of St. John the Evangelist in Cambridge, Massachusetts, and later moved to the Anglican Benedictine monastery of the Holy Cross in New York. He became a "lay reader and missionary" to the Indians on the Fort McDermitt Reservation in 1942. Marschall believes that Hughes took time off to become ordained in the Apostolic Episcopal Church, a dissenting sect of Episcopalianism, in 1945. This apparently led to his theological conflicts with Bishop Lewis and others. Marschall also repeats the story that Hughes's terminal illness, byssinosis, was caused by inhaling lint from the Hollywood clothing he distributed to the Indians. If true, he was martyred by wardrobe, a fitting death for the old actor.

Sometime in the early 1950s it became clear that revenue from six-week divorces might logically be supplemented by profits from quickie marriages. Unlike California, the state lacked a waiting period between application for a marriage license and the ceremony. Nor did Nevada require a blood test for venereal disease. Nevada's justices of the peace had always made a good living marrying out-of-staters who did not want more than a civil union, but why should those whose romantic souls craved more than the clammy handshake of an unctuous JP be denied a good show?

The rich and even the middle class have their long engagements, their June weddings in churches so filled with flowers that they resemble botanical gardens, and honeymoons at Niagara Falls or the Caribbean, but where could teenage runaways, three-time losers without tuxes and veils, and sailors due to ship out tomorrow get their share of nuptial bliss? They, too, had heard of "marriage ceremonies," and they were not unaware that weddings were "performed"; the hoi polloi, it seems, eloped with hope.

To meet the needs of this potential market, the wedding chapel was born. The first wedding chapel in Reno ("Think of us as a church with better hours") was located in a former residence across South Virginia Street from the county courthouse and jail. It was established by the father of a high school friend of mine. That pioneer in the theme-wedding business knew a good performer when he saw one and hired Brother David. Today you can be married by an Elvis impersonator, a Star Trek captain, or a pirate, but in 1954 the choice was limited to Brother David or the JP. More than a half century later, I doubt that brides and grooms get a better deal than they got from Brother David. I remember many young couples being dazzled by Brother David's Welsh lilt and hodgepodge recitation of the psalms and the soliloquies of Romeo and Juliet. Brother

David became a performer of weddings Monday through Saturday, but on Sunday he preached to the Paiutes.

He had a car, donated, it was rumored, by Marion Davies. Davies actually gave him a sedan that he traded for a used station wagon. Several of his old Hollywood colleagues regularly sent him clothing for the Indians, and Sunday service at Wadsworth (the Episcopalians prohibited access to their church at Nixon, early in 1955) began to resemble a Cecil B. DeMille production. As he told a reporter for the *Nevada State Journal* in May 1951, "I did get clothing from others, but high heels, John Frederic [*sic*] hats, Schiaparelli gowns! I wish people would send sensible clothing."

He had a wagon, but he needed a driver. I volunteered. I was already hanging around the wedding chapel, serving as the witness required by state law and collecting a few bucks in tips. Wedding chapel customers are couples, unencumbered by family or friends, the usual witnesses—or at least that is what I remember from my days as a professional witness. Brother David's need for a chauffeur gave me additional income and a nice Sunday drive on US 40, which, like its replacement, Interstate 80, paralleled the Truckee River and the Southern Pacific Railroad between Reno and Wadsworth.

Our Sabbath route took us past signs for old SP sidings, including Thisbe, about halfway between Reno and Wadsworth. Our weekly ritual involved a meditation on Thisbe. "Ah, Thisbe," Brother David would announce. "Do you know the story, Barney?" "A bit," I would aver in my best Reno Little Theater enunciation, and he would launch into a retelling of Ovid's story of the doomed lovers Pyramus and Thisbe, the inspiration for *Romeo and Juliet,* and the parody play-within-a-play in *A Midsummer Night's Dream.* From the latter he often recited Puck's concluding soliloquy:

> If we shadows have offended,
> Think but this, and all is mended,
> That you have but slumber'd here
> While these visions did appear.
> And this weak and idle theme,
> No more yielding but a dream,
> Gentles, do not reprehend:
> If you pardon, we will mend:
> And, as I am an honest Puck,
> If we have unearned luck
> Now to 'scape the serpent's tongue,
> We will make amends ere long . . .

Brother David was as fine a Puck as ever he was an Ariel. Indians, mostly elderly women dressed in long, full, tiered skirts with gray scarves covering their braided hair and a few old men in worn Levi's, plaid shirts with pearl buttons, and cowboy hats, greeted Brother David enthusiastically, asking what he had brought them. He usually had a box of clothes and costume jewelry sent by the aging princesses and princes of Hollywood. I maintain a fantasy that some future archaeologist will find the lost wardrobes of *The Ten Commandments* and *Ben-Hur* in the trunks and garages of Nixon and Wadsworth. After the distribution of gifts, the Indians truly seemed to enjoy Brother David's service, a mix of Christian liturgy and recitations from *Hamlet, Julius Caesar, Macbeth,* and, probably, though I do not really remember, *The Count of Monte Cristo.*

The fullest account of Brother David at his best is provided by the prolific journalist, playwright, and novelist Fulton Oursler in an article titled "Star in the Desert" in the *American Weekly*, February 2, 1952. Oursler was almost as colorful a character as Hughes, having written his way out of poverty with pulp fiction. Some of his stories were made into movies. In his late forties he had a religious crisis, converted to Roman Catholicism, and wrote the best-seller *The Greatest Story Ever Told* (1949) that became an epic movie partly filmed at Pyramid Lake in the 1960s. Oursler begins his piece on Brother David with the obligatory comment on Pyramid Lake's "sky-blue water" and then recounts Gareth Hughes's early career. "The famous Mrs. Fiske [Minnie Maddern Fiske was the most prominent American actress of the late nineteenth century] told Alexander Woollcott [*New Yorker* writer] that she could believe acting was an immortal act when watching 'the glow of a performance by Gareth Hughes.' And David Belasco [nineteenth-century American theater producer, director, and playwright] called one of his portrayals 'among the most magnificent that I have ever seen on the English-speaking stage.'"

Oursler continues with descriptions of Brother David at work among the Paiutes, recounting "not only the gospels, but also Aesop's tales of the Dog and the Shadow, the Wolf and the Lamb—animals they knew and could follow straight to the point of the fable." When two boys ask if they will turn white if they believe in God and follow the Commandments, Brother David opens a pocket knife and draws blood from his hand, and then he pricks the boys' hands and exclaims, "No difference, our blood is one and the same.... [T]reat every man like your brother, every woman like your sister." Oursler is especially impressed by Brother David's concern for the sixteen young men from the reservation serving in Korea. But it is the former star's performance on Sunday that fascinates him most.

Now comes the sermon. . . . Perhaps he will tell them the parable of the widow who lost a coin. To prepare, Brother David disappears into the sacristy. When he comes back he is wearing a gingham apron tied around his middle. In his right hand is a broom, the left holds a lighted candle.

"Where is my money?" a senile voice laments.

And down the aisle creeps the ex-star of Broadway and Hollywood, poking under the benches, causing small boys to stand aside, peering over window sills and into the baptismal font. When the coin is found, the old crone's joy electrifies everybody.

The parable, from the Gospel of Luke, is usually interpreted as symbolizing the loss of God's favor and the joy of reuniting with him. It may have had special meaning for Hughes and for Oursler. For the congregation it may have seemed more like a story of lost connections with their land and life before the Newlands Reclamation Project. As theater it was definitely an improvement over the flaming Santa in Janette Woodruff's Christmas play.

Regrettably, my association with Brother David ended in 1955 when Bishop Lewis sent an ordained Episcopal priest, Joseph Hogben, to replace Brother David, who went into a further desert exile on the Paiute Reservation at Fort McDermitt, where his health declined, leading him to retire to a home for actors in 1958. Before he left he gave me a copy of the Everyman Library edition of *Pre-Shakespearean Comedies*, with a line from Nicholas Udall's "Ralph Roister Doister" marked: "Mirth is to be used both of more and less, / Being mixed with virtue in decent comeliness." He also gave me three vellum pages from medieval Latin psalters. I had them framed, and they have traveled with me for more than fifty years.

From his papers in the Special Collections of the University of Nevada Library, we get a glimpse of Brother David in retirement and his relationships with his former congregation. He corresponded with some of the families at Nixon, Wadsworth, and Fort McDermitt, sending money when he could and encouraging them to be good. Letters from two men are particularly interesting. Through the fall of 1956 and the spring of 1957 he received several letters from James Jim, a prisoner in Steilacoom Prison (McNeil Island) in the state of Washington. He thanks Brother David for his letters and for his help in getting permission for his parents to visit. Jim tells Brother David that he has been working in a pear cannery and playing basketball and softball and has been given an award for "All Around Sportsmanship." Also in the Gareth Hughes Papers is a clipping from an unidentified newspaper about the conviction of twenty-one-year-old middleweight boxer James "Gentleman Jim" Jim for the murder of an eighty-eight-year-old woman, the last surviving daughter of Captain Dave Numana, a tribal policeman and one of the old-time chiefs.

Brother David was not the only person moved by Jim's plight. In the Leland Papers there is a letter, dated February 11, 1960, from Don Crawford, a Washoe County assemblyman, to Erle Stanley Gardner, author of the Perry Mason mystery stories, who had created a television series called *The Court of Last Resort,* which used real lawyers presenting cases of clients who had been unjustly convicted. Crawford made a case for James Jim and hoped that Gardner would help prove Jim's innocence. Gardner replied within two weeks that he had interviewed Jim and found him very forthcoming, but that Jim confessed that he had been drunk and Gardner implied that he was guilty. Gardner advised that because Jim would soon be eligible for parole, it would be better to wait. That this case could involve a state assemblyman, let alone a celebrated writer, is heartening. Perhaps it was unrelated to Brother David's work, but the combination of interests in the welfare of the most disadvantaged members of the tribe bespoke a new era.

The other correspondent was a mentally challenged young man Brother David had befriended and supported financially for several years. His letters to the missionary are filled with the pleasure he gets from movies and the Nevada Admission Day Parade. On November 5, 1959, he wrote Brother David that he saw "Charles Branson [*sic*] you know he was Captain Jack with Alan Llad [*sic*] in Drum Beat." This young man may have been struggling academically, but his sense of the importance of the Modoc War in Indian history was exact. The so-called Lava Beds War of 1872–73 was the final armed conflict between the Indians of southern Oregon and the US Army. For several months Captain Jack and a band of about fifty warriors fought a guerrilla war, but they were eventually captured and Captain Jack and three other Modoc leaders were executed. But Indian wars were not foremost in the young man's mind. On June 11, 1961, he wrote Brother David that he "still remembers the words Puck says, 'now the hungry lion roars,'" and he mentions a record called *A Midsummer Night's Dream* and knows that the play was written by William Shakespeare. A good performance is long remembered.

Brother David, the Puck of Pyramid Lake, was a trickster who carried the gifts of delight and laughter to audiences from Cymru to Coo-yu-ee Pah. The Paiute Reservation at Pyramid Lake in the mid-1950s was a bleak and impoverished place to which he brought the love of God and poetry in languages that transcended cultural barriers. A scrap of a letter found in the Charlton Laird Papers in the Special Collections conveys something of Brother David's wit. In an undated note to the university's distinguished linguist he assumes the persona of Geoffrey Chaucer's narrator of "The Nun's Priest's Tale": "From the pore wyddow dwelling in the narrow cottage at Wadsworth. Greetings." Brother David thanks Laird for a Kipling poem that he apparently read in one of his services. He concludes with a mock Chaucerian couplet in fractured Middle English: "If sometime you feelë nature pricking in hir corages—Come to Wadsworth in your horselessë carriages (wow!)." The note was signed "Gareth." The aging actor turned missionary found a boon companion in the professor who was also a novelist. They shared a love of language and theater, of the lake and its people.

Brother David's predecessor and replacement, Joseph Hogben, was no slouch as a self-promoter and mythologizer. In a signed but undated (probably 1956) legal-size three-page typed statement, "The Mission to the Paiutes," in the collections of the Nevada Historical Society, the "Buckaroo Priest" sets forth his creed. The opening paragraph announces in capital letters that the aim of the mission to the Paiutes is "REPARATION!" Linking "Our Dear Lord's Reparation on Calvary" and the "CENTURIES OF WRONG AND INJUSTICE TO THE TRIBES!" Hogben launches into a highly imaginative retelling of the Paiute origin myth, followed by a biographical sketch and a call for donations. Hogben adapts Chief Winnemucca's version of Paiute origins that asserts that two of the original four people were white and two dark. They quarreled and the white boy and girl were banished across a mighty ocean, while the darker pair remained and created the Paiute nation. When the first whites appeared, Winnemucca accepted them as the long-lost brothers and sisters of the Paiutes. This, says Hogben, is the "Good News" that the Episcopal Church brings to the Paiutes, "the beloved tradition of the 'great brotherhood' rested in the eternal truths of the Christian religion!"

Hogben is just getting warmed up. Claiming that he is the only white man ever formally adopted by the Pyramid Lake Tribe, Hogben describes the ceremony that took place on the Feast of the Epiphany 1956, when he received his Paiute name, "To-hah-ho-zee-guh," or "White Bird." The name, he says, was bestowed on him by Joe Wadsworth. The tribal council gave him a silver identification bracelet that serves "in lieu of the old blood rite of adoption." Aware of the mileage (forgive the pun) that Brother David got out of his gift from Marion Davies, Hogben is no longer "astride his great gelding," but is ministering to the Paiutes "with the aid of the Mission car, 'H. M. S. Ada,' (the beautiful station wagon given our Mission by Ada Francis, devoted Churchwoman of Santa Barbara)."

As revealed in the minutes of the Pyramid Lake Tribal Council found in the papers of Robert Leland, the missionary wars were constant from the 1930s through the 1950s. At almost every meeting the tribal council was beset by requests from Mormons, Assembly of God, and other sects to be allowed to proselytize and build churches. They were usually rejected or decisions postponed. The Episcopalian congregation within the tribe was strong enough to hold off the interlopers, and as noted above it was possible for a Paiute to be a shaman, a member of the Native American Church, and an Episcopalian simultaneously.

MOVIES

Brother David and Joe Hogben could put on good shows, but nothing beats the movies. Long before he became Franklin Roosevelt's commissioner of Indian affairs, John Collier was a young social worker in New York City. One of his concerns was the influence of motion pictures on immigrants and the poor. Writing in 1910, Collier thought that, "apart from wearing apparel, the illustrated magazine, and a church ceremonial, the motion picture is the leading artistic expression of the American masses." This is a penetrating observation and one that leads to the realization that the rituals of moviegoing and church ceremonials are closely linked. Both rituals involve surrender to authority. The priest or minister performs the rites and preaches according to conventions established decades, if not centuries, ago. The filmmakers also follow formulas of plot and character to instruct as well as to entertain. The man or woman in the pulpit may be more explicitly didactic, but within a dimly lit theater with its rows of confining seats an audience can become a congregation eager to be uplifted and transformed. I know of more than one occasion in which a momentarily transfixed teenager genuflected on leaving a Saturday matinee.

In his cleverly titled book *The Silents of God: Selected Issues and Documents in Silent American Film and Religion, 1908–1925,* Terry Lindvall, a professor of visual communications at Regent University, argues that "film was a primary vehicle in transferring social authority from the church to the larger secular culture." This insight offers a segue from missionaries to movies. Both Native and white religions were under assault from modernism and a more secular worldview conveyed by the movies. An aspect of that modern culture was a sense of multiple identities—for example, Indians learning from movies how to be Indians, or cowboys, or Mongolians.

Of the motion pictures made at or near Pyramid Lake, four make distinctive points about white American perceptions of the lake and the meaning of the surrounding desert: *The Winning of Barbara Worth* (1926), *Destination Gobi*

(1953), *The Misfits* (1961), and *The Greatest Story Ever Told* (1965). I have dealt with *The Misfits* in chapter 7, contending that it is *the* great film about the myths of the West that have shaped many of the interpretations of Pyramid Lake. One is the myth of an Eden in the wilderness where things were good until "they changed it around." Another is that there is some talisman—lake, fish, rock, man, or woman—that, if found and cherished, will bring happiness. Finally, *The Misfits* considers the tragedy of change: everything dies. "Honey," Gay says to Roslyn, "nothin' can live unless something dies." Gay's observation articulates the concept of the "limited good," the belief that the amount of land, natural resources, and good fortune is finite and the struggle for improvement is futile. Miller depicts his "misfit" mustang hunters as primitives unable to adjust to modern society. Miller and Huston offer the misfits an escape from this crippling idea by endorsing Unamuno's advice to live quixotically, to fight what they see as injustice and to pursue their dreams.

The pursuit of a dream, turning a desert into a garden by building dams and irrigation ditches, is the central theme of the silent film *The Winning of Barbara Worth*. Based on a 1911 novel by the once-popular Harold Bell Wright, the screenplay, by Frances Marion, a pioneer woman screenwriter, begins dramatically with a title card reading, "The Desert, 'Emperor of the Wilderness,'" followed by scenes of a woman burying her husband before being killed herself in a sandstorm. Her little daughter is rescued by kindly Jefferson Worth, who scratches out a living on the edge of the desert. Fifteen years pass and we see Mr. Worth receiving news that money is available to irrigate the land. Two men begin surveying. Willard Holmes (Ronald Coleman) is a well-educated easterner. Abe Lee (Gary Cooper) is a local boy; both are in love with Barbara (Vilma Bánky), the orphaned girl Worth rescued from the desert. Worth hosts a fiesta for the eastern guests, and a jealous Abe Lee says good-bye to Barbara in Spanish. Noticing Holmes's confusion, Barbara flirtatiously tells him (on a title card): "It's the language of the desert, you should learn it."

The next scenes are a montage of the "untamed Colorado"—a raging river, workers driving mules pulling Fresno scrapers to change the contours of the land, and settlers arriving by wagon and automobile. When the dam is completed, the farmers cheer until they learn that the banker owns all the stores and services in town and charges outlandish prices. Holmes, who knows that the banker has used inferior materials in his dam, tells Barbara he is returning to the East. She accuses him of complicity with the banker and sends him away. Mr. Worth cannot meet his payroll, and the workers and farmers begin to riot. The banker's goons stir up trouble. An old, Wovoka-like, Indian prophesies the biggest flood in history. Can things get any worse?

Holmes and Lee team up to bring money that Holmes has raised to meet the payroll, but the banker's gang attacks them and both are wounded, Lee seriously. He persuades Holmes to ride on while he holds off the gang. Holmes delivers the money and collapses, but not before telling Barbara to send help to Lee. She nurses Holmes, but when the rescue party arrives with Abe Lee, she rushes to him and Holmes realizes she loves Abe. Abe, however, tells Barbara that he loves her like a sister, but before they can acknowledge each other's noble gestures, a rider announces that a cloudburst has caused the dam to break and the happy valley to flood. There are scenes of panic—babies abandoned, confused animals, people running, and in the wonderful way of old movies a surrealistic moment when a man in a wheelchair tries to push himself uphill.

Even the banker is trapped, but rescued. The banker, in an act of atonement, begs Barbara to be fair to Holmes. She rushes to tell Holmes she loves him. He rides off, promising to tame the river better this time. Cut to the desert now covered with orange groves and Willard Holmes and Barbara Worth in a suburban setting with an energetic baby who crawls like a turtle. The dream has come true for them: the desert has become a garden.

Wright based his novel on the disaster that occurred in the winter of 1904–5 in Southern California when a levee broke, sending the entire Colorado River into the Imperial Valley, creating the present-day Salton Sea. The first breach and a subsequent one were finally successfully repaired in February 1907. The repair effort was largely paid for by E. H. Harriman, president of the Southern Pacific Railroad. Presidents Theodore Roosevelt and W. H. Taft recommended reimbursement for Harriman, but Congress refused to act. Although there are some parallels between the reclamation of the Imperial Valley and the Newlands project (the dam in the movie looks a lot like Derby Dam), the reader may well be asking, what else makes the movie relevant to the study of Pyramid Lake?

Thanks to the diligent research of Nevada historian Philip Earl, the answer is easy. Producer Samuel Goldwyn said that the Black Rock Desert resembled the Salton Sink and the Imperial Valley. Moreover, Wright could easily have set his novel in the Truckee and Carson River basins, and the extent of environmental damage caused by the irrigation projects makes *The Winning of Barbara Worth* a parable that illuminates the Pyramid Lake water wars.

Earl's detailed account of the filming of *The Winning of Barbara Worth*, published in the *Humboldt Historian* (available online), is a saga itself. Gold-wyn wanted to produce an epic western to rival James Cruze's *Covered Wagon* and John Ford's *Iron Horse* (partly filmed at Dodge Flat, north of Wadsworth). Goldwyn sent director Henry King and two associates on a scouting trip, and they were impressed by Gerlach as a potential site for the fictional town of *Barbara Worth*. The movie company set up headquarters in Winnemucca and began interviewing locals for bit parts and contacting local ranchers for livestock and horsemen. In early June 1926, Western Pacific Railroad workers began putting in water mains for the flooding sequences, and three false-front towns were constructed, one at Gerlach, sixty miles north of Nixon; another at Trego, a few miles east; and a third in the sand dunes near Blue Mountain, near the town of Winnemucca. Goldwyn, King, Gary Cooper, Ronald Coleman, Vilma Bánky, and a 150-person production unit arrived in Trego on June 21.

Nature provided some realism. When a sandstorm struck, King filmed it and used it in the movie. The temperature reached 124 degrees in the afternoons, so filming began at 5:00 A.M. Earl's essay contains many incidents that happened during the filming, including a visit by a reporter from the *Los Angeles Times* who was impressed by the scenery and the "striking cloud effects," and another visitor, Thomas E. Campbell, former governor of Arizona and chairman of the Federal Board of Surveys, who wanted to check out the movie's water-reclamation theme. This may have inspired Goldwyn to hold the movie's premier when the Los Angeles Chamber of Commerce was hosting a conference of state and federal reclamation officials. The officials were feted at the opening. Northern Nevadans hoped the movie would encourage Congress to appropriate funds for more irrigation projects in the state.

It probably did not, nor did it awaken an opposition to wasteful water practices and foolish geoengineering projects, but it certainly confirmed for many in the audience the redemptive power of love and the *winning* combination of eastern know-how and western can-do. Watching this movie today, it is easy to see Pyramid Lake Paiutes and hear them speaking the language of the desert. The lessons of the Imperial Valley disaster and the Newlands debacle are linked. Ignorance of local environmental knowledge can be fatal, as the residents of Fernley learned in January 2008, when one of the old and poorly maintained earthen canals of the Newlands Reclamation Project gave way and flooded hundreds of homes.

My favorite Pyramid Lake movie is the 20th Century Fox World War II adventure *Destination Gobi*. Based on a short story by Edmund G. Love and directed by Robert Wise, who went on to win Academy Awards for *West Side*

Story and *The Sound of Music, Destination Gobi* was filmed in July and August 1952. The locations included a site just north of Nixon, the dry bed of Winnemucca Lake, the Needles, and the sand dunes near Fallon. The film starred Richard Widmark as Chief Boatswain's Mate Sam McHale, who is sent, reluctantly, to Inner Mongolia with a meteorologist and six weather observers as part of a "Sino-American Combined Operation" to provide weather forecasts for the US bombing attacks on Japan. According to an effusive two-page story by Frank Johnson in the July 27, 1952, *Nevada State Journal,* the reservation was chosen as the movie's location by Cal Tech archaeologist Richard Rudolph "because its topography is strikingly similar to the Gobi and because the Paiutes bear close resemblance to the real Mongols." The only problem with Johnson's story is that Rudolph was a linguist who founded the Chinese studies program at UCLA in 1947.

The movie sets up a number of contrasts to build tension—old rule-book navy noncommissioned officer versus new PhD technocrat, sea versus desert, simple Mongolian nomads versus cruel Japanese soldiers and their Chinese collaborators. The *Journal* story highlights the thousand dollars a day that the 130 men, women, and children from Nixon were earning as extras. (This was about a dollar an hour per person for an eight-hour day, a little less than the national average in 1952, but women and children were probably paid less than men.) In one of the eight photographs accompanying the article, Paiutes Martin Green, Benson Aleck, and Edgar Pete pose with Widmark. In another, Sarah Moore, her son Raymond Moore, and Nina Winnemucca are shown in the shade of a Mongolian cart. Johnson notes that the Paiutes' "ability to fare so well in moviemaking is attributed by some to coaching from Gareth Hughes, a famed actor of silent films who, as Brother David, attends to the spiritual needs of the Indians at Nixon."

Johnson's article also introduces members of the cast, some of whom were well known, others just beginning their careers. Rodolfo Acosta, an established star of Mexican and US movies, played Tomec, the villainous Mongolian chief, while Murvyn Vye, a Yale-trained actor and opera singer, played Kengtu, the good Mongolian chief. Johnson is amused by the ability of these actors to invent a language that sounds Mongolian, while the Paiute extras "chattered conversationally in their native tongue." Vye was not totally winging it. I clearly heard a hearty Mongolian "sain bainuu" (hello) at the end of the movie when Kengtu returns to his wife in the Gobi.

Although Pyramid Lake does not appear in the movie, the Lake Range, Virginia Mountains, Pah Rah Range, and Nightingale Range are frequently seen in the distance. Cloud effects are terrific. The Needles provides an appropriately sinister location for one of the many betrayals. Winnemucca Lake's alkali flat is also menacing as a stand-in for the Gobi. Professor Rudolph should be honored. The plot is relatively simple. After the weather team, "Argus 6," arrives in Mongolia, they meet a band of Mongolians who first steal some of their gear and then return most of it, including a silver saddle paperweight. When McHale notices their interest in the saddle, he persuades their chief to protect the weather station in exchange for sixty saddles that he requisitions from the US Cavalry.

The saddles are dropped from a navy plane in what seems like record time, considering the military bureaucracies involved. Everything appears to be going well until the Japanese bomb and strafe the weather station and Mongolian camp, killing several nomads. The chief meteorologist also dies when he rushes into a burning tent to save his data. The attack is visually powerful as Paiute extras—men, women, and children—scatter frantically in a scene reminiscent of many massacres of Indians in western films and as described by Sarah Winnemucca. As in *The Winning of Barbara Worth,* an iconic scene occurs when a baby is stranded in the middle of the camp. As the Japanese planes open fire, one of the navy weathermen runs out and scoops up the child. Despite this heroic act, after the raid the Mongolians abandon the station.

With most of their equipment, including their radio, destroyed, McHale orders his men to follow him on an eight-hundred-mile walk to Northeast China and the sea. After many days they encounter a caravan led by a Chinese camel trader. The Mongolians are also camped with the caravan. McHale demands the return of the saddles because the Mongols failed to protect the weathermen. McHale then sells the saddles to the Chinese trader for four camels and passage with the caravan to the coast.

One night the duplicitous Chinese merchant tries to steal the camels, but the Mongol chief prevents the theft and agrees to resume his protection of the Americans. McHale orders his men to dress as Mongols in order to evade any Japanese patrols they encounter. This works at first, but when they arrive at an occupied Chinese village they are captured and treated as spies. The Japanese transfer the navy men to a prison in a port city where they are soon freed by Kengtu, the Mongol chief, who has also procured a boat for their escape. In a nice reversal of roles, the Mongolian predicts that rain will facilitate their escape. When the rain begins, one of the meteorologists admits that he failed to forecast it. With the Japanese in hot pursuit, the Mongol chief and a few of his men ride their horses onto the ship, and eleven days later the men are rescued at sea by the US Navy.

Pure Hollywood hokum, of course, but a treat for those who love the mountains near the lake, who may also be fascinated by the similarities between Mongols and American Indians, and who appreciate the work of weathermen (and jokes on them).

The Greatest Story Ever Told (1965), based on a novel by Fulton Oursler, is a seemingly endless series of scenes from the New Testament. Pyramid Lake gets a bit part as the Sea of Galilee. Most of the scenes are filmed inside the plaster walls of the biblical city of Capernaum, but the lake shows up briefly in the background from time to time with boats bobbing. The pyramid is visible in one scene, and inexplicably the Lake Range and the Virginia Mountains seem to be covered with snow. George Stevens, the director, had the set of Capernaum built near the Needles. In the scenes filmed there, Jesus Christ (Max von Sydow) converts Matthew (Roddy McDowall), heals a blind man (Ed Wynn), and prevents the first stone from being cast at Mary Magdalene (Joanna Dunham). Charlton Heston as John the Baptist did not appear in any of the Pyramid Lake scenes. Filming began in mid-April 1963, after problems with the Southern California contractor who was to build the ersatz city, according to a story in the *Journal*, April 4, 1963. The lake played its part with its usual dignity, but its power was apparently lost on some of the movie crew. "As one worker said," according to the reporter, "referring to the way the set is built into the surrounding terrain, 'This wall we built, now that's believable—but that rock over there (a Pyramid tufa formation)—who'd be-lieve that?'"

This was not the first time that the lake had been selected for its evocation of the Holy Land. On June 3, 1955, the Pyramid Lake Tribal Council heard from a man named Jacques Arlez. His proposal, as recorded in the minutes of the council and preserved in the Leland Papers, was to build a resort "for the poor and the rich people" at Pyramid Lake, where he would produce "passion plays" on the life of Christ. He assured the council that he had experience in producing such plays and that they were very popular in Europe. His plays would bring more than a million and a half people to Nevada and provide jobs for everyone on the reservation. Council chair Avery Winnemucca said it sounded like a good idea. "All I need is actors," Arlez declared. The project would take several years to develop, he admitted, but he would give a percentage of the profits to the reservation. He seems to have known a little about the short-term leases favored by the BIA, but, he pledged, if "you give me the 'o.k.' I will go see Cliff Young to change the length of lease to 20 years." Moreover, Arlez continued, Governor Russell had told him that if he got the lease, the state would build a four-lane highway to the lake.

The chairman suggested a secret vote, and the possibility of an all-Paiute passion play went down to defeat, five to one. Who was Jacques Arlez? The name does not appear in any American newspaper between 1940 and 1960, indexed in the online service "Newspaper Archive." How did he know Governor Russell and Congressman Young? Of all the development schemes proposed, this is surely the most mysterious. Had he been lured to the lake by *Destination Gobi*? Brother David? Fulton Oursler? Basil Woon? From his remarks to the council, he seems relatively unacquainted with the place. It is tempting to interpret this incident as some kind of practical joke, a clue hidden in the similarity of *Arlez* to *parlez*, French for "speak" or "negotiate." If it was a hoax, it was surely appreciated by the council for its similarity to Indian humor. Whatever the explanation, the passion-play proposal was just one of the many flights of imagination inspired by the lake.

PYRAMID POWER AND WINNEMUCCA WHIRLWIND

In the 1970s, 130 years after Frémont, a pyramid-power craze swept the United States and led back to the lake, thanks to the late Martin Gardner, a science popularizer whose "Mathematical Games" feature appeared monthly in *Scientific American*. In June 1974 Gardner took up the claims of various pyramid-power enthusiasts epitomized by Dr. Irving Matrix, Gardner's fictional renegade mathematician and magician. Matrix, in Gardner's fantasy, is operating Pyramid Power Laboratories near Pyramid Lake and advertising a six-foot-tall transparent plastic pyramid that promises to keep razor blades sharp, preserve rosebuds, restore old typewriter ribbons, cure bodily ills, raise intelligence, and build up sexual potential. It is an amusing article, illustrated with photos of the pyramid of Cheops and the lake's pyramid rock. Gardner frames his story with an explanation—he wants to fish and revisit a place he had first seen as a child with his father, a geologist. Gardner appreciates the beauty of the place and digresses from his satire to observe: "I could see, beyond the sagebrush, the deep Prussian blue of the lake. Jagged spires and pinnacles along the opposite shore were casting purple shadows over the water, and above the turrets the Nightingale Mountains undulated in soft shades of green and pink."

Gardner, quoting articles in *Time, enRoute, Other Dimensions,* and *Occult,* provides a brief history of the pyramid-power fad. The idea that pyramids have paranormal powers seems to have occurred to a French occultist in the early twentieth century, about the time of the discovery of King Tut's tomb, an event ballyhooed in the world's press. At first the pyramid's power was limited to preserving raw food, but in the 1950s a second pyramid-power craze broke out in the benighted Soviet satellites of Eastern Europe. Other paranormal phenomena such as Wilhelm Reich's orgone energy and Kirlian photography gained popularity at the same time, as did L. Ron Hubbard's Dianetics and similar "self-actualization" programs. The Kitselman family may have been attracted to the Pyramid Lake Guest Ranch because of their dabbling in mysticism.

De Quille was way ahead of his time in placing a magic green stone under the pyramid, but the "Eye of Providence" of the unfinished pyramid on the dollar bill and its purported link with Freemasonry suggest that pyramids and magic have an ancient pedigree. Gardner and Dr. Matrix banter over the numerological significance of a pyramid's dimensions, leading Gardner to ask if there is anything interesting numerologically about Nixon and Watergate. Matrix begs the question, but suggests that the president should retire to Nixon, Nevada, and spend a few hours a day sitting on top of the pyramid rock. In response to Gardner's question about whether it is necessary to be nude inside a pyramid to receive its full powers, Matrix responds: "No, but it helps. We have several opaque models on the beach for visitors too modest to use transparent ones. Last week Judy Clutch, a schoolteacher from Wadsworth, was inside one of them for only five minutes before she was so blue with psi-org that she leaped outside, ran all the way to Pyramid and streaked down the main street until the sheriff caught her and took her to lunch."

Nor do such singular ideas end with Dr. Matrix. An Internet site for artist and photographer Mark David Gerson features his energy-releasing prints. Print no. 49, titled *Ancient Egypt, Ancient Wisdom, Galactic Consciousness (Pyramid Lake, Nevada)*, is a red, gray, and yellow Anaho Island with Chinese calligraphy in the sky above and the lake below and hieroglyphics on the island's hills. Print no. 50 is of the pyramid, which seems to be erupting like a volcano. Gerson adds a brief explanation: "Using sacred geometry, sacred symbol and language of light in written form, this drawing contains light codes that will help you achieve your galactic chakras." If pyramid power fails, try whorls of energy.

From Gerson's low-end twenty-two-dollar prints to British artist Chris Drury's three-hundred-foot spiral *Winnemucca Whirlwind* (a piece of ephemeral earth art scratched into the alkali flat of the Winnemucca Lake bed in 2008), the lakes continue to attract the outré. A Nevada Museum of Art curator sees Drury paying homage to Wovoka and "symbolically reclaiming the lake for the Paiutes," by drawing his circles on BLM land adjacent to the reservation. Drury apparently sees his work more as a game, geocaching, inviting visitors to use their personal global positioning systems to find the site of *Winnemucca Whirlwind* and to leave their comments in a canister hidden nearby.

*　*　*

MISSIONARIES, MOVIEMAKERS, AND ARTISTS are presumably look-ing for locations appropriate for their dramas. Knowing when they have found it is another matter. Sometimes what is found is the process of seeking. Some-times the discovery is made by serendipity. Wovoka, desert father and Paiute dreamer, working with limited resources, made Mason Valley almost as famous as the Sinai, at least for a few years. Indians and anthropologists sought him out, and he continues to be remembered and respected as a skillful showman, and perhaps a real prophet. Idah Meacham Strobridge, in a desert a few miles to the north, found magic in the tricks played by mirages on unsuspecting travelers.

Brother David sought a stage more authentic than Hollywood on which to present his spectacles of redemption through faith and art. He created it near the shores of Pyramid Lake. Director Robert Wise sought an exotic locale to break the monotony of World War II films, disguise his sailors in exotic costumes, and send them on a voyage on the sagebrush ocean. Mathematician Martin Gard-ner, remembering the lake from a childhood visit, imagined it as the perfect set-ting for his scheming pseudoscientist, Dr. Matrix. Different as they were, these seekers all discovered joy in the desert. Deserts and their unexpected lakes are places for fun and play.

Epilogue

The less there was to see, the harder he looked, the more he saw. This was
the point.   —Don DeLillo, *Point Omega*

O n Sunday, October 10, 2010, I drove out to Pyramid Lake, hoping to
      meet with Ben Aleck, collections manager of the Paiute Museum and
Visitor Center in Nixon. When I arrived about noon he was busy with two
groups of foreign visitors. A small group, five or six people, was outside eating
lunch; the other larger group, about a dozen, was listening to Ralph Burns,
the museum's storyteller, talk about Paiute history and legends. He told them the
Stone Mother story in Paiute, then in English, so the translator could explain
what he said in Kazakh. The leader of the Kazakh delegation (I never did learn
the purpose of their visit) presented Aleck with a miniature yurt made of wood
that he placed in the museum's already extensive collection of gifts from visitors.
I hope that someday this souvenir will be placed on exhibit next to a photo of a
Mongolian *ger* in *Destination Gobi*.

Aleck had told the other visitors that he and Ralph would meet them at Popcorn Beach on the southwest corner of the lake. I drove Aleck and Burns to the
beach. This group turned out to be Buriat Mongols from Lake Baikal in southeastern Siberia who were visiting as part of the Tahoe-Baikal Institute program
in environmental education. When we arrived, two of the Buriats were dressed
in colorful *digil,* waiting for Aleck and Burns to participate in a blessing of the
lake. Aleck looked at me and said, "Come on," so the five of us walked to the
shore, where the Buriats burned incense, sprinkled milk (an ancient ritual for
honoring the earth), faced North, and chanted. We were handed the cup of milk
and invited to do the same. Our chants in Buriat, Numic, and English blew with
the wind over the lake. The shaman tied white (water), blue (sky), yellow (sun),
and red (fire and health) ribbons on a scrubby tamarisk. One shaman presented
each of us with a water-smoothed stone from Baikal and a quarter-size amulet
on a leather thong embossed with a petroglyph-like figure of a reindeer. Aleck
thanked the visitors, and we all did farewell hugs.

On my way back to Reno later in the afternoon, I tried to put these events in the context of this book. It certainly fits with the theme of the lake's exotic otherness, its oriental depictions. It also confirms the lake's power to transform those who seek to know themselves. Imagining I was standing in the whirlwinds of the Gobi or, hidden in thick sagebrush watching Wovoka, or on the back of a giant pelican flying over "the Land of Lakes," I was giddy with anticipation.

The lake of surprises, coincidences, conundrums. Frémont should have named it Serendipity, which would have evoked livelier connotations than the mute stones of Egypt. Frémont's "discovery" of the lake certainly fits the definition of "serendipity pattern" explored by the great sociologist Robert K. Merton. The lake was unanticipated: Frémont's expedition was looking for a river flowing west; it was surprising, how a large lake could be in the middle of a desert; and it was "strategic" information that confirmed the explorer's theory about the topography of the Great Basin. Serendipity, in other words, is not just an unexpected, lucky discovery; it is the convergence of seeker and something unsought but immediately recognized as significant. The appearance of Stone Mother, the preservation of Pirsig's letter, my meeting with the Buriat shaman, and other serendipitous occurrences in the history of Pyramid Lake are, for me, the essence of the lake's mystique.

I IMAGINE a hike around the lake starting at the Truckee River delta and walking northwest, east, and south back to the delta. My walk combines landmarks from a half-dozen maps of the lake made over the past seventy years. A couple of miles' stroll brings me to Popcorn Rock and Beach. Two miles north is Blockhouse Beach, probably named for a World War II facility removed long ago. A recent-looking sign by the highway identifies the next place as Rawhide Lookout, about where a 1997 map placed Sandhole Beach, and probably the same spots called Paiute Point and Zephyr Cove on the 1973 recreation map. These are followed by Wino Beach, a name that occurs on almost all the maps, made more offensive by its proximity to Indian Head Rock. A few hundred yards beyond Indian Head Rock is Tamaracks Beach, taking its name from the tamarisk planted by the US Navy during World War II to camouflage ordnance bunkers. Tamarisk, native to Mediterranean countries, ravenously consumes water, often killing off native cottonwood and willows. The Pyramid Lake Paiute Tribe is attempting to prevent tamarisk from spreading in the Truckee River delta.

A sign at the junction of Routes 445 and 446 calls the next point of interest Washout Beach, probably referring to flash floods in the usually dry Mullen Creek area. Next is South Net Beach, an area just south of Sutcliffe that takes its name from unsuccessful fish management efforts to raise LCT and cui-ui in net pens in the shallow water. Continuing north, Long Beach leads to Sutcliffe and the marina, where Hardscrabble Creek enters the lake. Beyond the collection of mobile homes and RVs that provide shelter for some of Sutcliffe's permanent and transient population are, according to a 1980 USGS map, Lombardo Point and then Pelican Point, the two points appropriately separated by Separator Beach. North of Pelican Point are Windless Bay, Spider Point, and Shot Dog Beach, the latter a place marked by a recent sign but unknown to my friends at the Paiute Museum and Visitor Center. (I like to think of this place as a memorial to Zoby.) Warrior Point, about two-thirds of the way up the west side of the lake, is on almost all maps, but Buck Wheeler calls the spot Bristol Point. Reaching Nine Mile Bay and Thunderbolt Bay, which are nine and ten miles from Sutcliffe, brings me to Letty Symonds's Ranch and Big Canyon, called the Willows on a recent road sign. The geologist Larry Benson places the tufa formation Blanc Tetons in this area. Beyond these landmarks is a tufa formation variously labeled George Washington Rock, Monument Rock, Castle Rock, and Cathedral Rock by mapmakers and magazine writers with different pareidolic visions. You see a cathedral; I see a castle. Wizard Cove and the Needles bring me within four miles of Fox Bay and the northernmost point of the lake, a place Wheeler divides into Enchanted Beach and Fox Bay. These two places were sharply divided in 1882, when the water level was higher, by what geologist Israel Russell called Terrace Point.

Traveling south on the eastern shore there are fewer named sites because there are no roads or boat landings. Hell's Kitchen Canyon is located about five miles down the beach, followed by Howitzer Slide, a reference to Frémont's little cannon that he abandoned before reaching California. A spit of land south of Howitzer is named Blizzard Camp Point on a USGS map, followed by Artillery or Anderson Bay, depending on the cartographer. Places called Grey Point and Standing Bear Rock appear on the 1973 recreation map, which encouraged boating and fishing in that area. Red or Reed Bay is tucked into a depression in the foothills of the Lake Range just north of the pyramid and Stone Mother. Two-thirds of the way back to the Truckee, Benson identified a formation he calls Doghead Rock, on the shore opposite Anaho Island. A little farther south are twin sphinx-shaped formations about fifty yards apart, a mile from the lakeshore. One is about seventy-five feet high, the other about fifty feet. About six miles south of Stone Mother is another tufa formation called the Bee Hives (closed to tourists), and farther on lies Dago Bay, the Marble Bluff Fishway, and the eastern part of the Truckee delta. Now I am back at Nixon.

I have been making this walk around Pyramid Lake, mile by mile, most of my life, completing it in my imagination. I will never finish. The lake is my white whale, my Sheep Rock. I reread George R. Stewart's 1951 novel while writing *At Pyramid Lake* and came to realize how much Stewart's *Sheep Rock* has influenced me. Stewart's story of a frustrated poet, who spends a sabbatical year living in an abandoned house in a desert north of Pyramid Lake, is a meditation on the meaning of place and time. The poet spends his days with his wife and two young daughters exploring the nearby hot springs, where he finds evidence of prehistoric animals, Paiute bands, immigrant wagon trains, military explorers, prospectors, and even a 1930s settler. Instead of finishing his poem, he writes long letters to a friend describing his discoveries.

The poet collects fragments of a blue-and-white pitcher that becomes a metaphor of his quest to understand permanence and change. Pieces of the puzzle are missing; some that he has do not fit. The unstated question is, was there ever a single shape to this relic? In *Sheep Rock*, Stewart, who was a professor of English at Berkeley and who is best known as a historian, onomatologist, and chronicler of American life, conveys the anxieties of annihilation in the nuclear

Storm, looking northwest, Nixon, Nevada. Photograph by Robert Dawson, 1989. Permission of Robert Dawson. Courtesy Library of Congress, USZ62-119148.

age and touches on some of the questions I have been raising in this book. Is the primary attraction of Pyramid Lake, as some suggest, that it is death defying? Do places like Pyramid Lake offer hope where many see oblivion?

Stewart makes two wise observations about places like Pyramid Lake. At one point he has the poet lie down on the ground in an effort to see what the desert looks like to a ground squirrel. "'Certainly, as I learned in that half-minute when I lay down and held my eye close to the ground,' the poet remembers, 'this blazing desert is, for a ground-squirrel, a beneficent park, full of shade. Oh, this place is like any other in the world, but perhaps a little honester than most.'" This might be called the microview, inviting us to see the desert or the lake from the perspective of a lizard or even a cui-ui. The macroview comes with trying to comprehend the whole. Stewart's poet observes that a river is not the water in it, since it is constantly changing, nor the land under it, because without the water it is a "riverbed." The same can be said of a lake, even an endorheic one, if its evaporating water is replaced by inflows. Rivers and lakes are, therefore, abstractions in the mind, "a kind of moving wateriness." The poet learns that physical places change over time, "that a drying lake drops a beach on a mountainside as casually as a passing prospector drops an empty whisky bottle." A peep under a sagebrush and a feel for wateriness are all most of us can ever achieve when we try to explain Pyramid Lake.

The meanings of the place for its original inhabitants are layered in past events remembered as stories. Some of those stories, as I have shown, were recorded by ethnographers with agendas of their own. The stories became arrows directed at colleagues. Most of the best stories may be lost. We are fortunate that some were preserved by listeners who did not claim to be scientists, but who were storytellers themselves. One of them was Frank McCulloch, born in 1920, the son of a rancher near Fernley. McCulloch returned from the Marine Corps in 1946 and established himself as a newspaper reporter, working at the *Reno Evening Gazette* until he left for *Time* magazine. From there he went as managing editor to the *Los Angeles Times*, the *Sacramento Bee*, and the *San Francisco Examiner*, with a four-year stint back at *Time* as a war correspondent in Vietnam.

In late 1947 McCulloch wrote a series of articles for the *Nevada Magazine* (a short-lived arts and history journal published in Gardnerville) based on stories told to him as a boy by elderly Paiutes. The first tale, which he titles "Death of a Great Warrior," had been related to him when he was eleven years old by a Pyramid Lake native known to whites as Jigger Bob. Jigger Bob was blind and estimated his age at 101, making 1830 the year of his birth. It is a story about his great-grandfather Paba Nona and a war between the Kuyuidokado and some

Shoshone. The Shoshone killed a number of Paiutes and trapped Paba Nona's family near the lake. With the enemy closing in, the Paiute warrior hid his wife, two young sons, a daughter, and four wounded braves in a cave and rolled a huge stone over its entrance. He then painted the story of his tribe and family on nearby rocks in the hope that some Paiute survivors might rescue those trapped in the cave. He fought the Shoshone until he was killed. Years later, descendants of the Paiutes who escaped the Shoshone found the drawings and opened the cave. On its walls they saw the sad story of the suffering and death of Paba Nona's family and the wounded warriors carved into the rock by the last survivor. The tribe decided the best thing to do was reseal the cave and keep its location a secret forever.

"That is why, boy," Jigger Bob tells the young Frank McCulloch, "the Indians did not like it when you and your friends were prying about on the black mountain last summer." Sixteen years after hearing this story, McCulloch remembers it as an admonition, but in the context of his more recent experiences in World War II, remembering and recording Jigger Bob's account of historic wars between Indian tribes and their tragic consequences for women and children must have added new meanings. Above all, McCulloch the journalist appreciated Jigger Bob's matter-of-fact telling of his ancestors' defeat. McCulloch prefaces his *Nevada Magazine* pieces with a qualification. The stories, he writes, "will be retold here in the same spirit in which the Indians related them—with no attempt made to establish historical veracity, but simply as tales, legends, folklore of the native people of this state. It is difficult to determine whether the Indians who told them believed them, but it is certain that they enjoyed the telling."

At about the same time that McCulloch was listening to Jigger Bob's stories, the elderly Kuyuidokado was posing for a portrait by Robert Caples. In his "Education Guide" for a Caples exhibition, art historian Russ Lindsay quotes the artist on Jigger Bob: "His face was lined as the desert is lined, it reflects for me, the stuff of the desert. I began to feel that these Indians were part of the scene, part of the mountains. Such landscape work I undertook to do in future years was definitely influenced by the weather-beaten faces I had looked at and admired."

The second story in McCulloch's series also came from Jigger Bob, in August 1933 when young Frank was again visiting the old man on the west side of Pyramid Lake. When Frank complains about the heat and drought, Jigger Bob launches into a story about a long ago time when the Great Spirit became displeased with the Paiutes because they did not appreciate the bounty of fish in

Blind Shaman. Charcoal by Robert Caples, ca. 1933, 16½" × 20". Courtesy Special Collections, University of Nevada, Reno, Libraries.

the lake and pine nuts in the mountains and fought among themselves. The deity punishes them by causing a drought and windstorms that kill the game and dry up the lake. Finally, the tribe begs their shaman to help them. The shaman builds a fire, burns hair from a deer's tail and "the eye of a qui-wui fish," and asks the community what they see. Where the smoke meets the sky everyone sees forests and rivers and green meadows and blue lakes, but one brave saw only "the face of a great and angry chief." This was the answer the shaman sought and chastised the rest for failing to see that they had offended the Great Spirit. The shaman made more smoke rise to the sky, and when the dissenting brave reported that he now saw the head of a great spear, the shaman asked to be left alone to pray for five days. On the fifth day a huge rock in the shape of a spear point rose from the dry lake bed, water began to pour from it, and clouds formed in the sky. In a few days the lake was full again, fish swam, and trees grew. After that the Paiutes never forgot to thank the Great Spirit for the earth's gifts. Jigger Bob sends McCulloch to look at the lake where he sees the spearhead that whites call a pyramid. When McCulloch reports this to Jigger Bob, the old man smiles and sends him inside because he smells rain.

Again, McCulloch clearly understands the moral of the tale, but offers it primarily as a kind of allegorical weather report, a disaster drama with a magical happy ending. As we know from the anthropological literature, a shaman was expected to be able to control weather by tapping powers in the natural world. Jigger Bob's story goes beyond mere faith in the supernatural, however, by demanding that at least one honest person in the tribe recognize that humans do not deserve an unearned cornucopia. Payment must be made in the form of good stewardship symbolized by living peacefully, in harmony with each other and the earth.

I CANNOT CLAIM to have found the meaning of Pyramid Lake any more than Stewart found the "tutelary spirit" of Sheep Rock. Some of my fragments fit together; others are "misfits." The solution to its puzzle is at Pyramid Lake. Above all, the truth I want to leave you with is that all the beauty, the enchantment, the healing powers of Pyramid Lake could vanish in a moment of thoughtless legislation or failure to take protective actions. The lake exists today because of a century of delicate political compromises. For it to live for another century requires that scientific knowledge be joined to moral wisdom. Nothing in nature is free. Human thirst and climate changes raise the value of water. What price are we willing to pay to keep the elusive blues of Pyramid Lake? To preserve its ancient fish? To make restitution for crimes against the lake's original human stewards? Remember this book as a ledger, an account of the values of the place—hydrological, piscatorial, historical, cultural, recreational, spiritual, and aesthetic.

 # REFERENCES

MANUSCRIPT COLLECTIONS

Special Collections, Mathewson-IGT Knowledge Center, University of Nevada, Reno
    Bean, Mary. Collection. 1934–67. Collection 95-10.
    Bundy, Gus. Photographic Collection. UNRS-P 1985-08.
    Creel, Lorenzo D. Collection. 1902–22. Collection 82-01.
    Drackert, Harry. Collection 91-49.
    Friends of Pyramid Lake Collection. 1968–97. Collection 94-54.
    Hughes, Gareth. Papers. 1925–55. NC803.
    Laird, Charlton Grant. Papers. AC0076.
    Leland, Joy. Collection 96-07.
    Leland, Robert. Collection. 1958–71. NC1035.
    Marshall, John Albert. Papers. 1933–34. 90-13 to 22.
    Pyramid Lake Water Papers. 1969–79. NC1202.
    Rowley, Gladys. Scrapbook Collection 84-26.
    Wheat, Margaret. Collection 83-24.

Nevada Historical Society
    Nevada Newspaper Index File
    Photographic collections
    Pyramid Lake Paiutes. Clipping File.

Harry Ransom Center, University of Texas at Austin
    Miller, Arthur. Papers.

PRINT SOURCES

"A. L. Kitselman Will Lecture on the Bridey Murphy Case at State Building on Wednesday." *Nevada State Journal,* June 15, 1956, 6.

Abbey, Edward. *Desert Solitaire: A Season in the Wilderness.* New York: Simon and Schuster, 1968.

Acton, Richard C. "Peace or Truce: The Truckee Carson Pyramid Lake Water Rights Settlement Act." PhD diss., University of Nevada, Reno, 2002.

Adler, Lee. "Ballet Brings Message of Harmony to Truckee River Water Fight." *Reno Evening Gazette,* January 10, 1976, 13.

Amaral, Anthony. "Idah Meacham Strobridge: First Woman of Nevada Letters." *Nevada Historical Society Quarterly* 10, no. 3 (1967): 5–12.

———. *Mustang: Life and Legends of Nevada's Wild Horses.* Reno: University of Nevada Press, 1977.

———. "Pelican Island." *Nevada* 29, no. 4 (1969): 20–23, 55.

The American Artist and Water Reclamation: A Selection of Paintings from the Collection of the Bureau of Reclamation. Washington, DC: US Government Printing Office, 1973. http://www.usbr.gov/museumproperty/art/.

Anderson, Ron. "Reno Mythbusters: The Water Babies of Pyramid Lake." http://news .travel.aol.com/2010/09/24/reno-mythbusters/.

Angel, Myron T. *History of Nevada.* Oakland, CA: Thompson and West, 1881. Reproduction, Berkeley, CA: Howell-North, 1958.

"Attorney Answers Attack Levelled by Indian Bureau." *Reno Evening Gazette,* October 25, 1950, 10,

Bandurraga, Peter L. "Gilbert Natches." *Nevada Historical Society Quarterly* 33, no. 2 (1990): 139–43.

Barber, Alicia. *Reno's Big Gamble: Image and Reputation in the Biggest Little City.* Lawrence: University Press of Kansas, 2008.

Barron, Terry. *Terry Barron's No Nonsense Guide to Fly Fishing Pyramid Lake: A Quick, Clear Understanding of the Nation's Top Lahontan Cutthroat Trout Fishery.* Edited by Jeff Cavender. Sisters, OR: David Communications, 1998.

Behnke, Robert J. *Trout and Salmon of North America.* Illustrated by Joseph R. Tomelleri. New York: Free Press, 2002.

Bellow, Saul. "Leaving Yellow House." *Esquire,* January 1958. Reprinted in *Mosby's Memoirs, and Other Stories.* New York: Viking, 1968.

———. *Saul Bellow: Letters.* Edited by Benjamin Taylor. New York: Viking, 2010.

Bengston, Ginny. *Northern Paiute and Western Shoshone Land Use in Northern Nevada: A Class I Ethnographic/Ethnohistoric Overview.* Reno: Bureau of Land Management/ SWCA Cultural Resources Report No. 02-551, December 16, 2002. http://www.blm .gov/pgdata/etc/medialib/blm/nv/cultural/reports.Par.99842.File.d at/12_N_Pauite .pdf.

Benson, Jackson J. *The Ox-Bow Man: A Biography of Walter Van Tilburg Clark.* Reno: University of Nevada Press, 2004.

Benson, Larry. "The Tufas of Pyramid Lake, Nevada." USGS Circular 1267. 2004. http:// plpt.nsn.us/geology/index.html.

Berkhove, Lawrence I. "Introduction to 'Pahnenit, Prince of the Land of Lakes.'" *Nevada Historical Society Quarterly* 31, no. 2 (1988): 79–86.

Bernstein, Alison R. *American Indians in World War II: Toward a New Era in Indian Affairs.* Norman: University of Oklahoma Press, 1991.

Bigsby, Christopher. *Arthur Miller, 1915–1962.* Cambridge, MA: Harvard University Press, 2009.

Bird, S. Elizabeth, ed. *Dressing in Feathers: The Construction of the Indian in American Popular Culture.* Boulder, CO: Westview Press, 1996.

Bordewich, Fergus M. *Killing the White Man's Indian: Reinventing Native Americans at the End of the Twentieth Century.* New York: Doubleday, 1996.

Borghi, Lillian. "Arts and Artists." *Reno Evening Gazette,* September 5, 1942, 14.

Bowen, Peggy Lear. "A Pa Oha Warning." Typescript, 1980. Special Collections, University of Nevada Library, Reno.

Brando, Marlon, with Robert Lindsey. *Brando: Songs My Mother Taught Me.* New York: Random House, 1994.

Bremner, Faith. "Fish Are a Part of Tribe's History." *Reno Gazette-Journal,* May 6, 1996, A4.

———. "Fish Now Rely upon Help from Humans." *Reno Gazette-Journal,* May 6, 1996, A1, A4.

———. "Water Wars to End?" *Reno Gazette-Journal,* September 28, 1994, A1, A6.

Brenn, Courtney. "Tribe Tries to Hold onto Heritage While Bolstering Business." *Reno Gazette-Journal,* December 1, 1991, A14, A15.

Brink, Pamela Jane. "The Pyramid Lake Paiute of Nevada." PhD diss., Boston University, 1969.

Browner, Tara. *Heartbeat of the People: Music and Dance of the Northern Pow-Wow.* Urbana: University of Illinois Press, 2002.

Bruder, Jessica. "The Changing Face of the Burning Man Festival." *New York Times,* August 28, 2011, Business, 1, 7.

Buchanan, Chester C., and Thomas A. Strekal. *Simulated Water Management and Evaluation Procedures for Cui-ui (Chasmistes cujus).* Reno: US Fish and Wildlife Service, Great Basin Complex; Carson City: US Bureau of Reclamation, Lahontan Basin Projects Office, 1988.

Burr, Aaron. "Roop County Notes: The Crops—the Fish—the Reservation and Matters in General." *Reno Weekly Gazette,* June 12, 1879, 6.

Cahill, Cathleen D. *Federal Fathers and Mothers: The United States Indian Service, 1869–1933.* Chapel Hill: University of North Carolina Press, 2011.

Canfield, Gae Whitney. *Sarah Winnemucca of the Northern Paiutes.* Norman: University of Oklahoma Press, 1983.

Carlson, Helen S. *Nevada Place Names: A Geographical Dictionary.* Reno: University of Nevada Press, 1974.

"Cast Announced for Indian Show." *Nevada State Journal,* October 9, 1941, 2.

Cerveri, Doris. *Pyramid Lake: Legends and Reality.* Sparks, NV: Western Printing, 1977.

Christensen, Rick, and Brent Mefford. "A Struggle of Needs: A History of Bureau of Reclamation Fish Passage Projects on the Truckee River, Nevada." In *The Bureau of Reclamation: History Essays from the Centennial Symposium,* edited by Britt Allan Storey, 1:209–20. Denver: Bureau of Reclamation, 2008. http://www.usbr.gov/history /Symposium_2008/Historical_Essays.pdf.

Clark, Walter Van Tilburg. *The City of Trembling Leaves.* New York: Random House, 1945.

———. "Pyramid Lake." *Troubadour* 4, nos. 4–5 (1932): 25.

Clemmer, Richard O. "Ideology and Identity: Western Shoshoni 'Cannibal' Myths as Ethnohistorical Narrative." *Journal of Anthropological Research* 52, no. 2 (1996): 207–23.

———. "Land Use Patterns and Aboriginal Rights, Northern and Eastern Nevada, 1858–1971." *Indian Historian* 7, no. 1 (1974): 24–47.

Clemmer, Richard O., Daniel Myers, and Mary Elizabeth Rudden, eds. *Julian Steward and the Great Basin: The Making of an Anthropologist.* Salt Lake City: University of Utah Press, 1999.

Cobourn, John. "Integrated Watershed Management on the Truckee River in Nevada." *Journal of the American Water Resources Association* 35, no. 3 (1999): 623–32.

Coetzee, J. M. "The Misfits." In *Writers at the Movies,* edited by Jim Shepard, 63–67. New York: Perennial, 2000.

Colby, Bonnie G., John E. Thorson, and Sarah Britton. *Negotiating Tribal Water Rights: Fulfilling Promises in the Arid West.* Tucson: University of Arizona Press, 2005.

Colgan, Helen Hope. "Journey to Pyramid: A Haibun." *Nevada* 33, no. 2 (1973): 37–39.

Collier, John. *Indians of the Americas: The Long Hope.* New York: Mentor Books, 1947.

———. "Motion Pictures: Their Functions and Regulation." *Playground* 4, no. 7 (1910): 232–39.

"Come to Nevada for Recreation." *Nevada Highways and Parks* 3, no. 5 (1938): 3–6.

Cosens, Barbara A. "Farmers, Fish, Tribal Power, and Poker: Reallocating Water in the Truckee River Basin, Nevada, and California." *Hastings West-Northwest Journal of Environmental Law and Policy* 10, no. 1 (2003): 89–136.

Cowger, Thomas W. *The National Congress of American Indians: The Founding Years.* Lincoln: University of Nebraska Press, 1999.

Culin, Stewart. *Games of the North American Indians.* Washington, DC: US Government Printing Office, 1907

Davis, Erik. "Is the 'Planetary Consciousness' of Neotribal Psytrance Gatherings Just Window Dressing for the Same Old Hedonism?" *Arthur Magazine,* October 2008. http://arthurmag.com/2008/10/17/is-the-planetary-consciousness-of-neotribal-psytrance-gatherings-like-portugals-boom-festival-just-window-dressing-for-the-same-old-hedonistic-consumption-and-pursuit-of-dis/.

Davis, Keith. *Timothy O'Sullivan: The King Survey Photographs.* New Haven, CT: Yale University Press, 2011.

Dawson, Robert, Peter Goin, and Mary Webb. *A Doubtful River.* Reno: University of Nevada Press, 2000.

Day, Vina. "The Myths and Legends of the Paiute Indians." Typescript, 1980. Special Collections, University of Nevada Library, Reno.

DeLillo, Don. *Point Omega.* New York: Scribner's, 2010.

De Long, Jeff. "Divers Remove All Ammunition from Pyramid Lake." *Reno Gazette-Journal,* June 12, 2005. http://www.plpt.nsn.us/inthenews/pyramiddivers.html.

Deloria, Philip J. *Indians in Unexpected Places.* Lawrence: University Press of Kansas, 2004.

Deloria, Vine, Jr. *Custer Died for Your Sins: An Indian Manifesto.* New York: Macmillan, 1969.

De Quille, Dan [William Wright]. *The Big Bonanza,* Hartford, CT: American Publishing, 1877.

———. "Pahnenit, Prince of the Land of Lakes." *Nevada Historical Society Quarterly* 31, no. 2 (1998): 87–118.

———. "Strange Lakes in Nevada." *New York Sun,* May 16, 1886, 3.

Dilworth, Leah. *Imagining Indians in the Southwest: Persistent Visions of a Primitive Past.* Washington, DC: Smithsonian Institution Press, 1996.

Dixon, Faun Mortara. "Native American Property Rights: The Pyramid Lake Reservation Land Controversy." PhD diss., University of Nevada, Reno, 1981.

Dobie, J. Frank. *The Mustangs.* 1952. Reprint, Austin: University of Texas Press, 1984.

Doermann, Julia. "Negotiating Conflict and Fostering Innovation: The Truckee-Carson–Pyramid Lake Water Rights Settlement." In *Our Lands: New Strategies for Protecting the West,* 107–19. Darby, PA: Diane, 1993.

Doten, Alfred. *The Journals of Alfred Doten, 1849–1903.* Edited by Walter Van Tilburg Clark. Reno: University of Nevada Press, 1973.

Duncan, David James. "Lake of the Stone Mother." In *Heart of the Land: Essays on Last Great Places,* edited by Joseph Barbato and Lisa Weinerman, 30–43. New York: Pantheon, 1994.

Dworkin, Dennis. "C. L. R. James in Nevada." *Nevada Historical Society Quarterly* 44, no. 2 (2001): 109–32.

"E. Griswold." *Reno Evening Gazette,* November 18, 1897, 3.

Earl, Phillip I. "Hollywood Comes to the Blackrock: The Story of the Making of *The Winning of Barbara Worth.*" *Humboldt Historian* (Winter–Spring 1988). http://www.gchudleigh.com/blackrock.htm.

"Editorials: "Push Too Hard." *Reno Evening Gazette,* April 10, 1973, 4.

Egan, Ferol. *Sand in a Whirlwind: The Paiute Indian War of 1860.* 1972. Reprint, Reno: University of Nevada Press, 2003.

Egan, Timothy. "Where Water Is Power, the Balance Shifts." *New York Times,* November 30, 1997, 1, 24.

Eldridge, Earle. "Senate OKs Water-War Pact." *Reno Gazette-Journal,* October 27, 1990, A1.

Ellis, Clyde, Luke Eric Lassiter, and Gary H. Dunham, eds. *Powwow.* Lincoln: University of Nebraska Press, 2005.

Ely, Joe. Interview with Donald B. Seney, Bureau of Reclamation, Mesa, AZ, May 20, 1996. http://www.usbr.gov/history/oralhist.html.

———. "More than Romance." *Nevada Public Affairs Review* 1 (1992): 60–63.

Espland, Wendy Nelson. *The Struggle for Water: Politics, Rationality, and Identity in the American Southwest.* Chicago: University of Chicago Press, 1998.

Essa, Ahmed. "Gus Bundy." *Nevada Historical Society Quarterly* 33, no. 2 (1990): 154–57.

"Eugene Griswold Is Trying the Experiment of Canning Pyramid Lake Cutthroat Trout." *Reno Evening Gazette,* March 11, 1880, 3.

Evans, Ingrid. "Ben Cunningham." *Nevada Historical Society Quarterly* 33, no. 2 (1990): 149–53.

"An Exciting Adventure with Pyramid Lake Fish Poachers." *San Francisco Daily Evening Bulletin,* December 21, 1877, col. B.

Fairbanks, Harold W. "Pyramid Lake, Nevada." *Popular Science Monthly* 58 (1901): 505–14. http://books.google.com/books?id=6KEVAAAAYAAJ&pg=PA505&1pg=PA505&dq=harold+j+fairbanks+pyramid+lake+nevada&source=bl&ots=_5kaP2OJJ&sig=QxfOwVMTwlHhltItQQal'.

Farrell, John Aloysius. "Paiutes Losing Long Court Battle for Water Rights." *Reno Gazette-Journal,* March 4, 1984, A1.

Fear-Segal, Jacqueline. *White Man's Club: Schools, Race, and the Struggle of Acculturation.* Lincoln: University of Nebraska Press, 2007.

"A Fish with Hook Bones: Researches into the Natural History of a Strange Fish—Not Cooyouie but Gooy oue—What Indians Say About It." *Reno Evening Gazette,* March 15, 1881, 3.

Fockler, Matthew N. "Plumbing the Truckee: Water Diversion and the Creation of Community Along the Truckee River." Master's thesis, University of Nevada, Reno, 2007.

Foley, Justin R. "In Defense of Self: Identity and Place in Pyramid Lake Paiute History." Master's thesis, University of Nevada, Reno, 2008.

"Folk Ballet School Tour Planned." *Reno Evening Gazette,* January 2, 1976, 30.

Forbes, Jack, ed. *Nevada Indians Speak.* Reno: University of Nevada Press, 1967.

Fowler, Catherine S. *In the Shadow of Fox Peak: An Ethnography of the Cattail-Eater Northern Paiute People of Stillwater Marsh.* Cultural Resource Series no. 5, US Department of the Interior, Fish and Wildlife Service, Region 1, Stillwater National Wildlife Refuge. Washington, DC: US Government Printing Office, 1992.

———. "What's in a Name? Southern Paiute Place Names as Key to Landscape Perception." In *Landscape Ethnoecology: Concepts of Biotic and Physical Space,* edited by Leslie Main Johnson and Eugene S. Hunn, 241–54. New York: Berghahn Books, 2009.

Fowler, Catherine S., and Joy Leland. "Some Northern Paiute Native Categories." *Ethnology* 6, no. 4 (1967): 381–404.

Francaviglia, Richard V. *Believing in Places: A Spiritual Geography of the Great Basin.* Reno: University of Nevada Press, 2003.

———. *Go East, Young Man: Imagining the American West as the Orient.* Logan: Utah State University Press, 2011.

————. *Mapping and Imagination in the Great Basin: A Cartographic History.* Reno: University of Nevada Press, 2005.

Frazier, Katie. "I Just Love to Dance!" *Nevada Public Affairs Review* 1 (1992): 64–65.

————. *That Was a Happy Time: A Paiute Woman Remembers.* Directed by JoAnne Peden and Mark Gandolfo. Produced by JoAnne Peden. Reno: University of Nevada, Teaching and Learning Technologies, 1993.

Frémont, John Charles. *The Exploring Expedition to the Rocky Mountains, Oregon, and California.* Buffalo, NY: Derby Orton and Mulligan / Auburn, NY: Darby and Miller, 1853.

Gammon, Clive. "Lost and Found: A Fish Story." *Sports Illustrated,* November 6, 1989. http://sportsillustrated.cnn.com/vault/article/magazine/MAG1068997/.

Gelvin, Ralph M. *Post War Planning Program for the Carson Jurisdiction.* Typescript submitted to the commissioner of Indian affairs, March 31, 1944. Reprint, Reno, NV: Desert Research Institute, University of Nevada, n.d.

Gerson, Mark David. "Ancient Egypt, Ancient Wisdom, Galactic Consciousness (Pyramid Lake, Nevada)." http://www.markdavidgerson.com.

Gilmore, Lee. *Theater in a Crowded Fire: Ritual and Spirituality at Burning Man.* Berkeley: University of California Press, 2010.

Gilmore, Lee, and Mark Van Proyen, eds. *After Burn: Reflections on Burning Man.* Albuquerque: University of New Mexico Press, 2005.

"Give Them a Chance." *Nevada State Journal,* March 22, 1931, 4.

Glotfelty, Cheryll. "Old Folks in the New West: Surviving Change and Staying Fit in *The Misfits.*" *Western American Literature* 37, no. 1 (2002): 26–49.

Gomberg, William, and Joy Leland. "'We Need to Be Shown': A Study of the Talents, Work Potential, and Aspirations of the Pyramid Lake Indians." Unpublished report to the Bureau of Indian Affairs, n.d. Robert Leland Papers, Special Collections, University of Nevada, Reno.

Goode, James. *The Making of the Misfits.* 1963. Reprint, New York: Limelight, 1986.

Goodyear, Frank H., III. *Red Cloud: Photographs of a Lakota Chief.* Lincoln: University of Nebraska Press, 20003.

Gorrell, Robert. "Walter Van Tilburg Clark and Trembling Leaves: A Review Essay." *Nevada Historical Society Quarterly* 35, no. 3 (1992): 149–61.

Gourley, Chad R. "Restoration of the Lower Truckee River Ecosystem: Challenges and Opportunities." *Journal of Land Resources and Environmental Law* 18 (1998): 113–21.

Grayson, Donald K. *The Desert's Past: A Natural Prehistory of the Great Basin.* Washington, DC: Smithsonian Institution Press, 1993.

Green, Rayna D. "By the Waters of Minnehaha: Music, Magic, and Princesses in the Indian Boarding Schools." In *Away from Home: American Indian Boarding Schools, 1879–2000,* edited by Margaret L. Archuleta et al. Phoenix: Heard Museum, 2000.

————. "The Indian in Popular American Culture." In *Handbook of North American*

Indians, vol. 4, *History of Indian-White Relations,* edited by Wilcomb E. Washburn, 587–606. Washington, DC: Smithsonian Institution Press, 1988.

———. "The Pocahontas Perplex: The Image of Indian Women in American Culture." *Massachusetts Review* 16, no. 3 (1975): 698–714.

———. "Traits of Indian Character: The 'Indian' Anecdote in American Vernacular Tradition." *Southern Folklore Quarterly* 39, no. 3 (1975): 233–62.

Greenan, Michael. "Pyramid's Cutthroat Mystique." *Nevada: The Magazine of the Real West* 41, no. 6 (1981): 16–19.

Gromme, Owen J. "A Sojourn Among the Wild Fowl of Pyramid Lake, Nevada." *Year Book of the Public Museum of the City of Milwaukee, 1930* 10 (1932): 268–303.

Growdon, Marcia Cohn. "Robert Cole Caples." *Nevada Historical Society Quarterly* 33, no. 2 (1990): 158–61.

Hale, Katharine G. "Lorenzo P. Latimer." *Nevada Historical Society Quarterly* 33, no. 2 (1990): 83–85.

Halverson, Anders. *An Entirely Synthetic Fish: How Rainbow Trout Beguiled America and Overran the World.* New Haven, CT: Yale University Press, 2010.

Hancock, Dale. "American Folk Ballet Makes Nevada Opening in Winnemucca." *Reno Evening Gazette,* January 7, 1976, 28.

Harner, Nellie Shaw. *Indians of Coo-yu-ee Pah (Pyramid Lake): The History of the Pyramid Lake Indians in Nevada.* 1974 Rev. ed. Sparks, NV: Western, 1978.

Harrison, Jim. "Passacaglia on Getting Lost." In *On Nature: Nature, Landscape, and Natural History,* edited by Daniel Halpern, 230–35. San Francisco: North Point Press, 1986.

Harry, Norman. Interviews with Donald B. Seney, Bureau of Reclamation, Nixon, NV, October 13, 1995, and March 20, 2008.

Henry, Marguerite. *Mustang: Wild Spirit of the West.* Chicago: Rand McNally, 1966.

Heth, Charlotte, ed. *Native American Dance: Ceremonies and Social Traditions.* Washington, DC: National Museum of the American Indian and Fulcrum, 1992.

Hittman, Michael. *Great Basin Indians: An Encyclopedic History.* Reno: University of Nevada Press, 2013.

———. *Wovoka and the Ghost Dance.* Edited by Don Lynch. Expanded ed. Lincoln: University of Nebraska Press, 1997.

Hopkins, Sarah Winnemucca. *Life Among the Paiutes: Their Wrongs and Claims.* Edited by Mrs. Horace Mann. New York: G. P. Putnam's Sons, 1883.

Hopper, Hedda. "Gareth Hughes Life Saga of Goodwill." *Los Angeles Times,* December 5, 1963, 14.

Horse Capture, George P. *Pow Wow.* Cody, WY: Buffalo Bill Historical Center, 1989.

Horton, Gary A. *Truckee River Chronology: A Chronological History of Lake Tahoe and the Truckee River and Related Water Issues.* 7th update. Carson City: Nevada Division of Water Planning, Department of Conservation and Natural Resources, April 1997.

———. *Water Words Dictionary.* 8th ed., 1st revision. Carson City: Nevada Division of Water Planning, Department of Conservation and Natural Resources, August 1999.

Houghton, Samuel G. *A Trace of Desert Waters: The Great Basin Story.* Glendale, CA: Arthur C. Clark, 1976.

House, Freeman. *Totem Salmon: Life Lessons from Another Species.* Boston: Beacon, 1999.

Hummel, N. A. "Mud Lake." *Reno Evening Gazette,* May 5, 1888, 3.

Huston, John. *John Huston: An Open Book.* New York: Alfred A. Knopf, 1980.

Hyde, Julia. "The Peaks of Pyramid Lake." *Atchison (KS) Daily Champion,* December 6, 1888, 3.

"Indian Pageant to Be Presented." *Reno Evening Gazette,* October 2, 1941, 14.

"Indian Pageant to Be Staged in Reno." *Reno Evening Gazette,* June 28, 1939, 3.

International Development Services. *Economic Development Plan for Pyramid Lake Indian Reservation.* Washington, DC: International Development Services, ca. 1963.

Jackson, Billy Morrow. "Pyramid Lake." http://www.usbr.gov/museumproperty/art /jackson3.html.

Jasper, David. *The Sacred Desert: Religion, Literature, Art, and Culture.* London: Blackwell, 2004.

Jeneid, Michael. *Adventure Kayaking: Trips from the Russian River to Monterey, Including Lake Tahoe, Mono Lake, and Pyramid Lake.* Berkeley, CA: Wilderness Press, 1998.

Johnson, Adrienne Rose. "Romancing the Dude Ranch, 1926–1947." *Western Historical Quarterly* 43, no. 4 (2012): 437–61.

Johnson, Frank. "Hollywood, Yourts, and Camels Transform Desert." *Nevada State Journal,* July 27, 1952, 6–7.

———. "Lake in the Blazing Sun Is Foe of Modern Times." *Nevada State Journal,* September 11, 1957, 4.

———. "Pyramid Lake Can't Exist—but It Really Does." *Nevada State Journal,* April 20, 1958, 10.

Johnston, Charlie. "Cultural Guardians." *Nevada Magazine* 71, no. 5 (2011): 16–25.

Josephy, Alvin M., Jr. "Here in Nevada a Terrible Crime . . ." *American Heritage* 21, no. 4 (1970): 93–100.

"Journal Takes You on Trip to Pyramid by Motor." *Nevada State Journal,* June 2, 1940, 10, 12.

Kania, Alan J. *Wild Horse Annie: Velma Johnston and Her Fight to Save the Mustang.* Reno: University of Nevada Press, 2013.

Kehoe, Alice B. "Where Were Wovoka and Wuzzie George?" In *Julian Steward and the Great Basin: The Making of an Anthropologist,* edited by Richard O. Clemmer et al., 164–69. Salt Lake City: University of Utah Press, 1999.

Kelly, Isabel T. "Ethnography of the Surprise Valley Paiute." *University of California Publications in Anthropology and Ethnology* 31, no. 3 (1932): 67–210.

———. "Northern Paiute Tales." *Journal of American Folklore* 51, no. 202 (1938): 364–439.

Khimm, Suzy. "Capitalism's Campgrounds." *Washington Post,* May 13, 2012, G4.

King, Clarence. *Mountaineering in the Sierra Nevada.* 1872. Reprint, Lincoln: University of Nebraska Press, 1970.

Kitselman, A. L. *E-Therapy.* New York: Institute of Integration, 1953.

———. *Tao the King (The Way of Peace) of Lao-Tzu.* Palo Alto, CA: School of Simplicity, 1936.

[Kitselman, Beau]. "The Parallel Universe of T. Townsend Brown." http://49chevy.blogs.com/ttbrown/2005/09/missing_persons.html.

Knack, Martha C. "The Effects of Nevada State Fishing Laws on the Northern Paiutes of Pyramid Lake." *Nevada Historical Society Quarterly* 25, no. 4 (1982): 251–65.

Knack, Martha C., and Omer C. Stewart. *As Long as the River Shall Run: An Ethnohistory of the Pyramid Lake Indian Reservation.* 1984. Reprint, Reno: University of Nevada Press, 1999.

Knobloch, Frieda. *The Culture of Wilderness: Agriculture as Colonization in the American West.* Chapel Hill: University of North Carolina Press, 1996.

Knudson, Tom. "Big Trout Saved from Close Call with Extinction." *Sacramento Bee,* May 5, 2013, A1. http://www.sacbee.com/2013/05/05/5395583/big-trout-saved-from-close-call.html.

Kouvaros, George. "*The Misfits:* What Happened Around the Camera." *Film Quarterly* 55, no. 4 (2002): 28–33.

Krutch, Joseph Wood. *The Voice of the Desert: A Naturalist's Interpretation.* New York: W. Sloan Associates, 1955.

Lacy, Steve, and Pearl Baker. *Posey: The Last Indian War.* Salt Lake City: Gibbs Smith, 2007.

Layton, Thomas N. "From Pottage to Portage: A Perspective on Aboriginal Horse Use in the Northern Great Basin Prior to 1850." *Nevada Historical Society Quarterly* 21, no. 4 (1979): 243–57.

"Legend of Paiutes to Be Recalled in Pageant for Rodeo." *Reno Evening Gazette,* June 29, 1940, 16.

Leland, Joy. *Firewater Myths: North American Indian Drinking and Alcohol Addiction.* Monograph 11. New Brunswick, NJ: Rutgers Center for Alcohol Studies, 1976.

———. "Women and Alcohol in an Indian Settlement." *Medical Anthropology* 2, no. 4 (1978): 85–119.

Lewis, Daniel. *The Feathery Tribe: Robert Ridgway and the Modern Study of Birds.* New Haven, CT: Yale University Press, 2012.

Liebling, A. J. "The Lake of the Cui-ui Eaters." Pts. 1–4. *New Yorker,* January 1, 1955, 25–41; January 8, 1955, 33–61; January 15, 1955, 32–67; January 22, 1955, 37–73.

———. "The Mustang Buzzers." Pts. 1–2. *New Yorker,* April 3, 1954, 35–51; April 10, 1954, 66–86.

Lillard, Richard G. *Desert Challenge: An Interpretation of Nevada.* New York: Alfred A. Knopf, 1942.

Limerick, Patricia Nelson. *Desert Passages: Encounters with the American Deserts.* Albuquerque: University of New Mexico Press, 1985.

———. "One Hundred Years of the Bureau of Reclamation: Looking from the Outside In." In *The Bureau of Reclamation: History Essays from the Centennial Symposium,* edited by Britt Allan Storey, 2:651–62. Denver: Bureau of Reclamation, 2008. http://www.usbr.gov/history/Symposium_2008/Historical_Essays.pdf.

Lindholdt, Paul. "From Sublimity to Ecopornography: Assessing the Bureau of Reclamation Art Collection." *Journal of Ecocriticism* 1, no. 1 (2009): 1–25.

Lindsay, Russ. "Robert Cole Caples: Rooted in Nevada." Education guide to accompany the Nevada Touring Initiative's Traveling Exhibition Program, 2008. http://nac.nevadaculture.org/dmdocuments/CaplesEducGuidelr.pdf.

Lindstrom, Susan G. "Great Basin Fisherfolk: Optimal Diet Breadth Modeling the Truckee River Aboriginal Subsistence Fishery." PhD diss., University of California, Davis, 1992.

Lindvall, Terry. *The Silents of God: Selected Issues and Documents in Silent American Film and Religion, 1908–1925.* Lanham, MD: Scarecrow Press, 2001.

Linton, Ralph. *Paiute Sorcery.* New York: Viking Fund, 1950.

Lomas, Marie. "Pyramid Lake, Mere Remnant of an Ancient Inland Sea, Is Now a Lake of Doom." *Nature Magazine* 36, no. 6 (1942): 321–23.

———. "Sphinx of Pyramid Lake." *Nevada Magazine* 2, no. 4 (1939): 25–28.

MacAgy, Douglas. Introduction to *The American Artist and Water Reclamation: A Selection of Paintings from the Collection of the Bureau of Reclamation.* Washington, DC: US Government Printing Office, 1973.

Mailer, Norman. *Marilyn: A Biography.* New York: Grosset and Dunlap, 1972.

Makley, Matthew S., and Michael J. Makley. *Cave Rock: Climbers, Courts, and a Washoe Indian Sacred Place.* Reno: University of Nevada Press, 2010.

Manzo, Peter. *Brando: The Biography.* New York: Hyperion, 1994.

Marschall, John. "Gareth Hughes: Unlikely Missionary to the Paiutes." http://online
nevada.org/gareth_hughes_unlikely_missionary_to_the_paiutes.

Martin, Fletcher. "Pyramid Lake." http://www.usbr.gov/museumproperty/art/martin
2.html.

Marx, Leo. *The Machine in the Garden: Technology and the Pastoral Ideal in America.* New York: Oxford University Press, 1964.

Matthiessen, Peter. *Indian Country.* New York: Viking Press, 1984.

McCandless, Erin. "The Pyramid Lake Case." In *Braving the Currents: Evaluating Environmental Conflict Resolution in the River Basins of the American West,* edited by Tamra Pearson d'Estrée and Bonnie G. Colby. Boston: Kluwer Academic, 2004.

McCool, Daniel. *Native Waters: Contemporary Indian Water Settlements and the Second Treaty Era.* Tucson: University of Arizona Press, 2002.

McCormick, Jim. "Hildegard Herz." http://www.onlinenevada.org/hildegard_herz.

McCulloch, Frank. "Death of a Great Warrior." *Nevada Magazine* 3, no. 2 (1947): 7–9, 54.

———. "The Golden One." *Nevada Magazine* 3, no. 7 (1948): 20–23.

———. "How the Great Spearhead Came to Pyramid Lake." *Nevada Magazine* 3, no. 5 (1947): 26–28.

———. "Tale of Two Lakes." *Nevada Magazine* 3, no. 6 (1947): 21–23, 30.

McCulloch, Frank, Sr. "A Day at Pyramid Lake." In *Just Thinking*. Gardnerville, NV: Academy Press, 1966.

McGee, William L., and Sandra V. McGee. *The Divorce Seekers: A Photo Memoir of a Nevada Dude Wrangler*. St. Helena, CA: BMC, 2004.

McKnight, Tom L. "The Feral Horse in Anglo America." *Geographical Review* 49, no. 4 (1959): 506–25.

McLane, Alvin R. *Pyramid Lake: A Bibliography*. Reno: Camp Nevada, 1975.

McMillan, Doug. "Agencies, Indians Begin New Push for Compromise." *Reno Gazette-Journal*, March 4, 1984, A1, A17.

———. "Lahontan Cutthroat Become a Sad Fish Story." *Reno Gazette-Journal*, August 23, 1988, A6.

———. "Orr Ditch Was 1st Suit in Truckee Legal Flood." *Reno Gazette-Journal*, August 21, 1988, A11.

———. "Rare Pyramid Fish Complicate Water Dilemma." *Reno Gazette-Journal*, August 23, 1988, A1, A5.

———. "Righting Wrongs of Truckee's Past." *Reno Gazette-Journal*, August 21, 1988, A9, A10.

———. "Water Settlement Eluded Laxalt." *Reno Gazette-Journal*, August 21, 1988, A10.

Meland, Carter, Joseph Bauerkemper, LeAnne Howe, and Heidi Stark. "The Bases Are Loaded: American Indians and American Studies." *American Studies* 46, nos. 2–4 (2005) and *Indigenous Studies Today* 1 (Fall 2005–Spring 2006): 391–416.

Mergen, Bernard. "Survivors, Seekers, Sojourners, Squatters, and Sportsmen: The Ineffable Attraction of Pyramid Lake." *Nevada Historical Society Quarterly* (forthcoming).

Mergen, Katharine Norrid. "Pyramid Lake." *Nevada Magazine* 3, no. 7 (1948): 3. Reprinted in *Sage in Bloom: An Anthology*, 55–56. Reno: Silver State Press, 1950.

Mergen, Kay. "Land Developers Eye Pyramid Lake as Prospective Resort Area." *Reno Evening Gazette*, May 20, 1959, 8.

———. "Reno Revue" [Wadsworth]. *Nevada State Journal*, August 14, 1941, 4.

Merritt, Dixon Lanier. "A Wonderful Bird Is the Pelican." http://en.wikipedia.org/wiki/Dixon_Lanier_Merritt.

Merton, Robert K., and Elinor G. Barber. *The Travels and Adventures of Serendipity: A Study in Historical Semantics and the Sociology of Science*. Princeton, NJ: Princeton University Press, 2004.

Merton, Thomas. *Ishi Means Man: Essays on Native Americans*. Greensboro, NC: Unicorn Press, 1976.

———. *The Wisdom of the Desert: Sayings from the Desert Fathers of the Fourth Century*. New York: New Directions, 1961.

Meyer, Carter Jones, and Diana Royer, eds. *Selling the Indian: Commercializing and Appropriating American Indian Cultures*. Tucson: University of Arizona Press, 2001.

Mieder, Wolfgang. "'The Only Good Indian Is a Dead Indian': History and Meaning of a Proverbial Stereotype." *Journal of American Folklore* 106, no. 419 (1993): 38–60.

Mihesuah, Devon A., ed. *Natives and Academics: Researching and Writing About American Indians*. Lincoln: University of Nebraska Press, 1998.

Milgrom, Melissa. *Still Life: Adventures in Taxidermy*. Boston: Houghton Mifflin Harcourt, 2010.

Miller, Arthur. Manuscript of first draft of script for *The Misfits* with emendations, 116 pages, n.d. Harry Ransom Center, University of Texas at Austin.

———. "The Misfits." *Esquire*, October 1957, 158–66. Revised and expanded in *I Don't Need You Anymore*, 78–113. New York: Viking, 1967.

———. *The Misfits*. New York: Viking, 1961.

———. *Timebends: A Life*. New York: Grove, 1987.

Miller, Arthur, and Serge Toubiana. *"The Misfits": Story of a Shoot*. London: Phaidon, 2000.

Miller, Jeannette. "Lo, the Poor Indian: The Piute Reservation at Pyramid Lake." *Reno Weekly Gazette and Stockman*, March 9, 1899, 2.

Misrach, Richard. "Pyramid Lake at Night." 2004. http://osxdaily.com/2010/02/16/the-ipad-background-picture/.

———. "Swimmers, Pyramid Lake Indian Reservation, Nevada, 1987–93." Museum of Contemporary Photography. http://mocp.org/collections/permanent/misrach_richard.php.

"Miss Sarah Winnemucca." *New York Times*, July 29, 1873.

"Monstrous Fish Reported Sighted by Railroad Men at Pyramid Lake." *Nevada State Journal*, May 6, 1952, 1.

Mooney, James. *The Ghost-Dance Religion and the Sioux Outbreak of 1890*. Washington, DC: US Government Printing Office, 1896.

Moore, Roberta, and Scott Slovic, eds. *Wild Nevada: Testimonies on Behalf of the Desert*. Reno: University of Nevada Press, 2005.

"Mornin' on the Desert." 1927. Reprinted in *Nevada Highways and Parks* 1, no. 2 (1936): n.p.; 13, no. 2 (1953): back cover; and 46, no. 1 (1986): 17.

Morrow, John. "Desert Lakes: The New Campground." *Nevada: The Magazine of the Real West* 40, no. 4 (1980): 15–17.

Mosby, Aline. "Silver Spurs Awaken Memories: Hughes Once Walked Glory Trail." *Nevada State Journal*, May 22, 1951, 9.

Moses, L. G. "James Mooney and Wovoka: An Ethnologist's Visit with the Ghost Dance Prophet." *Nevada Historical Society Quarterly* 23, no. 2 (1980): 71–86.

———. *Wild West Shows and the Images of American Indians, 1883–1933*. Albuquerque: University of New Mexico Press, 1996.

Murphy, Jacqueline Shea. *The People Have Never Stopped Dancing: Native American Modern Dance Histories*. Minneapolis: University of Minnesota Press, 2007.

Myers, L. Daniel. "Levels of Context: A Symbolic Analysis of Numic Origin Myths." PhD diss., Rutgers University, 1987.

Myrick, David F. *Railroads of Nevada and Eastern California*. Vol. 1, *The Northern Roads*. Berkeley, CA: Howell-North, 1962.

Nabokov, Peter. *A Forest of Time: American Indian Ways of History*. New York: Cambridge University Press, 2002.

———. *Where the Lightning Strikes: The Lives of American Indian Sacred Places*. New York: Viking Press, 2006.

"A Neglected Attraction." *Reno Evening Gazette,* October 26, 1916, 4.

Nevada: A Guide to the Silver State. Compiled by workers of the Writers' Program of the Works Progress Administration. Portland, OR: Binsfords and Mort, 1940.

Northern Paiute Nation and the Bands Thereof v. The United States of America. Docket No. 87, March 24, 1959, and July 3, 1961. http://digital.library.okstate.edu/icc/index/iccindex.html.

Numa: A Northern Paiute History. Reno: Inter-Tribal Council of Nevada, ca. 1976 [1988?].

Olds, Sarah E. *Twenty Miles from a Match: Homesteading in Western Nevada*. Reno: University of Nevada Press, 1978.

Oursler, Fulton. "Star in the Desert." *American Weekly,* February 3, 1952, 4–5.

"Pageant, Athletic Events Features of Holiday Celebration by Nixon Indians." *Nevada State Journal,* December 27, 1940, 12.

"Paiute Pageant at Pyramid Today Will Tell True Story of the Indians." *Nevada State Journal,* August 28, 1955, 8.

Parezo, Nancy J., and Angelina R. Jones. "What's in a Name? The 1940s–1950s 'Squaw Dress.'" *American Indian Quarterly* 33, no. 3 (2009): 373–404.

Park, Willard Z. *Shamanism in Western North America: A Study in Cultural Relationships*. Evanston, IL: Northwestern University Press, 1938.

———. *Willard Z. Park's Ethnographic Notes on the Northern Paiute of Western Nevada, 1933–1940*. Compiled and edited by Catherine S. Fowler. Salt Lake City: University of Utah Press, 1989.

Parman, Donald L. "The Indian and the Civilian Conservation Corps." *Pacific Historical Review* 40, no. 1 (1971): 39–56.

"Part of Pyramid Indian Reservation to Be Opened for Settlement Soon." *Reno Evening Gazette,* December 10, 1909, 1, 8.

Paulina, Mable Wright. "Pyramid Lake." Interview with Margaret Wheat, May 1964. Margaret Wheat Papers, Special Collections, University of Nevada, Reno, University Digital Conservancy. http://contentdm.library.unr.edu/cdm4/item_viewer.php?CISOROOT=/wheat&CISOPTR=51.

Pelcyger, Robert S. Interviews with Donald B. Seney, Bureau of Reclamation, Boulder, CO, September 27, 1995, and Reno, October 10, 1995.

Peppler, Randy A. "'Old Indian Ways' of Predicting the Weather: Senator Robert S. Kerr and the Winter Predictions of 1950–51 and 1951–52." *Weather, Climate, and Society* 2 (2010): 200–209.

Pinkoski, Marc. "Julian Steward, American Anthropology, and Colonialism." *Histories of Anthropology Annual* 4 (2008): 172–204. http://muse.jhu.edu/journals/histories _of_anthropology_annual/v004/4.pinkoski.html.

Pisani, Donald J. "The Strange Death of the California-Nevada Compact: A Study in Interstate Water Negotiations." *Pacific Historical Review* 47, no. 4 (1978): 637–58.

"Pogonip." *Monthly Weather Review* 22, no. 2 (1894): 76.

Põldsaar, Raili, and Krista Vogelberg, eds. *Points of Convergence: Selected Papers of the 5th Tartu Conference*. Cultural Studies Series no. 4, Baltic Centre for North-American Studies, University of Tartu. Tartu: University of Tartu, 2003.

Powell, John Wesley. *Anthropology of the Numa: John Wesley Powell's Manuscripts on the Numic Peoples of Western North America*. Edited by Don D. Fowler and Catherine S. Fowler. Washington, DC: Smithsonian Institution Press, 1971.

Pyle, Earl et al. "Cui-ui Recovery Plan." Typescript. Reno: US Fish and Wildlife Service, December 1977.

"Pyramid: A Strange Desert Lake." *Nevada Highways and Parks* 14, no. 1 (1954): 12–15.

"Pyramid Indians File Protest on Land Deal." *Reno Evening Gazette*, February 4, 1937, 14.

"Pyramid Lake." *Nevada Highways and Parks* 17, no. 2 (1957): 2–7.

"Pyramid Lake." *San Francisco Daily Evening Bulletin*, July 31, 1878.

"[Pyramid Lake]: A Beautiful Place of Summer Resort." *Territorial Enterprise*, June 20, 1868, 3.

"Pyramid Lake II." *Reno Evening Gazette*, June 24, 1880, 3.

"Pyramid Lake Economic Development Plan." Prepared by Scott H. Carey, tribal planner, approved by the Tribal Council of the Pyramid Lake Paiute Tribe, July 2, 2010. http://plpt.nsn.us/econdev/ApprovedPlan.pdf.

"Pyramid Lake Indians Belligerent; Threaten to Burn White's Boats." *Reno Evening Gazette*, June 14, 1915, 1.

"Pyramid Lake's Pyramid Is Larger by Far than Most People Believe." *Nevada State Journal*, April 3, 1955, 26.

"Pyramid Offers Facilities for Navy Training Center." *Reno Evening Gazette*, March 15, 1942, 5.

Quammen, David. "Desert Sanitaire." In *Natural Acts: A Sidelong View of Science and Nature*, 175–81. New York: Nick Lyons Books / Schocken Books, 1985.

Raymond, Elizabeth. "Middle Ground and Marginal Space: Sense of Place in the Middle West and the Great Basin." In *History and Humanities: Essays in Honor of Wilbur S. Shepperson*, edited by Francis X. Hartigan, 105–20. Reno: University of Nevada Press, 1989.

―――. "Sense of Place in the Great Basin." In *East of Eden, West of Zion: Essays on Nevada,* edited by Wilbur S. Shepperson, 17–29. Reno: University of Nevada Press, 1989.

―――. "When the Desert Won't Bloom: Environmental Limitation and the Great Basin." In *Many Wests: Place, Culture, and Regional Identity,* edited by David M. Wrobel and Michael C. Steiner, 71–92. Lawrence: University Press of Kansas, 1997.

"Reno Invited to Help Boost Pyramid Lake." *Nevada State Journal,* March 21, 1931, 6.

Rhode, David. "Two Nineteenth-Century Reports of Great Basin Subsistence Practices." *Journal of California and Great Basin Anthropology* 10, no. 2 (1988): 156–62.

Ridgway, Robert. *United States Geological Exploration of the Fortieth Parallel.* Pt. 3, *Ornithology.* Washington, DC: US Government Printing Office, 1877. http://openlibrary.org/books/OL14995868M/Report_of_the_geological _exploration_of_the_fortieth_parallel.

Robert Cole Caples: A Retrospective Exhibition, 1927–1963. Foreword by Walter Van Tilburg Clark. Reno: n.p., 1964.

Roberts, Kathleen Glenister. "Beauty Is Youth: The Powwow 'Princess.'" In *Powwow,* edited by Clyde Ellis et al., 152–71. Lincoln: University of Nebraska Press, 2005.

Rosenthal, Harvey D. "Indian Claims and the American Conscience: A Brief History of the Indian Claims Commission." In *Irredeemable America: The Indians' Estate and Land Claims,* edited by Imre Sutton et al., 35–70. Albuquerque: University of New Mexico Press, 1985.

Rosier, Paul C. *Serving Their Country: American Indian Politics and Patriotism in the Twentieth Century.* Cambridge, MA: Harvard University Press, 2009.

Rourke, Constance. *American Humor: A Study of the National Character.* New York: Harcourt, Brace, 1931.

Roush, John H. *Enjoying Fishing Lake Tahoe, the Truckee River, and Pyramid Lake.* Chicago: Adams Press, 1987.

Rowley, Gladys. "Reno Revue" [Pyramid Lake]. *Nevada State Journal,* May 6, 1941, 4.

Rowley, William D. *The Bureau of Reclamation: Origins and Growth to 1945.* Vol. 1. Denver: Bureau of Reclamation, US Department of Interior, 2006. http://www.usbr. gov/history/OriginsandGowths/Volume1.pdf.

―――. "The Newlands Project: Crime or National Commitment?" *Nevada Public Affairs Review* 1 (1992): 39–49.

―――. *Reclaiming the Arid West: The Career of Francis G. Newlands.* Bloomington: Indiana University Press, 1996.

Rusco, Elmer R., ed. *A. J. Liebling, a Reporter at Large, Dateline: Pyramid Lake Nevada.* Reno: University of Nevada Press, 1999.

―――. *A Fateful Time: The Background and Legislative History of the Indian Reorganization Act.* Reno: University of Nevada Press, 2000.

―――. "Formation of the Pyramid Lake Paiute Tribal Council, 1934–1936." *Journal of California and Great Basin Anthropology* 10, no. 2 (1988): 187–208.

———. "Julian Steward, the Western Shoshones, and the Bureau of Indian Affairs: A Failure to Communicate." In *Julian Steward and the Great Basin: The Making of an Anthropologist*, edited by Richard O. Clemmer et al., 85–116. Salt Lake City: University of Utah Press, 1999.

———. "The Truckee-Carson–Pyramid Lake Water Rights Settlement Act and Pyramid Lake." *Nevada Public Affairs Review* 1 (1992): 9–14.

Russell, Israel Cook. *Geological History of Lake Lahontan, a Quaternary Lake in Northwestern Nevada.* usgs Monograph no. 11. Washington, DC: US Government Printing Office, 1885. http://www.archive.org/stream/geologicalhistooorussgoog#page/n126/mode/2up.

Ruuska, Alex. "Ghost Dancing and the Iron Horse: Surviving Through Tradition and Technology." *Technology and Culture* 52, no. 3 (2011): 574–97.

Sampson, John [Timothy O'Sullivan?]. "Photographs from the High Rockies." *Harper's New Monthly Magazine* 39, no. 232 (1869): 465–75. Reprinted with an introduction by Michael J. Broadhead, *Nevada Historical Society Quarterly* 15, no. 1 (1972): 27–39. http://digital.library.cornell.edu/cgi/t/text/pageviewer-dx?c=harp;cc=harp;rgn=full%20te...

Sargent, Lyman Tower. "Utopia and the Late Twentieth Century: A View from North America." In *Utopia: The Search for the Ideal Society in the Western World,* edited by Roland Schaer, Gregory Claeys, and Lyman Tower Sargent, 333–43. New York: Oxford University Press and the New York Public Library, 2000.

Scherer, Joanna Cohen. "The Public Faces of Sarah Winnemucca." *Cultural Anthropology* 3, no. 2 (1988): 178–204.

Schwartz, William L. K., and David P. Fogel. *Economic Development Plan for Pyramid Lake Indian Reservation.* Washington, DC: International Development Services, 1963.

Schweber, Nate. "Pyramid Lake Journal: 20 Pounds? Not Too Bad, for an Extinct Fish." *New York Times,* April 24, 2013. http://www.nytimes.com/2013/04/24/us/lahontan-cutthroat-trout-make-a-comeback.html?hpw.

Scoppettone, Gary, Mark Coleman, and Gary A. Wedemeyer. *Life History and Status of the Endangered Cui-ui of Pyramid Lake, Nevada.* Washington, DC: US Department of Interior, Fish and Wildlife Service, 1986.

Scott, Lalla. *Karnee: A Paiute Narrative.* Reno: University of Nevada Press, 1966.

Seney, Donald B. "The Changing Political Fortunes of the Truckee-Carson Irrigation District." *Agricultural History* 76, no. 2 (2002): 220–31.

Septon, Greg. "Owen J. Gromme: Consummate Museum Man." Milwaukee Public Museum. http://www.mpm.edu/collections/pubs/vertebrates/owengromme.

Shaw, Hank. "Man, Nature, and Trout: Our Vanishing Traditions." *Atlantic,* April 12, 2011. http://theatlantic.com/life/archive/2011/04/man-nature-and-trout-our-vanishing-traditions/237139/.

Shepperson, Wilbur S. *Mirage-Land: Images of Nevada*. Reno: University of Nevada Press, 1992.

———. *Restless Strangers: Nevada's Immigrants and Their Interpreters*. Reno: University of Nevada Press, 1970.

Shreve, Bradley Glenn. *Red Power Rising: The National Indian Youth Council and the Origins of Native Activism*. Norman: University of Oklahoma Press, 2011.

Sigler, W. F., and Joseph L. Kennedy. "Pyramid Lake Ecological Study." Logan, UT: W. F. Sigler and Associates, 1978.

Silliman, Stephen W. "The 'Old West' in the Middle East: U.S. Military Metaphors in Real and Imagined Indian Country." *American Anthropologist* 110, no. 2 (2008): 237–47.

Simonds, William Joe. "The Newlands Project" (third draft). Denver: Bureau of Reclamation History Program, 1996. http://www.cityoffernley.org/index.aspx?NID=339.

Skillen, James R. *The Nation's Largest Landlord: The Bureau of Land Management in the American West*. Lawrence: University Press of Kansas, 2009.

Smith, Sherry L. *Hippies, Indians, and the Fight for Red Power*. New York: Oxford University Press, 2012.

Smoak, Gregory E. *Ghost Dances and Identity: Prophetic Religion and American Indian Ethnogenesis in the Nineteenth Century*. Berkeley: University of California Press, 2006.

Sokolov, Raymond. *Wayward Reporter: The Life of A. J. Liebling*. New York: Harper and Row, 1980.

Springmeyer, Don. "The Pyramid Lake Paiute Tribe, the Truckee River, and Pyramid Lake: Decades of Battles for Better Instream Flow Quantity and Quality." Paper delivered at the Twenty-Ninth Annual Water Law Conference, February 23–25, 2011, San Diego. http://www.wrslawyers.com/pdf/2011/Springmeyer-ABA-Conference-Paper-pdf.

Steward, Julian H. *Two Paiute Autobiographies*. Berkeley: University of California Press, 1934.

Steward, Julian H., and Erminie W. Voegelin. *The Northern Paiute Indians*. Typescript prepared for hearings held by the US Indian Claims Commission in Reno, 1956–57, in Special Collections, University of Nevada, Reno, Library. New York: Garland, 1974.

Stewart, George R. *Sheep Rock*. New York: Random House, 1951.

Stewart, Omer C. *Northern Paiute*. Anthropological Records, vol. 4, no. 3. Berkeley: University of California Press, 1941.

———. *Peyote Religion*. Norman: University of Oklahoma Press, 1987.

———. "Three Gods for Joe." *Tomorrow* 4, no. 3 (1956): 71–76.

———. *Washo-Northern Paiute Peyotism: A Study in Acculturation*. Berkeley: University of California Press, 1944.

Stewart, Omer C., and David F. Aberle. *Peyotism in the West*. Salt Lake City: University of Utah Press, 1984.

Stinger, Leslie, and Bobbie Ferguson. "Portraits of Reclamation." *Cultural Resource Management*, no. 4 (1999): 48–50. http://www.usbr.gov/museumprperty/art/.

Storey, Britt Allan, ed. *The Bureau of Reclamation: History Essays from the Centennial Symposium.* Vols. 1–2. Denver: Bureau of Reclamation, US Department of Interior, 2008. http://www.usbr.gov/history/Symposium_2008/Historical_Essays/pdf.

Strobridge, Idah Meacham. *In Miners' Mirage Land.* Los Angeles: Baumgardt, 1904.

———. *Sagebrush Trilogy* [*In Miners' Mirage Land, The Loom of the Desert, The Land of Purple Shadows*]. Reno: University of Nevada Press, 1990.

Swinth, Kirsten. *Painting Professionals: Women Artists and the Development of Modern American Art, 1870–1930.* Chapel Hill: University of North Carolina Press, 2001.

Sylvestre, Patrick David. "The Art and Science of Natural Discovery: Israel Cook Russell and the Emergence of Modern Environmental Exploration." Master's thesis, Colorado State University, 2008. http://digitool.library.colostate.edu//exlibris/dtl/d3_1/apache_media/L2V4bGlcmlzL2RobC9kM18xL2FwYWNoZV9tZWRp YS84ODMo.pdf.

Symanski, Richard. *Wild Horse and Sacred Cow.* Flagstaff, AZ: Northland Press, 1985.

Thompson, Renee. "Pelican's Island." *Nevada* 49, no. 5 (1989): 48–51.

Thomson, David. *In Nevada: The Land, the People, God, and Chance.* New York: Alfred A. Knopf, 1999.

"1,000 Persons Expected to Attend Paiute Dance." *Nevada State Journal,* August 18, 1955, 9.

Townley, Carrie M. *S-S Ranch and the Lower Truckee.* Reno: Agricultural Experiment Station, Max C. Fleischmann College of Agriculture, University of Nevada, Reno, n.d. [1978].

Townley, John M. *The Orr Ditch Case, 1913–1944.* Publication no. 43007. Reno: Nevada Historical Society in cooperation with the Water Resources Center, Desert Research Institute, University of Nevada, October 1980.

———. *The Truckee Basin Fishery, 1844–1944.* Publication no. 43008. Reno: Water Resources Center, Desert Research Institute, University of Nevada System, November 1980.

Townsend, William Kenneth. *World War II and the American Indian.* Albuquerque: University of New Mexico Press, 2000.

Trelease, Thomas J. "The Death of a Lake." *Field and Stream* 56, no. 10 (1952): 30–31, 109–11.

———. "The Rebirth of a Lake." *Nevada Outdoors and Wildlife Review* 3, no. 4 (1969): 10–14.

———. "What Lies Ahead for Pyramid Lake?" *Nevada Hunting and Fishing* 1, no. 2 (1949): 8–10, 23, 29–32.

"Tribe to Give Pageant Here to Open Show." *Nevada State Journal,* June 30, 1939, 2.

Trimble, Stephen. *The Sagebrush Ocean: A Natural History of the Great Basin.* Reno: University of Nevada Press, 1989.

Trotter, Patrick C. *Cutthroat: Native Trout of the West.* Boulder: Colorado Associated University Press, 1987.

Troutman, John William. *Indian Blues: American Indians and the Politics of Music, 1879–1934.* Norman: University of Oklahoma Press, 2009.

"Trout Running Up Truckee; Start Yesterday." *Reno Evening Gazette,* March 21, 1923, 6.

Tuohy, Donald R. "Notes on the Demography of the Kuyui̱-ti̱kadi̱, the Pyramid Lake Paiute." Typescript, n.d. Robert G. Leland Papers, NC1035/1/9A, Special Collections, University of Nevada, Reno.

Unamuno, Miguel de. *Tragic Sense of Life.* Translation of *Del Sentimiento Trágico de la Vida* (1912). New York: Dover. 1954.

Underdal, Stanley. "On the Road to Termination: Pyramid Lake Paiutes and the Indian Attorney Controversy of the 1950s." PhD diss., Columbia University, 1977.

Underhill, Ruth M. *The Northern Paiute Indians of California and Nevada.* Washington, DC: Bureau of Indian Affairs, 1941.

US Senate. Committee on Energy and Natural Resources. Subcommittee on Public Lands, Reserved Water, and Resource Conservation. *Pyramid Lake Paiute and Truckee River Settlement Act of 1985: Hearing Before the Subcommittee on Public Lands, Reserved Water, and Resource Conservation of the Committee on Energy and Natural Resources.* 99th Cong., 1st sess., on S. 1558, October 21, 1985. Washington, DC: US Government Printing Office, 1986.

———. Subcommittee on Water and Power. *Truckee-Carson–Pyramid Lake Water Rights Settlement Act: Hearing Before the Committee on Energy and Natural Resources.* 101st Cong., 2nd sess., on S. 1554, February 6, 1990. Washington, DC: US Government Printing Office, 1990.

US Senate. Committee on Indian Affairs. *Authorizing Patents Issued to Settlers, Pyramid Lake Indian Reservation, Nevada. Hearings Before the Committee on Indian Affairs.* 75th Cong., 1st sess., on S. 840, a Bill to Authorize the Secretary of the Interior to Issue Patents for Certain Lands for Certain Settlers in the Pyramid Lake Indian Reservation, Nevada. April 12–13, May 3, 17, 1937. Washington, DC: US Government Printing Office, 1937.

———. *To Settle Certain Claims Affecting the Pyramid Lake Paiute Indian Tribe of Nevada, and for Other Purposes: Hearing Before the Select Committee on Indian Affairs.* 99th Cong., 1st sess., on S. 1558, October 2, 1985. Washington, DC: US Government Printing Office, 1986.

"'Very Like a Whale' in Pyramid Lake." *San Francisco Daily Evening Bulletin,* July 25, 1860, 1.

Vetter, Don. "Dividing the Water." *Reno Gazette-Journal,* February 1, 1987, D1, D3.

———. "Water: Supply, Demand on Crash Course." *Reno Gazette-Journal,* March 22, 1987, A1, A19.

Vierra, Robert K., and John Jones. "A Cultural Resources Inventory for the Pyramid

Lake Paiute Tribe Proposed Broadband Project in Washoe County, Nevada." Type-script prepared for the Pyramid Lake Paiute Tribe, August 16, 2011.

Vitalis, Robert. *America's Kingdom: Mythmaking on the Saudi Oil Frontier.* Stanford, CA: Stanford University Press, 2007.

Voices of Nevada Indian Youth. Collected by Nevada Indian Rodeo Association under a grant by the Nevada Bicentennial Commission. Fallon, NV: Lahontan Valley News, 1976.

Voyles, Susan. "Pyramid Lake Area Closed." *Reno Gazette-Journal,* May 4, 2011, 2.

Wadsworth, Lorraine. *St. Mary's the Virgin: Centennial Celebration.* Reno: University of Nevada, College of Education, Center for Learning and Literacy, 1992.

Walsh, Phyllis. "From Lorgnettes to Lariats: In Loving Recollection of the S Bar S Ranch: Where Work Hardened Our Hands, While Visitors Lightened Our Hearts." Oral history by Mary Ellen Glass, 1971, University of Nevada, Reno, Oral History Project, Special Collections, Mathewson-IGT Knowledge Center.

"War Relief Rodeo Attracts Big Crowd to Reno for Holidays." *Reno Evening Gazette,* September 5, 1942, 14.

Warren, Louis S. "Animal Visions: Rethinking the History of the Human Future." *Environmental History* 16, no. 3 (2011): 413–17.

Washburn, Wilcomb E. "A Fifty-Year Perspective on the Indian Reorganization Act." *American Anthropologist* 86, no. 2 (1984): 279–89.

———, ed. *Handbook of North American Indians.* Vol. 4, *History of Indian-White Relations.* Washington, DC: Smithsonian Institution, 1988.

———. "Land Claims in the Mainstream of Indian/White Land History." In *Irredeemable America: The Indians' Estate and Land Claims,* edited by Imre Sutton et al., 21–34. Albuquerque: University of New Mexico Press, 1985.

Welland, Dennis. *Arthur Miller.* New York: Grove Press, 1961.

Wenger, Tisa. *We Have a Religion: The 1920s Pueblo Indian Dance Controversy and American Religious Freedom.* Chapel Hill: published in association with the William P. Clements Center for Southwest Studies, Southern Methodist University, by the University of North Carolina Press, 2009.

Wheat, Margaret M. *Survival Arts of the Primitive Paiutes.* Reno: University of Nevada Press, 1967.

Wheeler, Sessions S. *The Desert Lake: The Story of Nevada's Pyramid Lake.* Caldwell, ID: Caxton, 1967.

———. *Paiute.* 1965. Reprint, Reno: University of Nevada Press, 1986.

White, Richard. *The Organic Machine: The Remaking of the Columbia River.* New York: Hill and Wang, 1995.

"A White Chief Among Indians." *San Francisco Daily Evening Bulletin,* May 6, 1857, col. A.

Wihr, William Saxe. "Cultural Persistence in Western Nevada: The Pyramid Lake Paiute." PhD diss., Department of Anthropology, University of California, Berkeley, 1988.

Wilds, Leah J. *Water Politics in Northern Nevada: A Century of Struggle.* Reno: University of Nevada Press, 2010.

Wilds, Leah J., and Richard Acton. "The Saga Continues: Implementing the Negotiated Settlement." *Nevada Historical Society Quarterly* 48, no. 2 (2005): 315–32.

Wilds, Leah J., Danny A. Gonzalez, and Glen S. Kurtz. "Reclamation and the Politics of Change: The Truckee-Carson–Pyramid Lake Water Rights Settlement Act of 1990." *Nevada Historical Society Quarterly* 37, no. 3 (1994): 173–99.

Williams, Lucy Fowler, et al. *Native American Voices on Identity, Art, and Culture.* Philadelphia: University of Pennsylvania Museum of Archaeology and Anthropology, 2005.

Wilmer, S. E., ed. *Native American Performance and Representation.* Tucson: University of Arizona Press, 2009.

Wilson, Edmund. *Apologies to the Iroquois: With a Study of the Mohawks in High Steel by Joseph Mitchell.* 1960. Reprint, Syracuse, NY: Syracuse University Press, 1992.

Witt, Harold. "Pyramid." In *Beasts in Clothes.* New York: Macmillan, 1961. Reprinted in *Desert Wood: An Anthology of Nevada Poets,* edited by Shaun Griffin, 39–40. Reno: University of Nevada Press, 1991.

Wolfe, Ann M. *Chris Drury: Mushrooms/Clouds.* Chicago and Reno: Center for American Places and the Nevada Art Museum, 2009.

Wolfe, Patrick. "Settler Colonialism and the Elimination of the Native." *Journal of Genocide Research* 8, no. 4 (2006): 387–409.

Woodruff, Janette, as told to Cecil Dryden. *Indian Oasis.* Caldwell, ID: Caxton, 1939.

Woon, Basil. "Harry Drackert, Authority on Horses, Pyramid Lake." *Nevada State Journal,* July 26, 1953, 5.

———. "Indian Grant Pow-Wow Is Planned at Pyramid Lake Reservation Next Year." *Nevada State Journal,* July 25, 1954, 8.

———. "Indian Rituals of Centuries Ago Are Still Carried Out in Nevada." *Nevada State Journal,* October 18, 1953, 10.

———. "In Spite of Geiger Counters, Rain Making Machines, and Docks, Pyramid Lake Is Unchanged." *Nevada State Journal,* March 6, 1955, 8.

———. "Land of Ghosts from Pyramid Lake to Doyle Doesn't Include Highways." *Nevada State Journal,* June 13, 1954, 6.

———. "Lost Lands of Pyramid Lake Area Have a Constantly Changing Charm." *Nevada State Journal,* May 23, 1954, 6.

———. "Nixon, Lying on the Shores of Pyramid Lake, Has an Interesting Life of Its Own." *Nevada State Journal,* August 5, 1956, 26.

———. *None of the Comforts of Home, but Oh, Those Cowboys: The Saga of Nevada Dude Ranches.* Illustrations and cover by B. Kliban. Reno: Featured Features, 1967.

———. "Pyramid Lake, a Scant Century on the Map Centered the History of a Long-Gone Era." *Nevada State Journal,* June 27, 1954, 16.

———. "Pyramid Lake May Become a National Park If Some of the Current Plans Materialize." *Nevada State Journal,* June 6, 1954, 3.

———. "Roving Reporter Is Doing Research on Guest Ranches." *Nevada State Journal,* December 6, 1953, 29.

———. "Stage Road and Mine Created First Settlements on Pyramid Lake Shore." *Nevada State Journal,* May 30, 1954, 8.

———. "Thoroughbred Horses Prove They Can Take the Gaff Right Along with 'Cow Ponies.'" *Nevada State Journal,* July 31, 1955, 8.

———. "Traipsing Through Northern Washoe County Has Rewards Worth the Scarcity of Oases." *Nevada State Journal,* August 8, 1954, 5.

———. "Veronika Pataky Assumes Duties as Nevada Day Pageant Director." *Nevada State Journal,* September 20, 1953, 5.

Wright, Mervin, Jr. Interviews with Donald B. Seney, Bureau of Reclamation, Nixon, NV, October 13, 1995, and August 27, 1998.

Wunder, Delinda Day. "Performing Indianness: Strategic Utterances in the Works of Sarah Winnemucca, Zitkala-Sa, and Mourning Dove." PhD diss., University of Colorado, 1997.

"A Yacht for Pyramid Lake." *Territorial Enterprise,* April 23, 1868, 3.

Young, James A. "Israel Cook Russell in the Great Basin." *Nevada Historical Society Quarterly* 24, no. 2 (1981): 158–69.

Zanjani, Sally. *Sarah Winnemucca.* Lincoln: University of Nebraska Press, 2001.

INTERNET SITES

Art Collection, University of Nevada, Reno
  http://knowledgecenter.unr.edu/specoll/photoweb/artcoll/

Brother David
  http://www.desertpadre.co.uk
  http://www.intothelonging.com

Bureau of Reclamation History
  http://www.usbr.gov/history/index.html

John Cipollina
  http://www.johncipollina.com/
  Music and video clips

Jonas Dovydenas
  http://www.archives.gov/research/art/topics/environment/documerica-photographers.html
  Photographs of Pyramid Lake, 1973, "Documerica," Environmental Protection Agency, National Archives and Records Administration, Archival Research Catalog, nos. 52 and 53

Lahontan National Fish Hatchery Complex
http://www.fws.gov/lahontannfhc/lnfh.html

Nevada Fish and Wildlife Office
Cui-ui: http://www.fws.gov/nevada/protected_species/fish/species/cuiui.html
Lahontan cutthroat trout: http://www.fws.gov/nevada/protected_species/fish/species/lct.html

Newspaper Archive
http://newspaperarchive.com
A commercial index of thousands of newspapers, including the *Nevada State Journal* (1870–1977) and the *Reno Evening Gazette* (1876–1977)

Pyramid Lake Paiute Tribe
http://plpt.nsn.us

Sacred Visions Pow-Wow, Wadsworth, NV
http://www.sacredvisionspowwow.com

Truckee River Info Gateway
http://truckeeriverinfo.org

Truckee River Operating Agreement
http://www.troa.net

" 'What Continues the Dream': Contemporary Arts and Crafts from the Powwow Tradition," Nevada Arts Council, 2010
http://nac.nevadaculture.org/dmdocuments/powwowgallerynoteslr2.pdf

YouTube
The Dick Cavett Show, June 12, 1973, with Marlon Brando, Mervin Wright, and other Indian leaders: http://www.youtube.com/watch?v=fyUb2G2YQNo
Greg Douglass and John Cipollina play and sing "All Worth the Price You Pay": http://www.youtube.com/watch?v=DhTs_gSHEZA

INDEX